D0828457

Eastern Wisdom and Western Thought

Eastern Wisdom
and
Western Thought

A COMPARATIVE STUDY IN THE MODERN
PHILOSOPHY OF RELIGION

by

P. J. SAHER

London
GEORGE ALLEN AND UNWIN LTD
RUSKIN HOUSE   MUSEUM STREET

FIRST PUBLISHED IN 1969

This book is copyright under the Berne Convention.
Apart from any fair dealing for the purpose of private
study, research, criticism or review, as permitted under
the Copyright Act, 1956, no portion may be reproduced
by any process without written permission. Enquiries
should be addressed to the publishers.
© *George Allen & Unwin Ltd* 1969
SBN 04 141008 4

PRINTED IN GREAT BRITAIN
in 10 on 11 point Old Style type
BY C. TINLING AND CO LTD
LIVERPOOL LONDON AND PRESCOT

DEDICATED TO

George Grimm

The Trend Towards Integration in Modern Science
and its Counterpart in the Ancient Wisdom of the East

Saher is, as geniuses usually are, a philosopher who seeks *Integration*. Integration here means the inclusion of those factors which enable us to gain awareness of a thing in its totality. As applied to modern science it often means the inclusion of the spiritual dimension. For instance, people in general are still under the impression that the West lays particular emphasis on the rational function. During the last decades, however, the way was prepared for a decisive change. It stands in a reciprocal relation to the commencement of the Eastern turning towards the rational and technical. From this it becomes clear that East and West are by no means opposites, but *correspondences*. This distinction is of importance because it constitutes the basis for the encounter of East and West. Opposites are mutually hostile elements, whereas correspondences complement each other. Therefore a genuine meeting can only take place where there is a correspondence between the encountering elements, where they are complementary poles. This is true of East and West today, more than ever before.

From the Western point of view, this possibility of a genuine encounter is due to what one may call the circuitous European route. This roundabout way consisted of the West temporarily renouncing emphasis on the spiritual impetus. Instead it overstressed the intellectual, the rational, by the development of science, through which technology and industrialization became possible. This renunciation involved a loss which one can also call sacrifice—at all events, an unconscious sacrifice. Yet all the same, whether sacrifice or loss, the consequence common to both was unexpected gain. Surprisingly enough, it is rational science which has disclosed spirituality anew to the West. Taking a circuitous route via knowledge, it turned faith into certainty. This process is the result of what one may describe as the spiritual dimension of science. In reality, it was effectively disclosed only in the last decade. Here the term spiritual should be understood to mean that region which, from the human point of view, is closest to Ātman; on the other hand it by no means refers to the psychic-irrational and intellectual-rational possibilities of man. What the word Ātman really means is explained by Saher with unequalled lucidity in this book.

Western science proceeded from Aristotelean logic and Euclidean geometry. Both were supplemented, that is to say they both were partially surmounted, when laws were discovered by Gauss and subsequently by Riemann, which led to a non-Euclidean geometry. The latter was the starting point for Einstein's theories of relativity. Aristotelean logic was questioned by Max Planck's quantum theory. However, the inferences from this questioning were drawn only by the representatives of the generation succeeding Planck. In the German-speaking countries they were, above all, Werner Heisenberg and Carl-Friedrich von Weizsaecker. Both had the courage to acknowledge that by virtue of the discoveries of the new nuclear physics, the principal axiom of Aristotelean logic becomes untenable. This axiom stated that there is only an 'either-or'. It was formulated in the famous tenet: *tertium non datur* (there is no third). In other words, either something is or it is not; there is no other possibility.

The Aristotelean system of logic seems narrow compared with the *Seven Possibilities* of Mahavira, or even more so, with Shankara's system of logic; but it was precisely this restrictedness and exclusiveness that made science possible as such. Planck's quantum theory and Einstein's theory of relativity led to the Aristotelean 'either-or' being questioned. The result of the first was that the axiom, *natura non facit saltus* (nature makes no leaps), became untenable. As a consequence of the quantum theory, we know today that nature is very capable of making such leaps. This was the first intrusion into the Aristotelean 'either-or'. It gained support from biology, on the one hand through de Vries's mutation theory, from nuclear physics, and on the other hand, through Heisenberg's principle of indetermination and de Broglie's wave theory. Einstein's theory of relativity preceded the last two. By virtue of their work, we know today that matter is not merely a spatial element but also a temporal one. It is corpuscular as well as wave-like, so that both are merely different aspects of the same thing. In 'this as well as that' lies the decisive impetus which has led to questioning the Aristotelean 'either-or'.

This is a paradox the acceptance of which may lead to the discovery of a spiritual dimension which may help towards the understanding of *nirvāṇa* in the West. By the removal of the 'either-or' limitation the world or rather the universe has been transformed into a transparent or open one. In 1960 I mentioned this to Werner Heisenberg; for the open world by, the removal of rational restriction, reveals an unexpected wealth of relations. Since 'either-or' means giving up previous systematization, some people fear that they may lose all support and reliability, for they are faced with nothingness, with *nada* (in so far as nothingness can be an opposite). Here lies the root of the temporary Western nihilism, as for instance in existentialism. Werner Heisenberg confirmed that the transparent world is one of wealth and on no account a world of void even though it seems to *appear* void. If I am well informed, *nirvāṇa* is both fullness and void where the void has no nihilistic emphasis. The West can become conscious of this conception of *nirvāṇa* as a result of research in nuclear physics.

The 'either-or' belongs to the rational sphere of the mind—to that of strictly dualistic differentiation. The 'this as well as that' belongs to the mythical-irrational sphere, within which polarity and not the opposites are valid. One therefore reflects whether cognitional acknowledgement of the validity of both spheres—the irrational as well as the rational—is not in itself a step towards something which can be defined as a-rationality. This makes the spiritual dimension of science evident for the first time.

This spiritual dimension of science comes even more strongly to light in another result of nuclear research, our present knowledge of atomic structure. We know today that the elementary particles of which the divisible atomic nucleus is composed are so minute that we can no longer speak of them in terms of spatially perceptible matter. In other words, the basic elements of matter—the elementary particles of which atoms are constituted—are ultimately of non-material derivation. As a result, the atoms which form matter are themselves of non-material origin. But the non-material is at the same time the spiritual: it is at least a quality or characteristic of the spiritual. For the West, the world of material phenomena now becomes equivalent to *māyā*! However, the West does not consider this world of phenomena to be an illusion, but an aspect of the non-material, that is to say, of the spiritual, which one has to accept as a reality despite its unreal origin. It should be obvious that this way of looking at phenomena has nothing to do with materialism any more. This is further confirmed by the fact that neither pragmatism nor Marxist materialism recognizes this spiritual dimension, although it is a logical consequence of the scientifically investigated nature of matter.

Today a new consciousness is rising in the West. Or rather, a new kind of consciousness which forces its way towards an awakening, makes perceptions possible in the West today through which reality can be apprehended in an entirely new manner. It may be presumed that to the same extent—and there are Indian witnesses for this, as for example Sri Aurobindo—a new consciousness is arising in Asia today, which is called forth by the compulsion and the will to integrate technology and industrialization. It would be a serious mistake to see in Saher just one more great philosopher carrying on the good work of East-West understanding started by Max Müller, Radhakrishnan and others. Like Aurobindo, he is the living proof of that new (integral) consciousness in the dawn of which mankind is now living. It is that certain something which Teilhard de Chardin refers to as 'Superman' for want of a better name. The label 'Superman' is liable to be seriously misunderstood. Let me, therefore, illustrate what I mean. Evolution is mankind's progress towards a higher form of consciousness. This higher consciousness is beyond the understanding of those in whom it is still in the potential stage. Thus beings in whom this higher consciousness has developed appear to us to possess powers so extraordinary that the word genius is too feeble to describe them. We have examples in East and West of such marvellous occurrences. Take the case of Srinivasan Alyangar Ramanujam (1887–1920). At the age of fifteen, while fetching a book called *A Synopsis of Elementary Results in Pure and Applied Mathematics* from the town library in Madras, his mind was suddenly illuminated by the new (integral) consciousness. Effortlessly he could solve the six thousand mathematical equations in that book. In 1913 he got in touch with the Cambridge mathematician Professor G. H. Hardy, who invited him to England. Later he was elected a Fellow of the Royal Society and held the chair of mathematics at Trinity College. His achievements in this field were such that mere intellectual efforts would not have sufficed. A higher consciousness used him as its instrument. Then we have in the United States the case of Edgar

Cayce who died in 1945. With no knowledge of medicine, Cayce when in trance could diagnose all diseases and prescribe their correct treatment. In order to guard against fraud he had to submit to a check-up by the American Medical Association and the Federal authorities who cleared him. The former even gave him permission to practise without a medical degree!

From the correspondence of Dr Samuel Johnson and of Voltaire we know the case of Boskowitsch (1711–87), also a Fellow of the Royal Society (June 26, 1760) and one in whom the new consciousness had arisen as it will one day through the process of evolution in all mankind. Boskowitsch not only anticipated modern scientific discoveries (particularly Planck's constant and Einstein's relativity theories) but also those of several decades to come. The scientific world is not yet equipped well enough to test all his theories. Thus the Superman is only one in whom this new (integral) consciousness has burst forth before its time; he is a herald sent that we may know what evolution has in store for us. I have shown from the above examples that a Superman (in this legitimate sense of the word) may be born anywhere; in Asia, America or Europe. It is to be assumed that Asia and the West will mutually assist one another in order to help awaken this new consciousness. Seen from the viewpoint of man, only this new consciousness has the power to guarantee the continuation of human existence.

In this connection Jawaharlal Nehru, the then Prime Minister of India, said: 'The process of thinking has to be changed'. And this process we believe means what has been called here the formation of the new consciousness. For without the foundation of a new consciousness a new way and process of thinking are not possible.

This new consciousness, which is a-rational and therefore integral and so extending beyond the modes of consciousness of the merely prerational-irrational as well as the rational, does not manifest today only in the nuclear physics of the West. In order to be really effective, it must make itself felt in all spheres of life. That is the case: in everyday life as well as in the arts, in the epochal new way of thinking of the Christian churches, as well as, perhaps, in the spiritual dimension which Western science today attempts to realize. It may, however, be emphasized here that our references to Eastern terms like *nirvāṇa*, Ātman, and *māyā* are an attempt to explain the spiritual climax of the discoveries of Western science. Since it is commonly known that these discoveries were further advanced by the prominent scientists of Asia, mention will only be made of Japan's great contribution to nuclear physics and of Jagdish Chandra Bose who has proved by his experiments the untenability of the dualistic interpretation of nature, organic on the one hand and inorganic on the other.

This reference to Eastern terms should not be taken to imply that Western science will adopt the Eastern way of thinking. There is always the possibility of a mutual understanding. Still one should not forget the factor which is opposed to such an interpretation. For the Eastern way of thinking sometimes inclines towards the 'neither-nor' which is complementary to the Western 'either-or' and just as bad. On the other hand this 'either-or' is supplemented today by the more enlightened acknowledgement of the 'this as well as that'. In particular this way of thinking could help towards a mutual understanding of East and West as 'this as well as that' is no longer strange to the scientific thinking of the West.

The spiritual dimension under discussion, however, does not manifest itself only in nuclear physics. It is also being attained in all the other sciences; biology, psychology, even the study of history and law are examples. In the West, in all branches of learning there are references to the spiritual dimension which, as such, is a characteristic of the new consciousness. Everywhere representatives of the above-mentioned arts and sciences are to be found, whose manner of thinking already corresponds to the demands of the new consciousness. Moreover, almost all of them have an international reputation, so that their statements are typical of that new consciousness which makes itself known in the spiritual dimension of the sciences.

In biology it is Adolf Portmann in Basle who takes account of the spiritual dimension. He originated the concept of the undirected appearance, by so defining the result of a research which has been confirmed in other quarters. It consists of his proof that the inferences hitherto drawn from the behaviour of creatures are only of secondary value. He demonstrated that what he calls the directed appearance—for instance the camouflage colours and typical calls of animals—are special cases within a much more generalized category. This category, the undirected appearance, is an appearance which, to a certain extent, is purposeless. The undirected self-representation of the living, resulting therefrom, is non-material and so a clear example of the spiritual dimension which is now accepted by biology. Sir Julian Huxley is another example of a great scientist showing us the spiritual dimension in biology.

Let us take another case: Portmann proved that the songs of birds are not, as one believed hitherto, most beautiful and rich in modulations during mating time but only after the mating time. In other words, at a time when they are sung without purpose and are undirected (when they are not directed towards an object but are just an expression of abundance). Through an analysis of the smallest living beings of the deep sea Portmann further explained that their wealth of shapes and colours is not purposeful, for no living eye has so far been able to see this wealth. It is to a certain extent an undirected appearance in which the wealth of the spiritual comes to light.

In psychology C. G. Jung made the spiritual dimension accessible to the West as far as that is possible through psychological procedures. He prevailed over Sigmund Freud, who was bound to the instinctive factors, by not only taking the sexual-material impulse into consideration, but by also making the irrational-religious impulse valid again, even for science.

The following consideration shows the spiritual importance of C. G. Jung's psychological findings. A clear separation of the psychic sphere from the magical-instinctive-vital on the one hand and from the intellectual-rational on the other is only possible through these findings. This is at least true of those Westerners who do not remain within the limits of psychology (for example by seeing everything from the psychological point of view). The way to experimental realization of the spiritual dimension is thereby opened. Thus we notice the great controversy over Aldous Huxley's mescalin experiments.

In the field of history Professor J. R. von Salis from Zurich was the first to overcome the old Western conception. History had been pictured as a stream, as a one-way movement from a beginning to an end—that is to say, as purposive and material. Instead he presented it as a kind of network. By so doing he lifted the conception of history out of the dualistic material system of thought and placed it in the richness of that relative abundance which is the property of the whole, and which—as the whole—also includes the spiritual. Arnold Toynbee is another such spiritual historian.

What does this network-image mean? It is the acknowledgement that so-called reality is not a mere time-sequence but a complex process. A network is no system (which as such always fixes limits) but an expression of a texture of relations (and of the abundant possibilities suited to the network). In other words, historical realities are not, as thought hitherto, events succeeding each other consequentially, but are constellated by the interplay of many factors, the invisible among them. The meshes are the expression of the invisible in the structure of events; this form of the void, of the invisible, takes part in the abundance and wealth of the respective historical constellation. They are, so to speak, fragments of that *nirvāṇa*-like void which is creative fullness. Thus our conception of history surpasses the merely materialistic-causative conditionality which, in the Aristotelean manner, we projected into historical reality; and it opens the view to the wealth of the spiritual dimension. The network-image thus shows that the despair of nothingness can be overcome by the recognition of possible structures of consciousness yet to evolve.

In jurisprudence, besides Professor W. F. Burgi, the vice-chancellor of the Law School at St Gallen, Hans Marti, Professor of Constitutional Law in Berne, takes the decisive step in the spiritual dimension. His demand that the law should give 'a picture of the entire world' matches his demonstration that in the interpretation of a legal maxim 'something joins in always, which lies outside the merely judicial-political and completely outside every purposive consideration'. A maxim is not an isolated condition but always the creation of the whole man. That is why attitudes of mind pertaining to magic and myth find their necessary expression in law. At the beginning of the proceedings when the judge rises from his seat, he reproduces a magical image. He also repeats a magical spell while pronouncing a sentence of exile on the criminal. Every maxim is connected with the facts of a case and cannot be understood without their knowledge. Hence very often the whole reality is reflected in the law. Preambles to the constitution are the typical example of what should not only be interpreted rationally but examined on the basis of their whole contents. Similarly, a comprehensive understanding of the fundamental principles of the constitutional, criminal and matrimonial laws demands in particular the inclusion of all mental attitudes to reality, which only then appears as a comprehensive, legal reality. In the works of Burgi and Marti too there is a turning away from merely rational-material thinking towards the spiritual.

The new orientation of Western science and art illustrated by the examples just mentioned make, perhaps, a decisive Western contribution to the promotion of the encounter of East and West.

This spiritual dimension of science which has hitherto remained almost unnoticed indicates the new consciousness arising today. Its is perhaps the most important contribution of the West to the growth of this new consciousness amongst mankind.

University of Salzburg
Austria

CONTENTS

Part I

THE QUINTESSENCE OF EASTERN WISDOM

CHAPTER 1

Introductory Remarks

The human merry-go-round sees many changes: the illusion that cost India the efforts of thousands of years to unmask is the same illusion that the West has laboured just as hard to maintain and strengthen.[1]

The teachings of the ancient East have, in spite of all their manifold varieties, a hard core of fundamental ideas underlying them. This common pool of main ideas came through Eastern tradition to be called *wisdom*.

Undoubtedly there is a world of difference between the Sufism of Persia, the Zen and Shinto of Japan, the Universalism (Confucianism, Taoism, etc.) of China, and the Lamaism of Tibet; not to mention the countless other ways of thought in Asia. Yet there is supposed to be a very subtle unity of essence behind this diversity of forms. What this common substratum is will become apparent in due course.

The most outstanding representative of Eastern philosophy today is Vedānta. It is also of all forms of Eastern thinking the one with which the West is most familiar. A mastery of its first principles is also the key to the comparative study of Eastern wisdom in its other forms. Vedānta is the wisdom of the East *par excellence*. It is based on a spiritual experience of contact with the Higher Self present in each of us.

This spiritual experience of contact with the Higher Self can be had by any person so long as he is alive on this planet. Another necessary prerequisite is a modicum of ethical preparation. After ethical progress, which includes the ideal of self-effacing service to humanity as a whole, follows the exercise of certain psychological and physiological techniques collectively grouped under the term *yoga*.

Yoga is that part of Indian philosophy which deals with the discovery, classification and application of psycho-physiological aids for realizing of one's Higher Self. Specially conducive to such Self Realization are one or more of the following:

(a) inward contemplation (*rāja yoga*)
(b) fathoming one's innermost being through logical reflection on the question: 'who am I?' (*jñāna yoga*)
(c) extreme devotion, bordering on mysticism, through faith and love (*bhakti yoga*)
(d) disinterested and self-effacing service directed to any unselfish goal (*karma yoga*)

[1] Hermann Hesse, *Steppenwolf*.

In addition to the above, two other factors decide the success or failure of one's Self Realization:

1. *Anugraha:*
   an indefinable, unpredictable, and imponderable element, more or less like the grace of God, which descends when and on whom it will. It is a blessing, and like all blessings it appears to function arbitrarily though seers assure us that it works strictly according to laws which surpass ordinary human understanding. As with the laws of higher mathematics, the results appear to be the workings of chance rather than the product of exact calculation. Indian philosophy has, however, attempted to explain this somewhat enigmatic factor through the presence of the second one, namely:

2. *Karma:*
   in the popular but limited meaning of destiny or those currents which form the general trend of one's destiny. The force behind these currents is supposed to be the product of past (even pre-natal) conduct. That conduct, as expressed in thoughts, words or deeds, is considered to be the product of a parallelogram of forces arising from inborn attachments and aversions.

Thus seen as effect, it is grace; seen as cause, it is *karma*. The two are mutually related to each other as equity is to common law in the English legal system. And as equity follows law so does grace follow karmic deserts.

Only during or after the mystic self-realization of one's inmost being does Eastern wisdom enter upon its highest or third phase. The first phase is devoted to showing the necessity of freeing oneself from the dominion of the senses and the fallacy of mere sense-derived knowledge. The second or practical phase deals with how to attain a greater range of awareness. Equipped with this insight one begins the third phase in which the age-old, seemingly inexplicable problems of man's being and his place in the universal scheme of things are re-examined from the higher vantage ground. The origin of creation, the mystery of life, the secret of death, the cause of fate, the power of free-will, the significance of unearned sorrow, the presence of evil and similar problems are all explained in the third phase. But any effort to tackle these problems beforehand is severely denounced as a dangerous and vain presumption on the part of the unenlightened human intellect.

At this stage it is imperative to point out the dangers latent in the use of the term Higher Self. The most pernicious fallacy would be the misleading notion that there are two selves in man. No doubt one uses the term Higher Self for the sake of convenience. But that is merely a form of nomenclature and should in no way mislead us into imagining a second and lower self painfully trying to find its superior. The two selves of which we spontaneously think (because of the use of the comparative 'higher') are in effect one and the same; like, for instance, water and its wetness. Indeed the misconception of having more than one self can prove a serious obstacle to self-realization. To get rid of this dangerous notion Vedānta recommends unceasing reflection on the question: *who am I*? This draws the mind (or the ego or the so-called lower self) into a state of reverie wherein it looks for the source of its own essential being, namely the Higher Self. When mind is aware of naught but awareness-in-itself, it merges into its source. Suppose you stir your cup of tea with a spoon made of sugar. Here you have two concepts, the spoon, and the sugar out of which it is made. Both of them are necessary to sweeten your tea. In the process, however, the spoon soon disappears at the very moment it is no longer indispensable. Then you can see neither spoon nor sugar but the tea tastes sweet as it should. In the same way the ego (the Lower Self of popular belief, equivalent to the spoon in our example) disappears when it looks unceasingly (=the stirring of the tea) for its own essential nature which is *ānanda*, intrinsic bliss (=sweetness, an intrinsic characteristic of sugar). Just as the spoon is itself made of sugar, so is the ego constituted of self-awareness. A given quantity of sugar was called a spoon because of the shape into which it had been formed; so too pure consciousness, when it takes on the form of particular thoughts, is called mind. These constitutive thoughts then come to be identified as *my* mind by the individual concerned. In fact to him it is his *me*! It is his I or the ego, which is only the mind at one remove. And the 'my mind' of the individual is only a compendium of his thoughts.

Perhaps it would be best to give here an English translation of the famous Hastāmalaka Verses which are famous in India as being the gist of Vedānta philosophy. This poem which has earned loud praise from literary critics in Europe seems to be little known in English-speaking countries, though E. B. Cowell's version appeared in the *Indian Antiquary*.[1] I give here my own *free* translation from the original Sanskrit. The poem is sometimes attributed to the great Śaṅkara, the founder of Vedānta, and sometimes to Hastāmalaka, who lived about the same time as Śaṅkara (A.D. 788–820). It is said that the Brahmin Prabhākara had a thirteen-year-old son who was deaf, dumb and mentally retarded. On being introduced to the great Śaṅkara, the latter asked him casually, 'who are you?'. Thereupon a miracle took place. The boy recited the following verses which are meant to show that the Higher Self even of a dim-witted boy retains its absolute character. It is well to remember that it is the Higher Self, not the boy, who is here referred to as 'I'.

The Hastāmalaka

1　'Who are you? What are you?
　　Where are you going?
　　What does one call you? Have you a name?
　　Tell me, I would verily
　　Like to know your identity!'

2　'Neither man nor god nor ghost am I!
　　I belong to none of the social classes.

[1] Volume 9 (1880), p. 25 ff.

Neither prince nor pauper, neither saint nor monk am I!
I am the "I" behind the "I am"
To self-realized Awareness awakened.

3 To seek cause and identity within limits of sense-perceptions!
As if to cause the seasons
The sun its yearly movements makes!
Think of the cause-free, limitless interstellar space,
So limitless and uncaused is the secret essence of Being.

4 As the glow is to the fire
So is eternal Awakened-awareness to Being.
Even the stupor of the senses
Affects not the one and the Eternal.
That Awareness-in-itself am I,
That in truth is my very Being.

5 The face reflected in a mirror
Is devoid of all Being but for the real face:
So the Soul's reflection in the heart
Gives to mind the self-awareness which is my essence.

6 If the mirror were to break
So too would the reflection,
The face would remain unscathed
Alone without reflections.
So remains the *One*
Whose existence is original and not merely reflected.
This original Awareness-in-itself is true Being.

7 The pure *ONE* free from sense-perceptions
(For only the ego feeds on sense-perceptions),
His nature cannot be obscured by the senses;
That pure Self-Awareness is my real Self.

8 As the single sun reflects itself
On the surface of every water-jar
So are our minds enlivened
Through that common Cosmic Light;
That thought-free Awareness itself am I.

9 The sun simultaneously enables all eyes to see,
The *One* through the gift of awareness
Simultaneously equips all minds with consciousness;
That original consciousness itself am I.

10 The eye can perceive only what light illumines,
The light itself meets only objects devoid of light
The one illuminating power in both light and eye;
That unchanging Awareness is my very essence.

11 The sun's reflection in moving waters
Appears to move of its own accord.

The One True Light multiplies its image
In countless seas and pools.
So too does the *One* take its abode in countless hearts,
It remains as the Real-Self, the *One* behind the many.

12 Fools with beclouded understanding
Think the sun put out
When it's merely covered by passing clouds.
So is all perception conditioned by the sequences,
But the Self is Awareness itself, beyond the senses.

13 That unity in which all things are interwoven
Is itself untouched by any thing.
Like interstellar space, clear, eternal and pure,
Is my essence; I am the *integral* consciousness.

14 The glitter of gems is manifold
Depending on how they are cut and placed.
Thus do you sparkle in countless hearts,
O dearest God! Oh holy Vishnu!
As the reflected moon in turbulent waters
Provides the illusion of change and motion,
So only *apparently* does true Being change.'

The poem may seem unsatisfying as a description of so important a concept as the Higher Self. But can what is by definition beyond all attributes ever be described?

The Buddha, perhaps the wisest of the wise men of the East, knew the sheer impossibility of describing the self in any way whatsoever. The Self as pure being is devoid of every characteristic. Now Being, devoid of all characteristics, has a startling similarity to No-thing. Indeed the Buddhist *anattā* (not-self) doctrine equates it with Nothing! But the Buddha also knew the sheer impossibility of denying the self. He had, therefore, his own method of bringing home his point by using the *reductio ad absurdum*. This method is suitable when the truth of an assertion cannot be proved positively but remains as residue when all other possibilities have been eliminated. Supposing I cannot prove by the positive method that you are a human being and that only three other alternatives are possible. If I can show that the other three do not meet the case, I have proved the truth of the first assertion, which then remains as a kind of residuary legatee. This is the method that the Buddha often adopts.[1] He never says what the self is but lets the other party suggest what it could be. He then proceeds to demolish every possible assertion about the self. At last only one alternative remains, namely Nothing. This has misled many into thinking that the Buddha denied the self. But would a wise man like him deny what it is manifestly impossible to deny? Is such a denial possible without a self to do the denying? Is not the act of denying itself a proof of the very opposite of what is

[1] *Majj. Nik.* I, Suttam 35; *Majj. Nik.* III, Suttam 148; *Majj. Nik.* I, Suttam 22, etc., etc.

denied? The one thing not possible for anybody to gainsay is his own self. But what then is this self if it is nothing? 'I am, but my I is nothing.' This is not so absurd as it sounds. Let us first inquire into the opposite of nothing: everything. Everything means in effect all that I am *capable* of imagining, cognizing, perceiving, or at least thinking about. If a thing is unthinkable as well as imperceptible (that is, when its perception is *inherently* impossible), it is not included in 'everything'. It is then *similar to nothing*. But for anything to be perceived, or even thought of, there must be some subject-object relation, whereby the I is *always* the subject as in each case it is the perceiver, thinker, cognizer or the one who imagines. The I can, therefore, never be the *object* of perception or thought. It is consequently outside the sphere of everything and is akin to nothing. Perhaps it is better to call it no-thing in order to distinguish it from nothing.[1]

Now if the core of each individual's selfhood is no-thing (Buddhism) or pure Being (Vedānta), the individual has, as ontological essence, no separate individuality. There cannot be anything like *my* no-thing and *your* no-thing or *my* pure Being and *your* pure Being; there can only be no-thing or pure Being *per se*. Vedānta and Buddhism are on this point not in opposition but only the converse of each other.

The Far East under the influence of Buddhism has perhaps tended more towards the no-thing version which is particularly noticeable in Japanese Zen and the *shunyatā-shunyatā* (the emptiness of no-thing-ness) doctrine of Tibet. On the other hand Western Asia, more in keeping with the tradition of the revalatory religions, has tended more towards the pure Being version. Here the Higher Self is called the Soul in order to distinguish it from the ego. Much confusion is avoided by not using the same word 'self' for two such different aspects of selfhood. But then the use of the word Self, even in the sense of Soul, tends to intensify the notion that one *is* the Soul, rather than to strengthen the erroneous and hazy feeling that somehow one *has* one.

[1] Cp. Faust's reply to Mephisto: 'In this your Nothing, I find my All.'

CHAPTER 2

The Soul as the Higher Self in Man

IRANO-ARYAN AND INDO-ARYAN PARALLELS

The philosophy of six thousand years has not searched the chambers and magazines of the soul. In its experiments there has always remained, in the last analysis, a residuum it could not resolve. Man is a stream whose source is hidden. Our being is descending into us from we know not whence.[1]

In Manichaean writings we often come across a strange term called *manvahmēd vazurg* (the great soul). This has a startling similarity to the Ātman of Vedānta and the Zarathustrian *vohu manah*. When we recall that Mani, the founder of the Manichaean religion, was born in Persia and studied for a year or so in India, then the similarity acquires even greater significance.

On account of the familiarity between macro- and micro-cosmic conceptions in Gnostic teachings we may well assume that *manvahmēd vazurg* symbolized that spiritual element which as a part of the Cosmic Soul dwells in man as his Higher Self. A similar idea is found in the Hellenic mystery religions and the Mandaean religion of Mani's father where the individual soul is also identified with the Cosmic Soul. This too is the main thesis of Vedānta. Just as every individual is expected to have a soul of some sort so does he have his own *manvahmēd*. Still more arresting is the idea (hinted at when not expressly stated) that this cosmic soul when it descends on earth as a revealer of true religion is to be called a 'messenger' (*avatāra*) and so is both human and divine.[2] Mani considered Zarathustra (along with Christ, Buddha and himself) to be such an incarnation. This same idea, in a somewhat altered form, finds its counterpart in the Prophet and Apostle-of-God of the Semitic religions such as Judaism and Islam.

Now *manvahmēd* is a later derivation from the old Iranian *manah+vohu* as it originally appears in Zarathustra's *Gāthās*.[3] The Iranian *manah* like its Indian equivalent *manas* means mind. *Manah+vohu* means, therefore, 'good+mind' and is identical with *vohu manah* (the good mind, that part of the cosmic mind in man which leads him on to the lasting good).

In *Yasna* 28:5 we read:

> *ašā kat owā darasānī*
> *manascā vohū vaēdamnō*

---

[1] Emerson, *The Over-Soul*.

[2] Sri Ramakrishna laid particular stress on the fact that an incarnation has both a human and a divine aspect. See Swami Nikhilananda, *The Gospel of Sri Ramakrishna*, New York, 1952. This idea of incarnation finds its first clear elucidation in the *Bhagavad Gītā* although the technical term *avatāra* does not occur therein.

[3] *Yasna*, 28:5.

'O Truth! may I (be permitted to) see thee as (even) I myself (am like you a lover of) the good mind.'

We have a kind of parallel to it in the Upanishads:

'O Sun! the face of truth is covered with (your) golden disc. Uncover! so that I, a lover of the truth, may see it.'[1]

Vohu manah is, as we have seen, only the original term from which *Manvahméd* is derived and means like the Sanskrit Ātman either the Higher Ego (*manvahmēd*) or the Higher Mind (*vohu manah*). In fact it would not be altogether wrong to compare *vohu manah* (the Higher Mind) with the mind of Christ:

'For who hath known the mind of the Lord, that we may instruct him? But we have *the mind of Christ.*'[2]

According to Manichaean teachings Jesus, like other divine incarnations, is one in whom the Higher Mind (or Higher Self) was an *active* aspect, just as with us it is in the potential aspect. In a Manichaean tract praising Jesus we read:

'We glorify the great *vohu manah* (*vahman*) whom you have planted in the heart (*hṛdaya?*) of the good-intentioned ones'.

This cosmic principle which is planted in the hearts of mankind is also found in old Persian texts to be equated with *rōšn* (the Light (within) or the Light-particle). A certain resemblance to the 'Inner Light' of the Quakers is evident here and it also explains why the Parsis as legatees of the old Persian religion revere fire or flame as the most fitting emblem of God.

The Higher Mind is in all men and yet it is only an emanation of the still undiminished *vohu manah*. The latter is to be regarded as a Cosmic Principle and *simultaneously* as a divine power latent or active within the human organism, just as the *Tao* in Chinese Philosophy or the Ātman in Vedānta.

Thus not only in Vedic India but also in Zarathustra's Iran the soul of the individual was regarded as interrelated, participating and, in a certain sense, even identical with the *great vohu manah* or cosmic soul. The Higher Self is also referred to in Manichaean texts as the *saviour* to distinguish it from the ego (*jīvā?*) which is then called 'the I'.

We have many interesting dialogues between the heavenly Self and the earthly ego in Gnostic writings. Very significant for its similarity to Vedānta is the following:

'And to me did he speak: . . . and my ego was uplifted while he spoke to me:
"O soul [ego or *jīvā*], do not fear!
I am your *Manvahmēd* [*Ātman*],

[1] *Bṛhad-āraṇyaka Upaniṣad*, V.15.1. Also *Īśa Upaniṣad*, 15.
[2] I Corinthians ii. 16.

and a surety and a seal
and you are my body [like]
a garment [which I have put on].

. . . . . .

And I am your [Inner] Light,
the original effulgence,
the *Great Manvahmēd*,
and a perfect surety." "[1]

The word surety here means that the Higher Self guarantees the release
of the ego whose 'higher' Self it constitutes. An idea which appears with
considerable force in Vedānta.

The great *vohu manah* which in the macrocosmos represents all creation
is also present as the microcosmos in the individual. We are reminded here
of the description of the Ātman as 'smaller than the small, greater than the
great, the self is seated in the heart of every creature'.[2]

The cosmic *vohu manah* includes in itself the *vohu manahs* of all individuals but is nonetheless something apart and independent of them.
Even this feature is common to Indian and Iranian thought.[3]

All divine incarnations are emanations from the divine Cosmic Mind,
the universal *vohu manah*. Although they may seem to be distinct historical
personalities they are in effect the same as the single Power which sent
them out.[4] The salvation of the soul is often depicted in the allegory of a
son returning to his parental home from a foreign land. Now God is very
often mentioned as the father of *vohu manah* in Persian (Zoroastrian)
teachings. In one of his Gāthās the prophet Zarathustra speaks to God,
Ahura Mazda, the All-knowing Lord of All:

'Verily O Lord have I through observation and intuition realized Thee to
be the First and the Last. . . . Thou indeed art the father of *vohu manah*.'[5]

From this it is clear that between the *Absolute* (Ahura Mazda; corresponding to the Brahman of Vedānta and the Nameless Tao of the Chinese) and
the soul in man (the Ātman) there is an intermediate agency linking the
Absolute with its manifestation, the cosmic creation. Naturally this intermediary is the first in order of creation, or rather is ever prior to creation,
for the *Absolute* does not create. It merely calls upon an intermediary who
then thinks the Cosmos into creation. Understandably this intervening
Good Mind (*vohu manah*) or divine or cosmic mind has a much more

[1] Translated from the original printed in *Die Stellung Jesu im Manichäismus*,
Waldschmidt-Lenz, Berlin, 1926, p. 113.

[2] *Kaṭha Upaniṣad* I. 2. 20.

[3] Cp. *Bhagavad Gītā* IX. 4–7.

[4] Even in Islam we meet the idea that all the Apostles are one and the same Spirit.
Muṭahhar says that the *khurramdīnān* 'believe that all the Apostles, although the
Laws and Religions that they founded are different, are only one spirit and that
revelation never ceases'. *Le Livre de la Création* (IV, p. 30; 13 f. P. 28), Paris 1899–1919.

[5] *Yasna*, 31:8.

special relationship to God the father (the *Absolute*) than any created creature. In Indian thought this intervening agency is often ascribed to Ishvara (the personal God) or Hiraṇyagarbha (the Cosmic Egg). In Iranian thought this agency is fulfilled by the cosmic *vohu manah*, who then implants a spark of itself which later forms the spiritual substratum of each individual. A person lives by virtue of, by the permission of, indeed by the life-force (*ahū*) of the *vohu manah* implanted in him as a spark from the great or cosmic *vohu manah*.

'Even an opening of the eye can occur only by the entrance of *vohu manah* into the life-principle.'[1]

Like the Ātman, the *vohu manah* dwells in the heart of man, and the devotee implores its revelation. Zarathustra prays that *it* may descend upon him and his disciples:

'O God! as I am thy friend so ordain that through thy truth's grace the *vohu manah* be realized in us.'[2]

During his meditation before the holy fire Zarathustra recognizes God as *spenta*, the Holy Spirit. The Divine One grants him a boon in the form of a question and is willing to accept an appointed day on which Zarathustra may, in the form of an ecstatic dialogue, learn the sacred wisdom.[3]

Of particular interest is the passage where Zarathustra says:

'I recognized you to be *spenta* (the Holy Spirit) O God (only) when the *vohu manah* inspired me through asking the question "who art thou? To whom do you belong?"'[4]

The Higher Self is revealed when the ego is confronted with the question of its origin—who art thou?

The Manichaean scribes not only reproduce the identical idea, namely the presence of *vohu manah* in man, but even use the same words of the Zoroastrian texts.[5] As Zarathustra's version has its roots in the *Gāthās*, the Manichaean version must also be of Zarathustrian and Irano–Aryan origin. Its similarity with Upanishadic ideas goes to show the close interrelationship of Indo-Aryan and Irano-Aryan religious thought. Just as the Hindu devotee strives for union with the Ātman, so too does Zarathustra. He says in one of his hymns:

'tā vanhauš sara izyā mana vakō' So do I strive for union with *vohu manah*.[6]

---

[1] *Dēnkart* ed. Madan, p. 281, l.11 f. The complete text of the Pahlavi Dinkard, Part I, Bombay 1911.

[2] *Yasna*, 44:1.

[3] *Yasna*, 43:7.

[4] *Ibid.*

[5] See Widengren's *The Great Vohu Manah and the Apostle of God*, Uppsala, 1945, p. 49, where the original texts of both are placed side by side and compared.

[6] *Yasna*, 49:3.

Further, we learn from Zarathustra's writings the existence of an ancient doctrine according to which man has a share in the Cosmic Mind through the *vohu manah* within him. The latter is in essence identical with the Cosmic Mind, which includes at a lower level a collective organ composed of the minds of all human beings that are living, have lived, or will live. This collective organ is sometimes pictured as a mythical person who acts as a link between the cosmic *vohu manah* and its incarnation or apostle on earth.

Thus we see that even in the Irano–Aryan sphere of influence, and in the mystic lore of Western Asia, certain common conceptions are found which play a central role in Vedānta.

CHAPTER 3

Fundamental Ideas in the Vedāntic Conception of Salvation

In all directions the scientist's investigations bring him face to face with an insoluble enigma; . . . He learns at once the greatness and the littleness of the human intellect—its power in dealing with all that comes within the range of experience, its impotence in dealing with all that transcends experience.[1]

Certain fundamental ideas must be grasped before Vedāntic philosophy can be understood. These root ideas are intimately interdependent. Thus *karma* cannot be understood without *rebirth* and vice-versa. A list of such root ideas is useful in formulating the underlying structure of this system. The following list provides a bare skeleton:

1. *Enlightenment* (liberation or *mokṣa*) is possible *only*:
   (a) in *this* world
   (b) to one born as a human being[2]
   (c) and while he is awake (that is not asleep or dreaming)
2. This is the sole purpose for which man and creation were made:[3] that the former may recognize the latter as *māyā* (meaning not illusion but *illusory-like*)[4] and so have dominion over the entire cosmos as is his birthright.[5]
3. Between the *Absolute* (Brahman, or rather, that-which-cannot-be named —the *Father* of the Christian Trinity)[6] and a *jīva* (an individual human being) there are *two* connecting links:[7]
   (i) God (Creator; equivalent to the *Son* of Christian Trinity) also called *Īśvara* or *Brahmamāyi* the Divine Mother; similar to Demiurge; or scientifically speaking, the *Universal Cosmic Mind.*
   and
   (ii) a projection of this God[8] called Ātman or Soul (corresponding to the *Holy Ghost* of Christian Trinity), which, combining with other

---

[1] Herbert Spencer, *First Principles*, New York, 1910, p. 56.

[2] That is what makes our human life of such inestimable value. That is why, even in the worst situation, an individual feels 'as long as there is life there is hope'.

[3] See Radhakrishnan, *Eastern Religions and Western Thought*, p. 61 and p. 35.

[4] Radhakrishnan, *The Bhagavadgītā*, pp. 38 and 41; also *Religion and Society*, p. 103; also *The Reign of Religion in Contemporary Philosophy*, p. 334; also *An Idealist View of Life*, pp. 16 and 311.

[5] It is in this sense that God made man in his own image. This point is well developed by Carlyle in *Sartor Resartus*, chapters 'The Everlasting No' to 'The Everlasting Yea'.

[6] See Radhakrishnan, *The Bhagavadgītā*, pp. 21, 33, 58, 200, 314.

[7] *Kaṭha Upaniṣad* I. 3. 11.

[8] *Gītā*, XV, verse 7.

elements, composes the individual (*jīva*) of whom it is the sub-stratum.[1]

4. The individual by knowing this substratum, or essence, achieves the highest of which he is capable and wins liberation (*brāhmīsthiti*, or the life everlasting of Christian theology).[2] In the moments immediately prior to death,[3] this process may lead to a complete merger with the highest *Absolute*, unconditionally and *for ever*. That is *brahmanirvāṇa*, the ultimate climax.[4]

5. An individual's ego (psychological personality) must take repeated physiological-biological embodiments until he achieves *brahmajñāna* (knowledge of spontaneous identity with the *Absolute*).[5]

6. How to achieve *brahmajñāna* is meant to be the subject-matter of philosophy.[6]

7. God (Universal Cosmic Mind) through his power of *māyā* (*yogamāyā* or creative power in the sense of a cosmic illusion superinduced on the individual mind of a person as a kind of mass hypnosis)[7] prevents the individual from knowing himself[8] as he really is (as Ātman). The individual is, therefore, utterly dependent on the grace of God[9]—for his illumination is possible only when God gives him a respite from the imprisoning influence of His *māyā*. Hence the need for prayer and supplication. The individual's *sole* line of communication with God is through his Ātman (the Christ, or Christ-consciousness, in a person in Christian theology) which is God's plenipotentiary as far as the individual is concerned.

8. Whether a *jīva's* (individual's) request for Enlightenment should be granted or not is entirely at the discretion of his Ātman.[10] There is no appeal to some other authority. In the ordinary course of events, however, the Ātman is only too willing to permit Enlightment. On the other hand, the Ātman can at the most indefinitely postpone, but not alto-gether deny, Enlightenment to the individual (*jīva*).

9. The individual (*jīva*) and the Ātman are *not* two separate entities.[11] The Ātman is the individual's very being in the form of pure consciousness

---

[1] Radhakrishnan, *An Idealist View of Life*, pp. 269–72.

[2] *Gītā*, XIV, verse 20.

[3] *Gītā*, VIII, verse 5.

[4] *Gītā*, II, verse 72.

[5] *Gītā*, VIII, verse 16.

[6] Radhakrishnan, *An Idealist View of Life*, p. 311.

[7] There is a great, but seldom heeded, difference between a person's own individual mind and the Universal Cosmic Mind—specially when the latter is using the former as its base of operations. A careful analysis of this extremely subtle point is given by the Buddha in the *Suraṅgama Sūtra*. See his analogy of 'mistaking a thief to be one's own son'.

[8] *Gītā*, VII, verse 25.

[9] *Kaṭha Upaniṣad* I. 2. 23.

[10] *Ibid*.

[11] Radhakrishnan, *Indian Philosophy*, Vol. I, p. 194.

C

in its pristine state free of any and every thought.[1] The so-called individual *is* that very same consciousness[2] plus the colouring given to it
by the thoughts which flow through it. Of these the one thought, which
serves as fountain-head for all the rest, is the idea of existing (I am) as
a separate individual (ego).

10. What is called God (Universal Cosmic Mind) supplies an individual
with *pure* (free of thoughts) consciousness through Ātman and with an
ego through *māyā*. Thus conquest over *māyā* would abolish the ego
and conversely, conquest of the ego would abolish his subjection to
māyā.

11. Thus all Creation including all individuals (the phenomenal world) is
nothing but:

God per se   +   God disguised as creation

In other words:

Awareness in Itself   +   Awareness disguised as māyā as
creation, so to speak.

Just as an ocean full of icebergs is only H_2O as water $+$ H_2O disguised
as lumps of ice of some particular shape or form.

12. The individual's struggles for Enlightenment are, therefore, only
attempts to pierce through this disguise.

13. This disguise (*māyā*) is extremely difficult to pierce because the
Universal Cosmic Mind is constantly unloading its dynamic stream of
images into the individual mind (waking-state experiences or *viśva*).
In the dream-state (*taijasa*), the individual mind fabricates and pours
out its own images. Hence the vagueness of the latter relative to the
former.

14. The Universal Cosmic Mind (God) and the *Absolute* are *not* two
separate entities.[3] The Universal Cosmic Mind when 'at rest' or in a
state of pure awareness of itself alone is called the *Absolute* (*nitya*);[4]
that same entity when projecting, maintaining, or absorbing ideations
is termed the Universal Cosmic Mind (*līlā*) during the period of such
projection, maintenance or absorption (Cosmic Day). *The Absolute is,
therefore, the All Enlightened (Universal Cosmic), Mind itself.* It is the
pure consciousness-in-itself of the Universal Mind (just as the Ātman
is of the individual's) *above and beyond* the latter's alternating states of
ideation outwards (Cosmic Day) and reabsorption inwards (Cosmic
Night).[5]

15. It is not the individual's sin or stupidity which prevents him from
obtaining Enlightenment. The obstacle is in a sense God himself. For
the individual as 'Ego' is nourished from thought to thought by the
pure consciousness supplied through the Ātman. Through the Ātman
God pulls the individual towards Him and through His *māyā* pushes

---

[1] Radhakrishnan, *The Bhagavadītā*, pp. 57–8.

[2] Radhakrishnan, *An Idealist View of Life*, pp. 138–43.

[3] *Gītā*, VIII, verses 20, 21, 22.

[4] See also *Gītā*, VII, verse 24.

[5] *Gītā*, VIII, verse 17.

him farther and farther away from Enlightenment. The individual's spiritual evolution will depend on a balance of these forces. Enlightenment is, therefore, at the same time the easiest and most difficult thing in the world.

16. Enlightenment is an *irreversible* fact. Once the Universal Mind allows the individual to step outside its stream of *māyā* it cannot reverse the decision. But the Ātman remains subject to the Universal Mind in the sense that when the latter re-absorbs what it has given out, the former is included. It may well be that it also remains subject to another remanifestation[1] (or ideation-outwards in the next cycle).

17. Should, however, this 'liberated individual' (pure Ātman), during the period of *brahmajñāna*, merge itself in the *Absolute* (*brahmanirvāna*), then the Universal Mind forfeits all jurisdiction over it *for ever*.[2] Prior to this, however, no appeal lies to the *Absolute* from a decision of the Universal Mind to grant or withhold release from *māyā*;[3] and no appeal lies to the Universal Mind from a decision of the Ātman to permit or postpone Enlightenment.[4] Enlightenment is granted by God (Universal Mind) on the recommendation of and through the Ātman as the latter is in all respects the former's deputy.

The individual, being in *essence Ātman*, needs no liberation as he was never bound. Liberation is only a rediverting of consciousness from ego to Ātman.

The unliberated individual is *not* like a prisoner in a dungeon, but like someone in a mental hospital who is prevented from escaping by the superintendent who cajoles him into believing that he (the detainee) *is* the room in which he is confined. The wish to escape can hardly even arise as he now identifies himself with the walls within which he is confined.

An individual is whatever he identifies himself with. When, for instance, he does so with his body, he is no better than the man in the above example who identified himself with the walls within which he was confined. Such is *māyā*!

18. The purpose of yoga, as Indian philosophy sees it, is, therefore, to neutralize the hypnotic effects of *māyā*. Thus, instead of saying 'The truth will *make* you free', Indian philosophy says: 'The truth, if and when told, is that you always were free.' How so? Supposing a person is kept prisoner under an irregular warrant of arrest. The magistrate issues an immediate warrant for his release and posts it to the prison-governor. Now in legal theory that person never was a prisoner—

---

[1] *Gītā*, VIII, verse 16.

[2] *Gītā*, XV, verse 4; XIV verse 2.

[3] Cp. 'For the Father judgeth no man, but hath *committed all judgement unto the Son:* that all *men* should honour the Son, even as they honour the Father. He that honoureth not the Son honoureth not the Father which hath sent him.' John v, 22–3. See also Matthew xi, 27: 'neither knoweth any man the Father, save the Son, and *he* to whomsoever the Son will reveal *him*'.

[4] 'The Father loveth the Son, and hath given all things into his hand.' John iii, 35.

moreover he is 'liberated' the moment the magistrate issues the warrant. In practice, however, he will be set free when the prison-governor communicates to him the news of his release. (The warrant will also tell him that, since his confinement was unlawful, he had never been a prisoner but is and always had been a free citizen.) In a certain sense, therefore, he is 'not imprisoned', 'liberated', and 'to be set free', all at once while the release warrant is on its way to the prison-governor. In the same way Man is 'free', and yet to be liberated; 'liberated', and yet to be set free.

CHAPTER 4

Some Misunderstandings Cleared Up

The metaphysics of the Upaniṣads, when translated into the ethics of self-realization, provided and still provide for a spiritual need which has been felt in divers ages and which was never more urgent than it is today.[1]

Knowledge of the external world is possible *only* to whatever is aware of itself. That being so, our knowledge of the external world can only be of the nature of *phenomena*. The world is *not* a dream, but it is *like* one in the sense that both are phenomena.

Phenomena consist of consciousness plus particular thoughts. Actually, consciousness is only thought which is not about anything in particular.[2] That does not mean that a human mind is indispensable before the external world can be cognized. A camera will register things no human being ever saw. The mistake lies in supposing that it is the individual's mind which created the phenomena of which it is aware.

Here we come to an important difference between Eastern and Western philosophy. The former looks upon the universe as spontaneous ideation, while the latter can only explain it as a gigantic feat of engineering marvel.[3] The Eastern theory of spontaneous ideation is not so impossible as it may appear at first sight. For instance, when I see a railway-engine in a dream, I do not first have to manufacture it piece by piece before projecting it as a dream-engine. All parts of this engine are made of one stuff—my consciousness in the dreaming state. But what about phenomena in the waking state? The individual does not receive impressions from outside, as Western philosophy claims; he projects them outside. That both these kinds of phenomena can be indistinguishable is clear because an engine seen in a dream is as real, while the dream lasts, as one seen in the waking state. But, it will be argued, the engine seen while awake somehow appears to be more real than the one seen in a dream. This is because in the dream state the individual is projecting with the relatively feeble powers of his own individual mind whereas, when awake, his individual mind is a channel

[1] Edmond Holmes, 'The Philosophy of the Upaniṣads', an Introduction to, Appendix B in Radhakrishnan's *The Principal Upaniṣads*.

[2] Thought (meaning pure consciousness) resembles light in this respect. All things are seen with the help of light (reflecting from them) but *light in vacuo* or *per se* cannot be seen. Also: no man can see his own eyes except by way of reflection.

[3] It will be noticed that the second law of thermodynamics tends to support the Eastern viewpoint whereas the Western viewpoint tends to conflict with it.

for the much more powerful ideation-projection of the Universal Cosmic Mind. Thus phenomena, though not-Self, need not be not-God. As, however, *all* phenomena, whether while dreaming or awake, are entirely dependent on consciousness of some kind or other, a study of the various states of consciousness is the foundation of Eastern philosophy. Although the contents of a phenomenon may vary, the laws of its operation can be fairly well predicted. A mastery of the laws of how it acts would, therefore, give control over the phenomenon itself. To what end should the individual seek to control the workings of phenomena? To know their phenomenal nature is to know the non-phenomenal nature of 'not-phenomena', that is to say, the *Real*. 'The seeing of Reality, like a dream by one that's dumb, cannot be described in language to another.'[1] Why? Because all languages depend on phenomena-concepts arising from phenomenal experiences. Failure to realize this has led modern Western philosophy into that wild goose chase called 'logical positivism' and 'linguistic analysis'.

When the Oriental mind turns to study Western philosophy, it is at first shocked by the trivia with which it is sometimes faced. Logical positivism, pragmatism, and so on hardly deserve the name of philosophy by Oriental standards. But here the Orient is wrong. For even fifth-rate philosophy is, after all, philosophy.

The Orient is also wrong if it thinks it has *nothing* to learn from Western philosophy; but in practice it has never adopted this attitude. In so far as social and political philosophy is concerned, it has devoured it eagerly. As for philosophy of the other kind, the Orient must realize that in Western philosophy too, at the highest level, mystic illumination becomes the sole pursuit in life. St Augustine and St Thomas Aquinas can be a source of inspiration to good men in any country, at any time; *The Book of the Craft of Dying* teaches truths as important as the *Bardo Thödol*; the *Exercitia* of St Ignatius Loyola is as effective as yoga; *The Cloud of Unknowing* is as illuminating as the *Gītā*; *The Practice of the Presence of God* is as helpful as all the *Upaniṣads* put together. Western philosophy is not all materialism: nor is Eastern philosophy all illumination. Kauṭilya and Hsun Tze can beat Machiavelli in cynicism.

Nevertheless the plain fact remains that the Orient's misconceptions of Western philosophy are negligible in comparison to Western misconceptions of Oriental philosophy. Once more this is no accusation against the West. The reasons are partly historical, partly linguistic and partly connected with the subject matter itself.

It must be remembered that when the Orient calls Western philosophy materialistic, the adjective is not used to express hatred, ridicule or contempt. On the contrary, the Oriental viewpoint being that the paths to Enlightenment are innumerable, materialism itself *can* (but need not) be one more way leading to Illumination. Seeing the achievements of Western science, the Orient expects to see similar results in the realm of metaphysics—and is disappointed. That is where the Orient is mistaken. It thinks Western philosophy has a way to Enlightenment of which it is not

[1] Cp. Evans-Wentz, *The Tibetan Book of the Great Liberation*, London, 1954, p. 249.

aware. It thus expects Western philosophy to give what it has not got.

Oriental misconceptions about Western philosophy are relatively few. This is not to suggest that the Orient is any wiser than the West. The reason lies in that, because of historical conditions in the last few centuries, the Orient has been steadily importing Western philosophy on a sale or return basis.

An important result is that the Orient is more accurately informed of the *modern* than of the ancient West. Conversely, the West's knowledge of the Orient is relatively more or less confined to the *ancient* classics with a relative ignorance of the philosophy of the contemporary East. And so the Orient paints an exaggerated picture of Western materialism, and the West of the Orient's spiritual genius. *In medio veritas.* For instance, many accuse Eastern wisdom of being empty of ethical content, apparently unaware that ethical perfection is considered, in Eastern philosophy, as the *first* step towards spiritual enlightenment. It is taken for granted that a person comes to the study of philosophy only after having completed that of ethics. There is no need, therefore, to go over the same ground again. How can Indian philosophy be said to be empty of ethics when the highest state prior to *mokṣa* (final emancipation) is *sattva* (ethical perfection), the way to the state beyond the three *guṇas*, and so beyond good and evil. Even responsible Western critics believe that all these philosophers and holy men of India are egoists. The same failure to distinguish between *jñāna* and *bhakti* makes Evelyn Underhill state that Indian philosophy is empty of the *love* aspect. This accusation of lack of love and service to humanity seems rather curious. Have these critics then never heard of *karma marga*, the way of selfless service? Have they never heard of *Bodhisattvas*?[1]

The charges made against Eastern philosophy by Western scholars almost invariably show that a connecting link has been overlooked. This is natural as no one has hitherto realized that a definite interconnected system exists. Professor Tomlin is a learned critic but transparently partial in his religious views. Surely the idea of divine incarnation or the word made flesh existed in Indian philosophy centuries before Christianity, and was probably adopted from there by the latter. No philosopher has examined the theory of divine incarnations so thoroughly and with such wealth of detail taken from ancient Indian philosophy as Ramakrishna. Divine incarnation is certainly a very advanced spiritual principle, but Indian philosophy goes even further than that. When Arjuna called Krishna

---

[1] A *Bodhisattva* is a person who dislikes being reborn so much that he is ripe for the quest of Buddhahood. When after severe trials and sacrifice he has earned it, he voluntarily forgoes it (which for him means all that is best) and is willing to be born again and again (which for him must be far worse than hell) only to serve mankind. Whether we believe in rebirth or Buddhahood is irrelevant here, for the Bodhisattva certainly does. The main point to observe is that he voluntarily gives up that which *for him* means the highest happiness, in exchange for that which *for him* means the worst torture, merely to serve mankind. Is that egoism, lack of humanism, a heartless attitude towards mankind?

the only incarnation, Krishna showed him a tree which appeared to contain clusters of black berries. 'So do divine incarnations come and go on the tree of the Absolute', said Krishna.

It would appear that the Eastern system is based more on intuition than on logic. But Oriental civilizations have never made an artificial distinction between the two. Intuition is latent logic; logic is intuition highly organized. An important result is that it is the individual, not the *System*, that holds the central position in the System itself. Unlike other philosophical systems it does not demean the individual into thinking that he is only a cog in a big machine. An individual does not exist in order to study this system of philosophy or to attain *samādhi*. He is his own *raison d'être*. *Samādhi* is only a name given to the highest state of spiritual evolution an individual can hope to reach. This philosophy is organized as a system to help the growth of individuals each with a different temperament and rate of evolution. Neither the system nor *samādhi* has any value apart from some definite human being alive and in the flesh. Both exist for the individual, but the latter does not exist for anything or anybody—he is born to live, that is enough. The system and *samādhi* are there so that the individual may live more abundantly. The system is neither atheistic nor does it insist dogmatically upon the existence of a divinity. Where the individual accepts that existence, the system offers him a variety of techniques which he can apply within the framework of his own religion. If he denies the existence of the divine, the system offers him an opportunity of facing the implication that he may himself *be* the very divinity he denies.

CHAPTER 5

Radhakrishnan and Aldous Huxley as Ideal Exponents of East-West Integration

Besinne dich doch!
Nur einen Schritt,
so bist du frei.[1]

Reflect, consider, remember,
Resort to introversion;
But one step more
And thou art free!

The above quotation expresses concisely the exact message, which both Radhakrishnan and Huxley wish to convey to mankind. They both want to rescue modern man from the dangerous and unhappy situation of our times. This rescue can only be effected if man *reflects*[2] (on ideas common to the great religions of the world), *considers*[3] (the purpose of his existence on earth), *recollects*[4] (through developing his *latent* faculty of intuition), *remembers*[5] (his divine origin), *changes his mind*[6] (away from materialism and extraversion to introspection), *recovers*[7] consciousness (of his pure being), and *returns to his senses*[8] (restores a sense of proportion to his world-view). In short, just what the German word *Besinnung* so aptly conveys. With a little real and sustained effort (*nur einen Schritt*), man can find that there are friendly and co-operative forces in the universe which will assist him to that which will make him free (in the sense of 'the Truth will make you free').

Both Radhakrishnan and Huxley propound ideas of universal validity

[1] Goethe's *Faust*.

[2] Radhakrishnan, *An Idealist View of Life*, chapter III; Aldous Huxley, *The Perennial Philosophy*, chapter I.

[3] Radhakrishnan, *Eastern Religions and Western Thought*, p. 351; Aldous Huxley, *The Perennial Philosophy*, chapter XIII.

[4] Radhakrishnan, *The Bhagavadgita*, p. 194; Aldous Huxley, *The Perennial Philosophy*, p. 311, and *Vedānta for the Western World*, p. 126.

[5] Radhakrishnan, *East and West in Religion*, Lecture III, part V; Aldous Huxley, *The Perennial Philosophy*, p. 215.

[6] Radhakrishnan, *An Idealist View of Life*, p. 157; Aldous Huxley, *Vedānta for the Western World*, pp. 275–7.

[7] Radhakrishnan, *My Search for Truth*, p. 21; Aldous Huxley, *Ape and Essence*, p. 55.

[8] Radhakrishnan, *Contemporary Indian Philosophy*, pp. 478–83; Aldous Huxley, *Vedānta for Modern Man*, pp. 34–48.

instead of spinning narrow, private philosophical systems as is so fashionable today. Radhakrishnan reveals, in a comparative manner, the universally valid intuitions underlying all religions;[1] Huxley illustrates, by comparison and contrast, the perennial element in all the different philosophies.[2]
Radhakrishnan thus prepares the ground for inter-religious friendship;
Huxley, the basis of a universally understandable metaphysics. They have
both an anti-bigoted, anti-dogmatic character which is intellectually
objective and impartial. Huxley does not hesitate to write a ruthless satire
on the West; nor does Radhakrishnan hesitate to criticize India and
Hindu philosophy when they are found wanting. They are both fanatics in
their pursuit of truth, and have a monomania for ideas that are universally
valid, at all times and in all places. Neither of them is in the least interested in supporting this or that creed or dogma or some private interpretation of the universe.

Radhakrishnan and Huxley are both equally well acquainted with
Oriental and Western philosophy. Few writers in the West can equal
Radhakrishnan's intimate knowledge of Western philosophy, history and
culture. Not many *pandits* in India have Huxley's sincere intellectual
humility, which is so essential for an intuitive understanding of Indian
philosophy. Both know and appreciate German culture. Radhakrishnan
has a penetrating knowledge of German mystics, philosophers and poets.
For instance, on the two hundredth anniversary of Goethe's birth he
gave a brilliant lecture on Goethe which no German professor could have
equalled.[3] For an illustration of Huxley's defence of German values see his
The Perennial Philosophy.[4] German words often creep into his novels,
while he is also well acquainted with Sanskrit and Latin. Thus Radhakrishnan and Huxley are both able and willing to elucidate the philosophy of one part of the world in the language and terminology of the
other.[5] They can also place and express it in the framework of its cultural
history and psychological background. They are both equally at home, not
only in Oriental and Western philosophy and religions, but in literature,
history, politics, and allied topics as well. They are, therefore, able to
present an *integral* view of life and the universe.

The effect of their works is to revitalize Christianity in both East and
West. They give it a new dynamics with which to face the dangers of
secular humanism and communist materialism. It is proof of the sound-
ness of a religion, if others arrive independently at the same conclusions.
A knowledge of Oriental philosophy is indispensable to a correct understanding of the Oriental setting in which Christianity first found its
beginning. After all, the first worshippers of Christ were the three wise men

[1] The *locus classicus* being his *Eastern Religions and Western Thought*.
[2] The *locus classicus* being his *The Perennial Philosophy*.
[3] This lecture has been reprinted in Paris, Unesco Publication No. 411, pp. 99–108.
[4] p. 127.
[5] For illustrations of Radhakrishnan's equal fluency in both English and Sanskrit
see Dhirendra Mohan Datta's essay on Radhakrishnan and Comparative Philosophy
in *The Library of Living Philosophers*, New York, 1952, p. 674 (Vol. 8).

who came from the East. A proper understanding of Radhakrishnan and Huxley can save Christianity from its worst enemy, which is not Communism or materialism, atheism or agnosticism, secularism or humanism, but *inertia* and *indifference* within its own fold.

Both Radhakrishnan and Huxley are dynamic and not static. Religion in their hands is not dry theological dialectic but 'a fact of experience';[1] they 'testify to the felt reality of God'.[2] However much we may be inclined to disagree with what they say or write, their sincerity is unimpeachable. They speak first from the heart and then correct or justify it by the head. They are not mere scholars but creative artists with a wealth and dignity of learning that no bookworm can hope to acquire. They are saints first, artists next, and finally philosophers. They teach, not metaphysics, but the application of metaphysical wisdom to practical life. They are a living proof that philosophy, rightly interpreted, is not meant for ivory towers but for everyday life. They demonstrate by their own lives that philosophy, meditation and introspection make a person more efficient and not less; more useful to society, not less; more creative and not less. They are not philosophers, but philosophy incarnate.

They are also poets and literary giants in their own right. Even supposing that everything which Radhakrishnan and Huxley wrote can be proved to be wrong or meaningless, *still* the sheer beauty of their styles, that magic eloquence,[3] would make their works classics in literature. To a person who has a taste for English prose, their writing is a symphony in words. The poetic beauty of Radhakrishnan's commentary on the *Gītā* equals if not exceeds the beauty of the original. Aldous Huxley first acquired fame as a novelist. There was a time when one had only to mention his name in England and one was at once accepted as belonging to the most advanced cultural set.

They serve as ideal examples in our times because they have something *concrete* to say. It is, therefore, as refreshing as a pool of clear water at a time when much of contemporary philosophy claims that one cannot say anything that is not utterly meaningless, because of the so-called 'limits of language'. They are both men who have experienced the world in all its various aspects. There is hardly any corner of it to which they have not travelled. So when they conclude that the world belongs to the unworldly, they speak not as speculative philosophers but as people who know and understand. They offer not theories but concrete suggestions for the increased happiness of the individual, of mankind and of the world. They have a sense of the crisis under which the world exists today. They, therefore, do not mock mankind by offering an 'armchair philosophy'. They

---

[1] Radhakrishnan, *The Bhagavadgita*, p. 203.

[2] *An Idealist View of Life*, p. 91.

[3] The author once heard Radhakrishnan at a reception in London. His eloquence defied description. As Professor T. R. V. Murti wrote: 'He is not only one of the foremost writers, but an eloquent and inspired speaker as well . . . many of his books were first delivered as *extempore lectures.' The Philosophy of S. Radhakrishnan*, New York, 1952, p. 845.

recognize the moral expressed by one of the fables in the *Panchatantra*.

> The merely learned is a fool
> The wise man uses action's tool
> For no remembered drug can cure
> The sick, by name alone, it's sure.[1]

At the same time they recognize the need for balance and introspection. They, therefore, do not belong to that wing of contemporary philosophy which seems to suggest that life is at its best only when it is full of action.

Most important of all, they offer the best scope for a well balanced comparison and contrast between the so-called Indian and the Western philosophy of today. Other contemporary philosophers may have more to offer in the way of *knowledge*, but in Radhakrishnan and Huxley we find *Wisdom*. Moreover, it is not wisdom worshipped as a goddess but wisdom in the service of mankind. As that beautiful verse of the *Mahabharata* puts it:

> *dāsyam aisvaryavādena*
> *jnātinām tu karomy aham.*

(Under the nominal title of my suzerainty, I act as servant for the whole world.)

[1] Rider's translation.

Part II

RADHAKRISHNAN: OR THE EAST EXPLORES THE WEST

THE APPLICATION OF VEDĀNTIC WISDOM TO PRACTICAL LIFE

CHAPTER 6

Biographical Sketch

If only the good of others be sought in all that one doeth, no need is there to seek benefit for oneself.[1]

Our philosopher, Sarvepalli Radhakrishnan, was born at Tiruttani[2] on September 5, 1888. It would, however, be untruthful flattery to claim for him a place equal to Ramakrishna or Ramana Maharishi. His place is more comparable to that held by Mahatma Gandhi or Swami Vivekananda—and that is no mean honour. Details about his personal life are scanty, nor, for that matter, are they necessary in understanding his philosophy. With bashful modesty he refuses to write about himself: 'In the present account it is not my intention to speak of my personal life. . . . I have had my own share of burdens and anxieties of life. Although these are of immense importance to me, discretion forbids me to speak of them.'[3] We must not forget that our philosopher is also a diplomat, for he was the Indian ambassador in Moscow where discretion is most necessary. It is not, however, his astute diplomacy that prevents personal disclosures, but the sensitiveness natural in a poetic temperament. As he put it: '. . . of all writing, autobiographical writing is the most delicate'.[4] Because of this icy refusal to be personal or intimate on the grounds that 'any sensitive man who takes life seriously is somewhat inaccessible to the public', Radhakrishnan's biography reads like a network of intellectual achievements—an antarctic landscape consisting only of honorary doctorates and international conferences.

In 1909, after having been educated at Voorhees College, Vellore, and the Madras Christian College, he took his M.A. degree in philosophy by submitting a thesis on 'Ethics of the Vedānta'. It was 'a reply to the charge that the Vedānta system had no room for ethics'.[5] His professor, A. G. Hogg, praised it and Radhakrishnan became Assistant Professor of Philosophy at the Presidency College, Madras, where he distinguished himself as a 'very clear expositor of even the most abstruse problems of philosophy'.[6]

---

[1] Precepts of the Gurus. Cf. W. Y. Evans-Wentz, *Tibetan Yoga and Secret Doctrines*, Oxford University Press, 1958, p. 90.

[2] In the Chitur District of what is now known as the State of Madras.

[3] Fragments of a Confession in *The Library of Living Philosophers*, Volume 8 (on Radhakrishnan), p. 5.

[4] *Ibid.*

[5] Radhakrishnan in *My Search for Truth* (1946, separate offprint), p. 9.

[6] Proessor D. S. Sarma in *Great Indians*, Introduction, Hind kitabs, Bombay, 1956, p. 5.

In 1916–17 he became a full-time Professor and was then invited to Mysore University where he remained from 1918 to 1921. The young philosopher now attracted the eye of the great educationalist, Sir Ashutosh Mukherjee, the vice-chancellor of Calcutta University, who offered him the King George V Professorship of Philosophy[1] at Calcutta University (1921–31 and again 1937–41). Between 1931 and 1936 he served as vice-chancellor of Andhra University, Waltair.[2] He was also vice-chancellor of Benares Hindu University from 1939 to 1948.

He went to England first in 1926 to deliver the Upton Lectures, at Manchester College, Oxford, on 'The Hindu View of Life'. He then visited the United States on a lecture tour and in August became the Haskell Lecturer in Comparative Religion at the University of Chicago. He was now again invited to Manchester College, Oxford, this time to occupy the Chair of Comparative Religion.[3] In October 1929 he began the first of a series of lectures on 'East and West in Religion'. He was then asked to deliver the Hibbert Lectures which led later to the publication of his *An Idealist View of Life*. In the meantime, in 1927, he was also general president of the Indian Philosophical Congress, as well as chairman of its executive committee from 1925 to 1937. And during the period 1927 to 1931 he served as president of the Post-Graduate Council in Arts, Calcutta University. In 1931 came his nomination to the League of Nations' Committee for Intellectual Co-operation which he attended annually in Geneva till 1939.

With the founding of the Spalding Chair of Eastern Religions and Ethics in Oxford, it was only natural that Radhakrishnan should be invited to occupy it, which he did.[4] He thus had to divide his time between Oxford and Calcutta, lecturing two trimesters at the former and one at the latter. This arrangement worked well till the outbreak of the war.[5] Pressure was also brought upon him to accept the vice-chancellorship of Benares Hindu University. Radhakrishnan accepted the post while refusing the large salary that accompanied it. In 1941 he became Sir Sayaji Rao Gaekwad, Professor of Indian Culture and Civilization at that University. This meant giving up the Calcutta professorship; but in 1942 he was back at Calcutta University delivering the Kamala Lectures.

In May 1944 the Government of China invited him as a visiting lecturer to meet their leading academic figures. He stayed there for a fortnight and gave twelve major lectures, not counting informal talks on various subjects. This was followed in 1946 by still another lecture tour to the United States where he spoke at Harvard, Cornell, Yale, Michigan and Los Angeles universities. Having led the Indian delegation to Unesco's first

[1] *Ibid.*

[2] In 1930 he was also President of the All Asia Education Conference in Benares.

[3] Later Radhakrishnan was to play a leading role in the World Congress of Faiths, a practical experiment in comparative religion.

[4] 1936.

[5] In 1937 he was also the Niramalendu Ghosh Lecturer in Comparative Religion at Calcutta University.

conference in Paris, he became a member of its first executive board.[1] He attended its second conference at Mexico City in 1947, and at its third in Beirut (1948) he became chairman of the board.

However, Radhakrishnan's greatest distinction is that he was the first Indian to be elected a fellow of the British Academy. During his stay at Oxford, the British Academy had invited him to deliver the usual annual lecture in its *Master Mind* series. He chose Gautama Buddha, and the lecture was later described as '*on* a master mind *by* a master mind'. He then expanded it into his inspiring book, *The Dhammapada*.

In addition to all this he was president of the All India P. E. N. in 1949 and a member of the Indian Constituent Assembly[2] 1947–9. Surprising as it may seem, he was also India's Ambassador to the Soviet Union in 1949 where he met Stalin. He then became president of the Indian Philosophical Congress at its Silver Jubilee Session at Calcutta, in 1950.[3] In May 1952, Sir Sarvepalli Radhakrishnan, F.B.A., Fellow of All Souls College, Oxford, Hon. Fellow of the Royal Asiatic Society, Bengal, became *His Excellency, the Vice-President of India* (later also President).

In 1958 on a visit to Germany he received one more honorary doctorate, this time from the University of Mainz for his contribution to a better understanding between the East and West.

This is a short account of the career of a man whose philosophy is:

'To action alone hast thou a right and never at all to its fruits; let not the fruits of action be thy motive; neither let there be in thee any attachment to inaction.'[4]

In July 1959, on the occasion of the Thirtieth International Congress of P.E.N., Radhakrishnan received Germany's highest public tribute: the Goethe Medal of the city of Frankfurt. It was meant to honour 'the philosopher and statesman whose world renowned books and lectures serve to form a basis for the mutual understanding and appreciation of Eastern and Western cultural values. For even in his political career, he was inspired by the idea that the improvement of man's lot is not possible merely through scientific inventions and welfare-state legislation but require also the counsel of philosophy and religion'. Professor Heuss (the then President of Germany) further called Radhakrishnan's presence a living proof of Goethe's assertion that East and West are no longer separable.

[1] That is to say from 1946 to 1951.

[2] That is to say he was one of the framers of the new constitution of independent India.

[3] Even Canada came under Radhakrishnan's sway. The Sir Edward Beatty Memorial Lectures at McGill University were postponed for a whole year so that he could give the first lectures in this series. He spoke on the interrelationship between East and West. Thousands and thousands of people in Montreal came to attend his lectures so that the audience spilled over from Redpath Hall and sat outside determined to hear him in spite of everything and at the conclusion rose to its feet in a spontaneous ovation of sustained applause.

[4] *Gītā*, II, 47, Radhakrishnan's own translation.

D

Two years later Radhakrishnan received Germany's highest literary award, the Peace Prize of the German Book Trade. He was elected President of the Republic of India on May 11, 1962. His first act was to reduce his own salary to a bare minimum! After his retirement he brought out another excellent book called *Religion in a Changing World*.

CHAPTER 7

The Philosophy of the Spiritual Life

(a) THE SEARCH FOR INTEGRAL IDENTITY

Man is a religious animal. He is prepared to worship anything and many systems compete for his spiritual suffrage, fragmentary faiths, unaesthetic arts, and attractive panaceas.[1]

It is very difficult to write about Radhakrishnan without suffering the qualms of a guilty conscience. This is because what he may have said or written is of little value compared to what he *is*. That he is a philosopher is only a by-product of the fact that he is a holy sage and mystic in the full tradition of one who has had the experience of Self-Realization. Even if one has not had a modicum of this *Enlightenment*, one must at least be aware of it as a possibility before one can fully understand Radhakrishnan's works or write about him.

Otherwise we would resemble that amiable character in the Upaniṣads who confessed he knew everything 'from the Vedas to snake-charming' but did not know the Higher Self, had not *Erleuchtung* (mystic enlightenment). Radhakrishnan the philosopher can only be understood after Radhakrishnan the mystic has been comprehended. What then is the evidence that he is an enlightened mystic? If we leave aside *My Search for Truth*, with his autobiographical reference, we find it in *The Bhagavadgītā*, which is his most inspired book. The attitude in some academic circles is that a philosopher is all the more to be praised, for being objective, the less he believes in the philosophy he is interpreting. The *Gītā*, however, is not a treatise which can be translated and commented upon by one who has not to some extent experienced the validity of its premises. Since time immemorial it has been a tradition in India for every philosopher to write a commentary on the *Gītā*. The reason is not hard to seek. The commentary serves as a measuring rod for estimating the degree of genuine mystical enlightenment of the writer. Radhakrishnan's commentary gives one cause to believe that he is not devoid of that *Erleuchtung* which is the *sine qua non* of philosophy in India, and of mysticism and religion the world over. Emerson quotes the story of the ancient king of Persia who wanted to find out if Zoroaster had indeed the mystic enlightenment referred to. The king sent an expert judge of character to cross-examine him at a special ceremony in an assembly of the learned. The judge had only to see Zoroaster walk into the room and his mind was made up: 'This is not the gait of an imposter!' said he. So of Radhakrishnan's commentary to the *Gītā* one can also say: this is not the style of an imposter or of one who is deluded.

It is important to establish Radhakrishnan's claim to be a mystic and so to realize that he uses ordinary words like Religion, Soul, God, Self, etc., in

[1] Radhakrishnan, *The Brahma Sutra*, London, 1960, p. 9.

a very special sense. The most important of these words is *Religion* to which he attached a very special meaning. Failure to understand it is why his critics find so many contradictions in his attitude to religion and philosophy. Another reason for establishing his position as a mystic is to avoid the charge that his writings are only a collection of theistic platitudes, which they would be, were they not backed by the sincerity of his first-hand mystical experience.[1] A platitude uttered straight from the heart ceases to be one. Platitudes are like token money; their value depends on whether the person making them is sufficiently sincere or experienced. If you deny Radhakrishnan mystic-enlightenment (*Erleuchtung*) then his philosophy is only a string of elegant sayings, a rosary of rather second-hand gems.[2] His platitudes are so obvious that no writer would have dared to utter them had they not been forced from him by the overwhelming pressure of the genuine religious-mystical experience behind them. More-over, there is no reason to believe that a platitude cannot be true, or ceases to be so on repetition. It is well known that the founders of the great religions expressed themselves in statements which today sound like platitudes. But this is only because those statements were of such universal validity that they just had to be repeated over and over again. This is true in Radhakrishnan's case. A platitude indicates sincerity rather than rodomontade, just as the latter is notorious for its use of impressive eloquence. Besides, in the sphere of universal religious experience, which is the basis of Radhakrishnan's philosophy, there is little room for originality of expression. This all leads to the main point which we wish to establish:

Radhakrishnan's writings stand or fall on one issue: do they, or do they not, spring from a genuine mystical enlightenment (*Erleuchtung*)?

This further leads to the following points:
  (i) does such an experience exist?[3]
  (ii) if so, then can it be verified?[4]
  (iii) if so, then how?[5]
  (iv) assuming that it is proved valid, would it justify the entire corpus of Radhakrishnan's writings?[6]

[1] This is a charge easily levelled against Radhakrishnan's works but also against Pope's *Essay on Man*. This has not prevented the latter from being a classic in English literature.

[2] This is exactly what German Indologists accuse him of.

[3] Cf. 'Those who have this consciousness are the saintly souls whose lives are characterized by an unshakable faith in the supremacy of Spirit, invincible optimism, ethical universalism and religious toleration.' *An Idealist View of Life*, p. 126.

[4] Cf. 'The attainment of steady spiritual insight is the aim of religious endeavour and the means to it are an ethical life and the art of meditation.' *Ibid.*

[5] Cf. 'There is a mode of consciousness which is distinct from the perceptual, imaginative, or intellectual, and this carries with it self-evidence and completeness. Religious men of all ages have won their certainty of God through this direct way of approach to the apprehension of reality.' *Ibid.*, p. 125.

[6] Cf. 'The larger environment is of the nature of one's own self, with which the

Here it should be remembered that in Radhakrishnan's *Religionsphiloso-phie* it would be impertinent and blasphemous to discuss these points in detail when every spare moment should be devoted to attaining that very experience of Mystical Enlightenment (*Erleuchtung*) which we, at the theoretical level, are doomed merely to discuss. Perhaps we can atone for this sin of *superbia* by making it plain *why* this experience is so very important and *why* its attainment in life is considered so indispensable.

Radhakrishnan would answer, with Carlyle,[1] that nothing short of such attainment can bring *lasting satisfaction*[2] to an individual.[3] In this respect the quest for happiness is identical with that for *Erleuchtung*.[4] Radha-krishnan would go farther and say that without such attainment the individual is not only unsatisfied and unhappy, but also *incomplete*.[5] Spiritual regeneration is, therefore, in a very real sense our *need*.[6] For although *Erleuchtung* is a great comfort and privilege once it has been attained, we are under a duty and a necessity to strive for it until such attainment. Moreover, if you accept the general premises of this argument, it makes a colossal difference whether you die before such attainment, or after.

What then is the implication of what Radhakrishnan calls the *need for spiritual regeneration*? This need can be explained as follows: the only reason why man is born on earth is to find his spiritual self (what Radha-krishnan would call the Ātman) which is, at the same time, his *innermost being*. As this is the *sole* purpose of our earthly incarnation, the fulfilment

---

individual occasionally comes into contact. There are differences regarding the interpretation of the nature of this spiritual environment, while this at any rate is true, that it offers the only justification for a life of truth seeking and good realizing.' *Ibid.*

[1] Radhakrishnan's answer would find an echo in the writings of many Western thinkers. On this point Carlyle has been selected to give a closer comparison, especially in view of his unequivocal stand in *Sartor Resartus*.

[2] This word is not used here in any utilitarian sense. Many deny that man seeks happiness at all. For instance, Carlyle says that man does not seek it but seeks blessedness. For our purpose we define happiness as whatever a person seeks most, and finds satisfying to some degree or other when found.

[3] Radhakrishnan: 'It alone satisfies our total desire.' *An Idealist View of Life*, p. 302; Carlyle: 'Man's Unhappiness . . . comes of his Greatness; it is because there is an Infinite in him . . . in the Godlike only has he the Strength and Freedom.' *Sartor Resartus*, Bk. II, Chap. IX.

[4] Compare Radhakrishnan's: 'the heaven which is all the time here, *could we but see it* . . . a state of identification with the real *here* and now' (*Indian Philosophy*, Vol. II, p. 636) with Carlyle's: 'the thing thou seekest is already with thee, "*here* or nowhere", *couldst thou only see*' (*Sartor Resartus*, Bk. II, Chap. IX).

[5] Cf. 'Any one who has not had initiation (*Erleuchtung*) is only a half-man. Through it we enter into an awareness of our real selfhood, which is divine.' *Eastern Religon and Western Thought*, p. 139.

[6] Cf. 'Refined Paganism is not an answer to the problem of living.' *The Recovery of Faith*, p. 43.

of any other one would not result in lasting satisfaction.[1] Even to realize that life has such a purpose is a big step forward in spiritual regeneration. Just as a prudent merchant would not squander his capital, so also we should not fritter away in needless extraversion the precious opportunity afforded by birth in a human form, lest by our negligence of the spiritual we leave this world spiritually empty-handed. (Could this not be the hidden meaning of Jesus's parable of the servant who buried his talent?)[2]

Given the *need* for spiritual regeneration, what are the problems facing modern man in meeting and fulfilling this need? Today anything even remotely connected with the word spiritual is suspect. This is not so much due to a bias for what is commonly called materialism, as to a deep-seated prejudice that it is wiser and safer to leave certain things unknown. The word spiritual conjures up in the mind of the average person either the idea of saints and visions or that of rank fraud. Thus the first problem is that whereas many are eager and willing to find God, or the Ātman (as Radhakrishnan urges them to), they fight shy of having any extraordinary (what Radhakrishnan would call extrasensory) experience in which such 'finding' (or what Radhakrishnan would call self-realization) is most likely to take place. There is an inescapable penumbra, of what may be called the spiritual, around the experience of union with the divine (*Erleuchtung*). This, while it lures the curious, the superstitious, and the unbalanced,

---

[1] 'The *sole* spiritual vocation of man consists in the discovery of reality and not what serves our temporal ends.' *Indian Philosophy*, p. 655.

[2] The word religion is derived from the Latin *relegere* which originally meant meticulous heedfulness. It was also used in this sense by Latin authors of the pre-Christian era, such as Cicero (106–43 B.C.) in his *De Natura Deorum*. Not the unbeliever, but the person who lived heedless of the transcendental reality behind life, was considered to be irreligious. The opposite of *religio* would then be *neglego*, with its English equivalent negligence, which is the failure of a *duty* to take care. Are we then under a duty to take care that our life does not run to waste without earnest reflection on its inner meaning and transcendent purpose? So long as we do not call this in question, we are deeply religious even though we may harbour no other beliefs. This is also the sense in which the great contemporary theologian Paul Tillich understood religion.

Under Lactantius (A.D. +330), however, the word came to be coloured through his own preconceived Christian conceptions and was thus limited to mean: to bind. Accordingly the word came to mean the bond between God and man. For centuries thereafter, the word religion became almost a synonym for theism thereby doing serious injustice to so-called atheistic religions like Buddhism and Jainism. All Western polemic against religion, from Karl Marx to Bertrand Russell and G. Szczesny in our own day, has, therefore, concentrated its attack on theistic beliefs. It is high time to free the word religion from its Christian limitations, by restoring to it its original and universal meaning, if we are ever to have a science of religions. A beginning has already been made by Jose Ortega y Gasset in his *Concord and Liberty* (1946, p. 22 ff.) and by German theologians like Otto, Heiler, and Tillich, and also by the present Archbishop of Vienna, Cardinal Koenig, and by such authorities on comparative religion as von Glasenapp and Mensching. Even in Sanskrit the opposite of religious aspiration (*sattva*) is negligence (arising out of dullness, *tamas*).

Cp. also Tibetan *Clos* with its opposite *gTi-mug*.

frightens away the more deserving and better qualified group of genuine
seekers who are unwilling to risk their reputation of being practical men of
affairs for anything they feel would make them lose the ground under-
neath their feet. Radhakrishnan's philosophy, by its continual emphasis on
sarvamukti (universal salvation for *all* sentient beings), has to solve the
problem of how to reconcile the indispensability of *Erleuchtung* with the
sorry fact that even the best among us suffer from vertigo when faced with
'the flight from the Alone to the Alone'.[1] The choice is a very strict one:
either salvation (*Erleuchtung*), or acute suffering and dissatisfaction until
such salvation. Where the choice is so grim, any philosophy based on
universal salvation is inclined to apply mass-production methods to the
attainment of the goal. But, as Emerson pointed out, souls are not saved in
bundles.

Two factors aggravate the problem of spiritual regeneration in our times.
Firstly, the kind of life one is compelled to lead in our big cities all over the
world makes spiritual discipline appear far more extraordinary than it is.
A serious break with conformity is demanded which discourages the
beginner however earnest he may be. Although the goal (*Erleuchtung*) is
indispensable, city life makes that goal as difficult to attain as possible. For
instance, it would have been considered obvious in any period of history
except our own that periodical chastity and solitude are more or less
essential for creating an atmosphere in which spiritual experience can take
place. This though recognized and acted upon the world over, from the
early Christian saints and Tibetan students of philosophy to the witch-
doctors of Africa in our own day, comes as a puzzling surprise to the
modern city dweller. It is mainly for people of the last kind that Radhakrishnan insists on spiritual regeneration. What is demanded is not
asceticism, yet even the mildest form of austerity appears to us as the most
exasperating and painful asceticism. How tempting, therefore, to dismiss it
all as medieval superstition or as Oriental pessimism! Radhakrishnan
therefore has a hard time trying to convince his readers that what he means is
not asceticism. Judged by the standards consonant with so lofty a spiritual
goal as *Erleuchtung* (which Radhakrishnan also calls *mukti*), what is required is only a mild form of general restraint. Surely no one expects a smug
worldling to become an enlightened sage-mystic, or even a worthy student
of philosophy. Even an Egyptian snake-charmer demands seven days of
austere living from anyone who seeks the secrets of his trade. Curiously
enough, moderation and voluntary restraint appear alarming or ridiculous
to modern eyes only when associated with the religious life. People are
quite willing to grant that an austere life is necessary, and even inevitable,
in the case of a successful stock-broker, lawyer, or surgeon. Any serious
endeavour or lofty goal demands a disciplined life. Yet our modern society
is shocked and perplexed, when an individual decides to renounce family
ties and property in the interests of a spiritual quest. Great efforts are

[1] 'The silences and the eternities cannot be questioned without peril by the weak of
heart. The dizziness of the inquiry into the infinite is a vertigo which even mighty
minds try to avoid, if they can.' *Indian Philosophy*, Vol. II, p. 772.

often made to convince him that renunciation is irrelevant to religion.[1] But there is not half so much fuss when millions renounce home and family, even life itself, as soldiers sent to the front.[2] What people fail to realize is that austerity and renunciation are not peculiar to a religious life. They are attributes inherent in the successful execution of any great task. The second aggravating factor is that the word spiritual bears too close a resemblance to spiritualism or spiritualistic, meaning the so-called occult. The danger is that people come to think of *Erleuchtung* (or *mokṣa*) as some sort of occult, or at any rate abnormal, experience. From Radhakrishnan's point of view nothing could be more natural in the life of a human being than *Erleuchtung*. The ordinary man is wary and suspicious of any experience other than waking, or everyday, consciousness.[3] All unusual experiences are described, and then dismissed, as occult. This is commonsense yet a further unfortunate fact has to be faced. There is one so-called occult or unusual experience that cannot ultimately be put off, namely death. However much one may believe in immortality, or in everlasting life, the psycho-physiological experience of death has to be undergone at least on the earthly plane. No matter what one's beliefs about this may be, it is futile to deny that it lies outside the framework of everyday waking consciousness and, therefore, for the ordinary person must appear as something occult. If sleep and dreams did not occur so regularly, they too would be regarded in the same way. It is only through such occult experiences that we can overcome our habitual belief that matter is an abiding reality, and that the body is the real 'I'.[4]

Thus it is only natural that *Erleuchtung* should be an experience that is unusual when *judged from the waking state*. But it is no more unusual than dying, sleeping, or dreaming. These three experiences are so regular and unavoidable that they cease to be considered queer or occult however full of mystery they may be in themselves. Indeed, the modern man with his utter lack of a sense of ontological mystery does not even regard them as experiences. Since to him only the waking state is valid, he regards them as a cessation of experience. A person who feels that it takes courage to sacrifice his waking consciousness for an *Erleuchtung* would not hesitate to do so for the sake of an operation under anaesthesia. Yet logically to fall asleep shows as much faith and trust in a power higher than one's personal ego as the voluntary surrender of personal consciousness in the process of *Erleuchtung*. We may bury our caprices but they rule us from their graves, which lie in our own subconscious mind.

A very sharp look-out must be maintained to prevent the spiritual from

---

[1] Contrast this with Carlyle's: 'Well did the wisest of our time write: "It is only with Renunciation (*Entsagen*) that Life, properly speaking, can be said to begin".' *Sartor Resartus*, Bk. II, Chap. IX.

[2] Think of Viet Nam!

[3] 'The waking state is the normal condition of the natural man, who without reflection accepts the universe as he finds it.' *The Principal Upaniṣads*, p. 695.

[4] Cf. 'Though our age has largely ceased to understand the meaning of religion, it is still in desperate need of that which religion alone can give.' *The Recovery of Faith*, p. 204.

being mixed up with the occult tradition. The latter no more represents the former than Barbary Coast pirates can be said to typify a naval academy. Radhakrishnan says:

'Though intuitive wisdom is different from knowledge of the senses or anything we can achieve by logical reflection, it is not to be confused with occultism, obscurantism, or extravagant emotion. It is not magical insight or heavenly vision, or special revelation obtained through supernatural powers.'[1]

This danger is particularly acute in Indian philosophy where the genuine desire for self-realization (*Erleuchtung*) is too easily confused with the vainglorious desire for occult abnormalities. How great this danger is can be judged from the extreme virulence of Ramakrishna's warnings about it.[2] Yet there are so many superficial resemblances between the two that the average man can be excused for refusing to touch this matter for fear of catching hold of the serpent's tail. If one wishes to accelerate the coming of *sarvamukti* then what is needed most is not emphasis on the desirability and even indispensability of *mukti*, as a reliable means to prevent one getting lost in the uncharted, treacherous waters of the occult. After all, most of us are not hardened sailors lured by the rewards obtainable at the end of the voyage, but apprehensive passengers much concerned for our safety *during* the voyage. Radhakrishnan's reply would be that ethical discipline and austerity keep the aspirant clear of the occult; and in any case dangers cannot always be avoided, as the path to the goal is like a razor's edge. If courage is necessary for worldly adventures it is even more so for a spiritual one. Unfortunately all this talk will not make the modern man turn to spiritual regeneration. We are not heroes but people who need to be rescued.

There is a mild but disconcerting contradiction in Radhakrishnan's philosophy which unless resolved will discourage the modern man from ever taking the path of spiritual reawakening. On the one hand Radhakrishnan insists (and Aldous Huxley even more so) that the only insurance against suffering lies in realizing the *Real Self* or Ātman. This will give us 'the supreme and *only* blessedness . . . the heaven which is all the time here, could we but see it'.[3] This should fill the modern man with high hopes so that he turns to the path of spiritual regeneration full of good cheer. But we also read that: '. . . the Self (Ātman) cannot be realized except by those whom the Self chooses.'[4] Moreover, one has to be a very exceptional person indeed before one is so chosen by his *Self* (or Ātman).[5] How slender are one's

[1] *The Principal Upaniṣads*, p. 103.

[2] *The Gospel of Sri Ramakrishna*, New York, 1952, p. 745; also pp. 459, 547–8, 550, 624, 871.

[3] *Indian Philosophy*, Vol. II, p. 636.

[4] *The Principal Upaniṣads*, p. 103; also *Kaṭha Upaniṣad* 1.2.23.

[5] For a list of the necessary preliminary qualities to be acquired, see his very illuminating chapter 'God-Realization and the Way to It', where it is also mentioned that: 'The way to perfection is described as steep and hard, lonely and arduous, as sharp as the edge of a razor.' *The Recovery of Faith*, p. 161.

chances of being among the chosen can be seen from some of the hymns Ramakrishna used to sing:

> Can everyone have the vision of *Syāmā?*
>
> . . . .
>
> Oh what a pity that my foolish mind
> will not see what is true!
> [That] even with all his penances,
> rarely does Shiva himself
> behold the mind-bewitching
> [state of *Erleuchtung*]
> [Even] the prince of Yogis [and] the
> King of the gods meditate [for it]
> in vain![1]

What if in spite of ethical discipline, austerity and the like one does not happen to be chosen by the Self (Ātman)? Moreover, the idea of being so chosen is dangerously close to the Calvinist doctrine of predestination. Are we to understand that such a person may reach the goal without the need for ethical discipline? This for Radhakrishnan would be anathema and he would answer that ethical maturity is a *sine qua non* of being chosen by the Self.[2] But even then the great danger is that anyone who thinks he is 'chosen by the Self' is likely to neglect and discard ethical obligations in the comforting, if mistaken, belief that what is chosen cannot be forsaken. This type of difficulty does not occur within the strict framework of Indian philosophy for on the principle of *karma* such a person may even reach the final goal and yet continue on the ego-body plane to suffer for his past unethical conduct. But if, on the other hand, he does not regard himself as 'chosen' he has little incentive to take the path of spiritual re-awakening. The modern man can hardly be encouraged when Radhakrishnan suggests that very few reach the final goal of spiritual re-awakening.

It seems, therefore, that Radhakrishnan's besetting sin is over-simplification. But that would be to do him an injustice. According to him, the fact that very few achieve final emancipation does not invalidate his contention that suffering can best be eliminated or diminished if man, on a world-wide scale, turned to the practice of spiritual regeneration. This is irrespective of whether the goal in any particular case is reached or not, for as he says:

(i) 'It is not the end of the voyage that matters, but the voyage itself. To travel is a better thing than to arrive.'[3]

---

[1] *The Gospel of Sri Ramakrishna*, New York, 1952, p. 474.

[2] 'To be good,' as defined by Radhakrishnan, 'is to be capable of all evil and yet commit none.' *The Recovery of Faith*, p. 96.

[3] *Indian Philosophy*, Vol. II, p. 769. This is probably taken from R. L. Stevenson's *El Dorado* though Radhakrishnan does not mention it. It is also to be noted that here Radhakrishnan slightly contradicts himself. In criticizing the philosophers of 'endless progress' he hints that one cannot rest content with infinite progress without attaining the actual goal one is progressing towards. 'Progress is not its own end.' *Eastern Religion and Western Thought*, p. 81.

(ii) 'Even failure here is success and no sincere attempt will go without its reward.'[1] Again: 'The lesser ones bring lesser rewards while devotion to the supreme brings the supreme reward.'[2]

It is to be feared that when Radhakrishnan speaks of the eradication of suffering through *Erleuchtung*, the modern man may understand it in a purely utilitarian sense. He might overlook the fact that at the moment of release personal suffering may disappear only to be replaced by 'the Great Compassion' or non-egoistic suffering; a kind of *Weltschmerz*, which may even be more acute than the suffering he had hoped to get rid of through *Erleuchtung*.[3] Relating to this there is the following *koan* in Zen Buddhism:

'Before I understood the great affair (*Erleuchtung*), I felt as thought I had lost both father and mother (I was full of suffering). After I understood the grand affair, I felt as though I had lost my parents (i.e. vicarious suffering through compassion has replaced personal suffering).'[4]

Radhakrishnan teaches us that the most useful and valuable things in life are obtained through the cultivation of an attitude of anti-utilitarianism, by spurning calculations of pleasure and pain[5] in favour of a philosophy of duty (*karma-mārga*).[6] This hoary wisdom of anti-hedonism is then supported by a wealth of detail taken from the most recent findings of science and philosophy. The result is a *Religionsphilosophie* that stands in direct contrast to materialism, pragmatism, or utilitarianism of any kind, whether it be of the Marxist or the logical-positivist type. This part of his philosophy bears a striking resemblance to certain parts of Carlyle, both in regard to content and the attitude towards the *Zeitgeist*.

Carlyle was shocked by the godlessness of the industrial revolution with its prosperity of steam-engines and its social reformers anxious for the welfare of the masses while overlooking the fact that 'there is in man a *Higher* than Love of happiness: he can do without happiness, and instead thereof find Blessedness. Was it not to preach-forth this same *Higher* that

[1] *The Bhagavadgītā*, p.208.

[2] *Ibid.*, p. 248.

[3] 'Man is never nearer God than in the extremity of his anguish.' *The Recovery of Faith*, p. 73.

[4] Even this effect, which indicates the authenticity of an *Erleuchtung*, is to be found in Carlyle's *Sartor Resartus*: 'With other eyes, too, could I now look upon my fellow man; with an infinite love, an infinite Pity. . . . O my Brother, my Brother, why cannot I shelter thee in my bosom, and wipe away all tears from thy eyes. . . . The poor earth, with her poor joys, was now my needy Mother, not my cruel Stepdame; Man, with his so mad wants and so mean endeavours, had become the dearer to me; and even for his sufferings and his sins, I now first named him Brother.' This re-echoes Radhakrishnan's basic argument that *Erleuchtung* is not a diminution of humanism. It leads to a more profound and enlightened humanism in contrast to the sentimental, melodramatic kind of Leigh Hunt's *Abou Ben Adhem*.

[5] 'Profit and loss philosophy'—*see* Carlyle, Chap. VII of *Sartor Resartus*.

[6] Cf. Carlyle: 'The Situation that has not its Duty, its Ideal, was never yet occupied by man.' *Ibid.*, Chap. IX.

sages and martyrs, the Poet and the Priest, in all times, have spoken and suffered; bearing testimony, through life and through death, of the God-like that is in Man?'[1] Notice the words 'Godlike in Man'; can it possibly mean anything other than what Radhakrishnan calls Ātman or Higher Self? Radhakrishnan found himself in much the same position.[2] The dark night had grown darker. Prosperity had increased since Carlyle's time, so had discontent; the steam-engine had been developed and made obsolete by rockets; the atheistic social reformers now were no longer meek, middle-aged gentlemen but powerful and ruthless political organizations on an international scale; Carlyle's 'oceans of Hochheimer' had now become a flood of TV sets; and the idea of a 'Godlike in Man' had dis-appeared, to Radhakrishnan's horror, even in India. If Carlyle had to cry: 'Our Wilderness is the wide World in an Atheistic Century' in what words could Radhakrishnan describe his. The latter's idea, therefore, is that if man's attention could be brought back to his primary need and his primary duty (spiritual welfare), his secondary needs and tasks (socio-economic reforms) would to some extent look after themselves.[3] Radha-krishnan is decidedly *not* against the material prosperity and social welfare of the modern world, as Carlyle perhaps would have been.[4] His only regret is that we put the cart before the horse. The philosophers of utilitarianism insist on the welfare state first, with the kingdom of heaven added as an after-thought for those who still feel unsatisfied. Against this, both Radhakrishnan and Carlyle point out that there are contradictions inherent in every hedonistic approach to the problem. Firstly, the hedonistic ap-proach cannot explain that 'something extra' in man. 'How, with it, Martyrs otherwise weak, can cheerfully endure the shame and the cross; and without it, worldlings puke up their sick existence, by suicide, in the midst of luxury.'[5] As Radhakrishnan says: 'Man cannot live on doubt.'[6] The second fault of the hedonistic-utilitarian approach is that 'judgement on the world is passed on the unconscious assumption that the pleasure of man is the end of life'.[7] Radhakrishnan then explains that 'Happiness is

---

[1] *Sartor Resartus*, Bk. II, Chap. IX.

[2] He explains the predicament thus: 'Among the major influences which have created the problem of unbelief today are the growing scientific outlook, an awakened social conscience and interest in world unity.' *The Recovery of Faith*, p. 10.

[3] Cf. Carlyle: '*Do the duty which lies nearest thee*—which thou knowest to be a Duty! Thy second duty will already have become clearer.' *Ibid.*

[4] Cf. Carlyle: 'For a genuine man, it is no evil to be poor; . . . there ought to be Literary Men [who are] poor—to show whether they are genuine or not! Mendicant orders, bodies of good men doomed to *beg*, were instituted in the Christian Church; a most natural and even necessary development of the spirit of Christianity. It was itself founded on Poverty. . . .' *On Heroes, Hero-Worship and the Heroic in History*, Lecture V.

[5] *Sartor Resartus*, Bk. II, Chap. VII.

[6] *Indian Philosophy*, Vol. II, p. 19. Cf. Carlyle: 'for man's well-being, Faith is properly the one thing needful . . . for a (person of) pure moral nature, the loss of his religious Belief was the loss of everything'. *Sartor Resartus*, Bk. II, Chap. IX.

[7] Radhakrishnan, *An Idealist View of Life*, p. 57.

not to be confused with pleasure'.[1] He quotes Emerson, Descartes and even Dostoievsky to support his argument that we would not be aware of a sense of spiritual want if we did not have the idea of infinity all the time within us.

But what if a person does not feel this sense of spiritual want? Carlyle's standpoint was that it does not have to be a sense of any *particular* kind of want, such as spiritual want. What suffices is a general feeling of incompleteness or non-satisfaction. Beyond a certain point, the marginal satisfaction derived from the fulfilment of each succeeding wish tends to fall off. A person in such a position is, therefore, compelled to seek wishes more and more difficult to fulfil in order to derive the same amount of satisfaction. So that: 'Oceans of Hochheimer, a Throat like that of Ophinchus:— to the infinite [in a] Shoeblack they are as nothing. No sooner is your ocean filled, than he grumbles that it might have been of better vintage. Try him with half of a Universe, of an Omnipotence, he sets to quarrelling with the proprietor of the other half, and declares himself the most maltreated of men.'[3]

Again: '. . . for the Shoeblack also has a Soul . . . and would require for his permanent satisfaction: God's *infinite Universe altogether to himself.*'[4] Radhakrishnan would go farther and claim that even *that* would not lead to permanent satisfaction—not even if God gave man a delegated power to create entire universes at will. For this entire creation as well as the power to project universes belongs to the realm of *māyā*, of *phenomena*, or of the *not-Self*. By no amount of *not-Self* can man's need for the *Higher Self* be satiated, just as all things in existence put together do not add up to *being*. Radhakrishnan explains this as follows:

'It is because the Universal spirit which is higher than the self-conscious individual is present and operative in the self-conscious mind that the latter is dissatisfied with any finite form it may assume.'[5]

A critic of Radhakrishnan could argue that the very fact of temporary satisfaction being derived from the fulfilment of specific desires proves that the divine, the Ātman, the higher self, or the godlike in man is not indispensable to human happiness. Further, that permanent satisfaction is only a series of temporary satisfactions bound closely together. If one can have temporary satisfaction without God or Ātman, permanent satisfaction is only a matter of time or degree. The cardinal error here is to think in terms of:

(i) a permanent happiness derived from the realization of God or Ātman (*Erleuchtung*) and

(ii) a temporary one derived from the fulfilment of wishes.

[1] *Ibid.*, p. 58.

[2] One reason why the hero of Hemingway's novels is forever escaping into greatness.

[3] *Sartor Resartus*, Bk. II, Chap. IX.

[4] *Ibid.*

[5] *An Idealist View of Life*, p. 302.

In actual fact there is only one happiness-bestowing authority in an individual and that is the godlike or Ātman which he must learn to identify as his higher self. If the latter were not the highest and only form of happiness possible to him, the fulfilment of all his other desires would yield him nothing. This is because the moment any temporary satisfaction reaches its climax is when he effortlessly frees himself from that desire, which had been fulfilled, and also from the psychological-self [1] or ego which sustained that desire. [2] The result is an unintentional, lightning-like quasi-*Erleuchtung* of short duration. This temporary *Erleuchtung* causes the temporary satisfaction which follows on every fulfilled desire.

And so: 'at the human level the secret tendency of man's nature to be a superman is found at work. The destiny of man is to manifest this secret aspiration.' [3] Radhakrishnan maintains that we are not men but, as he puts it, 'God-men'.

Carlyle also refers to a superman, but this word has now fallen into disrepute. Moreover in his case it has been vulgarized and banalized as a cult [4] by his critics and linked up with Nietzsche and the political consequences of Nazism. For Radhakrishnan at any rate supermen are those who have found the higher self as their essence—what we ourselves will be after attaining *Erleuchtung* in the course of evolution. His *sarvamukti* is when all men are conscious of being supermen. As he says 'The supernatural is the natural in her true depths and infinity.' [5]

Appendix

Those who are interested in a more detailed comparison between the thought of Radhakrishnan and Carlyle may like to follow up for themselves the following points of resemblance:

(i) Radhakrishnan's view of political pacifism with Carlyle's passage beginning: 'What, speaking in quite unofficial language, is the net-purport and upshot of war?' in Book II, Chapter VIII of *Sartor Resartus*.

(ii) Radhakrishnan's view of non-violence, up to a point and only when free of cowardice, as illustrated by his *Gītā* commentary, with Carlyle's incident of the Hyperborean Bear (a Russian Smuggler) and its dark prophecy today illustrated by thermo-nuclear weapons: 'Such I hold to be the genuine use of Gunpowder' (or for that matter: thermo-nuclear weapons); 'that it makes all men' (or nations) 'alike tall'. *Ibid.*

---

[1] This psychological-self or ego must be destroyed (or at least eradicated in the case of a temporary *Erleuchtung*) before the higher self can be identified. Thus Carlyle: 'The first preliminary moral Act, Annihilation of Self (*Selbst-töting*), had been happily accomplished; and my mind's eyes were now unsealed.' *Sartor Resartus*, Bk. II, Chap. IX.

[2] 'Manu says that all desires are born of *samkalpa*. "O desire, I know thy root. Thou art born of *samkalpa* or thought."' Radhakrishnan, *The Bhagavadgītā*, p. 189.

[3] *An Idealist View of Life*, p. 302.

[4] *See* Eric Bentley, *The Cult of the Superman*.

[5] *An Idealist View of Life*, p. 59.

(iii) Radhakrishnan's protest that it is not possible to describe in words the integral experience or *Erleuchtung* (what Carlyle calls 'the hour of Spiritual Enfranchisement') with Carlyle's protest: 'How point to the sensual eye what passes in the Holy-of-Holies of Man's Soul; in what words, known to these profane times, speak even afar-off of the unspeakable?' *Ibid.*, Chapter IX.

(iv) Radhakrishnan's view of the underlying unity of all religions with Carlyle's statement: 'to a few some Solution of it [of spiritual tension] is indispensable. In every new era, too, such Solution comes out in different terms; and ever the Solution of the last era has become obsolete, and is found unserviceable. For it is man's nature to change his Dialect from century to century; he cannot help it though he would.' In Carlyle's terminology, Radhakrishnan's *Religionsphilosophie* could be 'the authentic Church Catechism of our present century' for which we seek.

(v) Radhakrishnan's disgust at all petty-minded quarrelling over dogmatic details at the expense of real insight with Carlyle's passage: 'what are antiquated Mythuses to me? ... Neither shall ye tear out one another's eyes, struggling over *plenary* Inspiration, and suchlike: try rather to get a little even Partial Inspiration, each of you for himself.' *Ibid.*

(vi) Radhakrishnan's idea of *karma-yoga* as a philosophy of action undertaken only for *dharma's* sake (i.e. out of a pure sense of duty) with Carlyle's closing words in the chapter 'The Everlasting Yea': 'Produce! Produce! Were it but the pitifullest infinitesimal fraction of a Product, produce it, in God's name! 'Tis the utmost thou hast in thee: out with it, then. Up, up! Whatsoever thy hand findeth to do, do it with thy whole might. Work while it is called Today; for the Night cometh, wherein no man can work.'

Readers who may be surprised to find any connection or resemblance between Carlyle and the essentially Indian philosophy of Radhakrishnan should learn by heart Carlyle's 'The World out of Clothes' (Chapter VIII in Book I of *Sartor Resartus*). There he stumbles upon the magic question, the golden key to every passage in Indian philosophy. The mere asking of this question sincerely, in solitude, and often enough, can sometimes lead to *Erleuchtung*. Carlyle says: 'With men of a speculative turn ... there come seasons, *meditative*, sweet, yet awful hours, when in wonder and fear you ask yourself that unanswerable question: "*Who am I*, the thing that can say 'I'? ... Who am I; what is this *Me*?"'[1]

He who can ask this in the right frame of mind possesses an open sesame to all the treasures of Eastern wisdom, including Radhakrishnan's contribution to it. The comparison with Carlyle should also help to show that the designation 'Eastern' wisdom is only a term of convenience and not intended in any parochial sense.

---

[1] *Sartor Resartus*, Everyman's Library Edition, London, 1916, p. 148.

(b) THE INTEGRAL CONSCIOUSNESS AS THE COSMIC CHRIST

(Reinterpretation of the Gospels in the light of Chinese and Indian Mysticism)

> All holy men have bequeathed this to one another: nothing is possible without contemplation (*fan chao*). When Confucius says: knowing brings one to the goal; or when the Buddha calls it: The way of the Heart; or Lao Tse says: Inward vision, it is all the same.[1]

Throughout the history of philosophy, whether it be Western or Eastern, we find two major but converse currents of thinking. These two seemingly contrary points of view are best illustrated in the person of Confucius and Lao-Tse respectively.[2]

Tradition speaks of a meeting between the two Masters, though recent research casts grave doubt on its historical authenticity. As each of them personifies one of the two major conflicting viewpoints, the anecdotes describing their supposed meeting, are instructive.

We are told that when Confucius tried to draw Lao Tse into a discussion on duty to society, obligation to one's neighbour and similar themes, the latter replied with cryptic brevity: 'Get rid of your affection and your extravagant aims. You sicken me with your constant talk of neighbourly love and duty. You first alienate the fish from its brook by bringing it on dry ground and then when it suffers from dryness you try to repair that loss with a little moist sponge. Would not the fish have been better off if it had been left to its own resources in the brook?'[3]

The fish in the above story symbolizes mankind. The philosophers of humanism by their positivistic emphasis (in particular, neglect of mysticism, self-realization, and the supra-human element in man) alienate the individual from his natural sources.[4] They do, however, seek to bring him social amelioration but no matter how good their will may be, the resources of society are as limited as the 'moist sponge' is for the fish.[5] In other

---

[1] Lü Tzu.

[2] Cf. Radhakrishnan: 'Different schools of thought arose of which the chief were those of Confucius and Lao Tze representing two different sides. . . . The social and the political was stressed by Confucius and the ascetic and the mystical by Lao Tze . . . Confucius adopted the ethical method of social reform . . . (while) Lao Tze suggested: Let each individual get into harmony with the spirit of the universe, let him not get confused by the social relationships. . . .' *India and China*, Bombay, 1954, pp. 75–6.

[3] See the last chapter in *The Wisdom of Lao Tse* by Lin Yutang, New York, 1948.

[4] Cf. Radhakrishnan: 'Inattention to the deepest part of our being is the fundamental defect of all humanist codes.' *India and China*, p. 86.

[5] 'There are humanists at the present day who believe in the force of moral ideals, the value of tradition, in international good behaviour which are all a part of the Confucian faith. . . . (But) the strict observance of ethical rules which Confucius lays down is possible only with the regeneration brought about by religion.' Again: 'Confucius requires us to fulfil our nature. But any view of human nature which excludes the spiritual in man is incomplete.' Radhakrishnan, *India and China*, p. 86 ff.

words, if man were to explore his own latent resources, he would find that nature has equipped him with so great an untapped source of strength that it is an impertinence to think that he depends on our 'duty-inspired' help or solicitude. We can help him most by distracting him as little as possible from his ground of Being, which as Pure Being is also his natural habitation.[1] In the words of Sri Ramana Maharishi: 'the attainment of one's true Self (one's true source of origin, Ātman) is the greatest blessing one can confer on society'.[2] This is the Taoist standpoint and provokes vehement opposition from those inclined to the Confucian viewpoint; the zealous if unwitting exponents of which in our times are Bertrand Russell and Albert Schweitzer. The Taoist viewpoint has hardly any chance of success in an age dominated by communism and concern for economically under-developed countries. The crying need for social reform being what it is, no Taoist viewpoints are now tolerated, least of all where they are most likely to be practised, in the under-developed countries of Asia. Moreover they are denounced in our civic-minded West as unethical, irresponsible or plain lazy. The Confucian idea of compulsory Civics is the order of the day.

The idea that under-developed territories should be developed by the use of machines appears to us as quite recent. But let us examine another anecdote of the Confucius-Lao Tse tradition. We are told that Tzu Kung a disciple of Confucius sought to instruct farmers in more efficient methods of cultivation. One day, finding a farmer watering his fields in a very simple way, he volunteered to make and explain the use of a more complicated watering gadget. The farmer being a Taoist replied that he would have nothing to do with him for he had been taught that people who can invent complicated machines may be very clever but are also likely to have a complicated character. A mind cunning enough to construct an ingenious machine can also devise an ingenious fraud.[3] This may sound quaint and illogical until we retranslate it as: minds clever enough to discover atomic energy can also release atomic bombs.

The Confucius-Lao Tse controversy is at bottom only a struggle for primacy. Which is our *first* duty, Self Realization or service to mankind in the sense of doing good? Vivekananda, the famous modern philosopher of Vedānta, answered this question on a geographical basis. To the West he said it was the former, to the East the latter. But this artificial division is unnecessary once the *karma-yoga* philosophy, as illustrated by the *Gītā*, has been understood. Radhakrishnan's commentary on the *Gītā* supplied the answer: Self Realization *through* unselfish service, that is to say, the *karma-yoga* way. *Erleuchtung* can be had through meditation and also through action, or work done as a sacrifice and without desire for reward. That is the message of the *Gītā* which Radhakrishnan brought into focus.

[1] 'The *dharma* (Tao?) is the true nature of Man.' *Ibid.*, p. 88.

[2] Cf. 'The Sage does nothing, yet achieves everything . . .' *Tao Te Ching*, XLVII, also XLVIII and LXXXI; 'Therefore the sage is all the time in the most perfect way helping men.' *Ibid.*, XXVII.

[3] Adapted from Lieh Tzu. See also Waley, *Three Ways of Thought in Ancient China*, Allen and Unwin, London.

E

For the chief aim after all is only to erase the false sense of 'I'. This can be done through constant meditation during which the 'I' sense is starved or through action performed in a self-sacrificing spirit, during which the 'I' sense is pulverized. Social service can lead to self-realization if the former is performed in a spirit of sacrifice. But every self-realization automatically results in a kind of social service which cannot be seen or measured and, therefore, is unappreciated. Moreover one should never forget that social service, if unenlightened, can do more harm than good. The very idea of service is a characteristic of the enlightened mind.

Let us analyse what Radhakrishnan has to say on this point:[1]

'Any ethical theory must be grounded in metaphysics ... a self-sufficient humanism has its own metaphysical presuppositions. ... It attempts to perfect the causes of human life by purely natural means. The subject of ethics is treated as a branch of sociology or a department of psychology ... [It thus] encourage[s] an acquiescence in the merely practicable.'[2]

But:

'An abundance of material things will not help to make life more interesting. The rich of the world are among those who find life stale, flat and unprofitable. *Even the social conscience that urges us to extend the benefits* of a material civilization cannot be accounted for by the principles of scientific naturalism.'[3]

Here, as in *India and China*, Radhakrishnan first points out the insufficiency of humanism, the so-called Confucian standpoint, but he does not rest at that.[4] He shows the equally damaging insufficiency of a mysticism that tends to escapism—the so-called Taoist standpoint.[5] 'The mistake of Taoism,' he says, 'is that it does not recognize the social side as natural to man.'[6] He envisages a harmonious combination making the best of both worlds.[7] Like St Theresa, he recommends rapt contemplation as the best possible source for finding the energy and aspiration for altruistic service in the common welfare of mankind. Nor is this an artificial compromise between two extremes. For a person who has understood the *Gītā*,

---

[1] See also Professor Edgar L. Hinman's essay on 'Radhakrishnan and Sung Confucianism', *Library of Living Philosophers*, pp. 609–32.

[2] *Eastern Religion and Western Thought*, p. 80.

[3] *Ibid.*, (our italics).

[4] *India and China*, pp. 85–9.

[5] *Ibid.*, pp. 113 ff.

[6] *Ibid.*; also: 'Mencius looked upon Taoism as leading to anarchy in social matters, for it rejects all forms of interference with nature and denounces government as unnecessary.'

[7] 'If Confucian ethics teaches us how to live together in harmony and good order, Taoist transcendental mysticism helps us to get out of society and realize the Tao. *We require a system of thought and belief which combines the strong points of these two cults.' Ibid.*, p. 117 (our italics).

such an attitude is as natural as breathing. It is a great mistake to think, like Albert Schweitzer for instance, that Taoism means harmless but lazy inactivity. For the attainment of Tao (*Erleuchtung* or *mukti*) simultaneously awakens the finest qualities of the heart. *Compassion arises automatically* and has not to be taught as in the Confucian schools. In the *karma-yoga* way, altruistic, ego-effacing service leads to *Erleuchtung*; in the *jñāna*, *rāja*, or *bhakti* way *Erleuchtung* leads to altruistic activity, visible or otherwise. That is the gospel of the *Gītā* as Radhakrishnan explains it. In other words: on attaining Tao, one behaves effortlessly like Confucius's ideal man. To do this unswervingly leads to the attainment of Tao! Radhakrishnan is inclined to recommend the former solution, and not without good reason.[1]

For:

'Only a philosophy which affirms that our ideals are rooted in the universal nature of things can give depth and favour to moral life, courage and confidence in moral difficulties. *We need to be fortified by the conviction that the service of ideals is what the cosmic scheme demands of us*, that our loyalty or disloyalty to them is a matter of the deepest moment not only to ourselves or to society, or even to the human species, but to the nature of things. If ethical thought is profound, it will give a cosmic motive to morality. Moral consciousness must include a conviction of the reality of ideals. *If the latter is religion, then ethical humanism is acted religion.* When man realizes his essential unity with the whole of being he expresses this unity in his life.'[2]

Further:

'[Man's] highest aim is release from the historical succession denoted by birth and death. . . . If we overlook this important fact, and make ethics or world affirmation independent of religion or world negation, our life and thought become condescending, *though this condescension may take the form of social service or philanthropy*. But it is essentially a form of self-assertion and not real concern for the well-being of others. If goodwill, pure love, and disinterestedness are our ideals, then our ethics must be rooted in other-worldliness. *This is the great classical tradition of spiritual wisdom.*'[3]

The synthesis, brought about in the *Gītā*, between the Confucian and Taoist viewpoints can be further extended to bring about a similar synthesis between the Christian and Vedāntic ones. This can best be done by interpreting each in the light of the other. Such a synthesis is of great benefit to all concerned.

[1] A magnetic needle spontaneously rests in a north-south direction; whereas a piece of iron must be allowed to rest in that position for a very long time before it is magnetized. In the same way it is easier for the spiritually awakened to manifest virtues in their ethical conduct than for one to attain spiritual awakening through the steady cultivation of ethical virtues.

[2] *Eastern Religion and Western Thought*, p. 82 (our italics).

[3] *Ibid.*, p. 83–4 (our italics).

'Christianity in India needs the Vedānta. We missionaries have not realized this with half the clearness that we should. We cannot move freely and joyfully in our own religion; because we have not sufficient terms and modes of expression wherewith to express the more immanental aspects of Christianity. A very useful step would be the recognition of certain books or passages in the literature of the Vedānta as constituting what might be called an Ethnic Old Testament. The permission of ecclesiastical authorities could then be asked for reading passages found in such a canon of Ethnic Old Testament at divine service along with passages from the New Testament as alternatives to the Old Testament lessons.'[1]

Now it will be clear that the essence of any Christian interpretation will depend on the meaning attributed to the word Christ. Many people think that Christ is the surname of Jesus instead of being a deferential title, like Buddha which means the Enlightened One. Much confusion would be avoided if people said 'Jesus, the Christ' or 'Gautama, the Buddha' instead of Jesus Christ or Gautama Buddha. The reason is that in the latter case people identify the second words (Christ or Buddha) exclusively with the first (Jesus or Gautama), whereas they are more or less synonymous for a certain state of *Erleuchtung*. Jesus and Gautama, however, refer to two different personalities distinct from each other in space and time. Yet people cheerfully call themselves Christians or Buddhists disregarding the fact that such adjectives are only valid for one who has attained the necessary *Erleuchtung*. From the Vedāntic point of view 'Christ' ('divine consciousness') can be translated as *svarūpajñāna*[2] which means the *real* as consciousness; the divine consciousness as the underlying *Reality* of creation. Moreover as Radhakrishnan says:

'*Svarūpajñāna* or the Real as consciousness always *is*.[3] Its constant presence does not dispel, according to Advaita Vedānta, *ajñāna* or ignorance. It rather reveals it.'[4]

'This consciousness [Divine Christ-consciousness or Christ for short] is not an abstract one. It is "that by which thou shalt see all existences without exception in the Self, then in Me".'[5]

Here the word *Self* of the Vedānta corresponds with the word *Christ* as used in the Christian teaching; and the last word *Me* (meaning in this case the Supreme) with God.

Thus in Vedānta Christ means one who has realized his self-identity in Ātman. It is a recognition of one's own inherent divinity, it is to be 'born

---

[1] R. Gordon Milburn in an article on 'Christian Vedāntism' in the *Indian Interpreter*, 1913. Re-quoted from Radhakrishnan's *The Principal Upaniṣads*, p. 19.

[2] *Svarūpatā*.

[3] Cf. 'Before Abraham was, *I am.*' John viii, 58. Also see *Gītā*, IV, v. 4 and 5.

[4] *The Bhagavadgītā*, p. 53, footnote 1.

[5] *Ibid.* (but not in footnote).

again' as the Bible puts it.[1] In as much as Jesus had killed his ego, he was attuned constantly with the omnipresent Christ-consciousness (*svarūpata*) and so identified himself completely with IT. He is, therefore, called Jesus the Christ, meaning Jesus, the *enlightened* one in unbroken contact with God.[2]

Thus according to Radhakrishnan's Vedāntic interpretation of Christ, the Christian teaching means that the underlying, pure or real consciousness in the heart of man and at the heart of creation is *Christ*.[3] Outside of it there is no reality.

Apart from it, all is unreal. The Cosmic Christ as omnipotent spirit symbolizes the highest state open to mortals. For:

'No man hath seen God at any time; the only begotten Son, which is in the bosom of the Father, he hath declared him.'[4]

But before the conception of the Cosmic Christ is even thinkable, its presence as the integral consciousness must have been realized.

This supreme state of the Cosmic Christ is so singular a spiritual attainment, that mankind, unable to find a term of veneration which would even remotely do justice to so unsurpassable an at-one-ment with the divine, has out of overwhelming devotion called Him the Son of God.

Even Lao-Tse gives a similar explanation in the first chapter of the *Tao Te King*. The divine as the unknowable Absolute is called the Nameless Tao and the Cosmic Christ the Tao with a name, a distinction almost identical with Meister Eckhart's *Gottheit* and *Gott*. Is this presumptuous, or even blasphemy on the part of Eastern wisdom? 'Is it not written in your law, I said, Ye are gods?' (*Ego disci, dei estis et filii excelsi omnes*). Jesus, in his controversy with the Jews in the temple expressly emphasized the universal validity of the statement contained in Psalm lxxxii, 6. This is again confirmed by the evidence of I John iii, 2, and even more unequivocally:

'But we all, with open face beholding as in a glass the glory of the Lord, are changed into the same image from glory to glory, even as by the Spirit of the Lord.'[5]

Indeed in our own day the French Jesuit and scientist Pierre Teilhard de Chardin calls this the supreme aim of evolution. He is praiseworthy for expressing anew what Eastern mysticism has always implied. *Nirvana* or

---

[1] Cf. Radhakrishnan: 'We must become different, change our natures, be born again. To be born again is to be initiated into a new life which is not a ceremonial act but a spiritual experience.' *Eastern Religion and Western Thought*, p. 172.

[2] Cp. *Gītā*, VII, 17: *jñāni nityayukta* = 'one who is ever in constant union with the Divine.'

[3] Cp. *Gītā*, VX, 15: *sarvasya cā 'haṁ hṛdi saṁniviṣṭo* = 'And I (Christ as Consciousness) am lodged in the hearts of all'; also *Gītā*, XIII, 17: *hṛdi sarvasya dhiṣṭhitam* = 'He (*Christ-Ātman*) is seated in the hearts of all.'

[4] John i, 18.

[5] II Corinthians iii, 18.

Erleuchtung, salvation or *Erlösung*, is in itself *a state of Consciousness*. It is a state in which one realizes the Christ-consciousness, Ātman or Buddha-nature to be one's real I.[1] The worst sin is to neglect one's potential *Christhood*. It is the innermost recognition of one's own divinity that brings *Erleuchtung* and *frees* one from bondage to the ego. Only through the attainment of this divine consciousness (called Christ-consciousness) do, or can we, become aware of the *Divine* which is called God or the Supreme. *No man cometh unto the Father* [to God, or the Supreme], *but by me* [Christ, Christ-consciousness].[2] In other words, one cannot attain to the Absolute, which the *Gītā* calls the unmanifest beyond the unmanifest, or the transcendent godhead *above and beyond* creation, until one has first realized the divine or Christ-consciousness *within and underlying* all creation.

Thus each and every individual has, or rather *is* though only potentially, the *mind* of Christ,[3] that underlying spiritual substratum which we may call Ātman or Christ-consciousness. Thus Radhakrishnan gives us a Vedāntic interpretation of the essence of the Christian teaching in the following words:

'When the individual is united with the Christ principle, his inward man,[4] his spirit, he realizes to the full his oneness with the Father, the supreme godhead. Each of us can become a perfect man unto "the measure of the stature of the fullness of Christ". When the spirit in us is realized, we shall see and know God as *He* is and knows us, by an immediate vision. "Now we see through a mirror" in which the reflection will not be clear and distinct, "but then face to face; now I know in part; but then shall I know even as I am known"[5] ... We must ... raise ourselves above the world to be able to assimilate the divine reality.'[6]

Thus we are led to the conclusion that: 'the Logos is the Absolute from

---

[1] Vide *Gītā*, VIII, 3: *Svabhavo adhyātman ucyate*: (one's) essential nature is called the Self. Radhakrishnan translates *adhyātma* as that 'phase of the Divine which constitutes individual self'. The individual's (higher) Self, which is the same as his (essential) nature, is a part of the supreme (God) in the same way as the force which makes any specific object fall to the ground is a part of the universal force of gravitation.

[2] John xiv, 6.

[3] 'But we have the mind of Christ'—I Corinthians ii, 16.

[4] See Romans viii, 9: 'But ye are not in the flesh, but in the Spirit, if so be that the Spirit of God [what Radhakrishnan calls the 'Christ principle' or 'inward man'] dwell in you.' See further Romans viii, 11: 'But if the Spirit of him that raised up Jesus from the dead dwell in you, he that raised up Christ from the dead shall also quicken *your* mortal bodies by his Spirit *that dwelleth in you*.'

[5] See I Corinthians xiii, 12: 'For now we see through a glass, darkly; but then face to face: now I know in part; but then shall I know even as also I am known.' Radhakrishnan also writes: 'the apostle of St John tells us that we shall see God "*as he is*". I John iii, 2.' ('Beloved, now are we the sons of God, and it doth not yet appear what we shall be: but we know that, when he shall appear, we shall be like him; for we shall see him *as he is*.')

[6] *Eastern Religion and Western Thought*, p. 223.

the cosmic end ... the divine Logos was identified with the gods of
ancient cults, and this general tendency is followed by the writer (of the
First Epistle of St John) when he looks upon Jesus as the incarnation, or
the manifestation in word and deed, of the eternal Logos by whom the
universe had been created and maintained.'[1]

He then goes on to say that this 'Logos is not merely the agency ... but
also the sustaining power of the universe. Though the revelation of God in
Jesus was complete, it is not intelligible to us without the help of Spirit,
which is the living and active principle operating in (us).'[2] Just as we are
incapable of seeing any object if there is no light, so, if there is no consciousness in us, we are utterly incapable of having any conception of,
or contact with, God, however well equipped our mind, heart, or soul
may be. By consciousness is meant the essential, pure-at-the-source
consciousness underlying the sleeping, dreaming and waking states. This
overall consciousness which supports our waking, dreaming, or unconscious states is known in Vedānta as *turīya*[3]—yet another name for Christ-
consciousness. As Radhakrishnan says: 'it is the deepest essence of the
soul, the image of Godhead'.[4] He is the (*Real*) *Self*;[5] He is to be known.[6]
Our metaphysical reality is cognized in Christ consciousness, or *turīya*,
just as objects can be cognized only in light. Thus 'the way to salvation is
through the purifying of the cognitive powers of the soul. The transcendental God is not an object of knowledge but can be approached only by
ecstasy.'[7] Ecstasy here means a rarefied state of heightened consciousness
entirely free of sentimentality, hysteria, or the like except where it is
achieved by following the way of *bhakti*, in which case certain symptoms
bordering on insanity sometimes arise. This explains the charge of being
'God-ravished' or 'gone mad for God' levelled against the dervishes of
Persia, Sri Ramakrishna and others. Thus 'we cannot reach God except
through the Logos. No one comes to the Father except through Christ.
The Logos is the rational law (*dharma*, or *lex aeterna*) of the world.'[8]

This does not necessarily mean that in the Vedāntic interpretation of
Christianity the position of Jesus is reduced to that of an average or normal
human being. Jesus as *avatāra*, (*īśvarakoṭi*) meaning a divine incarnation or
'the word made flesh', is something different from Jesus the Christ. For
whereas theoretically the Vedāntic viewpoint is that every individual has
in him the potentiality to attain to Christhood, it does not mean that
everybody is a divine incarnation in the sense that Jesus is generally
accepted to be. Thus even if an ordinary individual (*jīvakoṭi*) attains to

[1] *Ibid.*, pp. 224–5.

[2] *Ibid.*, p. 226.

[3] See *Māṇḍūkya Upaniṣad*, 7.

[4] *The Principle Upaniṣads*, p. 699.

[5] Clement says: 'If anyone knows himself, he shall know God and by knowing God, he
shall be made like unto him.' *Paed.*, i. 3.

[6] *sa ātma; sa vijñeyah.*

[7] *Eastern Religion and Western Thought*, p. 230.

[8] *Ibid.*

Christhood it does not mean that he is, therefore, equal to Jesus as an incarnation (*īśvarakoṭi*). The word incarnation implies a voluntary, temporary *descent* of the Divine to the level of the human; the word Christhood signifies a permanent *ascent* of the human and its amalgamation with the Divine. Thus Clement says: '*The word of God became Man* [this is what is meant by incarnation, *īśvarakoṭi* or *avatāra*] *so that thou* [any ordinary individual or a *jīvakoṭi*] *also mayest learn from Man* [from the incarnated one's earthly disguise as a human being], *how man becomes God.*'[1] The use of the word *how* is important here. It explains the purpose of an incarnation, which is to show ordinary mortals the way[2] and to speed up their efforts. The Vedāntic interpretation of Christianity, therefore, in no way detracts from the glory of Jesus either as the Christ or as the incarnation. In fact it enhances it: for according to the Vedānta the incarnation's power to assist man's liberation commences at his birth. Thus three wise kings of the East made a long journey to venerate Jesus in the stable although He was then only an infant and could not instruct them in any teaching or way. That is because from a Vedāntic viewpoint inherent in Eastern psychology, the *very presence of an incarnation, by itself speeds up one's progress on the road to salvation.*

Nor is there much substance in the contention that whereas the Vedānta admits the possibility of countless incarnations, Christian theology admits of only one. For, as Swami Siddheswarananda[3] has pointed out, although the Vedānta accepts many incarnations, it nevertheless considers the personality of all incarnations *as one unique person.* In each case it is, as Radhakrishnan says, 'the *cosmic Christ*'.[4] Does a person acquire an extra, separate personality every time he uses a different telephone? The conflict between the Vedāntic view of many incarnations and the Christian theologian's view of the one-and-only incarnation is only apparent, and arises because the former takes a post-Einstein, dynamic view of time whereas the latter takes a static, pre-Einstein view.[5] Once we have understood the mutual interrelation of *turīya* and *Christ-consciousness*, the folly of calling any religion non-Christian will be evident. For a religion which denies Christ (here meaning consciousness *per se*) is a contradiction in terms. No person on earth, whether he be a believer in any religion or a sceptic doubting everything, can possibly deny the fact of his own con-

---

[1] *Protrept.*, i. 8.

[2] Cf. Jesus: 'I am the Way, the Truth and the Life.'

[3] In a lecture given at the Sorbonne in a series on the Yoga of St John of the Cross.

[4] *The Principal Upaniṣads*, p. 131, note 1: 'The Cosmic Christ speaking through Jesus, "I am the Alpha and the Omega, the first and the last; for what was first comes at last and the last is the first".'

[5] Cf. Swami Siddheswarananda: 'I am thankful to the great Russian theologian, the late Professor Nicolas Berdyaev, who explained this to me and enabled me to understand how the notion of time as conceived in Judaic theology is the key to the differences in the Christian and Hindu (here meaning Vedāntic) outlook. Time in Indian Philosophy is not static but dynamic.' 'A Hindu View of Christian Theology', from *Vedānta for Modern Man*, p. 303.

sciousness. Denial of God we have known and of truth is possible, but who can deny the possession of consciousness? The very act would depend on the possession of consciousness. Consciousness is, therefore, the one *non-material* thing, fact or datum which it is absolutely impossible to deny. This consciousness in its unsoiled state is called Christ (short for Christ-consciousness) and experienced as *peace* ('the Peace that passeth understanding'); in its soiled state it is called ego (mind, or personality) and is experienced as sleep, dreams, or ideas. As no thought can arise prior to consciousness, even the idea of God is dependent on the presence of consciousness. If one were to deny that 'Christ' means consciousness, then whatever meaning you give to the word 'Christ' will depend on the prior presence (in you) of consciousness and will therefore, be subordinate to it. The reason why many people find this difficult is because of the age-long habit of always identifying the word Christ with the person of Jesus—and always identifying consciousness with the waking state.

This Christ-consciousness or *turīya* is no mere 'psychological state' or 'attitude of mind'—it corresponds to what the *Gītā* describes as:

'A fragment (or fraction) of My (God's) own self, having become a living soul, eternal in the world of life, draws to itself the senses (of which the mind is the sixth) that rest in nature.'[1]

When we ask what is this divine fragment that is given to every individual at birth and that is not to be found in a corpse, we find that it is consciousness. It is not the result of any effort on our part. It cannot be manufactured by laboratory methods. We do not owe it to our parents in the sense we owe our bodies to them. It is given. It is only because of consciousness that thoughts and dreams occur, and that one can fall into and out of deep sleep. As it is that which is most indispensable, it is in all probability also our link with the Divine. It is, therefore, in no light-hearted or superficial sense that the Vedānta interprets Christ as consciousness. Hence Radhakrishnan concludes: 'Each of us is a ray of the Divine consciousness into which our being, if we will only allow it, can be transfigured.'[2]

(c) THE UNIVERSALITY OF RELIGIOUS EXPERIENCE

(As the Basis for Interreligious Friendship)

All those in whom the Holy Ghost abides become deified by this reason alone.[3]

Before considering Radhakrishnan's definition of religion and religious experience it is important to note that he classifies the religions of the world into two broad groups: 'The religions of the world can be distinguished

---

[1] *Gītā*, XV, 7.
[2] *The Bhagavadgītā*, p. 329.
[3] St Athanasius, *Ep. ad Scrap.*, I, 24.

into those which emphasize the object and those which insist on experience. For the first class religion is an attitude of faith and conduct directed to a power without. For the second it is an experience to which the individual attaches supreme value.'[1]

It is more than likely that his definition of religion would fall in the second group because according to him, an experience which affirms the reality of the spiritual consciousness (*turīya*) can precede and exist without belief in, or the conception of, a deity but not vice versa.[2] For if one begins with a deity then: 'To say that God exists means that spiritual experience constitutes the most conclusive proof of the reality of God. God is given, and is the factual content of the spiritual experience. All other proofs are descriptions of God, matters of definition, and language.'[3] Thus we find that Radhakrishnan defines religion as:

1. 'An effort to unveil the deepest layers of man's being and get into enduring contact with them.'[4]
2. 'The perception of the eternal in the infinite.'[5]
3. 'The conscious union with the Divine in the universe with love as its chief means.'[6]
4. 'All religion is symbolic, and symbolism is excluded from religion only when religion itself perishes. *God is a symbol in which religion cognizes the Absolute.* Philosophers may quarrel about the Absolute and God, and contend that God, the holy one who is worshipped, is different from the Absolute which is the reality demonstrated by reason. But *the religious consciousness has felt that the two are one.*'[7]
5. 'It is an attempt to discover the ideal possibilities of human life, a quest for emancipation from the immediate compulsions of vain and petty moods. . . . It is an independent functioning of the human mind, something unique, possessing an autonomous character. It is something inward and personal which unifies all values and organizes all experiences. It is the reaction of the whole man to the whole reality.'[8]

The experience called Illumination (or Enlightenment), therefore, occupies the central position in Radhakrishnan's thought. Just as Zarathustra argues the righteousness of God from the presence of conscience, Radhakrishnan argues the very presence of God from the possibility of the transcendental, religious or spiritual experience. Hence the extreme

---

[1] *Eastern Religion and Western Thought*, p. 21.

[2] Thus: 'Real religion can exist without a definite conception of the deity. . . . Even in primitive religion with its characteristic phenomena of magic, we have religion though not a belief in God' *Eastern Religion and Western Thought*, p. 21.

[3] *Ibid.*, p. 22.

[4] *Ibid.*, p. 21.

[5] *An Idealist View of Life*, p. 212.

[6] *Ibid.*, p. 204.

[7] *Ibid.*, p. 209.

[8] *Ibid.*, p. 88.

importance given to *intuition* in his philosophy. This transcendental experience of Enlightenment, which gives validity to both God and religion, is attainable only through intuition (as distinguished from empiricological methods of perception). Radhakrishnan's *Religionsphilosophie* therefore, stands or falls on the reality of intuitive knowledge.[1] We are also told what he does not consider to be religion. It is *not*:

1. a mere feeling or sense of creaturely dependence—as Schleiermacher is inclined to suggest.
   (For in that case it could be argued that Schleiermacher's dog is more pious than Schleiermacher.)[2]
2. a mere consciousness of value, as Kant is inclined to suggest by assimilating religious experience to moral consciousness.
   (For in religious experience there is a 'mystical element, an apprehension of the real and an enjoyment of it for its own sake which is absent in the moral consciousness'.)[3]
3. a form of knowledge, as Hegel sometimes urged.
   (For although religion 'implies a metaphysical view of the universe, it is not to be confused with philosophy'.)[4]
4. a mere social phenomenon.[5]

Although Radhakrishnan distinguishes religion from philosophy, the two are not entirely disconnected. For 'it is the function of philosophy to provide us with a rallying centre, a synoptic vision, as Plato loved to call it, a *samanvaya*, as the Hindu thinkers put it, a philosophy which will serve as a spiritual concordat, which will free the spirit of religion from the disintegrations of doubt and make the warfare of creeds and sects a thing of the past'.[6] In other words, philosophy is 'an exhibition of insights'.[7] It is a preparation for the intuitive insight with which we may attain that experience which is of the essence of religion. The intimate interconnection between religion and philosophy in Radhakrishnan has led to much unjust, hostile criticism against his works, specially in non-German-speaking countries which have no word like *Religionsphilosophie* as something quite distinct from theology. Some critics take the view that if the word God is mentioned even once with conviction, then we are no longer dealing with

[1] 'If all knowledge were of the scientific type, the contemporary challenge to religion would seem to be conclusive. The problem thus narrows itself to the reality of intuitive knowledge and the conditions of its validity. Is there or is there not knowledge which by its nature cannot be expressed in propositions and is yet trustworthy?' *Ibid.*, p. 127.
[2] *Ibid.*, p. 88.
[3] *Ibid.*
[4] *Ibid.*
[5] *Ibid.*
[6] *Ibid.*, p. 83.
[7] *Ibid.*, p. 152.

philosophy but theology.[1] It is, therefore, of the utmost importance to note how Radhakrishnan distinguishes *Religionsphilosophie* from theology: 'Philosophy of religion as distinct from dogmatic theology refuses to accept any restricted basis but takes its stand on *experience* as wide as human nature itself. It rejects the high *a priori* road of speculative theology and the apologetic method of dogmatic theology and adopts a scientific view of religious experience and examines with detachment and impartiality the spiritual inheritance of men of all creeds and of none. Such an examination of the claims and contents of religious consciousness, which has for its background the whole spiritual history of man, has in it the promise of a spiritual idealism which is opposed to the disintegrating forces of scientific naturalism on the one hand and religious dogmatism on the other.'[2]

As Radhakrishnan's *Religionsphilosophie* provides us with one of the most enduring foundations for interreligious friendship, it is important to find out what exactly he means by it.

'Philosophy of Religion is religion come to an understanding of itself. It attempts a reasoned solution of a problem which exists directly only for the religious man who has *the spiritual intuition or experience* and indirectly for all those who, while they have no share in the experience, yet have sufficient belief that it does occur and is not illusory.'[3]

Further:

'If philosophy of religion is to become scientific, it must become empirical and found itself on *religious experience*.'[4]

Again:

'It is for philosophy of religion to find out whether the convictions of the religious seers fit in with the tested laws and principles of the universe.'[5]

Moreover:

'Just as we attempt to formulate in precise terms our sense experience in

[1] e.g. Swami Agehananda Bharati of Syracuse University in his essay 'Radhakrishnan and the Other Vedānta' (Chap. 13 in *Library of Living Philosophers*, Vol. VIII) where he says: 'Surety is for the theologian; doubt is for the philosopher'. To which Radhakrishnan replies: 'It is somewhat arbitrary to say that men of conviction are theologians and men who are in a state of doubt are philosophers. . . . It is one thing to say that we should question beliefs . . . another thing to say that we should not have any beliefs. . . . Whether a system is a philosophy or not depends on the methods employed and not on the conclusions reached. We cannot, for example, argue that all theistic systems are theological and that atheistic systems are philosophical', p. 817.

[2] *An Idealist View of Life*, p. 87.

[3] *Ibid.*, p. 84.

[4] *Ibid.*,

[5] *Ibid.*, p. 85.

the natural sciences, even so philosophy of religion attempts to define the world to which our religious experiences refer.'[1]

Just as all of Radhakrishnan's work centres round his *Religionsphilosophie*, so also does the latter centre around religious experience as is abundantly clear from the above quotations. Now what is this experience and why is it called religious?

It is one of spiritual rebirth—*dvitiyam janma*. This experience of Enlightenment or Higher Self Realization may also be called God Realization;[2] and the way to it is called religion. The experience is called religious because the methods which help to bring it about are by definition the functions of religion. Whereas the methods may differ according to time, race, country, beliefs, etc., the central experience brought about by such methods is universal. It is this universality of religious experience from Lao-Tze in ancient China to Emerson in America that provides us with a basis for interreligious friendship and mutual understanding. Thus when Radhakrishnan advocates a return to religion he does not mean a specific one but *sanātana dharma*[3]—the universality of an experience which forms the nucleus of all specific religions. *Sanātana dharma* is the other side of *iṣta devata*. Infinite variety is permitted in the latter (selection of a chosen deity and/or religion) because the former (the universal nature of the experience forming the nucleus of every religion) is invariable.[4] One will always get the same answer to a sum, irrespective of whether one counts a column of figures from top to bottom or the other way round, provided one adds correctly. Thus according to Radhakrishnan, the main thing in any religion is to repeat, realize, or reproduce in one's own case the central experience of the founder of that religion.[5] Without this direct experience[6]

---

[1] *Ibid.*

[2] Cf. Vātsyāyana's commentary to the *Nāyaya Sūtra*: '. . . *brahmaprāpti ṛṣi-arya-mlecchānām samānam lakṣaṇam*'—(God Realization is possible to all regardless of race, religion, etc.) Cf. also the *Koran*, II, 136 and also where it is said: 'There is no people among whom a warner has not been sent.' And the Bible: 'Now of a truth I perceive that God is no respecter of persons, but in every nation, he that feareth Him and worketh righteousness is accepted of Him.' St Peter, in The Acts of the Apostles, x, 34, 35.

[3] 'The religion outlined in these pages may be called the *sanātana dharma*, the eternal religion. It is not to be identified with any particular religion, for it is the one which transcends race and creed and yet informs all races and creeds.' Radhakrishnan, *Recovery of Faith*, p. 204.

[4] Vivekananda stresses the former aspect in his plea for interreligious friendship, Radhakrishnan the latter.

[5] Cf. 'The two, God's revelation and man's realization, though distinguishable, are inseparable from one another. They are two aspects of one process.' *An Idealist View of Life*, p. 337.

[6] 'Direct experience' also called *Kṛṣṇarjunasamvada* meaning 'divine-human encounter'. See Radhakrishnan's *Fragment of a Confession*, Part IX. (*Library of Living Philosophers*.)

we cannot realize God but only at the most acquire more and more highly evolved conceptions of God.[1] And being a mental concept it remains a figment of our mind or imagination. The direct or religious experience (*Erleuchtung*) is not an experience in the ordinary sense of the word. For all experiences are mental and, therefore, dependent on mind just as concepts of God are. But the direct experience does not take place within the framework of the mind,[2] for that would make it subordinate to mind. ('Mind' here means a stream of connected or disconnected thoughts.) In the direct experience it is the mind which is subordinated to or brought under control of the *Experience*. In other words, during the direct experience the mind vanishes[3] and with it the ego (mind as *subject*) and the so-called outside world as a separate reality in its own right (mind as *object*). Thus the direct experience is not like other experiences because during it there is *nobody who* experiences it nor (the mind being temporarily extinguished) is there anything to experience. The direct experience is therefore an *utter and complete lack of all experience, in fact there is not even the possibility of any experience*. But there is no loss of *waking*-consciousness as in dreamless sleep.[4] This experience being in essence a *non-experience*[5] cannot be adequately described in words.[6] This indescribable experience of no-experience is according to Radhakrishnan the most important part of any religion compared to which all else is as irrelevant.[7] It is also universal in its nature. How else could two or more people have an absolutely identical experience seeing that every person has a different mental and psychological background? This is true of the founders of religions who are widely separated from each other in place and time. In our own case, for instance, one can never be sure that any given experience as well as one's response to it will be exactly identical with that of anyone else *except* in one case: our experience of dreamless sleep is identical with that of anyone

[1] 'It is through religious contemplation that we realize the Holy.' *Ibid*.

[2] 'It is the act of recollection by which the recollecting self distinguishes its primal being from all that is confused with it. ... By recollecting the self is assured of its participation in ultimate being, the principle of all positivity, the ontological mystery.' *Ibid*.

[3] Thus it is said: 'The Absolute is the one in whom all is lost and yet all is found.' Cf. Goethe's *Faust*: 'In this your nothing I find my all.' Part II, line 6256.

[4] 'In the state of deep, dreamless sleep, the self wrapped round by the intellect has *no consciousness of objects*, but is not unconscious.' *The Principal Upaniṣads*, p. 75.

[5] This would again explain why the *Tibetan Book of the Dead* tries to tell the (dying) person: 'Thine own intellect, which is now voidness, *yet not to be regarded* as the voidness of nothingness, but as being the intellect itself (when unobstructed by thoughts, etc.) is the *very* consciousness. ... Thy own consciousness, not formed into anything, in reality void, and the intellect (unobstructed)—these two—are inseparable. The union of the two is the *dharma-kaya* state of perfect enlightenment.' *The Tibetan Book of the Dead*, ed. Evans-Wenz, London, 1957, p. 89 ff.

[6] 'The union of seer and seen is ineffable.' *The Reign of Religion*, p. 188.

[7] Cf. '... to cast off the unessentials and return to the basic truths. Whereas the principles of religions are eternal, their expressions require continual development.' *Fragment of a Confession*, Part X. (*Library of Living Philosophers*.)

else precisely because, like *Erleuchtung*, it is an experience of *no-experience*. This does not, of course, mean that the two are identical, any more than a dead body is the same as a sleeping one because of apparent similarities between the two. An *Erleuchtung* (direct experience) is not to be confused with an *Auslöschung* (dreamless sleep).

We can now recapitulate the points which explain the interconnection between the universality of religious experience and interreligious friendship in Radhakrishnan's *Religionsphilosophie*:

1. *Religion* is that which leads to a certain state called *religious experience*.[1]
2. *By definition*, this religious experience is the nucleus of each and every religion—so that either its actual attainment, *or* its having been attained through revelation by the founder of a historical religion, is the central point.[2]
3. This *direct experience* being one of *no experience* (as explained above) is universal and, therefore, identical in its finished state.[3]
4. This *experience* (*Erleuchtung*) is so all-important that all else fades into irrelevance in comparison.[4]
5. As *Sarvamukti* (the universal salvation, salvation for all sentient beings) is the goal or cosmic purpose set before mankind, all religions are jointly and severally liable for the non-salvation of any sentient being.[5]
6. The responsibility of a religion extends not only to those who follow it but also to those who do not. Therefore it is in its own interest to assist other religions (that is to say their followers) by a free, open and mutual exchange of ideas and information of the discovery of spiritual truths or methods, revelations and the like. So instead of trying to fit all people into the same religion the individual should be allowed to fit the different religions into his psycho-spiritual background, and in this his own religion should assist him. He should select the combination most conducive to his spiritual growth (paying due attention to differ-

---

[1] 'Religious life belongs to the realm of inward spiritual revelation, when exteriorized it loses its authentic character!' *Ibid.*

[2] 'Religion . . . is the cultivation of the interior life. It is the attainment of spiritual freedom, and is essentially the private achievement of the individual won by hard effort in solitude and isolation, on mountain-tops and in monasteries.' *East and West in Religion*, p. 54.

[3] 'The seers describe their experiences with an impressive unanimity. They are "near to one another on mountains farthest apart".' *Fragment of a Confession*, Part IX. (*Library of Living Philosophers*.)

[4] 'The differences among religions seem prominent because we do not seem to know the basic truth of our own religions.' *The Recovery of Faith*, p. 188.

[5] 'The prophetic souls who with a noble passion for truth strive hard to understand the mystery of the world and give utterance to it . . . are philosophers in a vital sense of the term. They comprehend experience *on behalf of mankind*.' *Indian Philosophy*, Vol. I, p. 46.

ences in temperament such as inclination to contemplation, devotion, metaphysical discrimination, etc.[1]

7. Any other alternative would postpone or defer *sarvamukti* on the cosmic plane; and lead to interreligious warfare, which in this atomic age might lead to mutual suicide on the worldly plane.

8. Therefore the choice before us is either universal salvation (*sarvamukti*) through interreligious friendship based on the universality of the *religious experience* revealing our unity of essence; *or* universal destruction through interreligious mistrust resulting from a misplaced emphasis on non-essentials and the diversity of forms.[2]

'—What will you have? quoth God; pay for it and take it—'.
                                        —Emerson, Essay on *Compensation*

(d) DOES ENLIGHTENMENT LEAD TO TOLERANCE OF OTHER FAITHS?

Gold does not cease to be gold, no matter what ornament it is shaped into; the inherently divine remains divine irrespective of what it worships or does not worship.[3]

Tolerance is a poor word to describe that spirit of active co-operation and mutual appreciation with which an illumined mind may be expected to respond. The word tolerance carries with it a ring of condescending pity; a mere enduring of mistaken notions in other creeds. Normally one tolerates only when one is unable to eliminate the object tolerated. Or one does so as one tolerates a nuisance; an irritating insect but not worth the bother of chasing out of the window. Such an empty and formal reaction can hardly be the fruit of so rich an experience as Enlightenment. As against this merely passive form of tolerance we have the active tolerance of mystic religions like Vedānta. The Vedāntic version of active or what I choose to call participating tolerance is best formulated in the words of Vivekananda:

'We not merely tolerate, we unite ourselves with every religion, praying in the mosque of the Mohammedan, worshipping before the fire of the Zoroastrian, and kneeling to the cross of the Christian. We know that all religions alike, from the lowest fetishism to the highest absolutism, are but so many attempts of the human soul to grasp and realize the Infinite. So we gather all these flowers, and, binding them together with the cord of love make them into a wonderful bouquet of worship.'[4]

[1] Cf. 'Each religion has sat at the feet of teachers that never bowed to its authority, and this process is taking place today on a scale unprecedented in the history of humanity and will have the most profound effects upon religion.' *Eastern Religion and Western Thought*, p. 348.

[2] 'If we have not the imagination and courage to work for world peace and unity, it will be effected violently through the demoniac agents of divine justice.' *Religion and Society*, p. 19.

[3] Shankara, *Aparokṣanubhuti*, 51.

[4] *Complete Works*, Part I, p. v.

It is this kind of participating tolerance that Radhakrishnan has in mind when he uses that much abused word. But it is doubtful if one can be tolerant merely by wanting to be so. What we are trying to elucidate here has nothing to do with that tolerance which springs from noblemindedness or generosity. It only comes into effect when the participating tolerance is the direct result of a recent mystic Enlightenment. It comes as a spontaneous reaction carrying with it an unshakeable inner conviction that in the sphere of spiritual experience there is no essential separateness. 'My Being is God, not by simple participation, but by a true transformation of my Being.'[1] From the standpoint of subjective phenomena just to taste salt water once is the same as having tasted all the oceans of the world. In the same way longitudes all lose their separateness at the poles. Perfect Enlightenment in the religion of one's choice gives one this polar point of view. The greater the distance from the peak of a mountain, the more ways lead up to it, and vice versa. Yet the polar view is possible only after reaching the pole. Till then one ought to stick steadfastly to one longitude only, since the shortest distance is the straight line. To mix up longitudes before one reaches the pole leads to needless deviations. The longitude to which one must keep is the *iṣṭadevata*—the chosen deity, the religion of one's choice, that form of devotion that most appeals to one. Thus perfect participating tolerance has nothing to do with that so-called open-mindedness which rejoices in studying various religions but fails to acquire the experience of insight in any one of them. Sri Ramakrishna used to compare that to a fondness for digging holes everywhere but never deep enough to strike water.

It is, however, dangerous to proclaim religious tolerance without laying down strict standards as to what is meant by religion. Some consider communism to be the religion of Russia or even cricket that of Australia! Indeed there are situations in which tolerance would be tantamount to suicide. One may with some justification compare theosophy with Christianity in a spirit of tolerance; but what are we to say if even Thuggism, with its rites of murder and robbery, claims to be a religion as it once did? Surely no amount of religious tolerance would ever justify the wilful destruction of human life. How then are we to define the limits of tolerance giving maximum scope when it is participating and yet excluding reprehensible and revolting elements masquerading in the guise of religion?

We can first define religion, very broadly, as a conviction of the reality and benevolence of any power which one considers to be either divine or transcendental. Tolerance, however, should be restricted to such religions as have a modicum of ethics as their basis. This modicum implies that the religion deserving tolerance must lay stress on the following two ideas:

(i) That our actions, sooner or later, result in consequences of a similar character (as judged by an impartial observer).

(ii) That ethical progress involving self-restraint of some kind is an indispensable preliminary to spiritual salvation.

[1] St Catherine of Genoa, *Vitta e Dottrina*, p. 36.

F

This may not be a perfect definition but it provides a handy test for the practice of tolerance while living in community with other religions. Radhakrishnan himself probably had something similar in mind when he recommended religious tolerance so warmly. Sri Ramakrishna, however, refused to accept any man-made limits to total tolerance on the grounds that it is God's special privilege to permit even ethically shady forms of religion as abortive attempts to reach Him. To quote his own words: 'If there are errors in other religions, that is none of our business. God, to whom the world belongs, will take care of that.' And conversely: 'Suppose there are errors in the religion one has accepted; if one is sincere and earnest, then God himself will correct those errors.'[1]

Ramakrishna always believed that human meddling (usually un-enlightened) would only make confusion worse confounded. He would have endorsed the letter sent by the king of Siam to Louis XIV of France:

'I am overwhelmed with astonishment that my good friend the king of France should concern himself with a matter wherein God alone has the say.'

F. S. C. Northrop objected strongly[2] to Radhakrishnan's famous thesis: 'Toleration is the homage which the finite mind pays to the inexhaustibility of the Infinite.'[3] Fearing that unbridled tolerance would weaken resistance against a creed like communism, he rightly warns us that:

'Unless India recognizes that an attitude of toleration which is appropriate for Oriental differences of belief is not appropriate for Western ones, she will have rid herself from the recent domination of the Western British only to welcome and find herself again under the yoke of the even more doctrinaire and dangerously intolerant Western Marxist communists.'

Further:

'. . . an end cannot be put to the present Cold War . . . after the manner of Radhakrishnan . . . nor by acting to Communists as if they were non-dualistic Vedānta pacifists.'[4]

Does this not mean mixing up religion with politics? No, answers North-rop:

'It means that there is a different concept of the spiritual in the West from the concept of the spiritual in the Orient.'[5]

---

[1] *Gospel*, p. 559.
[2] See his Essay 'Radhakrishnan's Conception of the Relation between Eastern and Western Cultural Values', No. 19 in the *Library of Living Philosophers*, p. 635.
[3] *Eastern Religion and Western Thought*, p. 317.
[4] Northrop, op. cit., p. 652.
[5] *Ibid.*, p. 648.

Specially:

'What it does mean is that the tolerant attitude does not apply between different Western religious, political, ethical and legal norms in the qualified sense in which it is appropriate between diverse Oriental religions.'[1]

Northrop insists that tolerance, as Radhakrishnan and Sri Ramakrishna understand it to be, is an excellent virtue as long as it is confined to Eastern cultural traditions; it only becomes dangerous and foolhardy when it is indiscriminately raised to the status of a universal virtue valid at all times and in all places. Such foolhardiness is 'a consequence of applying to the rest of the world the standards defined by the epistemology and specific philosophy of Oriental culture'. Why is that so? Because: 'ideological conflict is of the essence of the spiritual and cultural life of the West'.[2]

Does this mean that the West must be inherently and deeply intolerant? No, answers Northrop. It only means that: 'The Western method of knowing provides a novel basis for toleration. . . .'

Thus, whereas the Far East, as Radhakrishnan has emphasized, 'locates the basis for toleration between different religions and philosophies in the identity of the object known, the West locates it in the method of knowing'.[3]

This is the error in Northrop's argument. The basis of tolerance in the Eastern tradition does not lie in the identity of the object known, as Northrop suggests, but in that of the knowing subject. For in the highest experience open to Eastern tradition there is no object.

'The truth intended by all religions is the Ātman (the Self); and until we recognize the oneness of our Self . . . we shall revolve in the circle of saṁsāra (relative delusion).'[4]

The East does not recommend tolerance because God is the same to all but because the Self in all is the same. The highest mystic experience is described as 'that in which one beholds the Self through the Self and rejoices in the Self'.[5] That is also why tolerance should be extended even to atheists. The tolerance which arises spontaneously when the Higher Self is realized to be the Self in all beings, is such that one 'sees with an equal eye, a learned sage, a serving man, a cow, an elephant or a dog'.[6] That could hardly be the case if as Northrop suggests the basis of tolerance were traced to the identity of the object known. In the highest experience, on the universality of which Eastern tolerance is founded, one is enlightened. In other words:

[1] Ibid., p. 651.
[2] Ibid., p. 654.
[3] Ibid., p. 658.
[4] Radhakrishnan, Indian Philosophy, Vol. II, p. 653.
[5] Gītā, VI, 20.
[6] Gītā, V, 18.

'. . . we look at things from the standpoint of the Ultimate Reality present in all. . . .

'The characteristics of the Supreme, being consciousness and bliss, are present in all existences and the differences relate to their names and forms, that is their embodiments. . . .

'The fundamental dualism is that of spirit and nature and not of soul and body. It is the distinction between the subject and the object. Nature is the world of *objectivization*. . . . There we have the distinction of minerals, plants, animals and men, but they all have inner *non-objective* existence. The *subject* Reality dwells in them all. This affirmation of basic identity is not inconsistent with the empirical variety. . . . The empirical variety (of objects) should not hide from us the metaphysical reality (subject) which all beings have in common. This view makes us look upon our fellow beings with kindliness and compassion.'[1]

This kindliness and compassion, arising out of the realized identity of the *subject*, is the stuff out of which participating tolerance is made. Perhaps the real reason for Eastern tolerance can best be described in the following imaginary monologue:

'I am tolerant, co-operate with you and even participate in your religion, not necessarily because I think that what you worship and choose to call God, Allah or Spirit, etc. is the same as what I worship and choose to call Īśvara, Kṛṣṇa or Rāma, etc. For all we know, we may both be wrong and nothing of the kind may really exist. Nor does it make any difference if you, I or both of us should be atheists. You cannot deny your Self nor can I deny mine. But what do you call *your* Self and what do I call *my* Self? We both need some kind of awareness or form of consciousness before the idea of you and me can arise. It follows, therefore, that this awareness or consciousness is unsullied at its source by any such notions of you and me. Consequently this primordial awareness or consciousness is only Self and nothing more. *Tat tvam asi* (that thou art). Now you will object that you do not follow my reasoning. That was to be expected. Were it possible to grasp the underlying truth of what has been said above, it would mean experiencing the Great Liberation. Indeed, I hope one day to grasp this truth by having that experience. Till then I practise tolerance as one who knows that in the moment of illumination there will be no "you" (with retrospective effect!). That is to say, there never *was* any "you". In other words I am only being generous to myself although it may appear as tolerance to a given "you". It is, therefore, highly irrelevant whether you reciprocate my tolerance or not. Reciprocation is only possible where there are at least two separate entities (*ens individuale*). And that is precisely what I question. My submission is that there is, in essence, not more than one entity. For as far as spiritual salvation is concerned, all sentient beings together form one entity. A private or separate salvation for oneself, apart from cosmic salvation as a whole, is wishful thinking. For instance, a

---

[1] *The Bhagavadgītā*, p. 181 f.

drowning man can either be entirely saved (*corpore toto*) or he drowns completely. He is not in a position to choose and select what part of his body may get drowned and what part should be saved. He cannot say: "save my right hand, the left may sink". Or "let my stomach drown. It does not agree with me. But save my feet!" That certainly sounds ridiculous. A salvation that does not include all sentient beings is equally ridiculous to the Eastern mind.

'Now you may threaten me with the ugly prospect of religious persecution. But what will you persecute? At the most *my* body. But then should I identify my Self with my body? Or you suggest converting *my* mind (*ens spirituale; intellectualitas*) to *your* way of thinking. But this mind, the possession of which you attribute to me, is a mere conglomeration of thoughts, a *compilatio cogitationum.* It may be mine but it is not me.

'You now ask me, rather puzzled, what then am I? The answer will shock you.

'My I is nothing! That does not mean that it does not exist, but that its existence lies outside the field of cognition. I am. It is quite impossible to deny that. But this "I" before the word "am" is nothing. Just as we say it snows! But there is no it, apart from the snow. So the I is a kind of legal fiction that is placed before the word am in order to give it a coherence it would not otherwise have. As Being itself and Not-Being are both equally free of attributes, the statement "I am" conveys as much or as little as the statement "I am not". The I is of necessity a term whose meaning lies outside the realm of logical thought. Or, as the Buddha probably would have said, the I is *atakkāvacara*.'[1]

(The Pāli word *atakkāvacara* is a combination of three words: *a*, not included in; *takka*, logical thought; *avacara*, realm. It means what of necessity lies outside the realm of logical thought.) The I being the subject can never be the object of cognition. Therefore the I is not cognizable.[2] But if the ego is *atakkāvacara*, the experience of its so-called extinction is also *atakkāvacara*. So is *nirvāṇa*. It is here that the rationale of Eastern tolerance is to be found. Sri Ramakrishna tried to explain this rather enigmatic argument in the form of a parable. First he said:

'I have practised the disciplines of all the paths—I have practised all the disciplines; I accept all paths. Therefore people of all sects come here. *And* every one of them thinks that I belong to his school.'

Then he told the following parable which has a very profound meaning:

'A man had a tub of dye. Such was its wonderful property that people could dye their clothes any colour they wanted by merely dipping them in it. A clever man said to the owner of the tub, "Dye my cloth the colour of

---

[1] Cp. *Majjhima Nikāya*, 7 and 26 Discourse; *Saṃyutta Nikāya*, II, 1:1–3; *Itti-vutakka*, 43; *Dīgha Nikāya*, I, I, 36.

[2] Cp. The Buddha's answer to Sundarika: '*uda koci no mihi*' (I am not-I) in *Suttanipāta*, V, 455. Also Nāgārjuna in *Mādhyamika Kārika*, XXV, 19.

your dye-stuff". The "colour of your dye-stuff" is equivalent to *atakkāva-cara*! It can dye any colour but is itself devoid of colour. The different colours are symbolic of separate identities.'

What is the ego? Who is the ego? Whose ego is it? The *jñāni* searches for answers to these questions using the method of discrimination. He then makes a remarkable discovery. In isolating the ego through the method of discrimination, the ego, like the atom in physics, disappears revealing the stuff of which it was composed: the proton (Real Self) in the centre with the electrons (psychological selves) dancing round it. The *bhakta*, unlike the *jñāni*, de-electronizes his ego through the method of love and religious devotion. It is commonly believed that his love must be love of God. It need not be so. The object of the *bhakta's* devotion is unimportant provided his love is genuine and of the required intensity. An aboriginal savage on some far-flung island worshipping the devil, but worshipping and loving him intensely enough to submerge his own ego in the process of heightened devotion, will obtain the mystic Enlightenment just as readily as saintly mystics or *bhaktas*. Tolerance is to be extended to devil worshippers; for even that is a tortuous way to God. The final illumination will perhaps reveal that there is no devil apart from one's own ego-sense. For surely in the Eastern tradition the devil is but a symbol for that which obstructs our at-one-ment with God or the Absolute. And the most serious obstacle is, as the mystic religions have discovered, the ego-sense. That is why the mystic religions intuitively rejoice in tolerance while the revelatory or prophetic religions are hesitant to see in it an unqualified virtue.

Does Enlightenment lead to tolerance? According to Radhakrishnan it does. Sri Ramakrishna goes a step farther and holds even the converse to be true. That means, if one were to practise unbroken participating tolerance (on the strength of a belief in its justification through mystic Enlightenment) it would lead to the sought-for Enlightenment.

The general rule is that if the attainment of Enlightenment results in the spontaneous manifestation of a certain quality or virtue, then other things being equal, the deliberate cultivation of that quality or conduct also leads to Enlightenment. A powerful and sustained imitation of the effect conjures up its cause. If one knows one of the attributes of Enlightenment thoroughly, it leads to an insight into all the other aspects as well. This total insight is Enlightenment. That is why Sri Ramakrishna placed such emphasis on tolerance. As an experienced mystic he knew it to be an attribute of Enlightenment. But if participating tolerance is the consequence of Enlightenment it does not mean that we should postpone its practice until we are enlightened. We can begin with what may be called constructive participating tolerance until it matures into participating tolerance. Sri Ramakrishna believed in extending this kind of tolerance even to the different forms of yoga. And Radhakrishnan seems to agree:

'In its highest flights, *bhakti* coincides with *jñāna*, and both these issue in right *karma* or virtuous life.'[1]

[1] *The Hindu View of Life*, p. 82.

CHAPTER 8

The Revitalization of Metaphysical Thought

(a) INTELLECTUAL METHODS AND INTUITIVE RESULTS

When I have come to my work empty, I have suddenly become full; ideas being in an invisible manner showered upon me, and implanted in me from on high; for then I have been conscious of a . . . most penetrating insight. . . .[1]

Every age has its own metaphysics. Sometimes, as in our beat generation, it may consist of denial, of a non-acceptance of metaphysics in any form. But even a refusal to think metaphysically is a form of metaphysics. It is heartening at such a time to see a thinker of Radhakrishnan's status bring metaphysics back to where it belongs: in intimate relation to religious speculation on the imponderables of the universe.

The trouble begins when the religious of all sects think they have a vested interest in metaphysics. How to put a religious interpretation on the universe and its workings without adulterating metaphysics with theology is the key problem which Radhakrishnan has tackled. He solves the age-old dilemma of faith versus reason by giving intuition the central rôle of mediator.

Ever since Kant demolished the fallacy that reason is a sure guide to metaphysical thought, the validity of all religion has been reduced to the question: is there any reliable way of acquiring knowledge, apart from pure reason, that is also metaphysically acceptable?

Now if this can only be answered in the negative, then religion has lost its case. Radhakrishnan is convinced, however, that it can and should be answered in the affirmative. This source that is higher than reason is, according to him, *intuition*.

Kant demonstrated that it is equally possible to prove the non-existence and the existence of God through logical reasoning. Beyond a certain point, logic cannot reveal anything not already known. The fate of religion in a scientific age depends, therefore, not on reason but on whether there is or is not such a thing as intuition. The question of the existence or non-existence of God has been transposed to, and depends on, that of intuition.

Is there, however, such a thing as intuition? Is it reliable? Can it tell us more than reason? Can it be verified or refuted by reason? These are some of the questions on which the future of religion depends. Not worn out dogmas but an earnest inquiry into, and a revitalization of, metaphysical thought is the need of the hour. Radhakrishnan's thought will play a leading part in the integral *Religionsphilosophie* of the future because he has put the right questions and has also attempted to answer them. If

[1] *The Prophetic Spirit in Genius and Madness.*

you say no to intuition, you must also say no to God! That is why Radhakrishnan is so insistent that there *is* such a thing as intuition. A major part of his work, therefore, deals with intuition and the problems arising therefrom.

Radhakrishnan does not deny reason a place in metaphysics or for that matter in religion. Nor does he glorify intuition as the sole arbiter. For him intellect and intuition are not in antithesis. They complement each other. It is intellectual reflection based on intuitive insights that gives us knowledge in the full sense of the word. All religion is for Radhakrishnan *vibbhajjavāda*, that is to say reason plus meditation. Logic can help us to know something additional, something new, only when its premises are rooted in intuition.

'We are said to know a thing when we are able to place it in definite relations to other objects of experience. Empirical reality means necessary connection within the logical universe.'[1]

Radhakrishnan differentiates between intellect and intuition more or less in the same way as Hegel distinguished between *Verstand* (rational intellect) and *Vernunft* (reason guided by insight).

'While the indivisible unity is for intuition the primary reality, it is for Hegel something which is built up out of opposite parts which are logically prior to the whole. The unity appears as the result of a synthesis, the members of which are apprehended prior to the whole.'[2]

This type of thinking goes back to Kant who contested the existence of any unity prior to reflective thought. The sum and substance of it all is: 'Intuition is not alogical but supralogical.'[3] It is not irrational but only incapable of being expressed in set notions.

Now what exactly does the word intuition mean? Radhakrishnan says:

'Intuition is of two kinds, perceptual knowledge and integral insight. Personally, I use intuition for integral knowledge.'[4]

If we do not realize that faith and reason, intellect and intuition are interdependent, then Bradley's contention that metaphysics consists in finding bad arguments for our instinctive beliefs will be justified. Without rational inquiry faith will 'degenerate into credulity. Without the material supplied by faith, logical reason may become mere speculation.'[5]

While spiritual experience supplies the raw material (through intuition), philosophy shapes it into the finished product with the aid of rational intelligence. This problem has been searchingly investigated by Robert W. Browning in his brilliant essay *Reason and Types of Intuition in Radha-*

[1] *An Idealist View of Life*, Chap. IV.
[2] *Ibid.*, p. 151.
[3] *Ibid.*, p. 147.
[4] *The Philosophy of S. Radhakrishnan*, p. 791.
[5] *The Principal Upaniṣads*, p. 133.

krishnan's Philosophy.[1] There he shows how Radhakrishnan uses the word intuition in twelve different but related senses. He concludes that:

'Radhakrishnan's deployments of the term are normally clear for practical purposes in the actual contexts ... (and) the range of (his usages) is a tribute to his versatility in the artificially separated departments of human experience.'[2]

Radhakrishnan uses the word intuition

'... both to name a kind of intimate complete knowing of a concrete thing among the apparently plural entities of the realm of *māyā* and to name the consummatory toti-metaphysical insight in which empirical pluralities are transcended and all is apprehended as one.'[3]

In fact it would seem that intuition stands in the same relation to intellect as the latter stands to sensory perception. The word *intuitus* implies the sense of sight, hence *pratyakṣa*. He goes on to say:

'... reason and sense are outgrowths or determinations of intuition. Intuition is open to all men who possess the capacity for its acquisition, and there are ways and methods by which we can prepare for its reception.'[4]

In a certain sense, Radhakrishnan's metaphysics completes the task begun by Kant in his *Critique of Pure Reason.* The progress of man from magic and myth to rational thought need not bind us to a cult of reason-worship for its own sake.

'Both intellectual and intuitive kinds of knowledge are justified and have their own rights.... There are different types of knowledge: perceptual, conceptual and intuitive and they are suited to different kinds of objects. Plotinus tells us that sense perceptions are below us, logical reasonings are with us, and spiritual apprehensions are above us. The last type of knowledge may be called integral insight.'[5]

It is interesting to note that Radhakrishnan as far back as 1929 coined the phrase *integral* insight.[6] Today *integrale Bewusstsein* (integral consciousness) is the most hotly discussed topic in Continental circles. Moreover its adherents rebel against the tyranny of reason which they wish to replace with an all-round view of life in much the same way as Radhakrishnan had anticipated. The grand doyen of the *Integral* movement is the Swiss poet philosopher Jean Gebser, who is an ardent admirer of Radhakrishnan and Aurobindo. He developed a psychological theory of the history of man-

[1] *The Philosophy of S. Radhakrishnan.*
[2] *Ibid.*, pp. 178 f.
[3] *Ibid.*, p. 180.
[4] *Ibid.*, p. 195.
[5] *Ibid.*, p. 60.
[6] *An Idealist View of Life*, London, 1932.

kind which has won many followers. This theory is of considerable importance as it is relevant to the problem of intuition in metaphysics.[1] According
to it man must wander through different dimensions of consciousness. In
the beginning he lived in a magical world of fancy and superstition. Space
and time were devoid of meaning as belief in magic created its own space-
time chimeras. (This Age of Magic is estimated by Gebserians to have
lasted from 100,000–10,000 B.C.)

Then came the period of myth-derived consciousness. This also belongs
to the prelogical phase of human development, which is supposed to have
lasted till the Renaissance while others put its end as early as 500 B.C. In
any case the next period is called that of mental or rational thought-
patterns. Here at last is what we normally associate with logical cause-
and-effect thinking. The passing over from one phase to another is called
Bewusstseins-Mutationen (mutations of consciousness) and has some remote
similarity to Sir Julian Huxley's evolutionary Humanism. The main point
of the Gebserians, however, is that the phase of logical-rational consciousness has committed the blunder of overdoing itself. As a result it is now
fading and making room for a new mutation. In fact reason is already
regarded as dethroned. That we do not realize this, is considered a contri-
buting cause of our suffering and our inability to cope with modern
problems. Whereas the phase of magic-consciousness was irrational, that
of the myth-derived was non-rational and the mental period was rational,
so is the new phase, into which we are now supposed to have evolved,
suprarational. This phase of thought is called by the Gebserians *integrale
Einsicht* (integral insight) and has a startling resemblance to Radhakrishnan's conception of intuition. The attitude common to Radhakrishnan and
Gebser is the idea of an organic unity underlying the universe.

It was Radhakrishnan's genius for synthesis that led Charles A. Moore
into calling him 'the Thomas Aquinas of the modern age'.[2] Indeed,
Radhakrishnan is not only the Aquinas of our age but also its Kant for in
addition to proving the need for intuition in philosophy he has also proved
its value and validity in much the same way as Kant demonstrated his
a priori Grundwahrheiten (fundamental truths).

Compare Kant's:

'Experience is by no means the only field to which our understanding can
be confined. Experience tells us what is, but not that it must be necessarily
what it is and not otherwise. It therefore never gives us any really general
truths; and our reason, which is particularly anxious for that class of
knowledge, is roused by it rather than satisfied. General truths, which at
the same time bear the character of an inward necessity, must be independent of experience—clear and certain in themselves'[3]

---

[1] See my essay in *Wege zum integralen Bewusstsein*, Bremen, 1965, pp. 103–17.
[2] *The Philosophy of S. Radhakrishnan*, p. 282.
[3] *The Critique of Pure Reason*, London, 1881, p. 1.

and Radhakrishnan's:

'Absolute knowledge in its concreteness is more in the form of effortless insight or intuition. It is more immediate than mediate, perceptual than conceptual. Philosophy is not so much a conceptual reconstruction as an exhibition of insights. . . . the expression of all knowledge perceptual, conceptual, or intuitional requires the use of concepts. Only we have to remember that the rationalization of experience is not its whole truth. The great truths of philosophy are not proved but seen. The philosophers convey to others visions by the machinery of logical proof. . . . In moving from intellect to intuition, we are not moving in the direction of unreason, but are getting into the deepest rationality of which human nature is capable. . . . Even if intuitive truths cannot be proved to reason, they can be shown to be not contrary to reason, but consistent with it.'[1]

It is hazardous to make all knowledge dependent on external data. Every attempt to admit one kind of knowledge as evidence for the veracity of another leads to an endless chain of relations back to some proposition which is incapable of being proved either true or false. Radhakrishnan shows us the way out of this vicious circle just as Kant performed the same service to philosophy in his time.

Radhakrishnan constructs his synthesis by bringing evidence to show that both Eastern sages and Western philosophers have admitted the great certainties of life to be the products of intuition. For instance:

1. Socrates

'[He] preferred to rest his case not on inductive evidence from observed facts but on arguments based on axioms and intuitions.'[2]

2. Plato

'[The] theory of recollection is [only] Plato's name for that concentrated endeavour of the whole man by which (akin to intuition) the essential principles of life and logic are apprehended. The immortal soul learned all truth long ago, and it is reminded by sense experience of truths it once knew and has forgotten. Recollection (intuition?) is the basis of the logical process which consists in the discovery of ideas in which the particulars participate.'[3]

3. Aristotle

'*Nous* represents the intuitive apprehension of the first principles which all reasoning assumes to start with.'[4]

4. Descartes

'[He] admits that intuitive knowledge . . . is a knowledge different from the fluctuating testimony of the senses or the misleading judgments that proceed from the blundering constructions of imagination.'[5]

[1] *An Idealist View of Life*, p. 152–3.
[2] *Ibid.*, p. 158.
[3] *Ibid.*, p. 159; Cp. Plato, *Republic*, VI, 508.
[4] *Ibid.*, p. 159; Cp. Aristotle, *Metaphysics*, 997a.
[5] *Ibid.*, p. 160; Cp. also Descartes, *Intellectual System*, iv, pp. 31–8.

5. Spinoza

'In [his] *Short Treatise* [he says that] intuitive knowledge [does not] consist in being convinced by reasons but in an immediate union with the thing itself.'

Further: 'From intuitive vision arises the highest possible peace of mind.'[1]

6. Leibniz

'[He] does not favour the view that all knowledge is either perceptual or conceptual.'[2]

7. Pascal

'[His] saying that the heart has its reason which reason knows not is well known. Indeed his *ésprit de finesse* is but another name for intuition.'[3]

8. Kant

'[He] called the ideas, after Plato, Ideas of Reason. There are three ideas of reason—Soul, World in its entirety, and God. They cannot be construed as objects of experience, though they have a *regulative* use. . . .

'These three lines of reflection in Kant, Ideas of Reason, the forms of moral life, and the notion of adaptation, confirm the view that reason is in Kant another name for the deeper rationality or intuition.'[4]

9. Hegel

'[He] thinks that he makes little use of intuition . . . (but he) believes in a monistic view of the Universe. . . . This sense of the One which is the central feature of Hegel's system is an announcement of an intuition and not the result of a demonstration.'[5]

So long as the divine cannot be ascertained by logical evidence, intuition offers the only way out of the dilemma. That is why Radhakrishnan insists on intuition as an indispensable factor in all religion and metaphysics. Even meditation derives its value from the fact that it makes us receptive to intuitions.

Of course there is no overlooking the danger of wishful thinking masquerading as intuition. Intuition needs to be verified as far as possible by rational evidence. Although an intuition is sometimes at variance with a logical solution, this need not always be the case. Intuitions which contradict rational thought deserve even greater scrutiny to guard against their being false. An interesting case-study of pseudo-intuition is Hitler. At first he had genuine intuitions which contradicted the rational advice of his military experts. But success went to his head and from then on he regarded every quirk as genuine if only it happened to contradict the reasoned advice of his generals. Pseudo-intuitions lead to similar disasters on the

[1] *Ibid.*, p. 161; Cp. also Spinoza, *Ethics*, V, xxvii.

[2] *Ibid.*, p. 161.

[3] *Ibid.*, p. 161.

[4] *Ibid.*, pp. 162–5; Cp. also Kant, *Critique of Pure Reason*, London, 1881, vol. ii, p. xxiii.

[5] *Ibid.*, p. 172; Cp. also Hegel, *Philosophy of Religion*, E.T. (1895), vol. i, p. 4.

spiritual path. That is just the difference between the visionary and the false prophet. The former has access to intuition while the latter has been deceived by his ego into accepting its own caprices as intuitions from on high. Before one can have authentic intuitions one must be wary of deceptive hunches, which are no better than guesses. Only the self-mastered sage who has brought his ego under control can distinguish between false and genuine intuition. What the religions call revelation is only a collection of genuine intuitions from authentic sages. If, as we have seen, there need be no conflict between reason and intuition, there need be none between reason and revelation. Metaphysics can and should provide rational groundwork for the revealed wisdom of the sages. What one should always avoid is to try and force all life into some set framework or hide-bound system and then make a philosophy or religion out of it. Life refuses to be systematized. What fits neatly into a system cannot be life—cannot even be capable of life. Life is always contradicting itself. It laughs at all systems. How pathetic to see people worried to death while trying to find a meaning in life; as if it were all a game of hide-and-seek in which the meaning is the thing hidden. The paper cannot dictate to me what I shall write on it. We must add meaning to life (*Sinngebung*) and make it significant (*Lebensgestaltung*). Yet this meaning is not something static, but dynamic and has to be realized creatively in the living. This can only be done if we acknowledge intuition as an element of the total metaphysical world view.

Heidegger claims that the poet is the only true philosopher since through his intuition he receives what escapes the mere man of learning. This intuitive faculty of poetic genius was particularly stressed by Hermann Hesse who once put it as follows:

'When I gaze at anything, say a wood, and if I desire to purchase it or have it cut down or mortgage it or want to do anything with it then something escapes my cognition. I do not see the wood at all but am beclouded by a series of relationships between myself and my Will. When, however, I gaze into a wood without any such thoughts then the wood acquires a singular reality as well as a beauty all its own.'[1]

So we see that Radhakrishnan's plea for a return to intuition is well founded when he says:

'Knowledge of God is achieved not by intellect alone. Man's entire being—intellect and imagination, heart and will—is active. God is revealed through inner experience and not external observation.'[2]

Bergson came to more or less the same conclusion. Intuition alone enables us to appreciate the *Sinngebung* and the *Lebensgestaltung* without

---

[1] Requoted from the German in Werner S. Klar's essay in *Wege zum integralen Bewusstsein*, p. 57. Cp. also Wordsworth: 'Then my heart with pleasure fills
And dances with the daffodils.'

[2] *The Philosophy of S. Radhakrishnan*, p. 793.

which metaphysics as well as life would remain an arid desert. The wailing and moaning of the existentialist philosophers, from Kierkegaard down to our own days, is only a protest against the reign of intellect. All they want to say is:

'You cannot imprison my "me" in a system. For every system is all intellect but my "me" is a something more and beyond intellect.'

Whereas the existentialists wish to dismount reason without having anything, except perhaps an aggrandizement of the irrational in man, to put in its place, Radhakrishnan and Gebser offer us intuition and integral insight as worthy modes of acquiring a fuller depth and meaning to life. Schopenhauer called man a metaphysical animal. If we leave out the metaphysics, only an animal will be left. This is the danger which appears to threaten us. We cannot get a living impulse out of a dead metaphysics. In order to remain dynamic metaphysics must be nourished on intuitions.

(b) A CRITIQUE OF PURE BEING

(The *despair* of the Existentialists and its ontological roots)

The self subsistence of God is evident from the name of God, Iruvan='the one who exists.'[1]

Passing on from logical positivism to existentialism is like going from an uninhabitable desert, where nothing grows, to an equally uninhabitable jungle, where one is choked with excessive vegetation. Considering some of the wild extravagances of the existentialist philosophers one is tempted to believe that the logical positivists may be right in their insistence on language and logic.

To anyone well acquainted with the philosophy of China, modern existentialism appears to be no more than a bad paraphrase of the philosophy of the *Tao*. But this resemblance is superficial because existentialism belongs more to psychology than to philosophy.[2]

The *phenomenology* of Husserl, when combined with Kierkegaard's despair, on the basis prepared by Pascal and Nietzsche, created a kind of romantic revival generally called existentialism. Its chief enemy seems to be Hegel or rather any closed system claiming impersonal objectivity. It prefers to shift emphasis from phenomenal investigation (what Jaspers calls *Weltorientierung*) to the investigation of self and personality (what Marcel calls the ontological mystery). This aim made Sören Kierkegaard revolt against all merely rational and positivist systems, and declare that reality and truth, whether rational or not, are within man himself and his

[1] Father Heras, 'The Religion of Mohenjo Daro People', *Journal of the University of Bombay*, Vol. V, p. 3.
[2] The International Congress of Psychotherapy at Barcelona in September (1958) was centred on existential analysis.

actions. The Hegelian *Zeitgeist* is only capable of retrospective generalizations. The present and future are quite outside its ambit. According to Kierkegaard, the central, all-important fact about man is that *he exists*. But as he is the only self-conscious creature, he is also the only one who can be consciously aware of his existence. He can, therefore, also become aware of the possibility of *non-existence*. And this gives rise to the stress that existentialist philosophers put on *anxiety*. Kierkegaard's solution to this was Faith, in the most theological sense of the word—and his theology is evangelical protestantism. This theology disguised as philosophy found an eager follower in Karl Barth who insists on a vigorous return to the principles of the Reformation. Yet no one seems to fear the consequences of Luther's conception of Faith, which being a dynamically embracing force engulfs in its rash enthusiasm the other two members of the Pauline triad, Hope and Charity. The result of this insistence that all religious knowledge is due to faith leads to a theological trap in which knowledge can only mean that which supposedly leads to salvation.

Existentialism is usually divided into two branches
1. Religious existentialism (Kierkegaard, Jaspers, Marcel), and
2. Non-religious existentialism (Heidegger, Sartre).

Let us consider Heidegger and Jaspers briefly.

1. Martin Heidegger[1]

Heidegger's great feat was to combine Husserl with Kierkegaard. As a cure for the unceasing conflict between idealism and realism, Husserl recommended a sort of preliminary phenomenology for describing the contents of consciousness in neutral terms before coming to philosophical controversies. In *Sein und Zeit*[2] Heidegger emphasizes man's finite and contingent condition. Man is like a passenger on a railway journey from Nowhere to Nowhere, via Nothing—and the train has broken down *en route*. Hence arises that fundamental anxiety about the threat of Non-Being and Nothingness. It is in this concept of anguish that Heidegger assimilates Kierkegaard.

In *Kant und das Problem der Metaphysik*,[3] he enlarges upon the knowledge of the Self as admitted by Kant. According to Kant, our receptive knowledge can only be of its own products and its constructions of things as they appear—but the relation of such constructions to the thing-in-itself was in principle unknowable. Thus only the Self as *moral agent* could know itself in its reality. Heidegger fixes his attention on those passages in the first edition of the *Deduction of the Categories* in which the transcendental imagination is made the common root of both sensibility and understanding. He saves the knowledge of the Self from being drowned in Kant's phenomenalism, by arguing that time is not merely a subjective form of inner sensibility but the very condition of our existence. Man (*qua* ego) knows himself as a *temporal* existence. Transcendental imagination is

---

[1] The author of this book has had the good fortune to study under Heidegger at the University of Freiburg.
[2] Halle, 1927.
[3] Bonn, 1929.

anticipatory experience, because it involves a looking *forward* in time as opposed to the looking backwards of reproductive imagination. Heidegger claims that Being itself can become ours without ceasing to be Being itself. The secret lies in Being's transparency which he calls the non-concealment of Being (*die Unverborgenheit des Seins*). In his essay on *Platon's Lehre von der Wahrheit*,[1] he traces to Plato the main cause of difficulties and mis-understandings in European philosophy. Plato's mistake, he says, was in regarding the conception of truth as the correspondence of mind with fact. As we cannot leave the World-Cavern, for us, lost souls, the shadows are truer than the light. That is Heidegger's contention—but Indian philosophy is prepared to show a way out of the world-cavern for those who are willing to submit to *tapasya* or self-discipline. However, he allows man an anti-being (*Gegenwesen*) which consists of the changing and partial perspective of his consciousness through historical time. Death he explains as the clearing (*Lichtung*) in the destiny of Being, through the aid of which we can get a glimpse of 'the World as World'.

Heidegger prepares the way for a proper understanding of Indian philosophy by making *Death* a topic of central importance. But that does not mean that his philosophy is necessarily gloomy.[2] Besides death there is also genuine life. There is constructive joy (*das Freudige*) which makes the fear of death itself an ecstasy of joy (*Freudigschauern*). In his *Vom Wesen der Wahrheit*[3] we find an important change in terminology. The term decadence (*das Verfallen*) is replaced by insistence (*In-sistenz*). Just as opposed to the apparent (*das Offene*) we have the confused (*die Irre*), for rescue-through-excavation (*Ent-bergen*) there is rescue-through-concealment (*Ver-bergen*), so also for existence-outwards (*Existenz*) there is existence-inwards (*In-sistenz*). When he says that: 'the No-thing turns all to nothing' (*das Nichts nichtet*) we must not confuse it with Hegel's negation of the negation. Heidegger's Nothing is a tremendous contribution towards a proper understanding of the concept of Mind-in-its-nakedness in Tibetan philosophy. It makes man the last outpost (*Platzhalter*) of the void. Even in utter solitude an individual cannot separate himself from that Totality which is called the participated being (*Mitsein*). Heidegger's concept of existence (*Dasein*) includes a latent capacity for projection and discovery. It should not, therefore, be confused with the Cartesian sub-stance which merely cognizes and perceives. Moreover, it is a duty-for-me (*Verschuldung*) that arises out of a right-in-someone-else (*Schuldigsein*) and not the other way about. Creation, in so far as it is the foundation of negativity, is a debt-of-duty (*Schuld*) itself. For Heidegger, creation is

[1] Bern, 1954.

[2] In the Winter semester of 1955–6, Heidegger delivered at the University of Freiburg a course of lectures on *Der Satz vom Grunde* which the author of this book personally attended. Far from being gloomy the lectures fired the entire audience with enthusiasm and aspiration. The audience felt enlivened, rather than pessimistic at the end. The ontological *feel* that one got by attending his lectures cannot be reproduced by reading his books.

[3] Bern, 1947.

anxiety (*Sorge*) considered as man's liability to supply meaning to life (*Besorgen*). Genuine life means to accept and embrace one's liability (*Schuld*) of existence. From the sea of becoming-ness (*das Seiende, das Chtonische*) an infinite series of particles of existing be-bodies (*Dasein*) evaporate to condense and float down as bubbles.[1] Such is the analogy to Reality-in-the-process-of-becoming-Truth (*das Geschehen der Wahrheit*). Thus it will be seen that it resembles Leibniz's monad system as acted upon internally through Nothingness instead of externally by Harmony. What is called intention in Husserl's philosophy is called projection by Heidegger. Thus the formula:

'Nothing (*qua Selfness*) plus nothing (*qua Otherness*) equals *Being*—which says Heidegger is the soil of the Tree of Philosophy. He then asks: 'What is the soil into which the roots of metaphysics are plunged?'[2]

In his *Was ist Metaphysik*, Heidegger introduces a new term: Become-ness (*die Seiendheit*). The essence of being-there-in-the-world (*Dasein*) lies in its being-a-given-fact-of-existence (*Existenz*) which means transcending the world (*Transzendenz*) or rather anticipate becoming involved in the existence of the world (*Sich-vorweg-schon-sein-in-der-Welt*). The Becoming (*Seiendes*) when it means being-there-ness (*Vorhandensein*) is called a Becoming contrary to the laws of existence (*das nicht daseinsmässige Seiende*).

What then is so unique about Heidegger's thought? In what way does it differ from that of other philosophers in the past? The tradition of European philosophy from earliest times had been that the reality of the world is, in the last analysis, something intelligible. According to Heidegger, living in this world is utterly unintelligible because our lives are (and can at any moment be) terminated by an absurdity called death. We are *hineinge-worfen* on this planet, and the price to be paid for it is the perpetual *Angst* of a collision with Nothing.

Heidegger is quite right that it is to poets, rather than philosophers or scientists, that the ontological mystery is revealed. For the poet does not try to transcend himself but quietly waits for the transcendent. In the works of the Persian poet Omar Khayyam we have one of the finest expositions of *Existenzphilosophie*:

> One Moment in Annihilation's Waste,
> One Moment of the Well of Life to taste—
> The Stars are setting, and the Caravan
> Starts for the dawn of Nothing—Oh make haste!

2. Karl Jaspers

It is necessary to study Heidegger before one can understand the comparisons and contrasts in the philosophy of Jaspers, whose existentialism

---

[1] Cf. Shelley's *The Cloud*.

[2] *Was ist Metaphysik*, Bonn, 1929, p. 7. Cp. Descartes' comparison of philosophy to a great tree the roots of which comprise metaphysics.

is more religious and psychological. It is also more explicitly Kantian. He worked in a psychiatrist's clinic and one of his earliest books dealt with the general principles of psychotherapy. He was not alone in this. Eugène Minkowiski[1] (Paris), and Ludwig Binswanger (Switzerland) began applying what are now called phenomenological and existential principles to psychiatry. Binswanger called their method *Daseinsanalyse*, from Heidegger's *Dasein* which can best be translated as instant being—both here and now. The movement spread to Vienna, France and Spain culminating in the famous Barcelona Congress of Psychotherapy.[2]

Existentialism is not used directly to help patients but indirectly by providing a foundation for psychologists to widen the structure for their science and so to understand more intimately the problems of their patients. It means the introduction of an extra dimension, *ontology*. The therapist's own attitude to anxiety and guilt will naturally play an important role for the patient. In psychiatry before Jaspers there was no place for fundamental anguish about such essential issues as *Being* and *Non-Being*. Hence there was no method to cure it. Most anxiety was attributed to trauma or repression of instincts and so considered merely neurotic. This was perhaps true of the unconscious repression of the id-ego as explained by Freud. Now in a society so peculiarly organized and industrialized as ours, for the average person, sexual intercourse becomes the only available substitute for ontological fulfilment. This can be stated in the following formula: other things being equal, the compulsion of a person's biological urge will tend to vary directly with his *existential* anxiety and inversely with the fullness of his ontological satisfactions.

The reason why sex is so much sought after in our cities is not because it provides biological satisfactions but because it satiates the ontological hunger which is always extremely acute wherever a person is leading a functionalized existence. This implies constant activity, mainly in the form of *routine*. Although apparently most of the anxiety comes from the repression of instinctual drives, in reality it is because too many people lead lives devoid of ontological meaning. This brings to the surface existential anxiety. Successful psychotherapy demands that man be considered in his entirety. This from the existentialist view-point lies in his unique ability to see himself as a *finite* creature poised on the brink of Nothingness. In the words of Pascal, why 'here rather than there, now rather than then'?[3]

Jaspers speaks of *Existenzerhellung* but such *Erhellung* can never amount to an objective datum.

The mistake which permeates both existential and nearly all Western philosophy is the misleading meaning given to the word 'I'. The I is the pivot of existentialism. But this I is treated as objective and, as in general psychology, means no more than the totality of thoughts which make up the contents of a person's consciousness. It is then contended that the I, which I mean when I say 'I am', stands over against these contents as

---

[1] Editor of *L'Évolution Psychiatrique*.

[2] International Congress of Psychotherapy, Barcelona, September 1958.

[3] *Pensées*.

subject; so that when I try to regard this subject as an object, I find a contentless ego-point, which is not more than an empty form of the ego. But this so-called empty ego-form is the I; the mental contents constitute the false ego which plays a life-long deception on me. The anxiety, anguish or whatever else I may feel is because I mistakenly identify the false ego with the true I.

The pioneer work of Jaspers has created in America a keen interest in what is there called 'existential psychoanalysis'. Its leading exponent appears to be Rollo May whose *Existence: A New Dimension in Psychiatry and Psychology*[1] has awakened active interest in existentialism at the university level in the English-speaking world. Professor William Barrett of New York University wrote *Irrational Man: A Study in Existential Philosophy*, to show the increasing importance of existentialism in contemporary psychotherapy.

It is interesting at this stage to consider Radhakrishnan's criticism of existentialism. However much Heidegger, Jaspers and Marcel disagree with each other, they agree that Ultimate Reality cannot be proved in scientific terms, but must reveal itself to a certain kind of philosophical reflection. Here contemporary Western philosophy stands on the threshold of Eastern wisdom. But one step more and the existentialist's anxiety could vanish into the bliss of *bhramājñāna*.

'The human soul fascinated and tortured asks to be saved.'[2] Marcel says: 'So I am inevitably forced to ask: Who am I—I who question being?' That is the wisest sentence in contemporary Western philosophy. Only one should not attempt to answer it because it is not a problem but a *Mystery*. Marcel contends that it cannot be solved like a problem, for that would drag in the mediating work of the intellect, but it may be revealed or illuminated directly through participation or immediate contact. If one may not even attempt to answer this question, what should one do? Indian philosophy says we should wait for an answer. That is the art and secret.[3] 'By facing the bitter meaning of nothingness, we attain illumination of the Being in which existence dwells.'[4] But this asking and waiting is only possible for those who have been broken on the wheel of existentialist anxiety and ontological crisis. This extreme inward suffering and anguish is the kind cruelty of the surgeon's knife—a part of the therapeutic process. The greatest achievement of existentialism is that through anxiety, anguish and dread it shakes man out of his complacency and drives him on to the ontological mystery. In this sense a person tortured by existential anxiety is spiritually more advanced than he who never suffers this anguish but feels happy and accepts the world with a cheerful 'Yes'. The pessimism

---

[1] New York, 1958.

[2] Radhakrishnan, *History of Philosophy Eastern and Western*, p. 446. He compares existentialism with the symbolism of the second chapter of *Genesis*: 1. knowledge (the tree of) 2. sense of good and evil (Adam and Eve become smitten with fear) 3. insecurity, fear, anxiety 4. search for a way out. *Ibid.*, p. 443.

[3] Cp. Simone Weil, *Waiting on God*.

[4] Radhakrishnan, op. cit., p. 445.

of existentialism is an advance on the thoughtless and complacent optimism of what Heidegger calls the coward crowd, and Sartre *les salauds*. This so-called healthy optimism of the average person is like the health of someone who has a deadly cancer without knowing it—but which at any moment may give him a very painful surprise. The defect of Western existentialism is that it restores anxiety and anguish but shows no way out. It just tells the victim that he is suffering from a deadly ontological cancer. The remedy is to be found in Christ's and the Buddha's: 'I have overcome the world.' Existentialism symbolizes the darkest hours that precede dawn. The answer as Radhakrishnan explains is that: 'There are two elements in man, one in which he is involved in the flux of time and history and another by which he transcends it.' That is the promise held out by the New Testament's 'there shall be time no longer'. Existentialism has rendered yeoman service in *preparing* the soil in the West for a proper understanding of Indian philosophy. For it is only after one has suffered the most acute ontological anxiety that Indian philosophy begins to make sense. This bitter existential suffering is part of a purificatory process. Thus contemporary Western existentialism has come to agree with the Indian viewpoint that philosophy is not so much a matter of logical argument as an attempt at deepening our consciousness. But this deepening is possible only after acute anguish has cleared away the debris. Goethe seems to have guessed this when he said:

> Who never spent the midnight hours
> Weeping and waiting for the morrow,
> He knows you not, ye heavenly powers.

(c) THE ONTOLOGICAL IMPLICATIONS OF BEING IMMORTAL

(Radhakrishnan and the Systematic Theology of Paul Tillich)

We must make a distinction of the two great forms of being, and ask, 'What is that which Is and has no Becoming, and what is that which is always becoming and never is?'[1]

Is there such a thing as being-in-itself? Can we even imagine it? How does Pure Being differ from mere Being?

The concept of Pure Being (*Sein*; το εἶναι) as an abstraction above and beyond mere Being (*Seienden*; το ὄν) is attributed in modern philosophy to Hegel although in a certain form it is older than Plato and even Aquinas in his *De Ente et Essentia* had considered it. The existentialist philosopher Heidegger attributes the entire insufficiency of western metaphysics to its not having paid to the concept of Pure Being the attention it deserves. The whole forest of terms in Hegel's *Logik* can be traced to what he called Pure Being and to which he attributed the underlying basis of all harmony in nature. Nor must we forget that for Hegel his *Logik* was no mere logic but: 'God as he was before he created the world.'[2]

---

[1] Plato, *Timaeus*, §27.
[2] Deussen, *Allgemeine Geschichte der Philosophie*, Volume VI, p. 355.

Ever since Sartre's *L'Être et le Néant*[1] (Being and Nothing), the word Being has become a kind of magic codeword to be chanted by the elect who wish for a seat in the temple of the existentialists. Stripped of its French-Bohemian obscurantism this term has a very prosaic history. After Hegel it was Husserl who made Being the corner-stone of what he called *reine Phänomenologie* (pure phenomenology). This phenomenological ontology gave birth in its turn to the many different cults and sects of existentialism. England was spared Husserl's paradoxes while Germany was overrun by them. He founded a school of thought there to which many notables of his day came—and then went away discontented. The cruellest cut came in 1931 when Heidegger turned his back on the Master.

There is, however, more to Husserl than his contemporaries thought. If he could have had his own way Western philosophy would today be nearer to a *rapprochement* with Eastern thought. He wanted a return to the Subject of experience; that is to say, Consciousness should be considered the source of our knowledge of the external world. This is also the Eastern standpoint. It is a pity that Radhakrishnan did not pick up Husserl's line of argument for here indeed was the opportunity for building a bridge between East and West.

There is, however, a chance to make up for this in the existentialist theology of Paul Tillich. Husserl's stress on the Subject of experience is also to be found in Tillich, only his emphasis on the Subject is derived from Schelling. Still the latter's critical idealism was rather too subjective for the pious Protestant heart of a German theologian, which ever lives in dread of losing God through excessive subjectivism. This ghost of subjectivism (which still haunts German theology, as witness Karl Barth[2]) had to be exorcized within the rules of dialectical theology. Schelling's influence, in other words, had to be neutralized with elements taken from Kierkegaard in order to form a theology often called *transcendental realism*. This new theology working on the frontiers of knowledge has immensely impressed many Americans incapable of reading theology in German. Nevertheless Tillich stands head and shoulders above the theologians of our day and of all adherents of the dialectical school he alone offers ground for an East-West encounter in religion. He was so far ahead of his times that he wrote:

'Christ and the Buddha are symbols which at the same time have an empirical and historical side; the empirical is contained in the significance of the symbols. Therefore the empirical as well as the transcendental vibrates in their (holy) names and thereon rests their power as symbols. They are akin to the name of God: i.e. they are symbolic but in such a way that the unsymbolic reality is at the same time expressed therein.'[3]

Tillich is to Christian theology what Radhakrishnan is to Vedānta. Both rest their case on a critique of Pure Being. For Radhakrishnan it

[1] Paris, 1943.

[2] Cf. Pope's: 'Sworn foe to mystery yet divinely dark!'

[3] *Das religiöse Symbol*, Berlin, 1930, p. 288. (My translation; official English translation by James Luther Adams in *Journal of Liberal Religion*, 2 (1940).)

means the attitude of the Upaniṣads: 'Being is, is God.'[1] That emphasizes the primacy of Being. As also:

'The existence of the world means the primacy of Being. The very fact that becoming comes to be, that it has a beginning, means that there is something that has not itself become. The root principle is not the primordial night of nothingness but is Absolute Being. Being denotes pure affirmation to the exclusion of every possible negation. It is absolute self-absorbed Being, the one Supreme Identity beyond existence and non-existence, the universal reality.'[2]

Why should metaphysics pay such devout attention to the problem of Being? Has it any *practical* significance? It has indeed a far greater significance than the layman is apt to guess. Everyone has, tucked away somewhere in his mind, a metaphysics of some kind or other. This consists mainly of what he understands the word Being to mean. His view of Being will determine what he considers to be his Being, his 'I am'. This 'I am' notion, his concept of self, is in its turn the deciding factor of his version of death and immortality. How we will react to death in that fateful hour remains unknown to us until it arrives. Yet our reaction is prejudged and dependent on the ontological frame of our metaphysical world view. All those promises of everlasting life, rebirth, deathlessness, sojourns in heavens and Valhallas, so convincingly held out by the different religions, cannot enter a mind whose concept of Being is incompatible with such views on death and immortality. Before I can be deathless, I must have a metaphysics of deathlessness; before I can convince myself that I am immortal I must have an ontological basis to support that conviction. A mere Sunday-school belief in immortality, not grounded on or backed by a metaphysical view of Being consonant with such belief, is like a cheque drawn on a bank at which one has no account. At death such a cheque appears for what it is worth.

Being and Pure Being are not mere concepts for metaphysicians to toy with. They are vital in determining how you will feel when you know you are about to die. Nor is that all. The way a person thinks about death colours his whole attitude to life. Tell me what you think of death and I can estimate what value you put on life. The value one puts on one's own life is a reliable indicator of one's values-of-life. Just as there are certain things without which we cannot live, there are certain values-of-life without which we do not care to live. The mistaken belief that problems of Being may be left to professional metaphysicians and need not affect our practical day to day life is the main source of all psychic maladjustments. Anxiety, distress, depression, melancholia, neurasthenia, insomnia, nightmares; refuge-seeking in alcohol, speeding, LSD, drug-addiction—all point to the dangers of facing life without first having *consciously* analysed one's own metaphysical conception of Being. Every man his own metaphysician? This sounds alarming at first, but a quiet rumination will reveal its

---

[1] *The Principal Upaniṣads*, p. 448.
[2] *Recovery of Faith*, p. 82–3.

plausibility. Does not every man die his *own* death? Would not then some *unique* relationship between being and dying manifest in every individual, even in the insane? Has not everyone till now unconsciously played the metaphysician? Think of the last time you attended a funeral. In metaphysics we do openly and consciously what the masses have always done in a stifling and repressive way. It is only against this background that we can understand Tillich's and Radhakrishnan's preoccupation with ontology. So Tillich:

'Ontological concepts are *a priori* in the strict sense of the word. They determine the nature of experience. They are present whenever something is experienced . . . (but they are also) products of a critical analysis of experience. . . .'[1]

And Radhakrishnan:

'There would be no existence, no becoming, no manifestation at all, if there were not Non-Being. Without Non-Being, Being would be mere self-identity and there would be no manifestation, no expression. It is Non-Being that drives Being from its immovable self-identity and enables it to express itself. It is Non-Being that reveals God as power. No revelation is possible without the ground of Being and the principle of Non-Being. When we say that something *is*, we mean that it participates in Being but is not identical with Being.'

If Being is man's highest value and his ultimate concern then Pure Being is phenomenologically only another name for God. So we detect the existentialist in Tillich when he protests:

'This does not mean that there is a being called God and then the demand that man should be ultimately concerned about him. It means that whatever concerns a man ultimately becomes god for him, and conversely, it means that a man can be concerned ultimately only about that which is god for him.'[2]

Here Tillich comes very near to the standpoint of Vedānta. If Pure Being is the supreme reality then all existence is primarily but a symbol of that greater reality underlying it. He writes:

'But the term being means the whole of human reality, the structure, the meaning, and the aim of existence. . . . Man is infinitely concerned about the infinity to which he belongs, from which he is separated, and for which he is longing.'[3]

Is this longing then not for what Vedānta calls Ātman meaning the Self in its ontological depths, our essential Being?

[1] *Systematic Theology*, Chicago, 1951, I, p. 166.
[2] *Ibid.*, p. 211.
[3] *Ibid.*, p. 14.

Tillich says:

'What I mean is that the ground of being is at the same time the abyss of any definite being; and conversely that the abyss of being which transcends all special beings is at the same time the creative ground of all forms of existence. They are all conditioned by it; but it itself is not conditioned by anything; they all are contained in it but it itself is not exhausted in their infinity. . . .'[1]

Again:

'Therefore, instead of saying that God is first of all being-itself, it is possible to say that he is the power of being in everything and above everything, the infinite power of being.'[2]

This being-itself comes very close to the *svabhāva* of Indian philosophy. *Svabhāva* means own-Being, that is to say Being's own Being, and with *svadharma* becomes the law of one's own Being, the ground of one's own Being—in other words Pure Being. So Radhakrishnan:

'We mean by real any entity which has a nature of its own (*svabhāva*), which is not produced by causes, which is not dependent on anything else. . . . The real is the independent uncaused being.'[3]

And Tillich:

'. . . the unsymbolic statement which implies the necessity of religious symbolism is that God is being itself, and as such beyond the structure of everything that is.'[4]

A benevolent providence has so arranged things that what is best lies safest; it can neither be given nor taken away. This best in man is then the Ātman (Radhakrishnan) or our essential Being (Tillich). Indeed, all things share in that power of Being-itself. The revelation of Pure Being (Being-itself or *svabhāva*) manifests, according to both thinkers, as the unconditioned transcendental. This is described by Tillich as:

'the self-manifestation of the ground of the ontological structure of being'.

And by Radhakrishnan as:

'. . . behind and beyond the world and in the world; . . . a strife between being and non-being in the process of becoming. Pure being is above the world and pure non-being is below the lowest existent. If we go lower still we have nothing, it is absolute non-entity. In the world of true becoming,

---

[1] Symbol and knowledge. A response, in *Journal Liberal Religion*, 2 (1940), 202–6.
[2] *Systematic Theology*, I, p. 236.
[3] *Indian Philosophy*, I, p. 697.
[4] *The Theology of Paul Tillich*, p. 334.

samsara, we have the conflict between the two principles of being and non-being.'[1]

Pure Being is in practice equivalent to No-thing. The *Self* is Pure Being. As such it is a No-thing which cannot be described in words. A positive affirmation of *Self* (as Ātman) is logically difficult if not impossible. An ordinary person would even fall a prey to confusion. The Buddha, long before Radhakrishnan or Tillich, was aware of it and, therefore, bypassed this obstacle by using the method of *reductio ad absurdum.* This is permissible only when the positive proof of an affirmation is not possible but the number of negating alternatives is limited.

Suppose that I am not in a position to prove that what I hold in my hand is a pen. Suppose further that apart from it being a pen only three other alternatives are possible. Let these three alternatives be supposed as:
(i)   it is a bottle
(ii) it is a nail
(iii) it is a hat
If I can prove that what I hold in my hand is neither a bottle nor a nail nor a hat then I have also proved that what I hold in my hand is a pen by having made all the alternatives untenable.

This is the method that the Buddha adopts to drive home the truths about essential Being. He lets every contestant declare what the latter regards as his Self. He then shows him that that cannot possibly be his real Self.[2] After the adversary has thought out all the possibilities, he is at his wits' end and despairs to know what he is. So he thinks:

'That I am, cannot be denied. But what if the Buddha succeeds each time in proving that I am neither this nor that? The only alternative then is that I am nothing!'

The Buddha's aim was to provoke the adversary further into asking what this nothing is. In order to understand what nothing is, he is invited to contemplate its opposite. The opposite of nothing is everything or all. And what is all? It is composed of everything we can cognize with our senses plus all we can picture through our imagination.[3] What I can neither perceive nor cognize nor imagine is not included in my all. It is, therefore, *as if it were* nothing.

The I indeed cannot be cognized for it is the cognizer; it cannot be imagined because it is the imaginer. The I being always the subject of cognition can never be an object of cognition. The I being always the imagining subject cannot be the content of imagination. The I being always the thinker cannot be anything think-able, i.e. expressible in thoughts. The I is tantamount to nothing though not to be confused with nothing. So one may call this type of nothing a no-thing. According to the laws of

[1] *The Bhagavadgītā,* pp. 39–40.
[2] Cp. *Majjhima Nikāya,* 22nd Discourse.
[3] Cp. *Samyutta Nikāya,* XXXV, 24.

polarity, this no-thing is the metaphysical counterpole to every-thing. The I is the no-thing which makes our all cognizable and imaginable. Goethe put it succinctly:

In this your Nothing, I find my All[1]

Pure Being is transcendental. That means the I is outside the realm of conceptual thought. It is *atakkāvacara* (outside the realm of conceptual thought). If our I, even prior to death, is *atakkāvacara* then the question: 'What will happen to me after death?' is, metaphysically and logically, unaskable. The knowledge of the ontological constitution of my I cannot be of additional but only of the residuary-legatee type. Suppose I want more space in my room then I cannot fetch it from outside as I could a chair. I can only have more space in my room by removing the objects already there until only pure space (as a kind of residuary legatee) remains. The discarding of all thoughts, all signs, all characteristics reveals Pure Being. Having no distinctive traits it is hardly distinguishable from its opposite, Non-Being. The important point is that Pure Being is something more than a mere sum of all things having Being; just as Being is something more than the total of all things in existence. Here Jean Gebser has coined an important term, *Systase*. It means a convergence of a series of perceptions into a unity that is greater than the sum of its parts; an integrated whole is supposed to have a more complex Being. An integral insight into *Systase* gives us, according to Gebser, *Synairese*. This means an insight into the reality of Being through the acquisition of a new kind of consciousness; this intensified consciousness need not be mystical. According to Gebser's theory all things are transparent the moment we perceive them in their essential wholeness (*Ganzheit*). It is not indispensable to be a mystic to perceive that we live in a transparent world; the essential reality reveals itself to mystics and non-mystics alike. This revelation of transparence is called *Diaphanierung* which means here: the perception of the presence of anything simultaneously in all its aspects both past and present. This is the official ontology of the expressionist school on the Continent and is as such also called *expressionistische Phänomenologie*.

A similar Ontology is to be found in *Chassidism*, that East-European movement of Jewish religious revival which started at the beginning of the eighteenth century and whose exponent was the late Martin Buber. A central idea of Chassidism is the unity of God and Nature. The ablest exponent of this view was Maggid von Mesertisch to whom all phenomena are so many dresses put on by divinity. The Godhead is the inmost essence of all things, even those we otherwise condemn as filth. The devotee must, therefore, try to see *through* things until he perceives their core; for the inmost core of all things is divine.[2] The innermost Being of all existences is God. That is also the ontology of Vedānta and Taoism.

The secret of immortality is the insight that Being transcends Time. What is the correlation between Being and Time?—and how does it affect

[1] Faust's reply to the Devil.
[2] Horodetzky, l.c.p. 76 ff.

our attitude to death? That has been the main content of Western philosophy as represented by Heidegger and of Indian philosophy as represented by Radhakrishnan. For Heidegger, all existence is in bondage to Time. This gives rise to the radical insecurity of being which plagues man in the form of the fear that death could at any time upset his programme. But this insecurity should goad us into discovering the immortal in us. As Radhakrishnan puts it:

'In the uncertainty of life we feel a distant certainty through which alone this uncertainty is made possible.'[1]

The *Angst* of the existentialists can be conquered by a direct experience of the unchanging element of Pure Being through a process similar to what St Thomas Aquinas called *cognito dei experimentalis*. In such a direct experience man realizes that:

'time is not all, that death is not all, that it is possible to circumvent the time process. . . . Faith in such a non-object principle is the defeat of death, and the renewal of life. When the spirit is affirmed, dread is annulled.'[2]

This circumvention of the time process is possible only if you have an ontology in which Being stands outside Time. Although man thinks he lives in Time, there is something in him which *observes* how he lives there. This unchanging standpoint of the observer enables man to notice change and mark time according to such changes. This form of ontology is also implied by the New Testament with its promise: '. . . and there will be time no more'.

The earliest expression of this idea of the observer[3] is to be found in the Upaniṣads:

'Two birds, companions [who are] always united, cling to the self-same tree. Of these two the one eats the sweet fruit, and the other looks on without eating. On the self-same tree, a person immersed [in the sorrows of the world] is deluded and grieves on account of his helplessness. When he sees the Other, the Lord who is worshipped and His greatness, he becomes freed from sorrow.'[4]

On these verses Radhakrishnan comments:

'Our being in time is an encounter of empirical existence and transcendent reality. The eternal in itself and the eternal in the empirical flux are companions. The world is the meeting-point of that which is eternal and that which is manifested in time. Man as an object of necessity, a content of

---

[1] *The Philosophy of S. Radhakrishnan*, p. 57.

[2] *Ibid.*, p. 56.

[3] It is in a sense similar to Einstein's scientific conclusion that the observer enters into every observation.

[4] *Śvetāśvatara Upaniṣad*, IV, 6–7.

scientific knowledge, is different from man as freedom. In [the former] verse, the cause of sorrow is traced to the sense of helplessness induced in us when we are lost in the objective universe; in [the latter] verse freedom from sorrow is traced to our getting beyond object-thinking into contact with real being.'[1]

If we deny that Being transcends Time then we have the human predica-ment expressed in the question: 'Is the frightened individual the end of the cosmic process or has he another destiny?'[2]

A metaphysics that has explored the possibilities of Pure Being answers: 'The whole plan of evolution suggests that man has another destiny.'[3]

The despair of the existentialists need not be the summit of philosophical speculation. For it resembles a transitory phase, a kind of dark night of the soul in the spiral evolution of spiritual consciousness. This despair which arouses such diffuse reactions like protests such as 'God is dead', creating a theatre of the absurd, refusing to wash, growing long hair and so on is rather unconvincing so long as no genuine effort is made to overcome it. Would not this existentialist despair yield to what Radhakrishnan calls reintegration? The Self then finds itself securely founded in the depths of its own essential Being. The dreaded encounter with Nothing is only a psy-chological state and not an ontological dissolution. A great part of this despair is present because, as Sartre says, man cannot choose but choose. He is compelled to make decisions. According to him the torment of making an ontological decision is magnified enormously when man feels that he decides not only for himself but indirectly for all. This special kind of despair is not a discovery of the existentialists as they would have us believe. Its all too apparent ancestor was that peculiar Romantic faculty of making oneself artificially unhappy by gloating over the sorrows of the world, which in German is called *Weltschmerz*. Sober and healthy English commonsense has no equivalent for this word, but in Germany no one is ever called a genius if he is quite free from its devastating bouts. The enormous prestige accorded to the Buddha in German intellectual circles is in no small measure attributable to the part played by suffering in Buddhist teachings.

Sartre begins by insisting on man's freedom and then, on such hearten-ing premises, argues out a philosophy of despair fit for scarecrows. Radha-krishnan also begins with the premise of man's freedom but here we end up not in despair but in hope. Our freedom gives us grounds to hope that we are not subject to mechanical either-or solutions; even despair can be sublimated.

'It is the pressure of reality that provokes the disquiet in us. . . . The power of free choice gives us hope for the future.'[4]

---

[1] *The Principal Upaniṣads*, p. 733.
[2] *Recovery of Faith*, p. 92.
[3] *The Philosophy of S. Radhakrishnan*, p. 59.
[4] *Recovery of Faith*, p. 99–100.

Part III

ALDOUS HUXLEY: OR THE WEST EXPLORES THE EAST

THE PURSUIT OF WISDOM AS THE GOAL OF LIFE

CHAPTER 9

Experiments in Spiritual Consciousness

That so many philosophers and mystics belonging to so many different cultures,
should have been convinced, by inference or direct intuition, that the world
possesses meaning and value, is a fact sufficiently striking to make it worth
while at least to investigate the belief in question.[1]

So many good 'lives' of Aldous Huxley have been published that one can
say with confidence that he was a cynic turned saint. What caused this
drastic change? Suffering. Physical blindness led to the search for a cure
which he found in the Bates system. Spiritual blindness was cured by his
encounter with Vedānta in America. The clever knowing smile, the supercilious bantering, that inherent arrogance of the Englishman abroad that
we meet with in *Jesting Pilate*[2] mellowed until we have the saintly humility
of *The Perennial Philosophy*:

'The aim and purpose of human life is the intuitive knowledge of God.'[3]

That is Vedānta, that is the *philosophia perennis*. Here speaks the *fifth*
gospel: the gospel according to the seers of all times and climes, from
Lao Tse of China to Emerson in America, from the secret initiation
ceremonies of prehistoric Mexico to Radhakrishnan in our own day.
   The underlying unity of transcendental experiences, as mentioned in the
scriptures of divergent religions, had been studied closely in ancient India.
The metaphysics of this unifying aspect of a higher grade of consciousness,
recurring in the descriptions given by all mystics, evolved with time into
what is now called Vedānta. It is not an Indian gospel but the gospel one
can find in every religion if only one looks for what is meant rather than for
what has been said. Vedānta is no more Indian than a particular stretch of
salt water which for reasons of geographical convenience is called the
Indian ocean. Every religion has its own 'Vedānta' or subjective aspect.
Vedānta is the psychological, as opposed to the theological, or dogmatic
pole, of religion. Even so great an authority on Christian mysticism as
Evelyn Underhill, herself partial to the dogmas of the Church, confessed:

'Further, Christians may well remark that the psychology of Christ, as
present to us in the Gospels, is of a piece with that of the mystics.'[4]

It was only in this unconfined and creative sense of the word, that Huxley

---

[1] Aldous Huxley, *Ends and Means*, London, 1937, p. 277.
[2] London, 1926.
[3] *The Perennial Philosophy*, New York, 1945, p. 277.
[4] *Mysticism*, London, 1957, p. 448.

took Vedānta seriously; for he did not seek to elevate an ancient Indian dogma to the status of a universal religion for modern man. For him Vedānta was synonymous with his theory of the minimum working hypothesis, in which religion is something more than mere belief. It is among other things also research.

'To a Zen Buddhist the idea that a man can be saved by giving assent to the propositions contained in a creed would seem the wildest, the most unrealistic and dangerous of fancies.'[1]

No less absurd for Huxley was the idea that one could know the essence of one's own mind without experimenting with spiritual consciousness. The application of the empirical method to religion was thought of as the key that brought salvation in the form of Self Realization. This was Huxley's interpretation of Vedānta, for what in Vedānta is signified by Ātman (Real Self), is in Zen called non-ego.

'This cosmic non-ego is the same as what the Chinese call Tao, or what the Christians call the indwelling spirit, with which we must collaborate. . . .'[2]

Every individual is equipped with a kind of sixth sense for religion no matter how irreligious he insists on being. This inborn religious inclination may be termed *meta-aspiration*. This can either be cultivated and brought to flower or it can be destroyed, depending on how one lives. The life one is compelled to lead in the huge cities of industrial civilization wipes out this meta-aspiration altogether. Why this is so is explained by Huxley in what was almost his last work: *Brave New World Revisited*.[3]

'Life in large cities is not conducive to mental health. . . . Their [city-dwellers'] existence ceases to have any point or meaning.'[4]

According to Vedānta, religion is a kind of dehypnotizing process. Allegorically speaking an angelic being has been, through force of circumstance, reduced to a state of complete suggestibility; the sorcery of this world (*māyā*) then induced it to identify itself with the beast on which it rode (the body). That is the state of man seeking salvation. A divine discontentment plagues him even in the best of stables for his inmost essence feels that it does belong there.[5] Religion should, according to Vedānta, break this spell. But alas there are so many horses neighing their conviction that our social duty is to be good comrades.

---

[1] *Vedānta for Modern Man*, London, 1952, p. 369.

[2] *Ibid.*, p. 370.

[3] London, 1959.

[4] *Ibid.*, p. 118.

[5] 'Temporal conditions will be accepted as satisfactory only by those whose first concern is not with time, but with eternal Reality.' *Vedānta for the Western World*, London, 1951, p. 109.

To be enlightened means to be free from this trance condition, to be fully awake as the word *Buddha* suggests, for it means the fully awakened one. According to the Buddha an unenlightened person lives in a state of half sleep. Society, it is true, may nourish the individual but only meta-aspiration can fill him with enthusiasm for living—and also for dying. Meta-aspiration is the daily bread we ask for in the Lord's prayer. It is the only kind of bread worth asking for daily.

As man stands on the isthmus between God and beast, time and eternity, everything he achieves has a cosmic significance. Peace in the political sense and as a heavenly condition stand in mutual relation to each other.

'Consequently every violent extinction of a human life has a transcendent and eternal significance. Moreover the mind of the universe is, among other things, the peace that passes understanding. Man's final end is the realization that, in his essence, he is one with the universal mind. But if he would realize his identity with the peace that passes understanding, he must begin by living in the peace that does not pass understanding—peace between nations and groups, peace in personal relationships, peace within the divided and multiple personality. There are many excellent utilitarian reasons for refraining from violence; but the ultimate and completely cogent reason is metaphysical in its nature.'[1]

What Huxley saw and admired in Vedānta was the application of meta-physical wisdom to practical life. It was for him not only a light-giving but also a fruit-bearing science.

'The peace that passes all understanding is the fruit of liberation into eternity; but in its ordinary everyday form peace is also the root of liberation.'[2]

Vedānta is ideally suited to practical day-to-day life. This is because it channels our meta-aspiration according to inherent psychological laws. The moment man feels that his submerged meta-aspiration has a sporting chance of receiving proper attention, a strange kind of gladness seizes him. He begins to feel at home in the world and this has a soothing effect on all forms of aggression whether arising subjectively in himself or objectively in his environment. Even his presence is said to radiate peace. The actual and the metaphysical become blended.

'Man's final end is the realization that, in his essence, he is one with the universal mind.'[3]

Another great novelist who found in Vedānta the solution to the problem of peace in the world was Leo Tolstoy. It was this 'vedāntic' element in his

[1] *Vedānta for Modern Man*, p. 295-6.
[2] *The Perennial Philosophy*, London, 1957, p. 222.
[3] *Vedānta for Modern Man*, p. 295.

H

writings that Mahatma Gandhi developed into a phliosophy of *satyagraha*. The practical basis of which was aptly expressed by Huxley:

'The only sensible thing to do is to pay more attention to the things we can agree about.'[1]

As an essayist, on the other hand, who finds in Vedānta a source of inspiration, Huxley reminds us of Ralph Waldo Emerson who argued that:

'Society never advances. It recedes as fast on one side as it gains on the other. . . . Not in time is the race progressive.'

Is that not just what Huxley wants to point out?

'Technological progress does not abolish obstacles; it merely changes their nature.'[2]

The most Vedāntic essay Emerson ever wrote was on Self Reliance. This does not mean, for him, exclusive reliance on one's own efforts, but on the Higher Self for aid and intuition. It is this reliance on a higher-than-I which justifies that boundless freedom wherein alone a genuine conscience can develop. By what men fall, by that they rise.

'That is why, in spite of Buchenwald and Hiroshima, we have to give thanks for having achieved a human birth.'[3]

What Emerson called Self Reliance is the way to what Huxley calls Self Realization. He who has realized the Higher Self possesses naturally that quality of Self Reliance which Emerson so idealized. The Self Reliance which he preached is therefore only a concomitant of Enlightenment. Huxley describes this process in almost Vedāntic terms:

'The enlightenment is experienced as joy; but this bright bliss illuminates all that, within the self, remains unenlightened, dispelling our normal blind complacency in regard to faults and shortcomings and causing us to regret not merely what we are, but even the very fact of our separate individuality.'[4]

Huxley was a much deeper thinker than he is credited to be. He distorted his own image in the public eye by occasional bouts of levity. He had developed unawares rudiments of an important system of metaphysics, but a perverse predisposition to amateurism prevented him from completing its design in detail. His metaphysics may be called empirical neo-idealism

[1] *Ibid.*, p. 297.
[2] *Ibid.*, p. 37.
[3] *Ibid.*, p. 46.
[4] *Ibid.*, p. 47.

for want of a better word. Its unconscious aim was to exorcize the ghost of Locke out of European philosophy. Huxley regarded the industrial civilization of our day with more or less the same disenchantment as the poet Blake looked at the Newtonian physics of his time.

The key to Huxley's metaphysics is his concept of time. Progress is only possible through Self Realization because only therein is time transcended. Until that has happened we have not progress but mere change.

'It is by aiming at the eternal that we are able to make the best—and the best is a continuing progress—of our life in time.'[1]

The meaning given by Huxley to the word time is of central importance in his metaphysical interpretation of the cosmos:

'Time destroys all that it creates, and the end of every temporal sequence is, for the entity involved in it, some form of death. Death is wholly transcended only when time is transcended; immortality is for the consciousness that has broken through the temporal into the timeless. . . . time provides the embodied soul with opportunities for transcending time;[2] every instant of every temporal sequence is potentially the door through which we can, if we so desire, break through into the eternal.'[3]

Now there are three major metaphysical interpretations of time. First, as a straight line divided into three parts: past, present, future. Then as a circle, symbolically depicted by the Chinese as a dragon biting its own tail. This means that time, like a circle, has no specific beginning and no determinable end. The timelessness of time is eternity. Thirdly, we have the Hegel-Marx conception of time as a kind of historical staircase; a straight line which slides horizontally and then abruptly takes a vertical jump, sliding again horizontally higher up—until the next jump. Here the timelessness of time is not conceived as eternity but as History (written with an enormous H!). By taking an irrevocable decision the flow of time (horizontal straight line) is enabled to manifest the historical design inherent in it (vertical jump). If you believe yourself to be on the side of the coming historical design you need only do something irrevocable like shooting an archduke and you can then watch how History works itself out, with added speed, in your favour. Time here is the process through which the *Zeitgeist*, the spirit of History yet to be made, manifests itself. What the pious believer looked upon as the Will of God is here called the *Zeitgeist*, the inexorable force of historical necessity. The most dangerous form of fanaticism is founded on the metaphysics of time:

'. . . Those who regard time as the ultimate reality are concerned primarily with the future and regard the present world and its inhabitants as mere

[1] *Ibid.*, p. 45.
[2] Cp. T. S. Eliot, *The Four Quartets*: 'Only in time, is time conquered.'
[3] *Vedānta for Modern Man*, p. 118.

rubble, cannon fodder, and potential slave labour to be exploited, terror-
ized, liquidated, or blown to smithereens, in order that persons who may
never be born, in a future time about which nothing can be known with the
smallest degree of certainty, may have the kind of a wonderful time which
present-day revolutionaries and warmakers think they ought to have.'[1]

Huxley was opposed irreconcilably to this third conception of time as
History hypostatized as a temporal providence working for the realization
of the kingdom of heaven on earth. In this Hegel-Marx view of time he
saw the roots not merely of communism but of every kind of totalitarian
dictatorship:

'These views of history make the assumption that the divine, or history, or
the cosmic process, or *Geist*, or whatever the entity which uses time for its
purposes may be called, is concerned with humanity in the mass, not with
man and woman as individuals—and not with humanity at any given
moment, but with humanity as a succession of generations.'[2]

Ever since Einstein's *Theory of Relativity*, time has been inseparably
linked with space, so that we speak of the space-time continuum or of time
as the fourth dimension of space.[3] This has lead many serious writers like
T. S. Eliot, Huxley, Gebser and others to relate the time problem with
that of identity.[4] Huxley's preoccupation with the metaphysics of time
springs from his still greater preoccupation with modes of consciousness
and their transformation. All changes in the modes of consciousness are
correlated with changes in the perception of time. We must distinguish
between scientific time (the movement of a three dimensional thing in
space) and psychological time. The latter is a mental construction used as a
measuring rod by the mind to keep account of its own flights from thought
to thought. If, however, as Einstein demonstrated, the observer enters into
every observation, then even scientific time is subordinated to psychological
time. That Huxley devoted so much attention to time was symptomatic of
his shrewd intuition. He was on the right track. He who would unravel the
mind of the East must first be initiated into its special version of time.
According to Vedānta, all time is an eternal now. Its division into past,
present and future is not inherent in time but a function of the human
intellect which, when supported by memory, classifies thoughts as past
and, when assisted by anticipation, as future. As memories and anticipations
also consist of thoughts, there is no time outside the framework of thoughts.
Indeed, the aborigines of Australia depict both past and future with a word

---

[1] *Ibid.*, p. 121.

[2] *Ibid.*, p. 120.

[3] Lama Angarika Govinda's admirable essay on the 'Mystery of Time' (in *Trans-
parente Welt*, Bern, 1965, pp. 256–91) is perhaps rather unscientific but affords a
penetrating insight into the problem of time in Eastern metaphysics.

[4] See Eliot, *The Four Quartets* and *The Confidential Clerk;* Huxley, *Time Must Have
a Stop* and his essays on Vedānta.

that means dreaming. Thinking of the past or future—and what else can one do about it?—is a kind of day-dreaming. In this sense time is said to be illusory. It is the order in which thoughts follow thoughts that gives rise to the usual threefold classification of past, present and future. It is surprising that truths which were evident to the prehistoric savages of Australia have not yet been grasped by the logical positivists of our own century. How often is George Moore quoted as having said: 'Why is not time real? I have had breakfast and will soon take lunch.' This inanity is considered by logical positivists to be very clever. One fails to see how the remembrance of breakfast can be anything but an idea held in the mind; so too is the thought of the anticipated lunch. If the order of thoughts is disarranged, as under hypnosis or schizophrenia, the chronological coherence will also disappear. Huxley's attempt to experiment with different modes of consciousness revealed to him his interior relationship with time. He realized that the 'Golden-Now' of Eastern wisdom means that man has no other time to live in except the present.

'The universe is an everlasting succession of events; but its ground, according to the Perennial Philosophy, is the timeless now of the divine Spirit.'[1]

All time is movement. When this movement is recollected we have perception of time; otherwise it is mere duration as in dreamless sleep. The cohesive force of the recollecting faculty joins the successive instants of the present into a co-ordinated whole and it is the faculty of imagination that enables us to place a future in juxtaposition to the past. Man does not exist in time, time exists in his consciousness.

'What is ordinarily called God's foreknowledge is in reality a timeless now-knowledge, which is compatible with the freedom of the human creature's will in time. . . .

'The specious present in which human beings live may be, and perhaps always is, something more than a brief section of transition from known past to unknown future, regarded, because of the vividness of memory, as the instant we call "now"; it may and perhaps always does contain a portion of the immediate and even of the relatively distant future. . . .

'But according to the Perennial Philosophy, the eternal now is a consciousness; . . . a temporal world should be known and, in being known, sustained and perpetually created by an eternal consciousness. . . .'[2]

We all know the present to be more real than the past or future. Yet, is the present any less ephemeral?

'Time is only an idea. There is only the Reality. Whatever you think it is, it looks like that. If you call it time, it is time. If you call it existence, it is

[1] Aldous Huxley, *The Perennial Philosophy*, p. 212.
[2] *Ibid.*, p. 214 ff.

existence, and so on. After calling it time, you divide it into days and nights, months, years, hours, minutes, etc. . . .'[1]

Again:

'What is *time*? It posits a state, one's recognition of it, and also the changes which affect it. The interval between two states is called *time*. A state cannot come into being unless the mind calls it into existence. The mind must be held by the Self. If the mind is not made use of there is no concept of time. Time and space are in the mind but one's true state lies beyond the mind. The question of time does not arise at all to the one established in one's true nature.'[2]

The moment the present is experienced, it ceases to be the present and is the past. We experience past and future *in* the present and experience the present as if it were past. Huxley was fascinated by this theme because he expected to find in the interstices of time an outlet into eternity.

'The body is always in time, the spirit is always timeless and the psyche is an amphibious creature compelled by the laws of man's being to associate itself to some extent with its body, but capable, if it so desires, of experiencing and being identified with its spirit and, through its spirit, with the divine Ground. . . . the word "I" stands for the psyche, which passes from time to eternity when it is identified with the spirit and passes again from eternity to time, either voluntarily or by involuntary necessity, when it chooses or is compelled to identify itself with the body.'[3]

This is the Eastern standpoint as expressed by the Sage of Arunachala:

'There is no time and space in your sleep. They are concepts which arise when the "I"-thought has arisen. Before the rise of the "I"-thought the concepts are absent. Therefore you are beyond time and space. The "I"-thought is only limited "I". The real "I" is unlimited, universal, beyond time and space.'[4]

If one were to experience two (or more) instants of the present with the same thought content, there would be no notion of memory in the chronological movement from the former to the latter and, as such, no perception of time. Thus a deep sleep of several moments does not appear any shorter to the sleeper than one of several hours. Man would have no perception of time were there not something in him which, while keeping itself outside time, registered all mental movements from thought to thought. Only that

---

[1] The great Indian sage of modern times, Sri Ramana Maharshi of Arunachala; cited in *Talks with Maharshi*, Tiruvannamalai, 1958, p. 12.

[2] *Ibid.*, p. 673.

[3] *The Perennial Philosophy*, p. 215.

[4] *Talks with Maharshi*, p. 327.

can measure changes which itself remains unchanged. The eternal or time-less in man enables him to keep track of time. Even Kant conceded that time was correlative with consciousness by which he meant thinking or thoughts. To transcend time means, therefore, to transcend thoughts. Eternity is incompatible with thoughts for as soon as they arise a classification into past present or future takes place. It is by definition of the essence of eternity that it is outside such categories of time. An eternal hell must be a painless (because thought-free) hell and an eternal heaven equally devoid of experiences. Eternity does not and cannot mean limitless extension of time just as being does not mean the sum total of all things in existence. Eternity is a change in the mode of consciousness. There is one form of consciousness in which man experiences the categories of time (then-now-after); there is another in which all is timelessness.

'And I saw another mighty angel come down from heaven, clothed with a cloud: and a rainbow was upon his head, and his face was as it were the sun, and his feet as pillars of fire. . . . And swore by him that liveth for ever and ever, who created heaven, and the things that therein are . . . *that there should be time no longer.*'[1]

The angel symbolizes enlightenment, the book he brings is mystic wisdom, the many-coloured rainbow on his head represents mastery over the different modes of consciousness, and his face is lit up like the sun with the knowledge of Self Realization. For such a being there is no longer time. The life ever-lasting can be no empty promise for have we not already received its earnest? If the incessant movement of thoughts creates the time-sense, the cessation of such movement would mean entry into the higher consciousness of timelessness.

'Be still, and know that I am God.'

Huxley is not interested in either time or eternity for its own sake but only for his studies in the nature of the Real Self and the realization of those mystic modes of consciousness in which Enlightenment supposedly takes place. According to him, time merges into the timeless when it becomes the object of introspective concentration. As such he supports the second of the three major metaphysical conceptions of time, which is also that of Vedānta. Huxley quotes the *Gītā*:[2]

    ' "Tell me who you are, and were from the beginning,
    You of aspect grim. O God of gods, be gracious."

    "I am come as Time, the waster of the peoples,
    Ready for the hour that ripens to their ruin."

'But the God who comes so terribly as Time also exists timelessly as the

---

[1] *Revelation*, x, 1 and 6.
[2] XI, 31–2; also *kālaḥ kalayatām aham* ('of calculators I am Time'), X, 30.

Godhead, as Brahman, whose essence is Sat, Chit, Ananda, Being, Aware-ness, Bliss; and within and beyond man's time-tortured psyche is his spirit ... the Ātman which is akin to or even identical with Brahman. ... man can, if he so desires, die to his separate temporal selfness and so come to union with timeless Spirit.'[1]

Even science can only *measure* time but not produce it. Here again we notice the empirical character of Huxley's neo-idealism. He does not attempt to fit his speculations on time and eternity into a system but regards them as opportunities for gaining insight into the inner workings of that time-transcending experience by creating conditions propitious for its arrival.

Typical of Huxley's method is the gathering of stray facts, happenings, bits of knowledge, etc., and then seeing if they all fit into a specific thesis. If they do not then they are not discarded (as is usual with philosophical system-builders), but the thesis is modified till they do. In consciousness he saw the laboratory of the mystics, as yoga is of Vedānta. He did not rest content till the thesis gave practical demonstration of its value in the form of heightened or holier consciousness. The neo-idealism was not only a protest against Locke but also against the dull and dreary doctrines of materialism, determinism, logical positivism, linguistic analysis and the like. As a genius he was far ahead of his time and probably he died a saint. As he was wont to say:

'Let me emphasize that in regard to the end, all religions are in complete agreement. That end is the life in union with God.'

But how is one to achieve this union? Has Huxley illustrated its occur-rence in any of his novels?

His answer to the first question would be: Vedānta not in the sense of an Indian religious creed but as experiments in spiritual consciousness. The answer to the second question is his novel *The Devils of Loudun*[2] where we see how one of the characters, Grandier, and later also Surin, achieves that spiritual union through the process of untold suffering. Why does Vedānta have a special significance for Huxley? Behind the revelations of all the higher religions, the teachings of the wise and holy of all faiths and the spiritual experiences of the mystics of every race and age, Vedānta discovers a basic unity of experience which is the closest man can come to the divine and ultimate reality. If we compare the different religions that all take us to the same destination to so many different makes of car, then Vedānta is not comparable to yet another make but is analogous to the supplier of petrol for all those cars. The function of Huxley's Vedānta is to serve as a clearing house for the exchange of ideas and methods leading to Enlightenment, to that peace which passeth all understanding.[3]

---

[1] *The Perennial Philosophy*, p. 219.

[2] London, 1952.

[3] It is a pity that his brother, Sir Julian, has not yet found a way of making Aldous's

Surely Huxley must have been aware of the risks involved by openly recommending everyone to become a saint. The sharp barbs of irony, sarcasm and ridicule with which a society of well-fed TV-gazers greets the cynic turned saint could hardly have been unknown to him. Surely he did not expect to be spared that supercilious smile with which every sceptic feels authorized to greet the new devotee.

'Everything that's difficult and big, everything that needs thought and effort, repels.'[1]

Why did Huxley then venture to leave his secure stronghold? He had already attained worldly success as a novelist. He could have lived out his mystic life in secluded privacy. Why did he let himself become a target for Philistines and Pharisees?

'The theocentric saint is generally not content merely to be. He is almost always a teacher and often a man of action. Through teaching, he benefits surrounding society by multiplying the number of those who undertake the radical transformation of their character and thus increase the amount of antiseptics and antidotes in the chronically diseased body politic.'[2]

Huxley took upon himself a kind of voluntary crucifixion so that others might learn from his example. It was a piece of what may be called *applied* Vedānta! The wisdom of the East had always proclaimed that the finding of the real Self is not a mere act of cold metaphysics. The finest qualities of the heart burst forth simultaneously. It is a widely held misconception that the Eastern tradition emphasizes only wisdom (*jnāna*, *prajñā*) and not also compassion (*metta*, *karuna*). But the fully enlightened one is also a fully compassionate being. If Enlightenment were merely intellectual it would be one-sided. The laws of polarity, according to yoga, demand an integration of wisdom with compassion. This is true not only of Vedānta but of the entire Eastern tradition including Lamaism, Zen, Sufism *et al*. Huxley tried to live up to the words of Garmapa in the *Vow of Mahamudra*:

> During the moment of illumination,
> when I see the original face of mind,
> a limitless compassion ariseth.
> The greater the illumination,
> the greater is the compassion.

---

contribution the cornerstone of his evolutionary humanism. My own plan for linking up his perennial philosophy with Sir Julian's evolutionary humanism into an integral world-view is given in my *Evolution und Gottesidee* (*Evolution and the Idea of God*), Ratingen, 1967, where I have also pointed out the relationship between Teilhard de Chardin and Sri Aurobindo.

[1] Aldous Huxley, *Two or Three Graces*, London, 1926, p. 11.
[2] Aldous Huxley, *Vedānta for the Western World*, p. 269 f.

The greater my compassion,
the deeper is the wisdom I feel.
This unmistakable path of two-in-one
is the peerless practice of the *Dharma*.[1]

Zen too, has a similar sentiment to express in one of its *koans*:

'Before I understood the grand affair [Enlightenment] I felt as though I had lost my parents [i.e. was full of private sorrows]. After I understood the grand affair, I felt as though I had lost my parents [i.e. was full of compassion for the sorrows of others].'

Huxley's chief purpose was to show the way from the mundane to the supramundane; not only its intellectual understanding but the psychic realization of the spiritual goal. His perennial philosophy promises to become of epoch-making importance, both psychologically and culturally, and to foster better understanding between the East and the West.

[1] Requoted from the English version of Chang Chen-Chi in W. Y. Evans-Wenz, *Tibetan Yoga and Secret Doctrines*, London, 1958, p. xl.

CHAPTER 10

The Sources of the Perennial Philosophy

> I do not see why a critical Science of Religions . . . might not eventually command as general a public adhesion as is commanded by a physical science. Even the personally non-religious might accept its conclusions on trust, much as blind persons now accept the fact of optics. . . . Yet as the science of optics has to be fed in the first instance, and continually verified later, by facts experienced by seeing persons; so the science of religions would depend for its original material on facts of personal experience, and would have to square itself with personal experience through all its critical reconstructions. . . . In the religious sphere . . . belief that formulas are true can never wholly take the place of personal experience.[1]

We are told that the Amazon, the world's longest river, begins as a drop of water falling every thirty seconds from a glacier in the Andes. The source of the Ganges is an equally modest drip of water and is called Ganga-Gotri, which all pious pilgrims visit. The source of the perennial philosophy can also be traced back to a single, simple idea. The best formulation of this root idea became known to me in the course of the following episode:

An Oxford graduate and I once visited a hermit in the Himalayas. My friend asked him about the varieties of prophetic revelations. The hermit pointed to the sun and replied:

'Behold the sun! It shines indiscriminately on all days of the week. Its light is not trade-marked Monday or Tuesday. We have given names to the days of the week for the sake of convenience. So the sun of revealed wisdom shines at all periods of history and prehistory without calling itself by this or that name. Yet, for the sake of convenience, we talk of Hinduism here or Islam there, now of Judaism, then of Christianity and so on. The so-called varieties of religious experience are the fingers of God pointing to that unity underlying their diversity.'

It is this unity which Huxley referred to as the divine eternal ground of all being.

'God is. That is the primordial fact. It is in order that we may discover this fact for ourselves, by direct experience, that we exist. The final end and purpose of every human being is the unitive knowledge of God's being.'[2]

[1] William James, *The Varieties of Religious Experience*, requoted from *The World's Greatest Thinkers*, p. 557 (Random House Edition).
[2] *Vedānta for the Western World*, p. 163.

For him, the function of the perennial philosophy was to give an intellectual explanation for the gathering of intuitive insights. Classification of data, their critical examination and significance in the light of comparative study, to give a body of concepts to the supra-rational and so make it accessible to rational arguments, this was the self-imposed task of his metaphysics. He did not go out of his way to bring East and West together, for this was a natural corollary to his metaphysical inquiries. He did not begin like Radhakrishnan with the idea of an East-West synthesis and then set about collecting evidence to support it, for his earlier writings are hostile to such synthesis. The East-West integration came later as the fruit of his researches in comparative religion. Perhaps two factors in his psychological make-up made him more receptive to Eastern wisdom. Firstly he was always, even in his sceptical days, a convinced monist. As he put it:

'An ultimate physical identity underlies the physical diversity of the world.'[1]

Even his sociological essays were variations of the key idea that all individuals and all parts are inseparably linked up through the *Ur-Stoff*, the stuff of the Whole common to, and present in, all those individual parts.

'Scientific investigation reveals that concrete reality consists of the interdependent parts of a totality and that independent existents are merely abstractions from that reality.'[2]

What could be more Vedāntic than that? Monism, in some concealed form or other, is the life-breath of Eastern wisdom. In his novel *Eyeless in Gaza* this *Ur-Stoff* is no longer a static unity of matter but has become[3] a dynamic principle of spirit—a kind of *élan vital* called the 'stream-of-life'.

'Identical patterns and identical patternings of patterns. He [Anthony] held the thought of them in his mind, and along with it, the thought of life, incessantly moving among the patterns, selecting and rejecting for its own purposes. Life building up simpler into more complex patterns—identically complex through vast ranges of animate being'.[4]

From this to the Ātman of Vedānta is but a step.

'Each organism is unique. Unique and yet united with all other organisms in the sameness of its ultimate parts; unique above substratum of physical identity.'[5]

Every Monist is already half a Vedāntin, whether he knows it or not. Now if, as for the Monist, the *Urstoff* (primal and only substance) is the ultimate

[1] Aldous Huxley, *Ends and Means*, London, 1937, p. 295.

[2] *Ibid.*, p. 255.

[3] Probably under the influence of D. H. Lawrence and Henri Bergson.

[4] *Eyeless in Gaza*, London 1936, p. 612

[5] *Ibid.*, p. 613

reality, then the manifold appearances are a form of relative illusion cloaking the essential unity.

'Unity of mankind, unity of life, all being even.'[1]

This makes the monist in Huxley not only accept the ethics of the Vedānta (e.g. non-violence, because we are after all in end effect the same person in so many disguises) but also the central idea of māyā—that deception practised by the manifold in hiding or distorting the unity of essence. Once one accepts that, one is lead inevitably to consider the essence (underlying unity) as more real than the (manifold) forms which are supposed to mask it. Huxley would have become a Vedāntin even if he had never heard of Vedānta! His enthusiasm for this compendium of Eastern wisdom was aroused as he saw in it historical confirmation of his own devoutly-held private convictions. Once, however, the encounter was made, the piecemeal method gave way to a serious and heartfelt study of Eastern wisdom. The universe, once a jigsaw puzzle, which he tried painfully to fit together, became a book full of significance. Life is too short for each individual to solve all the Great Mysteries for himself, unaided by the wisdom of the past. This collected wisdom confirmed by and confirming personal experience became the *philosophia perennis*. In this sublime wisdom he found East and West to be at-one-ment.

The second factor drawing Huxley to Vedānta was that, like Dante, he had a concealed distrust for what we call the report of the senses. The metaphysical and benevolent Absolute is furthest removed from this world of sense-data. Note how frequently he quotes *The Cloud of Unknowing* where the cognition of the external world is made responsible for our isolation from the Absolute. This also fits very well into the Eastern conception of māyā—at least in its negative aspect as the curtain veiling reality. Even St Thomas Aquinas, like Huxley, came on this point nearer to Eastern wisdom than is realized.[2]

Although creation ultimately depends on a *latens deitas* and exists through the manifestation of powers and qualities inherent in Him, Huxley did not consider creation as something external to Him.

'If a human mind can directly influence matter not merely within but even outside its body, then a divine mind, immanent in the universe or transcendent to it, may be presumed to be capable of imposing forms upon a

---

[1] *Ibid.*, p.612

[2] The pious Catholic apologist (an author of good travel-books on Turkey), E. W. F. Tomlin, is singularly unfair to Huxley in damning his *philosophia perennis* as a pernicious breed of Gnosticism. In the last chapter of his *Great Philosophers of the Eastern World* (London, 1952, p. 279) Tomlin goes out of his way to glorify Christianity at the expense of all other religions, belittling Huxley into the bargain. A sad defect in a metaphysician of Tomlin's status. But then, even G. K. Chesterton suffered from this *superbia*. Overestimation of one's own religion is one of the favourite disguises of the devil.

pre-existing chaos of formless matter, or even, perhaps, of thinking sub-stance as well as forms into existence.'[1]

Here we have the third bond of sympathy linking Huxley to Eastern wisdom; namely, the idea of God, or the Absolute, as simultaneously immanent and transcendent.

'In other words, for the fully enlightened person, *nirvāṇa* and *saṁsāra* are one. God is perceived as being in creatures and creatures in God.'[2]

This is the *pan-en-theism* of Vedānta. Conversely, on the same grounds:

'When not I, but the eternal Not-I in me achieves this punctiform aware-ness of duration as a whole, man's life and the universe at large are under-stood as making sense. . . .'[3]

The search for the Absolute is a process of realization and not of seeking and finding. It is like a man who looks desperately for his wristwatch, thinking it to be lost while it is on his wrist all the time. When he realizes that, he knows that the watch was never really lost and so was never found. It had not been a losing but a forgetting. The realization of the Absolute is the realization of 'Something' that is both our essential Self and the essence of what appears as the external world. The *Ur-stoff* of the universe is no different from that out of which our thoughts are made. This is not yet another form of idealism but the conclusion to which modern nuclear physics is now tending.[4] Parallel to the *Ur-stoff* we have an *Ur-Energie* (Proto-Energy) which also is mind-derived; an activity of the Cosmic Mind (perhaps God) manifesting itself in the field of perception. In the last analysis we have no better explanation for why magnets behave like mag-nets (or heat like heat, etc.) except that God (Cosmic Mind) so decrees.

It is easy enough and even justifiable for the young to shout 'God is dead'; as a kind of protest against a stick-in-the-mud Church and a mori-bund theology. It is surprising that even this slogan should have been borrowed unthinkingly from Nietzsche and then quoted out of context. He makes his Zarathustra say:

'. . . *dieser alte Heiliger hat noch nichts davon gehört, dass Gott tot ist.*' (This old hermit has not yet received the news that God is dead.)

But that is not Nietzsche's *conclusion*. He went on to argue that if you contend that God is dead, you must have the moral courage to face the tremendous alternative of you yourself being the divinity you deny. He had the prophetic foresight to predict the coming of an atheism more fool-hardy than the theist platitudes it wanted to replace.

[1] *The Perennial Philosophy*, p. 36.
[2] *Vedānta for the Western World*, p. 189.
[3] *Ibid.*, p. 192.
[4] As, for instance, in the theory of anti-matter.

'To sacrifice God for nothingness—this paradoxical mystery of the ultimate cruelty has been reserved for the rising generation; we all know something thereof already.'[1]

Huxley, however, examined the other alternative: that behind the intellect affirming or denying God (i.e. the intellect's own conception of God) is the essential Self of man which, untouched by the vagaries of the intellect, represents divinity as the image in which he was made. Atheism is untenable until all alternatives have been examined. The present 'God is dead' fervour, inside and outside established theologies, is a boomerang of providence visiting those who dared to think up a God according to cherished dogmas.[2] To pretend to be dead is a favourite device to catch the unwary. It is not so much the absence of God as His apparent silence that arouses the righteous indignation of modern intellectuals. But if I do not reply does it *necessarily* mean I am dead? Nietzche foresaw even this and commented:

'Why Atheism nowadays? . . . he [God] does not hear. . . . The worst is that he seems incapable of communicating himself clearly. . . . This is what I have made out to be the cause of the decline of European theism; it appears to me that though the religious instinct is in vigorous growth, it rejects the theistic satisfactions with profound distrust.'[3]

To equate the so-called silence of God with the non-existence of God appears as an attempt to force the Almighty to reveal his presence.[4]

Nietzsche even saw in this kind of pious antitheism an opening to Vedānta:

'Modern philosophy, as epistemological scepticism, is secretly or openly anti-Christian, although (for keener ears, be it said) by no means anti-religious. . . .

'Kant really wished to prove that, starting from the subject, the subject could not be proved—nor the object either: the possibility of an *apparent existence* of the subject, and therefore of the soul, may not always have been strange to him—the thought which once had such an immense power on earth (*sic*) as the *Vedānta* philosophy.'[5]

To say God is dead means logically no more than that a particular conception, or mind-picture, of God does not fit into the structure of established realities. The death of a conception of reality does not change the nature of reality. As long as there is some kind of reality, that reality itself is God

[1] Nietzsche, *Beyond Good and Evil* (The Religious Mood), Random House Edition (The World's Great Thinkers), p. 501.
[2] Cp. T. F. Torrance, *Theology in Reconstruction*, London, 1965, p. 259 ff.
[3] Nietzsche, *Beyond Good and Evil*, p. 499.
[4] Cp. *Faith and the Philosophers*, ed. by John Hick, London, 1964, p. 103 ff.
[5] Nietzsche, *Beyond Good and Evil*, p. 500.

regardless of what it is called. Eastern wisdom calls this reality the *Self*, and for a very shrewd reason. It is possible to deny God, to deny truth, mind, soul, heaven (and so on)—but to deny the existence of one's own self is not possible for the very act of denial confirms the existence of someone who denies. It may be that this someone is called not-self, or a group of aggregates, or a thought-principle, and so on, but no conjuring trick of logic or linguistic analysis can ever make plausible one's own non-existence. Even the insistence on this non-existence would be an indirect confirmation that there is someone who insists. By positing Self as the ultimate reality the opponent of this thesis is drawn into an argument as to what constitutes the Self. This is precisely the situation into which Eastern wisdom aims at manoeuvring him. An analysis as to what constitutes the self takes us beyond intellect. The intellect can never give us God-as-He-is or Reality-in-itself but at most higher and higher evolved conceptions of God; the intellect can do no more than think, so we have to accept as God what it thinks of as God. Such a God would evidently be dependent on thoughts. Indeed, we notice that in deep sleep everybody is of the same religion! Such a thought-construction of a God need not even bother to die; it is enough if his votaries fall asleep. Thus the analysis of Self leads one beyond intellect into a study of the different states of consciousness. The God of the faith-religions depends on waking consciousness for his existence, in so far as every belief is a thought held by the mind. With the disappearance of waking consciousness all beliefs disappear as well. The fact of dreamless sleep teaches us many metaphysical lessons. Of course we cannot find consciousness-in-itself anywhere so long as we are examining the contents of consciousness. The God-who-is-dead was a *content* of consciousness but has his so-called death eliminated the fact of consciousness? Even the doubter needs consciousness to doubt. What is beyond consciousness is, therefore, also beyond comprehension. God (or Reality-in-itself) being the reality underlying all forms of consciousness (waking, sleep, dreams) is beyond comprehension. How easy then to imagine *Him* to be dead. If, however, ultimate reality as the substratum of consciousness never reveals itself in the contents of consciousness, is it anything more than a mere supposition?

'The Self is always aware. When the Self identifies itself as the seer it sees objects. The creation of the subject and the object is the creation of the world. Subjects and objects are creations in Pure Consciousness. You see pictures moving on the screen in a cinema show. When you are intent on the pictures you are not aware of the screen. But the pictures cannot be seen without the screen behind. The world stands for the pictures and Consciousness stands for the screen. The Consciousness is pure. It is the same as the Self which is eternal and unchanging. Get rid of the subject and object and Pure Consciousness will alone remain. Leave God alone! You do not know God. He is only what you think of Him. Is He apart from you? He is that Pure Consciousness in which all ideas are formed.'[1]

[1] Sri Ramana in *Talks with Maharshi*, p. 522.

Huxley saw in Vedānta the possibility of contacting what is called God through the transfiguration of the Self. Even Lord Tennyson defined prayer as: 'when God-in-man meets Man-in God'.[1] The same Reality which as macrocosmos is called the Absolute is in microcosmos the Self. Now everyone has his own idea of what, for him, constitutes God while this conception itself changes from time to time. All these different conceptions of God are attempts to reduce Cosmic Reality to the thought-forms by which all our thinking is conditioned. Even those who presume God to be dead are well advised to stand in adoring awe of the corpse.

The progress of human thought has reached a stage where the conception of God as a personal Being does not satisfy the intellectual demands of the man in the street. That is all there is to the 'God-is-dead' rage. We have still to face the possibility of God as a *Principle* of Being. Eastern wisdom took this step centuries ago and that is why Huxley was attracted to it.

'... the metaphysics that recognizes a divine Reality substantial to the world of things and lives and minds, the psychology that finds in the soul something similar to, or even identical with, divine Reality; the ethic that places man's final end in the knowledge of the immanent and transcendent Ground of all being—the thing is immemorial and universal.'[2]

In mysticism he saw the possibility of a fusion; the wisdom of the East revitalizing the dogma-sick but inherently healthy, and in some respects even superior, spiritual receptivity of the West.

'There is revealed from the earliest days of ancient Indian mystical speculation right on to the modern speculative system of Fichte, an astonishing conformity in the deepest impulses of human spiritual experience, which—because it is almost entirely independent of race, clime and age—points to an ultimate inward hidden similarity of human spirit and justifies us in speaking of a uniform nature of mysticism.'[3]

Huxley was as much impressed by the lives of the Catholic saints as he was by Vedānta. He accepted the fact of sainthood and saintliness but wanted to free it from all debris of theological dogma. His ideal was a form of mysticism founded on sound metaphysics:

'... a system of thought associated with a transforming discipline.'[4]

He laid down the main points of this metaphysical mysticism in his novel *Time Must Have a Stop*.

[1] *Enoch Arden.*

[2] *The Perennial Philosophy*, p. 1.

[3] Rudolf Otto in the Foreword to *Mysticism East and West* (E.T.); requoted from Aldous Huxley, *Entwicklung seiner Metaphysik*, by Suzanne Heintz-Friedrich, Bern, 1949, p. 65.

[4] *Time Must Have a Stop*, p. 280.

'That there is a Godhead or Ground, which is the unmanifested principle of all manifestation. That the Ground is transcendent and immanent. That it is possible for human beings to love, know, and from virtually, to become actually identified with the Ground. That to achieve this unitive knowledge, to realize this supreme identity, is the final end and purpose of human existence. That there is a Law or Dharma which must be obeyed, a Tao or Way, which must be followed, if men are to achieve their final end.'[1]

Accordingly, personality (in the sense of separateness) and time (in the sense of a flow of events) appear repeatedly in his writings as the twin principles of evil. He first tries to define what he means by personality, which for him is a form of unwarranted separateness, a particularization at the sacrifice of wholeness.

'The physical world of our daily experience is a private universe quarried out of a total reality which the physicists infer to be far greater than it. This private universe is different not only from the real world, whose existence we are able to infer, even though we cannot directly apprehend it, but also from the private universes inhabited by other animals—universes which we can never penetrate, but concerning whose nature we can make interesting speculative guesses.'[2]

Out of what the Buddha would probably have called the five groups of grasping, a voluntary or involuntary selection takes place.

'A lot of these atoms constitute normal experience, and a selection from normal experience constitutes "personality".'[3]

If one regards the Higher Self as the ultimate reality, the personality, or Lower Self, naturally appears as an usurper or, at least, as an obstacle on the path to Self Realization. As personality is nourished on impressions received from the external world, this world too becomes, even at its best, something less than desirable if not a positive source of suffering.

'Why do we imagine that solid matter exists? Because of the grossness of our sense organs. And why do we imagine that we have coherent experiences and personality? Because our minds work slowly and have very feeble powers of analysis. Our world and we who live in it are the creations of stupidity and bad sight.'[4]

Yet it is neither the world nor the personality *per se* which is the culprit but the mistaken notion of separateness arising therefrom:

'Only the rather stupid and insentient, nowadays, have strong and sharply

[1] *Ibid.*, p. 294.
[2] *Ends and Means*, p. 296.
[3] *Eyeless in Gaza*, p. 140.
[4] *Ibid.*, p. 141.

defined personalities. The civilized are conscious of what they may be, and so are incapable of knowing what, for practical social purposes, they actually are—have forgotten how to select a personality out of their total atomic experience. It is the end of personality in the old sense of the word.'[1]

This separateness is not to be viewed as an isolation from the society of others, for solitude is regarded as praiseworthy, but as an isolation from a metaphysical totality, a fall from integral consciousness.

'If you want to be free, you have got to be a prisoner. It's the condition of freedom, true freedom.'[2]

The remedy is not the company of others but reintegration; and through inner psychic reintegration an acceptance of social responsibilities:

'There were duties towards himself and others and the nature of things. He was committed to them as a hand is committed to the arm. Committed to his friends, even to those who had declared themselves his enemies. There was nothing he could do but would affect them all, enemies and friends alike—for good, if what he did were good, and for evil if it were wrong.'[3]

Self Realization is not a flight from the everyday world but a conquest of the processes by which it is cognized.[4] If normal cognition is the setting up of a relation between the personality (cognizer) and the external world (object of cognition), the condition of mystic or supranormal cognition is the transcending of the external word by the dissolution of the personality into its component parts. Where ultimate reality is attributed to the essential Self, the personality must be an impermanent and constantly changing *olla podrida* of inessentials.

'A swarm of constellated impulses and sentiments and notions; a swarm brought together by the accidents of heredity and language; a swarm of incongruous and often contradictory thoughts and desires. Memory and the slowly changing body constitute a kind of spatio-temporal cage, within which the swarm is enclosed. To talk of it as if it were a coherent enduring "soul" is madness.'[5]

Freedom and free will do not then mean the same. For:

'Every psychological pattern is determined; and, within the cage of flesh

[1] *Ibid.*, p. 149.
[2] *Ibid.*, p. 122.
[3] *Ibid.*, p. 616.
[4] See also *Grace*: a Comparative Study of the Doctrine in Christianity and Hinduism, by Bishop Kulandran, Lutterworth Press, London, 1964, p. 159 ff.
[5] Aldous Huxley, *After Many a Summer*, New York, 1939, p. 309.

and memory, the total swarm of such patterns is no more free than any of its members.'[1]

Free will can paradoxically increase bondage:

'Bondage is the life of personality, and for bondage the personal self will fight with tireless resourcefulness and the most stubborn cunning.'[2]

Again:

'Individuality is not absolute, personalities are illusory figments of a self-will. That all-important ego is a fiction, a kind of nightmare, a frantically agitated nothingness.'[3]

This personality for which Huxley has such an aversion is what Vedānta calls *jīva*, the ego, which from the Eastern standpoint is by no means inherently evil. It is, on the contrary, the fountain-head of even our spiritual achievements. Man is superior to other forms of creation precisely because he has evolved for himself a separate ego. It would be a costly mistake to sacrifice this, our most precious possession, for some kind of group-ego like country, race, state, nation, fatherland, workers of the world or the like. Here too lies the danger of Teilhard de Chardin's so-called Cohesion. The ego or the personality is to be treasured as a most valuable possession. The ego is even real as it proclaims the reality of the essential Self underlying it. Only when it presumes to be the sole reality or tries to usurp the place of the essential Self does Eastern wisdom treat it as an obstacle. A model company secretary need not be dismissed, yet must be cut to size if found arrogating to himself powers which belong solely to the chairman of the board. A good secretary, though not chairman of the board, is, analogically speaking, the ego:

'. . . self-will disastrously blind to the reality of more-than-personal-consciousness of which it is the limitation and denial.'[4]

The aim of Eastern wisdom is not to destroy the ego but to modify its claims to absolute reality and unconfined freedom, just as a dictator must be tamed before he can become a constitutional monarch. Once the sovereignty of the essential Self has been acknowledged, the personality or ego becomes the vehicle of enlightened service and integral living. Till the moment of illumination, however, the ego appears as evil incarnate to the mystic striving for union.

'Good is that which makes for unity, evil is that which makes for separateness.'[5]

[1] *Ibid.*, p. 310.
[2] *Ibid.*, p. 111.
[3] *Ibid.*, p. 109.
[4] *After Many a Summer*, p. 109.
[5] *Ends and Means*, p. 303.

In Huxley's attitude towards personality we find the fourth common feature between his ideas and those of Eastern wisdom: personality is not the whole of being.

'In so far as we think as personalities, we fail to understand what is below us no less than what is above.'[1]

Huxley often refers to the *philosophia perennis* as Western Vedānta or at least he recommends Vedānta for the Western world and for modern man. What does, what can Western Vedānta mean?

It is hardly necessary to explain that *Vedānta* as such can neither be Eastern nor Western. When called Western it merely implies the recently reawakened interest for Vedānta in Europe and, more particularly, in America. The word Vedānta has several popular meanings:

1. The entire philosophy of India in general
   and/or
2. the teaching of the *Vedas* including their elucidation, elaboration, explanation, etc.
   and/or
3. one of the six orthodox schools that sprang up as a reaction against scepticism at one period in the history of India
   and/or
4. those teachings which favour the impersonal (rather than the personal aspect of the goal of spiritual aspiration), the Monistic, and the *jñāna* (rather than the *bhakti*) method.

A Vedāntin is a person who, to begin with, understands *theoretically* the esoteric relationship of the Manifold and the One, and *a fortiori* of that which binds his idea of his I with the real I and, through the latter, with the Absolute; who, by virtue of such understanding, is resolved to convert this theoretical knowledge (*Vidya*) into actual Self Realization (*Vijñāna*).[2] It begins when he feels nauseated with theoretical discussion and willingly submits to a discipline not imposed from outside. The Vedāntin cannot allow himself to rest satisfied with any kind of 'I believe ...' but must plod on till he comes to the stage where he can say 'I know...' Yet he does not discard the 'I believe ...' until he arrives at the 'I know....'[3] He can belong to any religion, to no religion, or to all religions. ('By their fruits ye shall know them.') For Vedānta is to religion what possession (in the legal sense) is to ownership.[4]

---

[1] *After Many a Summer*, p. 179.

[2] That is *aikya-mukti*: Liberation through the experience of an experienced unity with the Absolute.

[3] 'You speak thus, Ānanda, because you so *believe;* the Enlightened One however *knows* that it is so.' The Buddha, on his deathbed.

[4] A person who only *believes* in a religion has 'ownership' (membership) but as he has not 'possession' (*possessio*)—that is to say possession of (the immediate presence of) God—he cannot *enjoy* God (i.e. actual God-contact). He is like a person who owns a

As Vedānta forms the very basis of Huxley's *philosophia perennis*, it is well to discuss it in detail. A *rapprochement* between Eastern and Western philosophy has already taken place in what is called Western Vedānta, through which the change-over from contemporary Western to Eastern ways of thinking is made easy and natural. Now *contemporary* Western philosophy[1] is like a spider entangled in the flimsy web it has spun out of its own body, which consists largely of insects devoured by it in the past (i.e. criticism and mutilations of bygone philosophers). As against this, Vedānta is like a bee which having found beautiful flowers (*yoga*), converts their essences into nourishing honey which has the sweetness of *bhakti*,[2] while its wax can be made into a candle which when lighted leads the way to *brahmajñāna*.[3] It is the Light, which the Bible tells us, 'lighteth every man that cometh into the world'.[4]

The critic may well ask: 'We know that, according to Vedānta, what is uncovered when the ego is cancelled is the Ātman; but what nourishment can that give us? Is it not like first cancelling and then propelling a zero into infinity? The airborne devotee of a metaphysical Absolute must return, if only to refuel, to the world he shunned; need he wonder that the more frequent and prolonged his absences, the more this despised territory has become a prey to weeds, vermin and decay?'[5] These are legitimate objections but not unsolvable enigmas. They arise out of an incomplete version that ignores the way of *karma-yoga* and its balancing effect. Thus for Tagore, who includes in his philosophy the *karma-yoga* viewpoint, they are invalid. As Professor A. N. Marlow points out: 'For Tagore every action in which man steps out of the narrow bounds of the *ego* helps to realize the supreme purpose of the world'.[6] He then explains Tagore's idea that *first* 'we must so withdraw into ourselves that we experience the truth of . . . mysticism'.[7] But we need not necessarily stop here for *we then return* and 'live our lives in the knowledge that a universal spirit is working through us and attempting to fulfil its purpose in every individual striving for an ampler scope and environment'.[8] The hypnotic glare and glamour of the Nobel Prize is so strong that Western critics explain the

---

magnificent palace but cannot enjoy it as he does not live in it. The Vedāntin having *possessio* does not worry over-much about the *dominium*. He is in the stronger position because possession, by mere lapse of time, tends to mature into and include ownership as well. Whereas ownership without possession is inclined to be lost through lapse of time.

[1] Logical positivism and the like!

[2] Divine, mystic love.

[3] *Unio mystica*.

[4] John i, 9.

[5] E. W. F. Tomlin, *The Great Philosophers of the Eastern World*, London, 1952, p. 278.

[6] 'Spiritual Religion' in *Library of Living Philosophers*, vol. 8, pp. 342–3.

[7] *Ibid.*

[8] *Ibid.*

above as if it were Tagore's own discovery, when in fact it has always been part and parcel of Vedānta.

The elucidation of the *karma-yoga* standpoint comes as a relief to an ego not inclined to lose itself in introspection. Delighted at being told that passivity is not necessary, it mistakenly takes this as an indirect corroboration of its inherent preference for extraversion, for life is lived at its fullest as in a cavalry charge.

Western Vedānta is not confined to Huxley. It is a world movement including such literary giants as Christopher Isherwood, Gerald Heard, Guido Ferrando, John van Druten, Carl Zuckmayer, Hermann Hesse and others. Isherwood in particular shows all the signs of a genuine saint.

As a writer, Isherwood has made a reputation equal to that of Huxley. With the poet Auden he belonged to the Group whose deep admiration for German culture wanted to turn Berlin into a second Athens. The rise of Nazism brought the Group into disrepute in England. Isherwood then seems to have travelled a lot, especially in China and the Orient. The philistine public had a shock when Isherwood, as a representative of the intellectual class at its literary best, openly acknowledged the value of Vedānta.[1] The time had now come for him to clear up misunderstandings, at least for the benefit of those genuinely interested. As a result we have two books edited by him: *Vedānta for the Western World* and *Vedānta for Modern Man.*[2] He co-operated with Swami Prabhavananda in translating the *Gītā* and wrote a new commentary to the Yoga Aphorisms of Patanjali and called it *How to Know God.*[3]

The first Vedānta Society in America was started by Swami Vivekananda. Vivekananda is a very important figure because he is the source from which both Radhakrishnan and Aldous Huxley derive much of their raw material. His visit to America led to the founding of the Ramakrishna-Vivekananda Centre, from which Western Vedānta sprang,[4] the sum and substance of Aldous Huxley's *philosophia perennis*. Vivekananda's philosophy was too rich and too deep to be fully appreciated by anyone less gifted with soul-force than Aldous Huxley. In the sphere of Spirit there is no such thing as Eastern and Western but one great soul-mind picks up from where another left off. Thus Vivekananda can be called the Emerson of India, and Emerson the Vivekananda of America.

Sri Ramakrishna (Vivekananda's teacher) preferred the way of *bhakti* and recommended it as ideal for modern times. With Vivekananda, however, the preference reverts to the way of *jñāna*—and that is what makes him so acceptable to the West and to westernized intellectual India.

[1] See his essay 'Hypothesis and Belief' in *Vedānta for the Western World*, London, 1951, pp. 36–40.

[2] London, 1952.

[3] London, 1953.

[4] 'In 1893, he (Vivekananda) visited the United States to attend the Parliament of Religions which was being held at the World Columbian Exposition in Chicago . . . he followed up this success by founding the first American Vedānta society in New York City.' *Vedānta for Modern Man*, pp. 405–6.

'I do not know how many of the younger generation reads Swami Vive-kananda, but I can say that many of my generation were powerfully influenced by him, and I think it would be well worth while, and would do a great deal of good to the present generation, if they also were to study his works and teachings. They would learn much from them. . . . If you read Swami Vivekananda's writings you will find that they are not old. They are as fresh today as when they were written, because what he spoke or wrote about dealt with certain fundamental aspects of the problems of the world today. . . . What Swamiji has written and said is still of interest and is likely to influence us for a long time to come. . . .

'He was, in my opinion, one of the great founders of the modern national movement of India. . . . Directly or indirectly, he has powerfully influenced the India of today.'[1]

Sri Ramakrishna left behind him two disciples. One was a great scholar and philosopher (Swami Vivekananda[2]), the other a deep mystic and seer (Swami Brahmananda). Of the latter's life and teachings we learn through his own disciple Swami Prabhavananda, an outstanding scholar of Vedānta philosophy and head of the Vedānta society of southern California. The *jñāna* aspect was emphasized by Swami Vivekananda (as his very name indicates[3]), leading on to one of the finest expositions of *karma-yoga* philosophy:

'The highest truth is this: God is present in all beings. They are his multiple forms. [For the *karma-yoga* philosopher] there is no other God than the souls [*Real Self*] of living beings. This is the only God that is awake [for the purpose of receiving our ego-eliminating service]; our own, [human] race; everywhere his hands, everywhere his feet, everywhere his ears. . . . The first of all worship is the worship [service] of those all around us [We serve God by serving those in whom he is embodied as their *Real Self*]. . . . He alone serves God who serves all other beings.'[4]

It was this masterly exposition of the *karma-yoga* viewpoint that prepared the ground for the *Religionsphilosophie* of Mahatma Gandhi, and that of Huxley and Radhakrishnan. Through the latter's exposition of the *Gītā*

[1] Pandit Jawaharlal Nehru in a speech delivered on the occasion of the birthday celebration of Sri Ramakrishna, at New Delhi in 1949.

[2] There is a seven volume edition of his collected works published by the Advaita Ashrama in the Himalayas, called the *Mayavati Memorial Edition*.

[3] When he was initiated, he received the name Vivekananda. That was not the name his parents had given him. They had called him Narendra. Vivekananda means *Bliss* (through the means of) discrimination.

We have already seen that the way of *jñāna* is characterized by discrimination through analysis. Hence *Vivekananda* indicates that by temperament, he belonged to the way of *jñāna*. Let it be repeated that success through one is success in all; success in *jñāna* includes success in *karma*, *bhakti* and *rāja* as well. Later on Vivekananda wrote a book on all four of these ways.

[4] See further Romain Rolland, *Prophets of the New India*, pp. 395 and 449–50.

we learn that the *karma-yoga* method was always an inalienable part of Eastern wisdom but was neglected until Vivekananda revived it. Moreover *karma-* and *rāja-yoga* methods lead to the same goal as *jñāna* and *bhakti*.[1]

At first sight it seems strange that even the Western mind should prefer *jñāna* as the Christian way belongs more to the *bhakti* group. Because of the modern scientific type of training and education, which involves discrimination and analysis, etc., the modern or Western type of individual is moulded, and remains by temperament, like one with a preference for *jñāna*. When he turns to his Christianity, which is based on the way of *bhakti*, he has to make a subconscious right-about-face and adopt another attitude involving a preference for the way of devotion. He, therefore, takes one attitude towards religion (faith-*bhakti*-love) and another (discrimination-*jñāna*-rational calculation) towards life in general. He is, therefore, constantly inventing conflicts between science and religion even where there are none. As a result he remains dissatisfied with both science and religion. While paying lip-service to the way of *bhakti*, he secretly cherishes a preference for *jñāna*. In order to conceal this subconscious conflict, he takes a violently dogmatic attitude towards both, to what he calls his religion and his science. This inner suffering and conflict is needless once one sees how *jñāna* and *bhakti* interpenetrate each other. Yet the one thing modern man is not willing to part with is this inner suffering. He has a most curious preference for inner suffering and conflict. Thus Ramakrishna was not quite correct in thinking that *bhakti* was the ideal method for the modern age, and Vivekananda was very wise in tilting the balance in favour of *jñāna*, specially in his teachings to the West. This is because modern man puts more trust in reason than in faith. Thus in modern Western philosophy the most eagerly hunted topic is a proof of God's existence or evidence for a soul in man, or the logical view of religion and the like. It is nearly impossible to live in this scientific age and not have a preference for *jñāna*. But once modern man realizes that *jñāna* and *bhakti* include each other, like the two sides of a coin, this inner conflict will disappear and he will see deeper into his own religion, Christianity. Because Christianity, as indicating success on the way of *bhakti*, includes automatically *jñāna* (see St Albertus Magnus[2]), *karma* (see St Theresa[3]), and *rāja* (see St John of the Cross[4]), it is, if properly understood, self-sufficient for Western man. The purpose of Eastern wisdom is to

[1] 'In this world a two-fold way of life has been taught of yore by Me, the path of knowledge for men of contemplation and that of works for men of action'. *Gītā*, III, 3.

[2] 'Happy is the man who by continually effacing all images and who by introversion and the lifting up of his mind to God, at last forgets and leaves behind all images.' *De Adherendo Deo.*

[3] 'Yours are the eyes through which is to look out Christ's compassion to the world, yours are the feet with which He is to go about doing good, and yours are the hands with which He is to bless us now.'

[4] 'He who does not withdraw himself from the things of the world is not qualified to receive the Spirit of God in the pure transformation.' *Ascent of Mount Carmel*, I, 5, 2, p. 22. (Translated by David Lewis: London, Thomas Baker, 1922.)

drive this home. Vivekananda's mission in the West was not to show any person the way but only, like a good surgeon, to remove the cataract from his eyes so that he might see that in each and every religion there are several alternative methods suited to one's temperament, education, upbringing or need. Every individual may reach the goal of Enlightenment or God-Union through his own religion. The purpose of Eastern wisdom, as Vivekananda saw it, was to remind him that as long as he did not turn theory into self-disciplinary practice he would not make progress. How to exchange dogmatic theological debris for direct perception, *Erleuchtung* or *Gotteserkenntnis* is what he meant by Vedānta—not a new religion but the science *underlying* a comparative study of all religions, just as philology is not a new language, but the science of comparative languages.

Vivekananda may, therefore, be considered the father and founder of comparative religion as a science in its own right. His entire philosophy may therefore be summarized in two words: *Ishta Devatā.*

Ishta Devatā means the right of each individual to select, from a religion of his own choice, that aspect or method which he finds most suitable to his temperament, as a means to Enlightenment or spiritual union. It is not a mere negative toleration of all religions but a positive acceptance. It involves:

'... praying in the Mosque of the Mohammedans, worshipping before the fire of the Zoroastrians, and kneeling before the cross of the Christians, knowing that all the religions, from the lowest fetichism to the highest absolutism, mean so many attempts of the human soul to grasp and realize the infinite, each determined by the conditions of its birth and association, and each of them marking a stage of progress.'[1]

That is the principle of *Ishta Devatā*; but what happens if we disregard it? The individual dissatisfied with one religion, or one aspect of a religion, denounces all aspects, and all religions, and embraces a violent atheistic materialism.

What happens if the principle of *Ishta Devatā* is accepted? Vivekanada says:

'I read my Bible better in the light of your Bible and the dark prophecies of my religion become brighter when compared with those of your prophets. Truth has always been universal. If I alone were to have six fingers on my hand while all of you had only five, you would not think that my hand was the true intent of nature but rather that it was abnormal and diseased. Just so with religion. If one creed alone were to be true and all others untrue, you would have a right to say that that religion was (so to say) diseased.'[2]

This synthesis is not static but dynamic. Vivekananda finds from his study

[1] *The Complete Works of Swami Vivekananda*, Part I, p. 25.
[2] *Ibid.*, pp. 23-4.

of the various religions that there are 'three different stages of ideas with regard to the soul and God':

1. All religions admit that apart from the body which perishes, there is a certain part or something which does not change like the body; a part that is immutable and eternal, that never dies. Let this for convenience be called the *Soul*.
2. If there is one universal truth in all religions it is in realizing something that is considered divine. Let this for convenience be called *God*.
3. Therefore the end of all religions is to teach us that the purpose of our life on earth is the realizing of God in the Soul. This realization may be called *Gotteserkenntnis, Erleuchtung, nirvāṇa, brahmajñāna* or just Self Realization—its only a matter of name.

This is the rough minimum working hypothesis underlying Vivekananda's philosophy of the universality of religion.

Vivekananda is a born philosopher and brings a wealth of learning to bear on whatever subject he has in hand. His approach is scientific rather than mystical. He presents Ramakrishna's philosophy in a more elaborate, elucidated, academic form, and, therefore, in a way more acceptable to the West. He even treats problems which Ramakrishna would have brushed aside as irrelevant on the ground that 'one is in the orchard to enjoy mangoes not count the trees and their leaves'. In other words man is born to enjoy God through Grace, and so it is idle to speculate on the metaphysical mysteries of the Cosmos. Vivekananda having once been an uncompromising atheist sympathizes with the average man's desire to *know* even when he cannot *believe*. He, therefore, gives an excellent philosophical explanation of the Cosmos first as Macrocosm and then as Microcosm.[1] 'The sum total of the intelligence displayed in the universe must, therefore, be the involved (as opposed to evolved) universal intelligence unfolding itself. This universal intelligence is what we call God.'[2]

There is a great similarity between the central idea of Vivekananda's thought and that of Hegel's system which no critic seems to have noticed till now. Both have the same idea of *freedom*, as the highest expression towards which all evolution strives.[3] Freedom is the final destination of the *Zeitgeist*. How then does Vivekananda explain our universal dissatisfaction?

'It is because freedom is ever man's goal. He seeks it ever, his whole life is a struggle after it. The longing for freedom produces the idea of a Being

---

[1] *Collected Works*, Part II, pp. 350–62.

[2] *Ibid.*, p. 353, from a Lecture delivered in New York, January 19, 1896.

[3] In this respect one should also remember the meaning attached to 'freedom' in Eastern and in Western philosophy—freedom of man and freedom of will. On this point refer to Chapter XIX in Radhakrishnan: *Comparative Studies in Philosophy* where Professor S. K. Maitra deals with 'The Gītā's Conception of Freedom as Compared with that of Kant', pp. 348–61.

who is absolutely free. [Thus] the concept of God is a fundamental element in the human constitution. . . . The embodiment of freedom, the Master of Nature, is what we call God.'[1]

This conception of God as a perfectly free Being incites man to struggle and rebel against his apparent bondage to the phenomenal world.

As Christopher Isherwood[2] points out, Vivekananda had two separate messages to deliver; one to the East, the other to the West. In the latter he attacked materialism and advocated spiritual experiment (*rāja yoga*), as against dogma and tradition. To the former he emphasized the ideal of social service (*karma yoga*). 'To each he tried to give what was most lacking.'[3] With variety and versatility, with humour, wit and wisdom he explains and gives authoritative instruction on not one but all the four major groups teaching various methods to Enlightenment. In dogma he saw an indication of decay; in variety he saw an indication of life and development. He realized intuitively that:

> God fulfils Himself in many ways
> Lest one good custom should corrupt the world.[4]

In January 1938, Swami Ashokananda and Swami Prabhavananda decided to start a bi-monthly journal which came to be called *The Voice of India*. The title was then changed to *Vedānta and the West*. The contributors were often famous authors[5] but the keynote was always sincerity and self-sacrifice. Thus what is called Western Vedānta received its organizational form.

In *Hypothesis and Belief* Isherwood shows us the hypocrisy and pedantry that lurks behind all such unrealistic controversies as the conflict between science and religion. (The less a person knows about a religion the more he finds it in conflict with everything else.) He then introduces two terms taken from English law, 'the credibility of the witness' and 'corroboration'. We are asked to 'behave like jurymen', when studying the various religions, and see what points are corroborated. In this way one can reconstruct what Aldous Huxley calls 'the Minimum Working Hypothesis'.[6]

Vedānta implies an obligation to put this Minimum Hypothesis into actual practice in one's own life. This leads Isherwood to ask the key-question: 'Am I dissatisfied with my life as it is at present? And, if so, am I sufficiently dissatisfied to want to do anything about it?' It is at this stage that some sort of division or grouping into esoteric and exoteric has to be

---

[1] *Collected Works*, Part I, pp. 181–3.

[2] In *Vedānta for the Western World*, p. 26.

[3] *Ibid.*

[4] Tennyson, *Mort d'Arthur*.

[5] Including of course our own philosopher Aldous Huxley.

[6] Aldous Huxley in *Vedānta for the Western World*, pp. 33–5. This article ('The Minimum Working Hypothesis') was later reproduced in his novel *Time Must Have a Stop*, as part of Sebastian's notebook.

made. Ramakrishna[1] gives an excellent example of this in his parable of
The Four Classes of Fish:

1st class: Fishes that never get caught in the net—eternally free, or rather
the ever free souls. Jesus.

2nd class: Fishes that get caught but struggle and succeed in getting
free—those great souls who win their way to salvation. The
saints of the church like St Thomas Aquinas and St Theresa
and saintly persons like Meister Eckhart, etc.

3rd class: Fishes that struggle but have still to succeed in getting free—
the genuine seekers, those interested in studying these things,
Vedāntists. Genuine priests, hermits, Trappist Monks, etc.

4th class: Fishes that, far from struggling to be free, seek to be at ease in
the net while they enjoy the murmur of the waters and the
splashing about of their fellow fishes. They forget that the
Fisherman will soon cast them on dry ground—this refers to
the rank and file. Those who make no effort at spiritual progress.
The murmur of the waters refers to the lisping of their children—
those who prefer the so-called 'joys' of family-life to the lasting
happiness of chastity. The splashing about of their fellow
fishes refers to small-talk and the usual trivia connected with
living in society—the underdeveloped who find solitude unbearable and, therefore, call it unnatural. 'But the poor things
do not know that the Fisherman will drag them out with the
net.'[2]

Of what use is Vedānta to one who is not seriously dissatisfied? It would
only cause him harm.[3] That is the type of which Jesus said: 'Thou shall not
cast pearls before swine.' Not that the pearls of esoteric wisdom would lose
their value thereby, but because the swine, being used to an exoteric diet,
would suffer from their inability to digest the esoteric. The great merit of
existentialism is that it makes men aware of the deep, underlying ontological
necessity of feeling dissatisfied. Vedānta begins where existentialism ends.[4]
Thus Vedānta is not for anybody and everybody, but for those who as a
result of extreme suffering are sufficiently dissatisfied to make a serious
effort at solving the root-cause of suffering *per se*. Suffering precedes
effort, as effort precedes assistance-by-grace. As Isherwood warns, 'they
[the obstacles] are tremendous'.[5]

In his essay on Vivekananda and Sarah Bernhardt, Isherwood examines
the medium of expression used by anyone who has had the Enlightenment
towards which Vedānta asks us to strive. He concludes that such a person's
'way of approach is more direct, more subtle and more penetrating. He
makes contact with you below the threshold of everyday awareness. No

[1] See *The Gospel of Sri Ramakrishna*, by M., New York, 1952, pp. 86-7.
[2] *Ibid.*
[3] 'The awakening of the *kundalinī* would be, for such a person, like the bite of a
poisonous snake.' Ramakrishna.
[4] Vedānta is health—existentialism is a disease.
[5] *Vedānta for the Western World*, p. 40.

matter whether he speaks of the Prince of Wales, or of God, or only smiles and says nothing, your whole life will be, to some degree, changed from that moment on.'[1]

In 'The *Gītā* and War'[2] Isherwood unfortunately overreaches himself. He is dealing with the most intricate, dangerous and slippery problem in the perennial philosophy, namely the ethics of action according to the *Gītā*. This is far too subtle to be explained away in a few pages.[3]

His 'The Wishing Tree'[4] is a thought-provoking, soul-searching parable. The idea is taken from Ramakrishna who used to refer to God as the *kalpataru* tree—the wish-fulfilling attribute of divine providence.[5] His excellent little story deals with the problem of desire *vis-à-vis* what the *Gītā* calls *dharmāviruddho*,[6] i.e. 'The desire that is not contrary'. This avoids an unnecessary self-contradiction for otherwise the desire not to have any desires, being itself a desire, would become confusing. The desire for Enlightenment, even when it means the total abolition of all desire, may legitimately be considered desirable. The central moral of the story has been put by Brother Lawrence in simpler words:

'For God will not permit that a soul which *desires* to be devoted entirely to Him should take other pleasures than with Him, that is more than reasonable.'[7]

We get a glimpse of the literary artist in Isherwood's 'The Problem of the Religious Novel'[8] where the tone is more intimate and personal. By 'the saint' he does not mean a person of a saintly character in a purely religious or ethical sense but one who has won his way to Enlightenment—which includes even one who 'goes in search of super-conscious, extraphenomenal experience'.[9] What Isherwood would like to prove is that every person is a potential saint. X may not, in the end, find anything in alchohol, sex, or speeding except misfortune, but this 'is not to be dismissed with a puritanical sneer, it is the crude symbol of [X's] *dissatisfaction* with surface consciousness, his [ontological] need to look more deeply into the *meaning* of life'.[10] Then his essay 'Religion without Prayers'[11] is a Vedāntist's answer

[1] *Ibid.*, p. 272.

[2] *Ibid.*, p. 358.

[3] The *Gītā* says in chapter IV, verse 17: 'One has to understand what action is, and likewise one has to understand what is wrong action and one has to understand about inaction. *Hard to understand is the way of work.*' One must be extremely slow in jumping to a conclusion when dealing with the *Gītā*, lest we rush in where angels fear to tread.

[4] *Vedānta for the Western World*, p. 448.

[5] The Western reader can understand this better by thinking of Aladdin's Wonderful Lamp in the *Arabian Nights*.

[6] The *Gītā*, chapter VII, verse 11.

[7] *Practice*—sixth letter.

[8] *Vedānta for Modern Man*, pp. 247–50.

[9] *Ibid.*, p. 249.

[10] *Ibid.*

[11] *Ibid.*, pp. 28–33.

to Professor Irwin Edman's article 'Religion without Tears' published in the *Commentary* of April 1946. His point is that you can love your neighbour only if you can regard him *sub specie aeternitatis*. But in order to do this, one must be able to evaluate oneself as the eternal reality that one is. The love-your-neighbour, serve-your-neighbour kind of sentimental humanism, so much in vogue today, can only end in frustration. As long as one has an ego, it is not possible to serve or love anything even remotely equal to oneself. Leigh Hunt's poem, *Abou Ben Adhem*, has misled countless people into thinking that loving one's fellow men or doing good is sufficient excuse to feel exempted from the inexorable imperative of searching for one's own ontological reality[1]—and this search necessitates, among other things, prayer, meditation, self-discipline, in one word: *tapasya*. It makes an important difference whether the love-your-neighbour comes before or after: 'Thou shalt love the Lord thy God with all thy heart, and with all thy soul, and with all thy mind'.[2] The Vedāntist does not deny neighbourly love, but only its primacy. In Christian terminology it means that to love one's neighbour, when one does not *first* of all love God, is to love the devil. For according to Vedānta the devil is a symbol for whatever obstructs a person's quest for God (Enlightenment). 'Thou shalt love thy neighbour as thyself'[3] because, says the Vedāntist, your neighbour when considered *sub specie aeternitatis*, is *no different* from though not identical with your own ontologically rooted *Real Self*. In other words many million pools of water reflect the same sun, though not the *identical* rays.

Gerald Heard is important for our study not only as a famous writer and lecturer on Vedānta but also as one of the most important of the influences under which Aldous Huxley came.[4]

Heard's many merits are overlooked by critics because of the rather overenthusiastic way in which he expresses himself. For instance he says: 'A new religion has come into history—that is Western Vedānta'.[5] Now Vedānta just *cannot* be Western, nor for that matter Eastern; it never was a religion;[6] and by no stretch of imagination can it be called new. What Heard probably means is that the study of Vedānta in the West has awakened there a renewed interest in the *essence* of religion.

His essay 'Is Mysticism Escapism?' is an excellent defence of the Vedāntist point of view, and the best possible answer to Bertrand Russell's comment on D. H. Lawrence's novel, *The Man who Loved Islands*. (Russell's conclusion was that, as long as one lives in society, Self Realization cannot

---

[1] Cp. G. Heard's Anniversary Address, 'My Discoveries in Vedānta', in *Vedānta for Modern Man*, pp. 59–63, loc. cit., p. 61.

[2] This is, so to say, the *greatest* and *first* commandment. (St Matthew, xxii, 38.)

[3] '. . . as thyself' should be read 'as *thy* (*Real*) *Self*'.

[4] Cp. Arthur Koestler, *The Yogi and the Commissar*, New York, 1946.

[5] *Vedānta and Western History*.

[6] Vedānta is often mistaken for a religion because it deals with the inner core of mystery to be found in every religion worth the name.

be the highest ethic.[1]) How and why the rediscovery of one's *Real Self* is the greatest possible service to humanity and to the society one lives in, is the most secret of secrets, kept hidden from all but the wisest mystics. This can be expressed in terms of Christian theology by referring to St Matthew, xxvi, 6–12. The precious ointment in the story refers to our own life-span; when it is poured over Jesus it means that one's life is spent in contacting the Christ-consciousness which is after all one's Real Self; when the onlookers complain 'to what purpose is this waste?', it refers to those good intentioned, ethically advanced, but social-minded (rather than spiritually mature) people who feel that a life spent in search of an inward divinity is a betrayal of social obligations. They prefer that the ointment be sold, meaning that the life-span is spent in some obviously lucrative profession. 'For this ointment might have been sold for *much*' and 'given to the poor' refers to social service (love for one's neighbour). But the Lord (through Jesus) replies: 'She hath wrought a good work upon me' (in other words, done the right or correct thing). This means that love for God as evidenced by a quest for the divine takes priority over, because it includes, social service. Social service in itself cannot bring lasting value, utility, or happiness to humanity. '*For ye have the poor always with you*, but *Me* (the possibility of God-contact through Christ-consciousness) *ye have not always*'—because our death puts an end to our chance of finding our Real *Self*. By spending one's life freely in the quest for the Christ-consciousness or the inward divinity ('for in that she hath poured this ointment on my body') one is safeguarded against ('she did it for') the time when such an opportunity is no longer possible—after the Christ-consciousness has been withdrawn from the bodily frame it sustained ('for my burial'). Since Christ-consciousness is one's very Self, its withdrawal is the real 'burial', for what is buried after that is only a collection of chemical components.

The phrase 'God is shy' was coined by a devout Jesuit and meant to refer to the divine as *Fascinans et Tremendans Mysterium*. Heard uses that phrase as the title of an essay[2] in which he applies Baudouin's principle, known in psychology as the law of reversed effort, to the study of theology. He then refers to what Radhakrishnan calls *integral knowledge*. As Heard rightly observes: 'Man cannot remember the saving knowledge he once had, but he can remember that he once knew what he has now forgotten. He is therefore driven to seek for he cannot say what. To his rational mind this need is inexplicable but for his entire nature it is peremptory.' The meaning of this passage is very deep and there is more in it than meets the eye. But seldom has so much of Vedāntic wisdom been compressed in so few words as when he says: '*Beware when you find what you are looking for.*'[3] Heard's merit is that he not only talks about Vedānta but has concrete suggestions to offer, as in his 'Guides to the Spiritual Life'. He is a living proof that it is possible for a Western intellect to grasp all the subtleties of Vedānta. Seldom was the wisdom of the East planted abroad

---

[1] *History of Western Philosophy*, London, 1948, p. 710.

[2] *Vedānta for Modern Man*, pp. 277–80.

[3] *Ibid.*, p. 279.

in such fertile soil. Being a practioner of the integral life himself, he speaks at first hand as in 'Three Answers to Three Key Questions'.[1] They are answered through the teachings of the three great geniuses of the 'integral' or spiritual, life: St Thomas Aquinas (the devotional aspect); Meister Eckhart (the psychological aspect); St Ignatius Loyola (the practical aspect). Those who wish to fit the Vedāntic technique of *Gotteserkenntnis* into the Christian framework can learn much from 'the great catholic directors' because they are 'always precise, always great diagnostic pyschologists and, even when their letters are found for centuries to be applicable to thousands of souls, they seem like all great physicians actually prescribing for a specific, individual case'.[2]

Heard's 'The Inner Voice'[3] is an amusing and instructive little story in the form of a parable. Three devils in disguise try to hinder a man on his path to Enlightenment. They are: lust ('There are a lot of first rate girls coming but we're short on men'[4]); greed ('Capital is zooming'[5]); and pseudo-civics ('It isn't democratic to desert your social duties'[6]). It is a concealed satire on Hollywood's version of the true life. In 'Is Old Age Worth While?' we realize the value of the ancient Indian tradition of dividing and organizing life into *four* periods,[7] with Enlightenment as the goal, as contrasted with the dangerous, haphazard way it is led in the modern West. The reason underlying this fourfold division is that man differs from the animals in that 'only when our reproductive acme is over do we enter into our particular, outstanding way of life'.[8] Thus our modern way of living puts the cart before the horse.

In 'The Return to Ritual'[9] Heard compares the Puritan's *via negativa* with the importance of ritual for those who intend to use the method of *bhakti*. Ritual need not be confined to sight and touch (as in relics, sacraments, etc.). It can also use sound (music) or even a kinesthetic expression of worship (as in the religious dance).[10] The main thing is to express a condition or create a state of mind 'whereby man reminds himself of the Inexpressible',[11] of the *Real Self*.

Suffering is a kind of vitamin without which spiritual growth is unattainable. Moreover spiritual growth takes a spiral form (more or less like what economists describe as the trade-cycle). It is obvious, therefore, that

---

[1] *Ibid.*, pp. 351–64.
[2] *Ibid.*, p. 291.
[3] *Ibid.*, pp. 381–6.
[4] *Ibid.*, p. 381.
[5] *Ibid.*, p. 383.
[6] *Ibid.*, p. 385.
[7] The four stages of life (*āshrama*) are: (1) *brahmachārin* (chaste student); (2) *grihastha* (professional and married life); (3) *vanaprastha* (renunciation and preparation); (4) *sannyāsin* (pilgrimage to liberation).
[8] See Sir Julian Huxley, *Uniqueness of Man*.
[9] *Vedānta for the Western World*, pp. 89–93.
[10] *Ibid.*, p. 92.
[11] *Ibid.*

K

the downward movements of the spiral are accompanied with acute suffering for the spiritual aspirant. This has the advantage of eliminating half-hearted beginners who may have turned to things spiritual only out of curiosity or as one of their many hobbies. But in addition to these spiral depressions 'there are deeper dips' as Heard tells us in 'Dryness and Dark Night'.[1]

An elucidation of Dryness (spiral depression) is found in Ruysbroeck; and of the dark night of the Soul ('deeper dip') in *Theologia Germanica*. Now whereas the first is the normal psychological result of acquiring any new skill such as learning a foreign language, playing the piano, etc., the latter is confined to those using the method of *bhakti* and does not affect those using that of *jñāna*. This is because the former uses, and is therefore entirely dependent on, *Emotion*—a quality notorious for its fluctuations. The *jñāni* on the other hand relies on what may be called discrimination through *analysis* which induces stability. *Jñāna* is like the first gear in a car; it does not have a wide range of speed but can climb the steep slopes of a mountain. As against this the *bhakta* is like a bird that flies over the mountain and so gives the impression of being the faster of the two. But after a time the bird is exhausted ('dark night of the Soul') and must recuperate, while the car needs no such rest and after having climbed the mountain catches up with the resting bird.

Heard's 'The Philosophia Perennis' deals with Coomaraswamy's contribution to a synthesis between Eastern wisdom and Western thought.[2]

Like Huxley and Radhakrishnan, Coomaraswamy is equally at home in both oriental and occidental culture; in science as well as art; in not only one but several religions. The width of his culture and learning can be estimated from his published work: *Mediaeval Sinhalese Art, Rajput Painting, The Dance of Śiva, History of Indian and Indonesian Art, A New Approach to the Vedas* and *The Transformation of Nature in Art*. But it is chiefly as a philosopher that Coomaraswamy interests us, and his contribution is the pertinence of philosophy to the problem of immortality. Now as material things cannot be immortal in *esse per se*,[3] wisdom is primarily concerned with immaterial things.[4] The conclusion he comes to is that 'metaphysics can in no way be thought of as a doctrine offering consolations to a suffering humanity'.[5] Although the metaphysical concept of perfection may be regarded as *non*-human, it certainly is not *in*human. For 'it is maintained that such a state is always and everywhere accessible to whoever will press inwards to the central point of consciousness and being on any ground or plane of being. . . .'[6] What is required from any one to actualize his inherent immortality is 'a total and uncompromising denial of

---

[1] *Ibid.*, pp. 136–41, loc. cit., 139.

[2] *Ibid.*, pp. 294–7.

[3] Not even from one moment to another because science demonstrates that they are continually in flux.

[4] In *Contemporary Indian Philosophy*, London, 1952, p. 161.

[5] *Ibid.*, p. 7.

[6] *Ibid.*, p. 169.

himself and a final mortification'.[1] It is here, from the religious point of view, that one's realization of immortality lies. For as St Thomas Aquinas said: 'the duration of eternity is infinite'.[2] What is required in order to conquer contingent death (*punar mṛtyu*) is 'to be dead and buried in the Godhead';[3] in the *Real Self*. It is a state of which St Thomas Aquinas says: 'Certain men even in this state of life are greater than certain angels, not actually, but virtually.'[4] And again St Augustine: 'Even we ourselves as mentally tasting something eternal, are not in this world.'[5] The Godhead being a noumenal principle is to be differentiated from the subtle and gross bodies. This explains the remark of St Thomas Aquinas: 'things belonging to the state of glory are not under the sun'.[6] Because in that state, as St Gregory explains: 'Some men are taken up into the hlighest angelic orders.'[7]

Coomaraswamy's masterpiece is, however, a small book called *Hinduism and Buddhism*. In it he tries to show that the Northern (esoteric) and Southern (exoteric) schools of Buddhism should not be treated as if in opposition to each other. But what is more important is his second point, that Buddhist and Hindu philosophy are not in conflict. The former has grown out of the massive and fertile field provided by the latter. 'Still further, Dr Coomaraswamy wishes to show—and certainly his scholarship would seem to sustain it—that the *essentials* of Christianity, of Buddhism in its two forms, and of Hinduism are one. Here is the *philosophia perennis*, here the eternal gospel.'[8]

George Grimm[9] was a judge of the High Court of Bavaria and as such famous for the justness and equity of his decisions. However, he soon felt the urge to seek spiritual truth and something told him to look for it in the ancient wisdom of India. So he gave up his lucrative office to study Sanskrit and Pali, and became an intimate friend of Paul Deussen, the famous translator of the Upanishads.

George Grimm studied Buddha and his teachings with extreme thoroughness and was aghast at the superficial attitude to Buddhist thought in Europe. People considered it to be a kind of oriental pessimism caused by malnutrition. *Nirvāṇa* was regarded as an atheistic invention to abolish a self that was non-existent.

His researches convinced him that the Buddha formulated a philosophy and a technique of logical thinking combined with meditation which helps us to understand our personality and the world around us as it really is. In *The Doctrine of the Buddha* he took great pains to prove that the Buddha's teachings are not at variance with the main tenets of Indian

[1] *Ibid.*, p. 171.

[2] *Summa Theologica*, i.q. 10, a. 5, a.d. 4.

[3] *Contemporary Indian Philosophy*, p. 171.

[4] *Summa Theologica*, i, q. 117, a. 2, a.d. 3.

[5] *De Trinitate*, i, v. 20.

[6] St Thomas Aquinas, *Summa Theologica*, iii, Sup., q.I, a.I, XXXIV in Ev.

[7] St Gregory, *Hom.*

[8] Gerald Heard in *Vedānta for the Western World*, p. 295.

[9] 1868–1945.

philosophy. Grimm argued that the Buddha belongs to the mainstream of Indian thought because He tried to draw our attention to the cardinal problem of Self in contradistinction to ego.

If one accepts the Buddha one ought also to accept Western Vedānta because the latter illuminates the same truths from a different angle and for a later generation. Pure Being is equivalent in practice to No-Thing. The *Self* is Pure Being. As such it is a No-Thing which consequently cannot be described in words. A positive affirmation of *Self* (as Ātman) is logically difficult if not impossible. An ordinary person may even fall a prey to confusion. (We notice this on almost every page of Huxley's later novels.) The Buddha was aware of this danger and, therefore, bypassed this obstacle by using the method of *reductio ad absurdum*. Indeed the *neti neti* of the Upanishads is a case in point. George Grimm saw deeper than most scholars of Buddhism. In *The Doctrine of the Buddha*[1] he shows how the Buddha came to the same conclusions as Ramana Maharshi[2] by using the *reductio ad absurdum* method. This is permissible when the positive proof of an affirmation is not possible but the number of alternatives is limited.

The Ātman or our essential *Self* is always in a condition of *nirvāṇa*. The metaphysics of Ramana Maharshi enables us to understand Buddhist philosophy in its pristine purity. Grimm freed Buddhist thought from the mountains of prejudice under which it was submerged (in Europe). Thanks to him we now see how the Maharshi and the Buddha complement one another, thus giving us one of the most perfect systems of metaphysical thought known to man. Indeed the combined metaphysics of the Maharshi and the Buddha enable us to understand the secret truths of the *Tibetan Book of the Dead* in a meditative-intuitive way.

I am convinced that the *Tibetan Book of the Dead* (*Bardo Thödol*) is an authentic record of the dying hour and of the post-mortal state. I myself have tested it involuntarily. Twice in my life I have been very close to death and have had experiences which agree with the accounts given in the *Tibetan Book of the Dead*. The dying hour brings with it such a turmoil that one can preserve one's calm and make use of the golden opportunity only if one has mastered the epistemology[3] common to the Maharshi and the Buddha. A mere superficial knowledge of it would be more a hindrance than a help. George Grimm has worked out step by step this *Erkenntnistheorie* (epistemology and ontology) common to the Maharshi and the Buddha. The Maharshi's cardinal question was 'who am I?'; the Buddha's 'what am I not?' By using the latter method one eliminates all one had superimposed on the Real Self till there remains only the 'Unborn, Unoriginated, Unmade, Unformed' which is the Clear Light of the Void. 'If there were not, monks, this unborn, unoriginated, unmade, and unformed, there would be no way out for the born, the originated, the made and the

---

[1] English Edition, Akademie-Verlag, Berlin (East), 1958.

[2] 1879–1950; for his life and teachings see Arthur Osborne, *Ramana Maharshi*, Rider, London, 1957.

[3] Theory of knowledge: the process of our cognition of the external world.

formed'.[1] I, therefore, suggest that in order to understand the *Tibetan Book of the Dead* one should master Grimm's works on Buddhist philosophy.[2]

What then is the *essential* underlying idea of Western Vedānta? It is summed up in a single statement of Meister Eckhart: 'The kingdom of God belongs only to those who are thoroughly dead while still alive in this world.' It is the death of the ego, *prior* to that of the body, which leads to the *life everlasting*. As Coomaraswamy says: 'For the Supreme Identity is no less a Death and a Darkness than a Life and a Light. . . . And this is what we understand to be the final purport of the First Philosophy.'[3] The First is also the *Perennial* Philosophy.

In 'Unknown Indian Influences' Heard traces how the *Religionsphilosophie* of ancient India influenced and inspired the saints of the Christian church. This is further proof that Vedānta cannot be geographical, national or in any way exclusive.[4] For instance, St Thomas Aquinas had as his revered teacher St Albertus Magnus who in later life wrote a masterpiece called *De Adherendo Deo* which, along with *The Cloud of Unknowing* and Brother Lawrence's *The Practice of the Presence of God*, are the three holiest, wisest, and most profound books the Christian West has ever produced. In *De Adherendo Deo* we are told that: 'To mount to God is to enter into oneself' (into one's *Real Self*). The Christian reader will find in that book an excellent example 'of that Western mysticism which has such strange parallels with the East'.[5] The *Adherendo* favours the *rāja yoga* method, just as *The Cloud of Unknowing* illustrates a method of the *jñāna* type and *The Practice of the Presence of God* that of the way of *bhakti*. The first and last also partake very much of the nature of *abhyāsayoga* —the frequent, loving and intense recall at all times and places, of the Christ-conscious nature of one's *Real Self* until an inward presence of divinity becomes a felt reality.

'How far have the mystics of the West following the Christian tradition succeeded in rendering in Western terms thoughts which we today would mainly classify as Oriental?' Heard attempts to answer this in his 'Mysticism in the *Theologia Germanica*'.[6] He seems to possess the gift of spotting genuine spiritual vitality under any disguise. His 'Is There Progress?'[7] provokes one into asking what kind of progress? For it may well be that one kind is in inverse ratio to another. Technological progress, for instance, involves a movement away from *natura naturans* to *natura naturata*. Whereas spiritual progress is usually accompanied by a renunciation of the *natura naturata* in the favour of the *natura naturans*. 'The first thing that is

---

[1] Cp. *Itivuttaka*, 43.

[2] An English version of Grimm's works is to appear soon, published by George Allen and Unwin, London.

[3] *Contemporary Indian Philosophy*, p. 171.

[4] *Vedānta for the Western World*, pp. 294–7.

[5] *Ibid.*, p. 373.

[6] *Ibid.*, pp. 383–8.

[7] *Ibid.*, p. 432.

obvious,' says Heard in his 'Future of Mankind's Religion',[1] 'is that the Indian contribution will be fundamental. . . . Scholarship has now proved as a fact . . . that the specific concepts which gave to Western religion its deepest insights and its most effective techniques were all imported from the Indian areas.' Heard maintains that every faith needs a frame of reference.[2] 'For Christianity that frame—the form in which a faith becomes amalgamated with philosophy and culture—was found in Greek thought.'[3] This blending of faith with frame was the great merit of St Thomas Aquinas. But in our times this Greek frame of reference is exhausted and out of date. Hence the crisis. What Christianity needs today is another Aquinas. One who can realize and elucidate that 'the great religions do not so much borrow from each other as all draw from a basic philosophy, a way of life, an apprehension of reality *which has been there all the while but which we have forgotten'*.[4] Heard then examines 'the part that India might play in that new system to embrace mankind'. If religion in general and Christianity in particular are to be revitalized, we must have the vision to combine Shankara's insights into Vedānta philosophy with Aquinas's technique of interpretation—we have to put the faith that is taken from revelation in the Gospels within a frame of reference taken from pre-Gospel revelations. Thus we retain and preserve that wholeness which comes through keeping in touch with the past, and the past, after all, is something that neither man nor a religion can cast off at will. Thus we find in the *Vedas* that same chant which through Persia, Bagdad, Alexandria, Cordova, Padua, and Paris, reformulates the same essential message in Europe and Western Christianity. We find it in the writings of Meister Eckhart, of Suso, of William Law and others. 'Though Christ be born a thousand times in Bethlehem, if HE [as the Real-Self] be not born [realized] in thee, all is in vain!'

Another great literary figure who together with Aldous Huxley in America started the movement which came to be called Western Vedānta is Guido Ferrando. Ferrando was a professor of Italian, an authority on Dante and a very profound student of Vedānta. His comparison of St Francis with Sri Ramakrishna[5] is a product of great insight. It is a successful pioneer attempt at linking up faith with its framework as discussed in the preceding pages. These 'perfect images of God in the mirror of humanity' enable us to realize that 'Vedānta' is the fundamental unity of every true religion. Thus it was St Francis's *Laudes Creaturarum* that the World Congress of Religion[6] selected as its hymn, for it can be sung by representatives of all creeds. This is an example of constructive Vedānta in a Western Christian framework.

In Ferrando's essay on 'The Spiritual Message of Dante'[7] we see how the

[1] *Ibid.*, pp. 442–6, loc. cit., 442.
[2] *Ibid.* (See also *The Flowering of Mysticism*, by Dr Rufus Jones.)
[3] *Ibid.*, p. 294.
[4] *Ibid.*, p. 296.
[5] *Vedānta for the Western World*, p. 253.
[6] London, 1931.
[7] *Vedānta for the Western World*, p. 389.

Vedāntic idea of life as a quest for a Vision, which can see the Manifold *as* the One, and the One *underlying* the Manifold,[1] inspired Dante, through the influence of St Francis, to write about it in the form of an allegory, now famous as *The Divine Comedy*. (This should be read together with Bunyan's *Pilgrim's Progress* to get the full effect.) Just as St Francis is an example of Vedānta within the framework of mediaeval Christianity, so in Emerson we have an example of it in the Christianity of modern America. Now Ferrando proves that Emerson was directly influenced by the books on Indian philosophy which he had so eagerly read. To quote Emerson: 'in all nations, in all times there are minds which incline to dwell in the conception of the fundamental unity. This tendency finds its highest expression in the religious writings of the East, and chiefly in the Indian Scriptures'.[2] This is the sum and substance of Vedānta in a nutshell. Now Mary Baker Eddy, who founded Christian Science, had read and studied Emerson and often quotes him in great detail. In this way a garbled version of Indian philosophy became the inspiration and substratum of what is called Christian Science. People who ignored, ridiculed, or scoffed at Indian philosophy in its original form as something heathen and Oriental and therefore unscientific accepted it wholeheartedly as soon as an Americanized version was given out under the title Christian Science. Such is the power of prejudice!

The gifted dramatist John van Druten scored a big success in London with his play *I am a Camera* which is a stage version of Christopher Isherwood's stay in Berlin. In a later book, *The Widening Circle*,[3] van Druten writes of the effort to put Western Vedānta into practice. In 'One Element'[4] he describes his progress and that of his generation, from what Aldous Huxley described as 'the philosophy of meaninglessness' to Western Vedānta. Huxley was the leader of this generation and so this essay is important in dealing with Huxley's *philosophia perennis*.

In 'Prayer'[5] van Druten explains what he calls petitionary prayer and describes the standpoint of Vedānta with reference to Christian Science. His 'Māyā and Mortal Mind'[6] examines the Vedāntic interpretation of what is called the sin against the Holy Ghost. Why is Enlightenment also called *Liberation* in Indian philosophy? In what way are we unliberated before Enlightenment? Our freedom is restricted by *māyā*, but as *māyā* is unreal our freedom is not really restricted for we only delude ourselves into putting on imaginary fetters—just as if someone were told of a non-existing law and behaved as if he were bound by it. As a man, not knowing he has

---

[1] Cp. 'Sustanzia ed accidenti, e lor costume,
        Quasi conflati insieme per tal modo,
        Che cio ch'io dico è un semplice lume.'
Dante, *Paradiso*, XXXIII, 88–90.
[2] Ferrando's requotation in *Vedānta and Modern Man*, p.213.
[3] New York, 1959.
[4] *Vedānta and Modern Man*, pp. 372–80.
[5] *Vedānta for the Western World*, pp. 184–8.
[6] *Ibid.*, pp. 350–4.

crossed the frontier from a totalitarian to a free country, will continue to act as though still oppressed by the rigours of the former.

To realize mystically that the kingdom of God is within means we have crossed the frontier to spiritual freedom, but until we have done so we feel and behave as if in bondage. This false but effective sense of bondage is called *māyā*. Enlightenment is like a notice-board proclaiming that the frontier has long since been crossed and so the escapee may drop his self-imposed limitations. That is why Enlightenment is called the Great Liberation. This experience has been described by van Druten in 'I Am Where I Have Always Been'[1] which also dispels some popular misconceptions about Christian Science. Vedānta helps to correct misconceptions because it emphasizes again and again that:

'The desire to *get* must be replaced by an understanding and acknowledgment of that which one already spiritually is.'[2]

As Huxley points out, spiritual experience can only be talked about inadequately but never shared.[3] The method of *rāja yoga* emphasizes (psychologically planned) meditation just as the way of *bhakti* stresses devoted worship. What then is the difference between them? For one thing *rāja yoga* can be used even by atheists and agnostics. Secondly it does not require that intense *emotional* power so necessary in *bhakti*, and therefore is more suited to our prosaic and Protestant North. But there are also two other important differences to note:

1. *Bhakti* is like a radio which can transmit but not receive while *rāja yoga* is like one that can both transmit and receive. In *bhakti*, or worship, the person communicates with a 'God' of his own choice but in so far as the devotion is active (as in prayer) the communication is always in one direction—from the devotee to his God. In order to receive a return message one has to be passive.[4] Undoubtedly passive-receiving forms of worship exist in *bhakti yoga* but as far as the West is concerned, what the average person understands by worship is usually prayer.

2. In *bhakti* the aspirant's aim is to *dissolve* the ego through a constant recognition of his utter dependence on the divine. He, therefore, cultivates a feeling and attitude of *powerlessness*. For only thus can he realize that what he worships is alone the efficient cause. He attempts through prayer to contact the 'Higher Power'. Therefore, to begin with, there is that awful sense of separation from that power. The conviction that there is a God, which is also a power greater and mightier than his own feeble and borrowed resources, keeps the aspirant humble and dependent because the *separation* has been emphasized. Success in *bhakti* is conditional on a deep sense of separation, forlornness, weakness, dependence, and above all humility.

[1] *Ibid.*, pp. 212–15.
[2] *Ibid.*, p. 214. (Requoted.)
[3] *Adonis and the Alphabet*, London, 1956, p. 39.
[4] Cp. Wordsworth's 'a wise passivity'.

On the other hand in *rāja yoga* the aspirant's aim is to *destroy* the illusion of having an ego by cutting off its supply line. This he achieves through a re-identification, during deep meditation, with 'God' as his *Real Self*. He tries through repeated and systematic meditations to bring about a kind of re-assimilation with the Higher Power. This then leads to an intense inner conviction that this Higher Power is identical with his *Real Self*. 'Not I but Christ (i.e. Christ-consciousness) in me.' That is why *rāja yoga* leads to a feeling of *power-full-ness* as the aspirant progressively approaches a state of re-assimilation, or rather his *Real Self* which is after all the source and junction of such re-assimilation. Moreover it is usually only after some initial success in *rāja yoga* that *karma yoga* becomes practicable. This is because the power generated by the former is later used to keep the ego-sense out of whatever one does. How else can the ego be eliminated when it is at its strongest, as when we undertake some action. As Swami Prabhavananda says: 'Without meditation (*rāja yoga*), *karma yoga* is impracticable'[1]— though not impossible. Religion, he points out, is a *dehypnotizing* process. What mesmerizes us is *māyā*, or what in Tibetan philosophy is called *bardo*-hallucinations. But we are only capable of being hypnotized because of the errant notion that there is in us a single permanent I: yet in fact this 'I', ego or *self* with a small 's', is only an endless collection of fluctuating I's which follow one another so quickly that they induce the sense of being a separate ego. Actually, this ego-sense is only a distorted version of the pure consciousness of the *Real Self* on which the I-sense is fed. As the human body changes slowly and as the person has a name by which he is called, he identifies himself with his *name*; the illusion is fostered that he is a specific *someone*, only because of that permanent name. This combined with a seemingly permanent body, creates the hallucination of a fixed, separate, unchanging permanent I. The hallucination is all the more difficult to overcome as it is indirectly supported by the *Real Self*. The ego-sense exists only because of, by, and through the *Self*. Thus, as Swami Prabhavananda points out, both Christian theology and Indian philosophy, both *rāja*- and *bhakti-yoga* are unanimous on one point: *through divine grace alone* is Enlightenment *possible*. This on the path of *rāja-yoga* means that the *Self* cuts off its supply of pure consciousness to the ego which thereupon vanishes, as it was entirely dependent on that supply. But this raises the problem:

'If I have to depend upon divine grace, if I have to wait until that grace descends upon me, what is the use of my efforts?'

In spite of everything, however, we are compelled to end on a note of mystery. Since the 'grace of God' on the way of *bhakti* or the 'grace of the Ātman' on the way of *jñāna* is indispensable, and also the most decisive factor, it is possible, though improbable, that a person can win Enlightenment in a single moment through such grace.[2] Although this grace operates

---

[1] *Vedānta for the Western World*, p. 421.
[2] 'Take the case of a room that has been dark a thousand years. If somebody sud-

with a kind of higher mathematics of its own we do not as yet know how its calculations work out. The only explanation that Ramakrishna gives is:

'God has the nature of a child. A child is sitting with gems in the skirt of his cloth. Many a person passes by him . . . [who] prays to him for gems. But he hides the gems with his hands and says, turning his face away, "No, I will not give any away". But another man comes along. He doesn't [even] ask for the gems, and yet the child runs after him and offers him the gems, begging him to accept them.'[1]

What conclusion is one to draw in the face of this explanation? On the one hand death and life come down with cruel force on a person who has not realized the *Real Self* (or found God); yet on the other hand this achievement depends on a variety of factors outside one's calculation or control. The most one can hope is:

> Still achieving, still pursuing,
> Learn to labour and to wait.[2]

Just what is the difference between *jñāna* and *bhakti*? An apt comparison is that between a democratic republic like the U.S.A., and a democratic state with a constitutional monarchy such as England. In both cases the State is the real power and the entity to which the subject owes allegiance. But in the first case it is an entirely invisible, abstract legal fiction, personality or concept. Although real enough to those who understand constitutional law, it is something inconceivable to the masses. For the benefit of the latter, the state must first be embodied in some *form* or symbol like a flag or an eagle, etc. But human nature being what it is, the best form it can understand is a human one. Thus in the second case (democratic monarchy) the imaginative and emotional needs of the masses find ample fulfilment, for the State is here embodied in the person of a living king or queen. In this case the masses understand better to *whom* they owe allegiance. The average person finds it easier to believe that he should die for his king than for the state.

In the above comparison the divine power was likened to the State. In its formless aspect the State can be understood only by a study of constitutional law. The divine power is understood as formless and impersonal by *jñānis* through deep insight and study—but the broad masses cannot give allegiance to what they cannot see. For the benefit of the latter the divine power takes a form—the best, as explained above, being a human one. Hence the idea of a personal God, divine Incarnation, or the Word made Flesh. It is far easier for a person to concentrate attention and devotion on

---

denly brings a lamp into it, the room is lighted in an instant' (The thousand years long darkness disappears in an instant and not bit by bit). *The Gospel of Sri Ramakrishna*, by M., New York, 1952, p. 769.

[1] *Ibid.*

[2] Longfellow, *The Psalm of Life*.

a definite form, such as Jesus or Krishna, than to meditate on a formless Absolute. That is Ramakrishna's argument for the method of *bhakti*—namely its relative simplicity for the average person. In his words: 'In learning archery one first aims at big things (like a tree-trunk) easy to shoot at and then progresses on to difficult targets (such as a flying bird).' So one should begin with the usual practice of devotion to a personal saviour or God. When this is intense it automatically leads to a realization of the *Self* and the *bhakta* or devotee gets the same Enlightenment as the *jñāni*. In each case the *ego* (and so the phenomenal world as an objective reality in its own right), which is after all the only obstacle, is eliminated but by different processes. In the one case it is *dispelled* like darkness before light, revealing what is called the *Self* and the completion of this process is called Enlightenment. This is the method of *jñāna*. In the second case, the ego through intense devotion (*bhakti*) *dissolves*, like sugar in tea, into that which it worships, revealing what is called 'God'—and the completion of the process is called *unio mystica*. As in the latter case the ego, just prior to union, amalgamates with that particular form which the devotee may have selected (Jesus or Krishna, etc.), it fosters in the devotee a more or less fanatical belief that that form alone is the one true God, or the only road to union. Ramakrishna's outstanding genius led him to show that: *once* the *required white-hot intense devotion* (depending on the melting-point of one's ego) has been reached, the *same result* (union) will follow no matter what other object of devotion is substituted for the form originally selected. If, *after* union, the *bhakta* experiments by worshipping a form other than the one first selected, he finds that the same result takes place no matter what form he reveres. Thus like the *jñāni* he too comes to the conclusion that all roads lead home. The reason is that it is not the *object* worshipped but the fact of worship that dissolves the ego and leads to union. Thus supposing that some primitive tribe worshipped the devil, it would not *necessarily* prevent a member from reaching union provided his devotion was sufficiently intense to dissolve his ego. For, after all, the latter is the only devil which can hinder union with God. The ego is like a disease which prevents the Enlightenment or union which is potentially present from being realized. *Jñāna* is like surgery. It operates upon the patient and removes the ego with the scalpel of keen analysis and discrimination. *Bhakti* is like a medicine, which through regular dosage progressively weakens the ego.

Ramakrishna points out how in *bhakti* there are several traditional ways which can be divided roughly into two broad groups. The one may be called the Monkey (personal effort) Group and the other the Kitten (receptivity) Group. A new born monkey makes every effort to cling to its mother, while a kitten mews and its mother comes and lifts it up. Thus aspirants of the Monkey Group have to make, because they *think* they should, strenuous efforts in the form of spiritual discipline, etc., while those of the Kitten Group have to become acutely receptive (self-surrender).

'All that they can do is to cry to God with yearning hearts. God hears their cry and cannot keep Himself away. He reveals Himself (as their *Real Self*)[1] to them.'[2]

The way of *jñāna* leads to Enlightenment as does the way of *bhakti*. Still, says Ramakrishna, 'as long as God keeps the feeling of ego in us, it is easier to follow the path of *bhakti*'.[3] But as this ego exists by the presence, permission and power of the *Self*, it is eliminated not whenever it wants to be but only when the *Real Self* stops nourishing it with pure consciousness. An aspirant trying to abolish his ego by his own personal efforts is, therefore, trying to lift himself up by his own shoe-laces. What is called the grace of God is necessary. The normal channel through which this grace is communicated is someone who is already enlightened. Therefore such a person is considered even more precious than the philosopher's stone—which can only convert other metals into gold, not into another philosopher's stone.

The *jñāni* tries as far as possible to avoid using the word God for it can easily be misleading. That is why the Buddha whose method was of the *jñāna* type, was reputed unjustly to be an atheist. The method of *jñāna* can be used by, and is even recommended for atheists. Unlike *bhakti* it has no God or something to believe in. From the *jñāna* point of view a person who looks for God without having understood the interpenetrating relationship of ego-*Self*-God is like someone with a bright lamp on his head searching for darkness.

As God has no quantity, He is only quality. Thus even a part of God is, for all purposes, as good as the whole. This is not so absurd as it may sound. For example even our own mind has no quantity of thoughts—in the sense that it does not become empty or even reduced by thinking. And so even a part of our mind such as a thought, is *qualitatively* of the same nature as all other thoughts put together—this refers to thought as thought and not to its idea-content. The *Self* being a projected particle of God (Universal Cosmic Mind) is for all purposes the same as God. It is so to speak not God's ambassador but His *plenipotentiary*. To have contacted it is the same as having contacted God. For example, if I say 'I have seen the Thames', is it necessary that I should have seen every square inch of it from its source to its mouth? It is enough to have seen it at London, Tilbury or some such place.

Yet it is important to clear this up in a little more detail because Ramakrishna strove hard to show the folly of a certain idea popularly misunderstood in India and elsewhere. It springs from *soham*, one of the sacred formulas of the non-dualistic Vedāntists, which means literally 'I am *He* [God]'. The deluded aspirant repeats this regularly in the naïve hope that by so doing he will *become* God. This outrageous piece of blasphemy arises from a misunderstanding of what Vedānta means by *soham*. In the

[1] 'Thus did they realize Brahman ("God") as their own inner consciousness'. *The Gospel of Sri Ramakrishna*, p. 103.

[2] *Ibid.*, p. 369.

[3] *Ibid.*, p. 104.

first place it is valid only for those who are already enlightened so that the I at the beginning of the formula is not the ego but the Christ-conscious-ness or the *Real Self*. Now as this Christ-consciousness (*Self*) is the pleni-potentiary of God ('I and my Father are One'), it so to speak radiates of itself a powerful innermost conviction: 'I am Supreme Spirit' in the case of a *jñāni* or 'I am God' in the case of a *bhakta*. As even *after* Enlightenment the successful aspirant remains in that exalted state, the steady unbroken realization of the *Self* (on a principle similar to that of induced magnetism), may in time induce an intuition of *soham*. Here it is not the aspirant who claims to be God but the *Self* or the Christ-consciousness in him, his I as ego having been long since eliminated. As Meister Eckhart put it: 'God is at the centre of Man'. In the case of genuine *soham* it is this *centre* which says 'I am He' and not the man. If, therefore, a person indulges in *soham* or says 'I am God' *before* Enlightenment it is only a case of ignorance, blas-phemy or both.

But here we have reached a point where Ramakrishna would agree with Wittgenstein that words cannot communicate further. Ramakrishna also says that 'the God of the *jñāni* is full of brilliance, and the God of the *bhakta* full of sweetness'.[1] But whereas in order to *know* God (*jñāna*) a complete merger of the ego with the *Self* is necessary, in order to *enjoy* God it is equally necessary that the merger remain incomplete (by an extremely small fraction). Enjoyment implies a duality however minute. Would this not mean that the nearer anyone comes to God (on the *bhakti* way) the greater would be the inertia *against* going further? As we have seen, most people take to the path of seeking God only after being torn by ontological anxieties. If on approaching the goal of union with God that anxiety disappears in a glow of ontological bliss, the impelling force of the original anxiety would also be lost. Therefore, it is likely that although he may go further *the relative rate of progress may fall*. The beginner-aspirant should, therefore, make the most of the early stages of the quest when the impelling drive of anxiety is stronger. After that he can only depend on the impelling force of the incentives of bliss and peace.

'There are two ways,' so Sri Ramakrishna used to say, 'one is the path of discrimination, the other is that of love.'[2] Discrimination means to know the distinction between the *Real* (*Self*) and the Unreal (ego) through the process of analysis. The magician (*Real Self*) alone is real; his magic show (created by his ego) is illusory. This is discrimination.

As Ramakrisha explains: 'One ultimately discovers God by trying to know who this "I" is.'[3] Is this I the flesh, bones, blood, marrow or the like, of which the human body is physiologically composed? Is it the mind, emotions, or thinking apparatus? *Analysing* thus, one realizes at last that one is none of these nor the sum of them. Ramakrishna calls this the pro-cess of *neti neti*[4] (not this, not that *ad infinitum*). 'One can neither compre-

---

[1] *The Gospel of Sri Ramakrishna*, p. 768.

[2] *Ibid.*, p. 179.

[3] *Ibid.*, p. 180.

[4] 'Supposing the husband of a newly wed girl is sitting in a room with several other

hend nor touch the Ātman (*Real Self*). It is without qualities or attributes.'[1]

It seems that this path of *jñāna*, or the scientific analysis of one's ontological existence and essence, is ideal for the sceptical and rationalistic twentieth century. But Ramakrishna suggests that *bhakti*, the form of devotional worship most popular in Christianity, is the ideal way for our times. Yet the drawback of this method is that it requires sustained emotion of a very sublimated and refined quality, not easily achieved in our anti-mystical and phlegmatic times.

The best solution is not to rely on one method alone, but to combine all the ways to transcendental consciousness into an integral system. This is what the famous Indian sage of Pondicherry, Sri Aurobindo (1872–1950) has done. His great merit lies in interpreting yoga in the light of evolution and evolution in the light of yoga. He has thus anticipated many discoveries mistakenly attributed to Teilhard de Chardin.[2] Sir Julian Huxley's evolutionary humanism often provides scientific corroboration for Aurobindo's intuitive findings. The secret of Aurobindo's genius is that he, like Aldous Huxley, goes back to the source of the *philosophia perennis* for his inspiration. This is none other than yoga. No self-discipline, then no spiritual insight; no spiritual insight—no Self Realization; no such realization—no far-reaching wisdom; no such wisdom—no lasting peace; no such peace or contentment—no lasting happiness; no lasting happiness causes dissatisfaction with life as led on the surface of consciousness; recurring dissatisfaction leads to recurring and habit-forming desires for substitute satisfactions which may take the form of drugs or drunkenness, excitement, or even extroverted activity. Such substitute satisfactions may increase the need for self-discipline to restore balance and so it goes on like a vicious circle. The end result of it is, in Emerson's words, 'Things are in the saddle and ride mankind.' The best way to break this vicious circle is by self-discipline of all kinds—physical, ethical, intellectual, emotional and the others included under the one word yoga. Radhakrishnan explains this scientifically and philosophically, but Tagore, being a poet, expresses it with a touch of sentimental idealism:

'Life of my life, I shall ever try to keep my body pure, knowing that thy living touch is upon all my limbs. I shall ever try to keep all untruths out of my thoughts, knowing that thou art that truth which has kindled the light of reason in my mind. I shall ever try to drive all evils away from my heart and keep my love in flower, knowing that thou hast thy seat in the inmost

---

young men. The girl and her friends (who are not as yet acquainted with him) are peeping through a window. They point to one man after another asking "Is that your husband?" "No" replies the girl. When at last they point to her husband and ask: "Is he the one?" she says neither yes nor no, but only smiles and keeps quiet. Her friends *realize* that he is her husband.' The significance is that one becomes *silent* on realizing the true nature of one's Self [Real Self]. *Ibid.*, p. 280.

[1] *Ibid.*

[2] See my *Evolution und Gottesidee*, Ratingen, 1967.

shrine of my heart.[1] And it shall be my endeavour to reveal thee in my actions, knowing it is thy strength [that] gives me strength to act.'[2]

The bulk of Sri Aurobindo's philosophical writing is concentrated in *The Life Divine, The Synthesis of Yoga, The Ideal of Human Unity, On the Veda*. He claimed to have arrived at his philosophy through mystical insight; and how this was achieved is explained by his theory of Integral Yoga which is thus the centre round which his philosophical ideas revolve. His philosophy, though in a sense Vedāntic, is seriously critical of Shankara's Advaita Vedānta on many points. In particular, he denounces what he calls the illusionism of Shankara as untrue to the spirit of the original Vedānta. Matter[3] is not always to be explained away as an illusion. On the contrary, like the modern scientist, we should analyse and study its innermost nature. Ramakrishna often stressed that as long as one lives on the material plane one should respect the laws of matter. Thus Jesus refused to jump off the temple tower at the devil's suggestion that angels would hold him up. As matter is transformable into energy, it is more than probable that it is also *relative*, like space and time as Einstein proved. For instance air as well as iron is 'matter'—but what a difference between the two. Here Aurobindo's philosophy has more affinity with Ouspensky's explanation that if all created things are regarded as matter in a state of vibration, the rate of vibration will determine, or vary with, its density. As Ramakrishna illustrated, we reach the roof (Absolute) by denying (leaving behind) stair after stair (the relative planes). But once we reach the roof we find that the stairs were made of the same material as the roof. So that 'after finding [the Absolute] one reaffirms what one formerly denied'. The relative is only a denser manifestation of the Absolute. Knowing, and having *realized*, this one accepts *both nitya* (the Absolute) and *lila* (the Relative as a manifestation of the Absolute)—otherwise 'one gets short weight'.[4] A practical

[1] Not meaning the mere physical heart but rather *hridaya; hrid-guhā* in ancient Indian religions, means cave of the heart. It is *ullam* in Tamil; also *ashtānga-hridaya* (i.e. the centre of the eight-fold science) or *ojas-sthāna* (i.e. centre of life-consciousness). Anatomically that part of the physical heart which is at the extreme right, so that it lies over the meridian line of the body and falls on the right side of the line. This is also called *samavid*, the centre of Awareness-aware-only-of-itself.

[2] Tagore, *Gitanajali*, 4.

[3] 'The affirmation of a divine life upon earth and an immortal sense in mortal existence can have no base unless we recognize not only eternal spirit as the inhabitant of this bodily mansion . . . but [also] accept Matter of which it is made, as a fit and noble material out of which He . . . builds recurrently the unending series of His mansions.' *The Life Divine*, p. 7. See also *Taittiriya Upanisad*, III, 2, in Radhakrishnan's translation: 'For truly, beings here are born from matter (and) when born, they live by matter. . . .' *The Principal Upaniṣads*, London, 1953, p. 554.

[4] In Ramakrishna's illustration, when a person considers, say, for instance, a walnut, he thinks at first only of the nutty part inside it as walnut. But in order to get the 'full weight' of the walnut one must include the shell, inner coverings, etc., as well. In the same way after realizing the Absolute one knows that It is both the Absolute and the Universe. 'It is *HE* (the Absolute) who has *become* the Universe and its living beings' *as well. The Gospel of Sri Ramakrishna.*, p. 779.

corollary of this, as Ramakrishna found out from his own experience, is that as long as one lives in the human world one can express one's love for the divine only by loving that in which the divine is incorporated and through which it manifests—namely all sentient beings.[1] But this has meaning only when the ego has been eliminated. Thus the word love as used in everyday parlance has no meaning here. It is to this ego-eliminated love that Sri Aurobindo refers:

'. . . We must assume first that the supreme Existence is not an abstraction or a state of existence, but a conscious Being; secondly, that he meets us in the universe and is in some way immanent in it as well as at its source . . . thirdly, that he is capable of personal relations with us . . . finally, that when we approach him by our own human emotions, we receive a response in kind.'[2]

According to Aurobindo, there is no particle of creation which is not to some extent infused with absolute spirit. Thus *involution* from higher to lower forms of supramental self-consciousness is as inevitable as *evolution*. Our purpose in life is to attain identity with the Absolute by surpassing the realm of the mental through a *supramental* change.[3] But this requires strenuous effort and self-discipline. A mere increase in knowledge is not enough, and even dangerous if the ontological base of our Being is not correspondingly broadened. But the effort and discipline required seem so hard and difficult that we are discouraged from even making a start. Moreover society has an ingrained hostility towards those who plan any kind of spiritual development for themselves or others. It, therefore, keeps a man busy by filling up his time with what it calls *duties* in the hope of making him forget that he also owes a duty to himself—to his *Real Self*. It keeps on pushing him from one duty to another with such rapidity that his own spiritual development must be neglected. The cost of this has to be borne eventually by society, which never thinks either in the long or the short run. It is influenced by emotions. Thus it surrounds the word *duty* with a fictitiously pious aura, till all duties come to be called holy. First of all there is one's holy duty to society or the state, backed by a holy police force armed with holy weapons. Then duty to the profession, duty to the family, to one's club, to one's old school, and so on *ad infinitum*. The philosophy of duties is the philosophy of a slave. But a slave who has decided to fight for his freedom has half ceased to be one. And so too has a

[1] Cp. O mortal, turn back to thy transient kind;
    Aspire not to accompany Death to his home,
    As if thy breath could live where Time must die.
From Aurobindo's poem *Savitri*, Book IX (The Book of Eternal Night), Canto I, p. 655.
[2] *On Yoga*, Part III, p. 629, loc. cit., p. 635.
[3] Cp. '"Transformation" is a word that I have brought in myself (like "Supermind") to express certain spiritual concepts and spiritual facts of the integral Yoga.' Sri Aurobindo, *On Himself And On The Mother*, Part I, p. 168.

man who says: 'My *first* duty is to my *Real Self*. To find out who I am and what are my ontological roots.' But to take up this attitude requires great courage,[1] and great energy to overcome inertia. Where is this added courage and energy to come from? Just as a merchant needs capital to start his business career, so an aspirant needs a kind of spiritual capital or *grace* to start him off and keep him going. This extra grace which lightens his efforts and so prevents him from getting discouraged is the esoteric meaning of what Aurobindo sometimes refers to as *mother*; symbolizing mercy, or the mother aspect of the divine, in contrast to justice, or the father aspect.

Another means to lighten his efforts is *integral* yoga.

'All *life*, when we look behind its appearances, is a vast Yoga [or methodized effort towards self-perfection] of *Nature* attempting to realize her perfection in an ever increasing expression of her potentialities and to unite herself with her own divine reality.'[2]

And yoga, as we have seen, is a methodized effort towards self-perfection as a means of *compressing* one's evolution into a shorter period of bodily existence.[3] Therefore '*all life is consciously or subconsciously a Yoga*'.[4] But the greatest tragedy that ever fell on India was that yoga as a science was ruined by the wrong kind of people practising it. The harmony of the whole (of yoga) was mutilated by overdeveloping some aspects, while neglecting others, usually out of egoistic or foolish motives. This brought about a sharp incompatibility between ordinary life and yoga.[5] 'So strongly has the [false] idea prevailed, . . . that to escape from life is now commonly considered as not only the necessary condition, but the general object of yoga.'[6] This is the very worst that could have happened. In order to safeguard one's spiritual evolution from the plethora of duties imposed by society, it is not necessary to escape to a jungle or a desert island.[7] What is needed is a changed attitude towards such duties: not extreme renunciation but balance and harmony. The yoga of work or duty must be supplemented and complemented by the yoga of meditation; the yoga of wisdom is to be enriched by the yoga of devotion; and the whole is to be kept going by a

[1] Because society in its folly does not understand that the realization of one's *Self* is the greatest blessing that any of its members can confer upon it.

[2] *On Yoga*, p. 4.

[3] 'As life has developed mind, and the embodiment has modified itself to suit this development . . . so mind can develop Supermind which is in its nature knowledge not seeking for itself, but manifesting itself by its own automatic power, and the embodiment can again modify itself or be modified from above so as to suit this development'. Aurobindo, *Correspondence with Sri Aurobindo*, p. 122 (Re: 7/7/1936).

[4] *On Yoga*, p. 4.

[5] 'Whatever the ideas or ideals which the human mind extracts from life or tries to apply to life, they can be nothing but the expression of that life itself as it attempts to find more and more and fix higher and higher its own law and realize its potentialities.' Aurobindo, *The Ideal of Human Unity*, p. 176.

[6] *On Yoga*, p. 7.

[7] See Hazlitt's essay, *On living to oneself*.

L

sound yoga of physical health and well-being. For yoga is a means to *more abundant* life and not less.[1] 'For man is precisely that term and symbol of a higher Existence descended into the material world in which it is possible for the lower to transfigure itself and put on the nature of the higher and the higher to reveal itself in the forms of the lower.'[2] It should, therefore, be more than clear that self-discipline in yoga leads to positive sublimation and not to negative repression. It is a confident *Yea*-saying to life.[3] For 'to avoid the life which is given him for the realization of that possibility, can never be either the indispensable condition or the whole and ultimate object of his supreme endeavour or of his most powerful means of self-fulfilment.'[4]

Aurobindo's philosophy may therefore be called Spiritual Virility or life led as the harmonious whole it is meant to be.[5] The goal is really reached when 'the conscious yoga in man becomes, like the subconscious yoga in Nature, outwardly conterminous with life itself.'[6] This was just the kind of philosophy which the unbalanced extremists of both the Orient and the West needed to restore a sense of balance in life—and Sri Aurobindo has provided it through his idea of an Integral Yoga. In him we find the *philosophia perennis* in its pristine purity.

[1] 'The manifestation of a supramental truth-consciousness is therefore the capital reality that will make the divine life possible.' Aurobindo, *The Supramental Manifestation*, p. 79.

[2] *On Yoga*, p. 7.

[3] 'As the eyes of the sage are opened to the light, so is his ear unsealed to receive the vibrations of the Infinite; from all the regions of the Truth there comes thrilling into him its Word which becomes the form of his thoughts.' Aurobindo, *On the Veda*, p. 533.

[4] *On Yoga*, p. 7.

[5] Cp. 'It may well be that both tendencies, the mental and the vital and physical stress of Europe and the spiritual and psychic impulse of India, are needed for the completeness of the human movement.' Aurobindo, *The Foundations of Indian Culture*, p. 24.

[6] *On Yoga*, p. 7.

Mescalin and LSD: the Problem of Synthetic Sainthood

Now from my own unforgettable experience I know well that there is a state in which the bonds of the personal nature of life seem to have fallen away from us and we experience an undivided unity.[1]

Huxley was not the first to experiment with the psychological effects of mescalin. Ever since the German scientist Ludwig Lewin published his work *Anhalonium Lewinii*, famous psychologists like Janesch, Weir Mitchell, Havelock Ellis and others have tried out this cactus containing the active principle of peyote. Huxley, however, may have been the first to suggest the use of this chemical aid for the production of bigger and better mystics.

'For an aspiring mystic to revert, in the present state of knowledge, to prolonged fasting and violent self-flagellation would be as senseless as it would be for an aspiring cook to behave like Charles Lamb's Chinaman, who burned down the house in order to roast a pig.'[2]

Concepts as tremendous as Grace, Transformation, Beatific Vision, the Dharma-Body of the Buddha, Mind, Suchness, Void, even Godhead become quite clear ('as evident as Euclid') to Huxley when under the influence of mescalin.[3] Were we not taught to believe that only the pure in heart see God?

'For what we are, that we intently contemplate, and what we contemplate that we are; for our mind, our life and our essence are simply lifted up and united to the very truth, which is God. Wherefore, in this simple and intent contemplation we are one life and one spirit with God. And this I call the contemplative life. In this stage, the soul is united with God without means; it sinks into the vast darkness of the Godhead.'[4]

Even yoga warns that:

'The barriers to interior consciousness which drive the psychic nature this

---

[1] Martin Buber, *Between Man and Man* (E.T.), Routledge and Kegan Paul, 1947, p. 24.

[2] *Heaven and Hell*, London, 1956, p. 64.

[3] *The Doors of Perception*, London, 1954, p. 13.

[4] Jan van Ruysbroeck, 'The Sparkling Stone', 43 in *The Adornment of the Spiritual Marriage* (E.T.), C. A. Wynschenk, London, 1951, p. 203.

way and that are these: sickness, inertia, doubt, lightmindedness, laziness, intemperance, false notions, inability to reach a stage of meditation, or to hold to it when reached.'[1]

Can these barriers be overcome merely by taking mescalin?

'We must be careful to distinguish between contemplation of the Mystical Life and the special gifts which accompany it, such as ecstasies, ravishments, and visions, either bodily or imaginary. It is forbidden to desire these gifts and to ask for them, but to strive to reach them would be madness.'[2]

Mescalin experiences seem to be more akin to this madness than to genuine mysticism. The real danger begins when Huxley goes out of his way to praise mescalin as 'completely innocuous'.[3] Intensive research by German scientists have shown that this is not the case. Given below is a summary of the investigations under Professor Esser:[4]

'Another dangerous drug is mescalin. Its homeland is Mexico where it is found in a small prickless cactus of the peyote. The peyote is to be eaten to get the effects. After the First World War, the German chemist Späth discovered ways to produce mescalin in the laboratory. Thus doses suitable for injections could be manufactured on a commercial scale. We debated a long time whether it did any good to the patient and then decided in the negative. Mescalin works by disturbing sense-responses. After a short spell of heightened tipsyness follow a phantasmagoria of richly coloured pictures of rapidly varying patterns and shades. The patient (or victim) loses the ability to distinguish between one sense-impression and another so that he sees melodies and hears colours! Vague recollections of the past rise up to add to the confusion and the feeling of 'I-am' (the Ego) is all but lost; a disorderly and disrupting mess of visions, fancies and feelings sets in. After this confused ecstacy comes usually a hangover followed by vomiting. This drug enjoys enormous prestige in advertisements for the sale of magic-occult intoxicants. For example:
"Take this harmless wonder producing drug. It will enable you to see into the future, to communicate with those who are far away, and converse with the spirits of the dead."
We wish to warn all what this claim actually boils down to: a wilful damaging of brain-functions brought about by *Alkaloidvergiftung* (slow poisoning through overdoses of alkaloid).'

Professor R. C. Zaehner, a violent opponent of Huxley's mescalin theory

[1] Patanjali, *Yoga Sutras*, Bk. I, 2, 30 (E.T.); Charles Johnston, *The Book of the Spiritual Man*, New York, 1912.
[2] Alvarez de Paz; requoted in *An Introduction to the Mystical Life*, London, 1915, p. 11.
[3] *The Doors of Perception*, p. 52.
[4] *Volksbibliothek* Nr. 1007.

of mysticism, made himself the subject of an experiment with mescalin in the course of his endeavours to discredit Huxley's theory.

Huxley, however, seems to have been misunderstood by his critics. First of all the essence of his argument is that physiological changes brought about in body-chemistry through controlled external and synthetic means do *not* invalidate the spiritual significance of mysticism. As long as man has a body, it is in the fitness of things that even Enlightenment is accompanied by such side-effects as a change in body-chemistry. But can such side-effects bring about the main cause? A typhoon changes the barometer in my room. But can I bring on a typhoon by manipulating the barometer?

'One of the chief charges against me is that I am a magician. Have I not myself distinguished between two kinds of magic? One which the Greeks called *goeteia* depends entirely on alliance with evil spirits and deserves to be regarded with horror and punished; the other (*theurgia*) is magic in the proper sense of the word. The former subjects man to the evil spirits, the latter makes them serve him. The former is neither art nor science; the latter embraces the deepest mysteries and the knowledge of Nature with her powers.'[1]

Do mescalin and LSD belong to *goeteia* or to *theurgia*?

Dr James Olds has made an interesting experiment on rats. At the University of Michigan rats were given an inducement in the form of an electric shock in the brain that released a pleasant sensation. So enticing was this electrically induced joy that the rats were willing to endure even severe physical pains (asceticism!) for the privilege of touching the joy-giving wire; they even neglected food and drink (fasting!). The joy did not lessen through habit. More important still, the rats did not show the expected signs of fatigue or illness even after interminable and exhausting jumps to touch the wire; instead they appeared all the more reinvigorated. The results of these experiments were confirmed by those of Dr Robert Heath in Tulane (U.S.A.) and of Dr Carl Sem Jacobsen at the Mayo clinic. Can it not be that the innermost essence of all beings, including rats, is itself the source of, and in a state of, unending bliss? That this state or source has been through some chance or mischance veiled from us by brain-functionings? That a reduction or radical alteration in the activities of the brain restores the original source or state of bliss? Is it all that ridiculous to compare the bliss of the mystics with the artificial exuberance derived from mescalin and LSD or the electrically induced joy of the rats? The mystic must earn his bliss through mortification or by Grace; to get it by mescalin would be to get it only very temporarily (if at all) and that too by subterfuge. There is righteous indignation on the part of honest men like Zaehner that it should be even possible to replace the mystic's way by chemical means—for then even the undeserving many would be able to enter that hallowed realm. But is not alcohol already doing very much the

[1] 'Apology of Pico della Mirandola' in *Christian Mysticism*, Dean Inge, p. 269 n.

same? ⟨Take the case of someone who has suddenly received very bad news—so bad that, if left to himself, he would have been downcast and melancholy. Supposing further that, had he received good news, he would have danced and sung. If now, under the influence of strong drink, he dances and sings, then he pretends a joy to which he has no title by right of his reactions in the ordinary course of events. Moreover this momentary joy has been obtained by subterfuge.⟩ At first sight, the difference between this case and that of mescalin appears to be more of degree than of kind. If spiritual progress can be bought by a change in body-chemistry is there not the danger that ethics and self-discipline will be neglected as superfluous? Surely it is ethics and the cultivation of virtues, love and compassion, wisdom and renunciation that differentiate the *nirvāṇa* of a Buddha from the peace of an opium-eater. Could not this be why great sages like the Buddha, Mohammed and Zarathustra strictly forbade the use of intoxicants and similar drugs? Was it out of devotion to God (*bhakti*) that saints and mystics chanted hymns or, as Huxley darkly suggests:

'to increase the concentration of CO_2 in the lungs and blood and so to lower the efficiency of the cerebral reducing valve until . . . [it] permits the entry into consciousness of experiences, visionary or mystical, from out there.'[1]

A far more important feature of Huxley's mescalin experiment lies in the light it throws on problems discussed in *The Tibetan Book of the Dead*.[2] This singular masterpiece of Eastern wisdom attempts to deal with the problem of changes in consciousness which take place shortly before, during, and immediately after death; the first two are dealt with metapsychologically, the last on a more or less cybernetic basis of the metaphysical possibilities and consequences of any given change.[3] In so far as mescalin and LSD also work by bringing about revolutionary changes in consciousness, it was very thoughtful of Huxley's wife to ask him during the experiment: 'Would you be able to fix your attention on what *The Tibetan Book of the Dead* calls the Clear Light?' After considering the question for some time, Huxley answered:

'Perhaps I could—but only if there were somebody there to tell me about the Clear Light. One couldn't do it by oneself. That's the point, I suppose, of the Tibetan ritual—someone sitting there all the time and telling you what's what.'

At a later stage he added:

'What those Buddhist monks did for the dying and the dead, might not the modern psychiatrist do for the insane?'

The problem of death and the Hereafter had always loomed large in the

---

[1] See *Heaven and Hell*, p. 64 and pp. 54–5.

[2] Ed. by W. Y. Evans-Wentz, London, 1957.

[3] See also Chapter 13 in Part IV of this book.

works of the later Huxley. Already in *Grey Eminence* we have the figure of the twins (success-in-life and failure-in-death) portrayed by Father Joseph:

'When I thus think and then look and see how I and the most part of creatures live our lives, I come to believe that this world is but a fable. . . .'[1]

His novel *Time Must Have a Stop* makes a bold attempt to convey the ideas of *The Tibetan Book of the Dead* in the imaginary postmortal state of its non-hero Eustace Barnack:

'Abruptly, almost violent the beauty of the light and the anguish of participating in its knowledge were intensified beyond the limits of possibility. But in the same instant he realized that it was in his power to avert his attention, to refuse to participate. Deliberately he limited his awareness. The light died down again into insignificance. He was left in peace with his little property of memories and images.'[2]

In the same novel Sebastian relates how even great art can be a distraction from the mystic's point of view: '. . . some God-centred saints have condemned art, root and branch'. We have an example of this, for instance, in the later Tolstoy's vituperation against Beethoven's music. Romain Rolland was puzzled by this polemic against the great composer; Huxley saw deeper, he makes Sebastian say:

'Man has to remember that what he does as an artist or intellectual won't bring him to knowledge of the divine Ground, even though his work may be directly concerned with this knowledge. On the contrary in itself the work is a distraction.'[3]

This phobia of distractions is explainable only from 'the enormous importance attached, in all the great religious traditions, to the state of mind at the moment of death'.[4]

Nowhere is the value of this moment so convincingly elucidated as in *The Tibetan Book of the Dead*. For mysticism, as for romanticism, it is death that gives significance to life. Yet by death is meant the time immediately prior to clinical decease—the moment when one is still alive but so utterly involved in the process of extinction that dying is here interchangeable with death. This moment is regarded as particularly important because if

'consciousness survives bodily death, it survives, presumably, on every mental level.'[5]

[1] *Grey Eminence*, London, 1941, p. 228.
[2] *Time Must Have a Stop*, London, 1944, p. 158.
[3] *Ibid.*, p. 192.
[4] *Heaven and Hell*, p. 52.
[5] *Ibid.*

Again:

'Something of the same [mescalin-visionary] kind may happen in the posthumous state. After having had a glimpse of the unbearable splendour of ultimate Reality, and after having shuttled back and forth between heaven and hell, most souls find it possible to retreat into that more reassuring region of the mind where they can use their own and other peoples' wishes, memories and fancies to construct a world *very like that in which they lived on earth.*'[1]

It seems to me that there are two, and *only* two, alternatives as to the post-mortal state: nothing whatever happens (total extinction); or something or other happens (arrival in heaven, burning in hell, visit to astral worlds, etc.). In the case of the second alternative, a form of cognition is explicitly or by implication admitted. The Great Mystery is thus reduced to: cognition or no cognition. If the former then all post-mortal states must also be subject to the laws of cognition (even should it be non-sensory as, for instance, in dreams). Whether I arrive in heaven or land in hell, see my dead daughter in a dream or in my own post-mortal state—there must in every case be an I (the one who cognizes) and an object or state that is cognized. All interpretations of post-mortal states are, therefore, determined by what we conceive this I of ours to be. The deceased takes with him into the Hereafter his own conceptions of it. Studies of psychic processes and changes of consciousness could well patch together a fragmentary mosaic of the *structure* though *not* the content of the post-mortal state. For instance, I cannot tell the *contents* of the dream I am going to have tomorrow yet I can explain its structure: I shall imagine seeing, feeling, hearing whatever it may be. The imaginary seeing, feeling, hearing are linked to an I (perhaps a fictitious or a dream I). The I is the structure of all cognition, even in dreams and after death. Alterations in the psychic content of the I would then mirror themselves in the visions cognized, as the *Tibetan Book* rightly deduces. Huxley and C. G. Jung may not be too far off the mark when they draw parallels between the states of schizophrenia and (possible) after-death cognitive processes.

'At any rate, it is unexpectedly original, if nothing else, to find the after-death state, of which our religious imagination has formed the most grandiose conceptions, painted in lurid colours as a terrifying dream-state of a progressively degenerate character. . . . The supreme vision comes . . . in the moment of death. . . . Human life, therefore, is the vehicle of the highest perfection it is possible to attain; it alone generates the *karma* that makes it possible for the dead man to abide in the perpetual light of the Voidness without clinging to any object, and thus to rest on the hub of the wheel of rebirth, freed from all illusions of genesis and decay. . . . this eschatological goal is what he himself brings to birth as the last and high-

---

[1] *Ibid.*, italics mine.

est fruit of the labours and aspirations of earthly existence. This view is not only lofty, it is manly and heroic.'[1]

Why should such visions (cognitive processes) mar the serenity of the dead? Huxley answers:

'Of those who die (only) an infinitesimal minority are capable of immediate union with the divine Ground ... but there is also a heaven of blissful visionary experience; there is also a hell of the same kind of appalling visionary experience, as is suffered by schizophrenics and some of those who take mescalin. ...'[2]

The mescalin-sponsored heaven and hell are however not quite divorced from ethical conduct. We learn from Huxley that:

'Fear and anger bar the way to the heavenly other world and plunge the mescalin-taker into hell.'[3]

Further:

'Negative emotions—the fear which is the absence of confidence, the hatred, anger or malice which exclude love—are the guarantee that visionary experience, if and when it comes, shall be apalling.'[4]

Yet the mere absence of negative emotions is no guarantee that only the ethically deserving will attain mescalin's heaven; nor are negative emotions necessarily unethical. Otherwise Huxley would have to admit that a reckless (no absence of confidence) and merry gambler would obtain mescalin's Beatific Vision; yet a frightened, ill-tempered (but otherwise honourable) widow would be condemned to hell.

A serious difference between the chemically obtained states of mescalin and the hard-earned experiences of the mystics lies in the importance attached to *deeds*. 'By their fruits shall ye know them' is the standpoint of all religions. For the Buddha, deeds alone determine who gets to *nirvāṇa* and who is kept out; who becomes happy in this and future lives and who miserable:

'Owners of their deeds are men, children of their deeds, victims of their deeds; my inheritance consists of my deeds, my deeds determine my lot in life—that which I have gained and that which I missed. My works will reward me, my works punish me, my works protect me. My works are my refuge.'[5]

As against this our Prophet of Mescalin advises:

[1] Psychological Commentary in *The Tibetan Book of the Dead*, London, 1957, p. li.
[2] *Heaven and Hell*, p. 53.
[3] *Ibid.*, p. 5.
[4] *Ibid.*
[5] *Anguttara Nikāya*, V, 57.

'Works alone are powerless.'[1]

A heaven that can be attained without works is a dangerous temptation to hold out to the masses, for man, by nature, inclines to sloth:

'As a rule the mescalin taker discovers an inner world as manifestly a datum, as self-evidently infinite and holy. . . .'[2]

Again:

'For the artist as for the mescalin taker, draperies are living hieroglyphs that stand in some peculiarly expressive way for the unfathomable mystery of pure being.'[3]

Would not this mescalin solipsism lead to serious neglect of ethical values, to an irresponsible shirking of civic, moral and social duties? Unselfish service to mankind is not compatible with mescalin escapades and without unselfish service all heavens are worthless. Huxley says:

'the will (under mescalin) suffers a profound change for the worse. The mescalin taker sees no reason for doing anything in particular.'[4]

That alone should be reason enough to condemn the drug. Society has an adequate supply of ne'er-do-wells who even without mescalin see no reason for doing anything in particular.

It cannot be contested that it is possible, through the use of mescalin, LSD and other psychedelic drugs, to induce a substitute and inferior form of mystical consciousness in a controlled laboratory environment. The result of recent experiments confirms this.[5] What Huxley, as well as Zaehner, overlooks is that mescalin, LSD and similar chemicals, being psychedelic drugs, depend for their psychic effects on the psyche of the person taking them.[6] The more introverted a person is the less extra-ordinary are his visions. The tense, withdrawn person wishing to avoid contact with the world will neither panic under the drug (hell) nor experience hallucinated heavens. Here lies the greatest weakness in Huxley's

[1] *Heaven and Hell*, p. 51.

[2] *The Doors of Perception*, p. 35.

[3] *Ibid.*, p. 25.

[4] *Ibid.*, p. 18.

[5] *Journal of Religion and Health*, September 1966. Professor Walter Pahnke and Professor William Richards (Andover–Newton Theological School, U.S.A.): 'Religious services were held for twenty divinity students, half of whom were given *psilocybin*. All those who had taken the drug claimed to have experienced mystical states resembling those described by saints and mystics. They beheld "white light of abso-lute purity"; and had the feeling of "going deep within . . . to the self stripped bare of all pretence and falseness".'

[6] A. M. Becker, *Zur Psychopathologie der Lysergsäurediathylamidwirkung*, Wiener Zeitschrift für Nervenheilkunde und deren Grenzgebiete, Vol. II, No. 4.

apologia for the therapeutic use of mescalin. The emotionally ill (through over-introspection) are not affected by it whereas the sensation seeker (over-extraspection) reacts with wild enthusiasm. In genuine yoga it is the other way round—the excessively introverted is reintegrated through *karma-yoga* therapy and the over-extravert is brought to self-reflection through the psychologically devised methods of *rāja-yoga*. No doubt mescalin and LSD can be of considerable use in drug-assisted psychotherapy but curing certain forms of insanity is not the same as attaining the status of a mystic.

'Psycholytic treatment, i.e. psychotherapy activated by means of Delysid (R) or Indocybin (R), provides a very effective method of drug-assisted psychotherapy. Successful treatment is possible in cases of severe character neuroses and even patients with psychopathic disorders of personality development, chronic neuroses, including those previously regarded as incurable, and borderline psychoses. A remarkably high success rate of 65 per cent has been obtained. The way in which the treatment is carried out is of importance: special rooms and personnel must be available. Due care must be paid to indications and prognosis if the method is not to fall into disrepute.'[1]

As other experiments go to show:

'On the same experimental subject, a physician, mescalin and lysergic acid diethylamide (LSD) respectively produced different psychopathologic reactions, the former one of catatonic, the latter one of hebephrenic type. These differences could be demonstrated also by means of a drawing test. Drawings produced under the influence of LSD showed a tendency to expansion, while the "Mescalin pictures" showed a withdrawal reaction. Both tests show some relationship to the pictures produced by psychotic patients.'[2]

Perhaps the reason why LSD experiences are equated with mystical consciousness is that in both states there is a feeling of timelessness. The most frequent assertion of patients under LSD is summed up by the following:

'I do not feel as if there can even be such a thing as the next moment; past, present and future appear to be simultaneous. As if the last moment were complete in itself, a thing apart! No chronological connections anywhere at all.'[3]

The word mysticism is conveniently vague. It means all things to all

[1] H. Leuner and H. Holfeld in *Psychiatria et Neurologia*, 143: 379–91. See also F. K. Taylor, *The Analysis of Therapeutic Groups*, Oxford University Press, 1961.

[2] László Mátéfi in *Confinia Neurologica*, Basel, Vol. 12, p. 3.

[3] Requoted in: *Schweizer Archiv für Neurologie und Psychiatrie* (Zürich), Vol. LX, p.15.

men. It has been confused with magic, it was attributed to Hitler, Catholics use it in describing miracles caused by suspension of the laws of science, politicians use it to describe Mao-Tse Tung's inscrutability, Huxley links it up with mescalin visions and now, the ultimate insult, it even denotes the ungrasped significance in beat music or beatnik poetry. The definitions of the authorities on mysticism offer, however, no ground for vagueness:

(i) Evelyn Underhill:
   'Mysticism is the art of union with Reality. The mystic is a person who has attained that union in greater or less degree; or who aims at and believes in such attainment.'[1]

(ii) Dean Inge:
   'Religious Mysticism may be defined as the attempt to realize the presence of the living God in the soul and in nature, or more generally, the attempt to realize in thought and in feeling, the immanence of the temporal in the eternal, and of the eternal in the temporal.'[2]

(iii) Margaret Smith:
   'Mysticism is an attitude of mind; an innate tendency of the human soul, which seeks to transcend reason and to attain to a direct experience of God, and which believes that it is possible for the human soul to be united with ultimate Reality, when "God ceases to be an object and becomes an experience".'[3]

The above three are excellent definitions; were I allowed to give my own definition of mysticism, it would run as follows:

Mysticism is the conscious or unconscious practice of becoming responsive to ineffable impulses from whatever source one considers to be so holy that one is prepared to sacrifice everything else for the opportunity of either coming in contact with it, or remaining thus in contact through the ties of veneration; and this contact causes such intense happiness that one becomes thereby incapable of thoughts, words or deeds which in the common ethical tradition of mankind are taught to be unkind.

'Nothing is more individual to each soul than the form of its intimacy with our Lord'[4] says the Abbé de Tourville, and with good reason. 'He who knows the Tao,' assures Chuang-Tze, 'is sure to understand how to regulate his conduct in all varying circumstances. Having that understanding he will not allow things to injure himself . . . nothing can injure him.'[5] Sainthood and saintliness go hand in hand; if the latter is conjured up by synthetic means the former becomes a counterfeit. Mysticism through mescalin resembles paper currency during inflation; it was valid, yet its validity was a joke for it was without value.

[1] *Practical Mysticism*, p. 3.
[2] *Christian Mysticism*, London, 1948, p. 5.
[3] *An Introduction to the History of Mysticism*, p. 3.
[4] *Letters of Direction*, Westminster, 1939, p. 38.
[5] Bk. XVII, 7, in Legge's translation.

'It is therefore supreme ignorance for any one to think that he can ever attain to the high state of union with God before he casts from him the desire of natural things, and of supernatural also, so far as it concerns self-love, because the distance between them and that which takes place in the state of pure transformation in God is the very greatest. . . . until the desires be lulled to sleep by the mortification of sensuality, and sensuality itself be mortified in them so that it shall be contrary to the spirit no more, the soul cannot go forth in perfect liberty to the fruition of the union with the Beloved.'[1]

The genuine mystic experience comes after hard effort—prayer, fasting, chastity, devotion. Asceticism alone cannot lead to it as an inexplicable something called Grace is necessary. Grace stands to effort as equity to law; it follows effort. St Paul meeting the Risen Christ on the road to Damascus, St Theresa of Avila seeing visions, Simone Weil enraptured by a recitation of George Herbert's 'Love bade me welcome'—were all those events brought about as a result of some change in body chemistry? At first sight it seems grotesque that someone merely by swallowing a pill can have that which another has attained by dint of ethical or spiritual merit. But consider, only a few decades ago we were told that one of the worst punishments for having a guilty conscience was insomnia. Even Lady Macbeth complains of sleeplessness after murder. Today a strong sedative would wipe out those tormenting thoughts disturbing her good night's rest. If sleep can be obtained by chemical means (without the old-time necessity of having a good conscience) why not rapture, ecstacy, even illumination—and that too, without moral or spiritual effort? C. G. Jung has even hinted darkly that what we so reverently look up to as Grace need not be the grace of God at all but rather the co-operation of the unconscious mind; 'the self-liberating power of the introverted mind'.[2] Huxley often takes Jung for granted. The purely rational explanation of the universe is incomplete for both. There is an inner world yet to be explored. To get there, Huxley examines three means: mescalin, LSD and hypnosis. According to him the last is not the best of the three. Mescalin is supposed to reduce the efficiency of the brain and thus permit the exploration of inner space. Very important in this connection is Huxley's lengthy quotation from C. D. Broad:

'. . . we should do well to consider much more seriously than we have hitherto been inclined to do the type of theory which Bergson put forward in connection with memory and sense perception. The suggestion is that the function of the brain and nervous system and sense organs is in the main *eliminative* and not productive. Each person is at each moment capable of remembering all that has ever happened to him and of perceiving everything that is happening everywhere in the universe. The function of the

---

[1] *Ascent of Mount Carmel*, I, 5, 2.

[2] Psychological Commentary in *The Tibetan Book of the Great Liberation*, ed. by Evans-Wentz, London, 1954, p. xxxviii.

brain and nervous system is to protect us from being overwhelmed and confused by this mass of largely useless and irrelevant knowledge, by shutting out most of what we should otherwise perceive or remember at any moment, and leaving only the very small and special section which is likely to be practically useful.'[1]

Assuming for a moment that this is correct, we can guess how mescalin produces those mystic effects, specially that *sine qua non* of all mystic experience: timelessness. If the function of the brain is indeed eliminative and if mescalin disturbs brain-functioning, then the removal of such an eliminative function would result in apparently heightened cognitive abilities. In the ordinary process of cognition, time always flows forward for all beings and for the processes in which beings or even particles of matter are involved. If a radioactive atom splits up into subatomic particles, the particles never unite to reform the original atom. Like an unwinding clock the cosmos radiates its energy and expands. Yet everything in the universe is subject to the laws of polarity. Eastern wisdom says that if the conscious mind registers time only in the forward direction, there must be, embedded in our subconscious mind, an arrangement that registers time in a chronologically reverse direction. For instance, the drowning swimmer who sees his life pass by in review sees it from the moment of drowning backwards to youth, childhood and infancy. The intersecting of these two contrary orders of time can result in a feeling of being outside time. Huxley's explanation is built on Jung's theory of the unconscious. Jung explains Grace (the grace of God) as something which always appears to come as if from outside because it comes from a realm lying outside the conscious. It comes suddenly and unexpectedly, for what we call Grace means, according to Jung, that the subconscious is temporarily refraining from its habitual opposition to the conscious. Now suppose that mescalin or LSD or any other chemical has the effect of reducing or numbing this habitual opposition of the subconscious. The resulting conciliatory attitude of the subconscious will then mean (on the Jung–Huxley line of reasoning) that Grace has been produced synthetically. For what is Grace other than the conquest of the arbitrary and capricious opposition of the subconscious? Do we not see examples of the synthetic, if not divine, grace-of-alcohol giving millions a consolation without which they would not care to live? And tobacco? And opium? Do not the severest physical pains yield to the synthetic mercy of morphia? The mistake lies in attributing to alcohol, morphia or mescalin an efficiency which is only ancillary to them. The reason why any substance can influence the mind lies in the purely mentally formed structure of what, when cognized, is called the external world.

The title of Huxley's book is taken from Blake's:

'If the doors of perception were cleansed, every thing will appear to man as it is, infinite.'

[1] *The Doors of Perception*, p. 16.

As there is nothing infinite in the external world, the w
refer only to the mind. Everything would appear infinite,
because the cognizing mind itself is infinite; the mind not o
lends a portion of its own reality to the external world so tha
appears to be even more real than the mind itself. (Just as t
film appear more real than the invisible screen which makes t____ ___g of
the film possible.) Indeed, as the Tibetan sages say, the *Trikāya*, the three
mythical bodies of the Buddha, is the all-enlightened mind itself! The
Buddha was right in attributing the failure of mankind to attain *nirvāṇa* to
an ignorance of the original and essential nature of mind. This essential
nature of our own mind may be called Mind-in-itself.

What one calls mind is the sum total of all thoughts put together; mind-
in-itself does not mean this totality of thoughts but the metaphysical
source from which they originate. Huxley calls it 'Mind at Large':

'The various other worlds with which human beings erratically make
contact are so many elements in the totality of the awareness belonging to
Mind at Large.'[1]

This Mind at Large (which I prefer to call Mind-in-itself) is constantly
broadcasting a plethora of thoughts which are picked up by individual
minds acting like receiver sets. Through the variation in awareness and
intensity of the receiving minds this stream of cosmic images is particular-
ized according to the situation into a partial and specified process of
cognition. Why do we not know mind in its essence, in itself? Because we
are always thinking of something in particular. Thoughts bar us from the
source of all thoughts. That is why thinking cannot solve the ultimate
mysteries of the universe. To get at the source we need a method which
bypasses thinking. *The Cloud of Unknowing* recommends not-thinking as
the best form of meditation. This cloud of unknowing means a process of
stopping thoughts without losing hold of waking consciousness. *The Cloud
of Unknowing* is the best treatise on Eastern wisdom ever written west of
Suez and east of San Francisco. This process of stopping the arising of
thoughts can, however, be made easy or more difficult through certain outside aids. Rhythmical breathing, fasting, even mescalin can be a help—
which is not the same as saying they *cause* the mystic's illumination. A
physiological process that enables mind to become an undisturbed reflector
of Mind-in-itself does not *per se* degrade or discredit the spiritual significance of mystic illumination. Nowhere is it suggested, not even by
Huxley, that mescalin or LSD can give us illumination, let alone Enlightenment. The most that we are promised is a galaxy of visions. No amount of
these, whether synthetically or mystically induced, can make up for
Enlightenment. Ramakrishna, the greatest mystic visionary of his day, was
not allowed to rest by his master Totapuri, until he had got beyond seeing
visions of the Cosmic Mother. Even the most lofty visions belong to the
world of phenomena and are, as such, inferior to the Enlightenment which

[1] *Ibid.*, p. 17.

ᴀᴇs place at the level of Mind-in-itself. It is wrong, however, to accuse Huxley of making this error. He knew better than his critics that:

'Visionary experience is not the same as mystical experience. Mystical experience is beyond the realm of opposites. Visionary experience is still within that realm. Heaven entails hell, and "going to heaven" is no more liberation than is the descent into horror. Heaven is merely a vantage point from which the divine Ground can be more clearly seen than on the level of ordinary individualized existence.'[1]

Again:

'I am not so foolish as to equate what happens under the influence of mescalin or of any other drug, prepared or in the future preparable, with the realization of the end and ultimate purpose of all human life: Enlightenment, the Beatific Vision.'[2]

Righteous indignation so often clouds reason that some critics are prevented from giving Huxley's thesis a fair hearing. No doubt visions are not a substitute for illumination (final emancipation accompanied by the peace that passes understanding) or Enlightenment (final emancipation accompanied by such peace *and* insight into Ultimate Reality equals wisdom). For the sage seeking Enlightenment, mystic visions can be an annoying source of hindrance. Huxley's point, however, is that the vast majority of us are not sages seeking Enlightenment and obstructed in this pursuit by visions, but woeful beginners so lost in materialism that the merest fragment of anything even approaching vision, would be a tremendous encouragement for us to strive further on the spiritual path. It is to the latter class that Huxley's mescalin promise is held out. What is hindrance to a sage can mean an incentive for a poor beginner just trying to get out of the rut of daily routine.

'For a person in whom the candle of vision never burns spontaneously, the mescalin experience is doubly illuminating. It throws light on the hitherto unknown regions of his own mind; and at the same time it throws light, indirectly, on other minds, more richly gifted in respect to vision than his own.'

The Mescalin Experiment is the last phase of Huxley's spiral evolution as a great writer. Asceticism, he wants to say, is not necessary; it is only needlessly painful.

'When they [old-time ascetic-mystics] were not starving themselves into low blood sugar and a vitamin deficiency, or beating themselves into

---

[1] *Heaven and Hell*, p. 52.
[2] *The Doors of Perception*, p. 58.

intoxication by histamine, adrenalin and decomposed protein, they were cultivating insomnia and praying for long periods in uncomfortable positions, in order to create the psycho-chemical symptoms of stress. . . . Today we know how to lower the efficiency of the cerebral reducing valve by direct chemical action, and without the risk of inflicting serious damage on the psycho-physical organism.'[1]

In asceticism he saw only a means for altering body chemistry. The weakened physical condition reduces the efficiency of the valve regulating cerebral activity; the previously restrained contents burst upon the mind in the form of heightened perceptivity. Is that true? The Buddha, we are told, fasted till he became a mere skeleton without obtaining either visions or Enlightenment. This compelled him to resume a normal diet in order to continue his quest for *nirvāṇa*. More or less the same occurred to the Tibetan hermit Milarepa. Asceticism does not lead to Enlightenment and visions are a tricky business at best. Thus the Buddha, in keeping with the tradition of Eastern wisdom, *condemned* asceticism as being hedonism in disguise. Body chemistry is not all. Nor does asceticism consist solely of physical pain and discomfort. The mystic seeks to cultivate humility, which is the only chemical that will dissolve the ego. If the ego is the main obstacle to Enlightenment, a mere change in body chemistry will not eliminate or sublimate it. Unless we can produce drugs that make us humble, synthetic grace will not suffice. The function of grace is to demolish the ego.

The price of freedom is Enlightenment. Grace makes Enlightenment possible. Humility enables us to become fit recipients of grace. Suffering and self-control teach us humility. How is it even possible to profit from the lessons of suffering if we allow ourselves such chemical lost week-ends on the sly? Huxley himself was aware of this problem:

'Reflect that we all have our Poonas (Poona, a city in India renowned for its huge lunatic asylum). Bolt-holes from unpleasant reality. The danger, as Miller is always insisting, of meditation becoming such a bolt-hole. Quietism can be mere self-indulgence. Charismata-like masturbations. Masturbations, however, that are dignified, by the amateur mystics who practise them, with all the sacred names of religion and philosophy.'[2]

What one critic wrote of Huxley's career as a novelist has perhaps a grain of truth in it:

'So long as Huxley confines himself to the task of a collector he is interesting, though even here one suspects a good deal of "reading into". But when he tries to classify or dogmatize he becomes at once feeble and is in a hurry to gloss over.'[3]

[1] *Heaven and Hell*, p. 64.
[2] *Eyeless in Gaza*, London, 1936.
[3] Sisirkumar Ghose, *Aldous Huxley: cynical salvationist*, Asia Publishing House, London, 1962, p. 174.

M

Yet it would be going too far to say:

'... it has become increasingly clear that Huxley's inability to develop characters and situations and his failure to dramatize his ideas in fictional terms have diminished his stature as a serious novelist, even though his ideas, while not profound or wholly original, are sufficient for work of greater literary quality than he has given us.'[1]

Jocelyn Brooke has probably come to the most balanced judgment on Huxley:

'One can say, then, that he has progressed from a purely aesthetic, through a politico-ethical to a predominantly religious point of view. This, of course, is a drastic simplification: in reality, his development has been far more complex—for ... most of the beliefs he has embraced in his maturity are in fact latent in his earliest published works.'[2]

The real Aldous Huxley was a genuine representative of that illustrious family and was, as the Huxleys so often are, a genius. Yet he died a saint. Anyone who seeks God or the Ground of Being (or however we wish to put it) with such single-minded devotion, as in the last phase of his life Aldous did, is in death united with Him or It—so says Eastern wisdom.[3] This brings us to the question: what is God or the Ground of Being? Are they just words? Perhaps just

'... a noise such as a man might make involuntarily, feeling the nail go through his hands into the wood.'[4]

For contemporary theologians, the concept of God has begun to fade.[5] Anglican bishops have tried to redefine God as the Ground of Being.[6] In keeping with Greek tradition, medieval scholastics defined God as subsisting Being itself, and thus a supreme Creator whose essence was identical with his existence.[7] Modern philosophy limits the word Being to cognizable or created things.[8] God is becoming more and more the symbol for an outdated supernatural idol.[9] Even the church has betrayed, by silence, this reality-beyond-being it should serve and preach. Christianity, if it is to survive, will have to incorporate portions of Eastern wisdom into its teachings. Till now the attitude of the church to any wisdom except its

[1] Karl Magalanar, *A Reader's Guide to Great XX-Century English Novels*, New York, 1960, p. 284.

[2] Jocelyn Brooke, *Aldous Huxley*, London, 1954, p. 9.

[3] For instance, the *Gītā*, VIII, 5–7.

[4] Ernest Hemingway, *The Old Man and the Sea*.

[5] See also T. F. Torrance, *Theology in Reconstruction*, London, 1965.

[6] Cp. Leslie Dewart, *The Future of Belief*, Herder & Herder (U.S.A.), 1966.

[7] Cp. J. V. Langmead Casserley, *Toward a Theology of History*, London, 1965.

[8] Cp. L. Addis and D. Lewis, *Moore and Ryle: Two Ontologists*, Iowa (U.S.A.), 1965

[9] Cp. Ervin Laszlo, *Beyond Scepticism and Realism*, The Hague, 1966.

own has been one of arrogant apartheid.[1] Eastern wisdom is in a good position to deal with the atheistic arguments of our time. It had heard all this even before the Buddha was born.

Our present-day atheists do not use arguments very different from those of the *Cārvāka* Materialists of the pre-Buddhist era.

Even if there be no God as a world cause there is still a hidden, mysterious factor in world events. This factor explains the occasional causes that are knowable through their occurrence as inconceivably marvellous effects; indeed from it world events draw the substance of their *potenz* to occur at a given time in the flow of what we call history.[2] Even Marxism has its God; it is the inexorable Will of that history.[3] The name God, which embraces everything mysterious and miraculous, is intended to indicate just that mysterious and miraculous factor.

Can mysticism define this God more closely? It can. We need only call to mind in what way that occasional cause, from which our own astonishingly complicated and technically perfect organism has originated, namely the fertilized cell in our mother's womb, obtained its causality. It was by our grasping and clinging to this seed in our unfathomable inner nature. If no grasping, no clinging had arisen, this fertilized seed would have again been swept away without a trace. Consequently, our own essential and inner nature is that mysterious factor in world events from which they draw their entire substance, at any rate in so far as we are concerned. But then there is no longer any need for lengthy statements that underlying everything there is a mysterious inner essence which is concealed behind the mask of all visible phenomena as its attribute; and from which that attribute radiates like light from the solar body that eludes our perception. For example, underlying fire there is this unknowable inner essence which, due to a pressing desire, seizes the fuel; and then the fire *reveals* itself in the fuel. Therefore, if the *underlying essence* of fire were capable of knowing, it too would be bound to recognize the fire as a mere attribute of itself, since it would be forced to say: 'I am *not* this, this is *not* my Self; I have merely seized the fuel, and in it bring forth the phenomenon of fire.'

Thus it is quite definite that our world is not the entire world; it is merely the *phenomenal* world; and opposed to it is the world's unknowable *inner essence* from which the energies and forces conditioning world events and everything rational in them have sprung.

The concept of God in its proper sense indicates that which first endows the knowable occasional causes with their causality, and in which, for that reason, there already lies the possibility of the phenomenal world. The mystic's concept of God is the unknowable, mysterious *essence-in-itself* of the cosmos. This is the foundation of the phenomenal world, and hence in this sense the *ground of Being*.

Thus the mystic can exclaim like Sister Catherine to Meister Eckhart:

[1] Cp. Ernest Best, *The Temptation and the Passion*, Cambridge, 1965.

[2] Cp. Kees W. Bolle, *The Persistence of Religion*, Leiden, 1965.

[3] Cp. Josepf P. Fell, *Emotion in the Thought of Sartre*, Columbia University Press, 1965.

'Rejoice, Lord, I have become God!'

This means simply that, as soon as we withdraw into our real Self by seeing through our entire personality as a mere sorrow-bringing attribute of ourselves, we recognize that our nature is similar to that of the Ground of Being. We are of the same stuff that God is made of. That is the standpoint of monistic Mysticism. In this way, the concept of God becomes immensely more profound; there can no longer be any talk of an almighty personality, of a person who could be addressed as God, and thus of an extramundane personal God. On the contrary, the true content of the concept of God is the world ground, but this is the kernel and essence of the world itself, the embodiment and quintessence of the *essential nature* of all things. The mystic who has delved so deeply will, therefore, drop the concept of God in which the personal element appears to be intimately associated. If he is still unwilling to dispense entirely with the concept of God, he will at first substitute for it the concept of the impersonal *deity*. It is the favourite description of the mystics, for they use it to describe the world ground to which they attained by withdrawing into their own essence; first by hard asceticism, then by poor and scanty feeding, and in particular through perfect chastity, they assuaged their appetites and desires until it was easy for them to become the pure spirit that could dispose of the phenomenal world, including every recollection thereof. Can one achieve this through mescalin or LSD? In a certain sense, yes; but on the whole, no. Through mortification the mystics experienced something quite singular and strange: *nothingness*. For what else could present itself to cognition beyond the phenomenal world that alone is knowable? They no longer perceived even themselves; for pure spirit that is detached from the grossly material body is imperceptible. But this nothingness in which they floated was peculiar; for the spirit 'which had slipped from time' and 'withdrawn into eternity' had indeed experienced this 'nothingness with its profound silence', that 'complete calm and void above time and space'. It had experienced this 'groundless abyss', the 'non-existent being', in which all 'figure and form' is extinguished, and that 'which causes the soul full of joy and bliss to flow from itself'. Not only did Meister Eckhart, from whom the above passages are quoted, contemplate thus but also all mystics who have attained to these heights. Hence the statement *Sensuum occasus veritatis exortus est* (the decline of the senses is the dawn of truth). The ancient sages of the *Vedas* had similar visions. All mystic knowledge consists of intuitive perception and reflection. After the seers had returned to the material world, their reflection was bound to manifest itself in the 'intuitively perceived marvel'. It is an abyss in which 'the soul for ever sinks and yet can never reach the bottom', and in which it feels unutterable bliss. What could this abyss be except its *abode*, that realm in which it is *rooted*? What could that 'complete calm and void' be, looming behind the conditioned and accidental of the phenomenal world, if not the counterpart to that phenomenal world, the domain of the kernel and essence, and thus of the unconditioned and immovable Ground of Being? The intuitively perceived marvel was recognized by the Indian genius as that domain of the *kernel and essence* from which the phenomenal world emerges, like land formed from the ocean. Thus it became the 'all-active, all-desiring, all-fragrant, all-seeing, all-embracing, silent, unconcerned: This is *Brahman* [the Vedic equivalent of the impersonal deity] in whom the world has its only nest.' Meister Eckhart was also clear that he had become quite 'torpid and numb' in the marvel, had come under the spell of the 'boundless and inexpressible essence', and that he had thus found the 'secret approach to God' who 'dwells in a silence beyond all silence'. And so he never wearied of extolling and glorifying, as 'the true vision of the divine mirror', the 'pure nothingness' in which a mystic finds himself when in that state.

'There then comes forth the pure and clear spring of the tincture of grace which illuminates the inner eye, so that in a blissful vision it experiences the supreme delight of the divine visitation.'

'It arose and shone forth to me that it wished to reveal something to me, and gave me tidings of God.'

The concept of an *impersonal* God is (as in the *Vedas* and Meister Eckhart) the mystic's description for the Ground. In the first place, there is the element of spirituality which all mystics associate with it. From their point of view this could not possibly be otherwise; for all mystics, from the ancient sages of the *Vedas* to Meister Eckhart, had recognized themselves, from the heights they attained, to be pure spirit. Since our essence is identical with that of the Ground,[1] they suffused with the semblance of their own spirituality the domain of the Ground which they had entered, and then showed how it consisted of pure formless spirituality.

A second element in the mystic's concept of the deity is that of the only one; indeed this element of the one is regarded by all mystics as a self-evident attribute of the deity, and hence of the Ground. Even Plotinus, the great Neo-platonist, who expressly withdraws from the ONE not only the will (*boulesis*) and every activity (*energeia*), but also all spirituality because it is superior even to these qualities, still calls it the *ἐν*, the ONE, although more in the sense that it excludes from itself and denies all plurality.

Our phenomenal world, and with it our thought and speech, do not contain a single element which could be used to define or construct the essence and kernel of the world, of the Ground, and so we cannot attribute to this even the predicate of unity. This is because the essential world Ground is only the quintessence of the kernel of phenomenal things. Therefore, whoever maintains the unity of this Ground, thereby asserts that all things have the same essence, are essentially one. Naturally, one cannot assert that the kernel or essence of the phenomenal world is something in itself distinct or different. 'The essential nature of things before or beyond

[1] Cp. Eckhart: 'Whoever will fathom the miracle of God draws his stock of knowledge from himself.'

the world is not open to any investigator.'[1] Indeed this is what mystics mean when they say that the kernel or essence and its possible relations are transcendent.

In conceiving the world essence as the ONE, it induced mystics to conceive the return to the essential kernel as a self-dissolution or as a flowing away into the deity in the form of a union with it (unio mystica).

'Whoever knows this, is without craving, of stilled craving, free from craving, is himself his craving; for he is Brahman, and melts and dissolves into Brahman,' proclaims the Vedic saint.

'Escape from all you possibly can; slip wholly into his inmost calm; what first was by itself, he there you here, now forms into the united We. Where you, now he, see him with eternal mind, a nameless nothing, an Am not yet become,' as Meister Eckhart exclaims in mystic ecstacy. The final words of Plotinus, who according to his statement awoke to himself from his body even during his lifetime, were that he wanted to unite the divine within himself with the divine in the universe.

Thus all mystics represent the essential kernel of the world as an ocean into which beings sink back are dissolved, and flow away. But whoever has recognized that the world's essential kernel rises above even the concept of unity, in that it is completely inaccessible to our knowledge, will guard against describing that absolutely transcendent realm in words which are drawn from the phenomenal world and thus have meaning only for that world.

> Om Amitaya! Measure not in words
> The immeasurable! Rise not with thoughts to the inscrutable.

The realm of the unoriginated is, according to mysticism, the realm of the essential. In the first place, there is concealed in it our own essential kernel; for it arises precisely through our withdrawing ourselves from the phenomenal world into our real essential nature. 'Those who imagine the essential (sāra) to be in the non-essential (asāra), and see the non-essential in the essential do not arrive at the essential but follow vain imaginings. But they who know the essential and the non-essential, reach the essential element.'[2] 'Not in the attributes do we arrive at the essential element: na so upadhīsu sāram eti.'[3]

What is the world's essential kernel? All our concepts are valid within the phenomenal world; indeed only there have they any meaning. Thus they can never have transcendent value. The realm where the essential kernel of the cosmos lies must be transcendent. Nothing whatever can be ascertained about it except its mere actuality since in the kernel of our essential nature, we are never touched by the decline and end of the entire phenomenal world. Thus no positive concept is any longer valid for that realm: 'I shall go to that which is immovable and unshakeable, and

---

[1] Schopenhauer.
[2] Dhammapada, 11 u. 12
[3] Suttanipāta, v. 364.

to which there is nowhere any likeness.'[1] Not even the concept of the Absolute is wholly conclusive. Nevertheless it is the most appropriate concept with a positive element, in that it expresses what is detached from, and therefore unconditioned by, all expressions, conditions and limitations. But it also misleads one into conceiving this unconditioned something as a unity. Only a thoroughly negative concept would be perfectly adequate, since the essential kernel of the world appears to our cognition, for which the phenomenal world is the only positive thing, as something thoroughly negative. Such a negative concept can be drawn only from those events in which there is a withdrawal from the phenomenal world to the essential kernel. The most striking and obvious event of this nature is a fire that goes out. If the fuel is used up, the fire *is extinguished*; in other words, the inscrutable something, rid of its attribute, again withdraws into its primary and unknowable state. The Christian mystic, Meister Eckhart, recognized this, as is clear from his words:

'Where fire is within its true nature, it burns not and causes no harm. Only the heat flowing from the fire burns here below. Yet where the heat is still contained in the nature of the fire, it burns not and is harmless. And yet where it is still contained in the fire, it is as remote from the true nature of the fire as heaven is from earth.'[2]

This idea is chacteristic of the mysticism of the *Upaniṣads*.

'*Brahman* [the essential kernel lying beyond the phenomenal world] is by its nature pure thought, comparable to *fire after it has used up the fuel.*'

'Just as when the principle of fire has returned to its source, it continues to exist invisible according to its nature, and flares up afresh from the source [new fuel]; so does he become extinguished.'

This describes the return into the world's essential kernel by using the analogy of a fire going out.

'The perfectly redeemed is like the fire [*aggi va gacchati*] that has gone out; *he is extinguished.*'[3]

'The sages are extinguished like the lamp [*nibbanti dhīrā yatha yam padīpo*].'[4]

This, like the other frequently used expression 'the *nibbāna* of a lamp' (*pajjatassa nibbānam*), shows that, at the time of the Buddha, men were generally aware that this extinction had nothing to do with annihilation. The lamp itself remains wholly untouched by its extinction. On the con-

---

[1] *Ibid.*, v. 1149.
[2] *Meister Eckharts Schriften und Predigten*, by Hermann Büttner, Vol. I, p. 7 f
[3] *Dhammapāda*, 31.
[4] *Suttanipāta*, v. 235.

trary the extinction of a saint meant simply the casting off of the burning attribute of personality which incessantly disturbs and troubles the mystic. This is confirmed by the other expressions with which this extinction is frequently paralleled by Buddhist saints:

'Where perception and sensation have come to be abolished, those *continue to live* who have brought perception and sensation to an end, and are the venerable saints *no longer hungry*: they are extinguished, have escaped, *have reached the other shore.*'[1]

Accordingly, even in his lifetime, the Buddha was addressed by Kakudha:

'Indeed I see a Brahman *who for long has been perfectly extinguished*, a mendicant without joy or sorrow who has overcome a clinging to the world.'[2]

'Full of peace am I, extinguished [*nibbuto*] am I.'

'I am detached, full of peace, extinguished.'[3]

'I have become cool, extinguished.'[4]

'Revere the great lords, the perfectly extinguished.'

Indeed in the *Majjhima Nikāya* even a horse, which has lost its wild impulse through being broken in, is repeatedly mentioned as being perfectly extinguished (*parinibbuto*).

And so the Buddha describes the realm of the essential kernel as the *nirvāṇa* principle (*nibbāna-dhātu*), or briefly *nirvāṇa*; the realm of extinction in which everything *knowable* is extinguished.

This significance of *nirvāṇa* as the world's essential kernel finds expression in the passages:

'*Nirvāṇa* is the supreme essence [*para matthasāro nibbānam*].'

'What are the things that have not become? *Nirvāṇa*: this is amongst the things that have not become (in so far as they have not come into existence, and hence remain their essential kernel).'

'A Perfect One is extinguished into this principle of *nirvāṇa* that is free from all attributes [*Tathāgato anupadisesāya nibbānadhātuya parinibbāyati*].'

By expressing himself thus, the Buddha describes perfectly the mystic Ground of Being and the sage's withdrawal thereto. By describing the

[1] *The Book of Nines*, Nr. 33.
[2] *Samyutta Nikaya.*
[3] *Therīgāthā*, v. 66, 86.
[4] *Ibid.*, 76.

withdrawal from the phenomenal world into the unknowable essential kernel as an extinction, no scope is given for conclusions concerning the state of perfect extinction; neither the assumption that it flows into a unity with the world's essential kernel, nor that it retains its individuality therein. Therefore the Buddha says elsewhere that the perfect ones who have died are submerged in deathlessness; like a stone cast into the sea, of which we cannot say that it is part of the sea nor that it retains its individuality apart from it. In the realm of *nirvāṇa* there reigns the Great Peace, eternal calm, and unshakeable bliss. But how can peace reign, if *nirvāṇa* is the essential kernel of the world? The mystics have solved this difficulty. The Vedānta distinguishes between the visible and the invisible Brahman. In the former sense, Brahman is the principle that brings forth and shapes the world, in the latter, the primordial essence 'free from good and bad, free from happening and not happening, free from past and future', into which everything can again return. Accordingly, it is also called: 'The kingdom, the highest, the hidden, three quarters of which lie in secret, while there is one quarter about which men speak.' The redeemed returns home into the secret invisible Brahman. 'To the bustle and turmoil of this world I shall belong only until I am redeemed, whereupon I shall go home.'

In a similar way, Meister Eckhart with his 'deity' also distinguishes between the essence and its realization.

'The essence designates the Deity in the narrower sense and is the first thing that we apprehend in God. Accordingly, it is itself immutable harmony and a hovering silence, and yet at the same time a fountain-head of separation and singularity.'

'God, as he is in himself, has essence, and the essence dwells in unrevealed silence. Therefore it is an immovable: it speaks not, it loves not, it does not bring forth, and yet it moves the movable.'

The ego, being grounded in the deity, naturally takes part in *both* states, and finally again withdraws from separation, the immovable, into the 'hovering silence of the Deity in itself which is free from and rid of all activity'.

'In this unity of the divine essence the father has never had any knowledge of a son, or the son of a father; for there is neither father, son, nor Holy Ghost.'

'Test it, noble soul, with this splendour and majesty! Of course, so long as thou dost not drown thyself in this groundless ocean of the Deity, thou canst not come to know him, this divine death.'

The Buddha's method of presentation is somewhat different. He does not speak of the world's essential kernel in its activity as such, and hence in the sense in which the Vedānta speaks of the world-creating Brahman and Meister Eckhart of the realization of the essence of his deity; for to this extent they assumed, or indeed merely imagined, a single, harmonious, spiritual, primordial being which becomes active. On the other hand, the Buddha speaks of the only knowable fact that, in any case, the phenomenal world (*papañca*) is *not* our real and essential kernel; that it exists for us because we cling to it. Those who do not so cling, who therefore no longer have any attributes, and who thus withdraw into the essential kernel, are no longer touched by the restlessness of the phenomenal world, and so pass over into the eternal silence, into the Great Peace. This can be made clear by the following analogy. Our living rooms are pervaded day and night by lectures, talks, concerts, and plays in the form of electrical oscillations transmitted by different broadcasting stations, which in no way disturb our peace; indeed, they do not even exist for us. Only when we install a receiving set and an aerial do we become conscious of this whole world of sights and sounds which encircles us. On the other hand, it vanishes completely the moment we switch off the set. In a similar manner, our sense-organs, as an *apparatus* of cognition, convey to us the entire phenomenal world. The mystic who has discarded for ever this apparatus of cognition has also withdrawn for ever from the influence of the phenomenal world, and, although this continues to exist, he enjoys for all time supreme peace.

The mystics are so called not because their path is mystical, not further communicable, but because they claim to have reached the primary mystery, the mystery of the world; they first of all perceived the miracle, and then recognized it as the magic circle of the world's essential kernel to which they gave names familiar to them, such as Brahman, God, Deity. The Buddha went the opposite way. First of all he made it clear that our own essential kernel lies beyond the phenomenal world, and thus beyond all knowledge in general. Then in the realization of this knowledge, he inwardly detached himself from this entire phenomenal world that alone is knowable, and in particular from the whole of his personality.

'There is, mendicants, that realm where neither earth nor water exists, neither fire nor air, neither the infinite province of space nor the infinite province of consciousness, neither this world nor another, neither moon nor sun. This, mendicants, I call neither coming nor going, neither arising nor passing away; without point of support or basis is this. Just this is the end of suffering.'

'There is, mendicants, a not-born, not-become, not-created, not-originated. If, mendicants, there were not this not-born, not-become, not-created, not-originated, then here it would be impossible to discern an escape from the born, the become, the created, and the originated.'

Transcendental mysticism or *Transparenz* (reintegration through methodical self-inquiry) is the essence of the way to integral consciousness; and the question 'Who (or rather *what*) am I?' is indispensable to it.[1] So important is this question that it is also the title of one of the very few books written by the sage and mystic of Arunachala. *Who am I? (and Self-knowledge)* consists of instructions issued in writing by Sri Ramana Maharshi during the years 1901 and 1902.[2] It is the most authoritative classic on the method of *jñāna*—a gem of transcendental mysticism equal to the Vedas and Upanishads. Why is this question 'Who am I?' so very important? For that we must examine three main points and three sub-points made by the Maharshi:

1. The first and foremost of all the thoughts that arise in the mind is the primal 'I'-thought. It is only after the rise or origin of the 'I'-thought that innumerable other thoughts arise.
   (*a*) *Therefore:*
   Every other thought can arise only *after* the rise of the 'I'-thought.
2. What one calls the mind, meaning the intellect or thinking apparatus, is a *śakti* (attribute or unique power) of the Ātman (*Self*), whereby thoughts occur to one. On examining what remains after eliminating all thoughts, it will be found that there is no such thing as mind apart from thoughts. So thoughts themselves constitute the mind.
   (*b*) *Therefore:*
   The mind is nothing but a composition composed of thoughts.
3. Unless the illusory perception of a serpent (seen in a piece of rope) ceases, the rope on which the illusion is formed is not perceived as such. Even so, unless the illusory nature of the perception of the world as an objective reality ceases, there is no realization of the true nature of the *Real Self*, on which the illusion is formed.
   (*c*) *Therefore:*
   The world is perceived as an apparent objective reality when the mind is externalized, *thereby* forsaking its identity with the *Self*. When the world is thus perceived, the true nature of the *Self* is not revealed. In other words, mystic Enlightenment is obstructed and so does not take place.

Conversely, when the *Self* is realized the world ceases to appear as an objective reality. Putting (*a*)+(*b*)+(*c*) together we conclude:
  Since every other thought can occur only after the rise of the 'I'-thought and since the mind is merely a composition of thoughts, it is only through the enquiry 'Who am I?' that the mind subsides perfectly.
  Moreover, the integral 'I'-thought, implicit in this enquiry, having

[1] On the Continent *Transparenz* is a word often used to distinguish mysticism of the serious kind (a rise to integral consciousness; supra-rational) from emotionalism, obscurantism, mystification and the like (a relapse into the subconscious; irrational). The word was coined by Jean Gebser, whose theory it is that in the highest stage of integral consciousness the whole world becomes as if transparent. Then there is no other, no not-self. The *Self* is alone with the *Self*.

[2] Arthur Osborne, *The Collected Works of Ramana Maharshi*, Rider & Co., London, 1959, pp. 39–48.

destroyed all other thoughts, is finally destroyed or consumed. Since there are now no thoughts, there is also no mind; hence the world ceases to appear as an objective reality and the Great Enlightenment becomes an accomplished fact.

In dealing with existentialism we saw how, sooner or later, ontological necessity drives each and every individual to ask the question: Who *am* I? At once the problem arises: to whom is this question to be put and how does one ask it? Eastern mysticism says:

'Put the question to whatever you consider to be your self and then try to *feel* your way through to the *source* from where your idea of 'I' seems to spring up. After some time whose length may vary from minutes in one case to decades in another, the answer will dawn on you.'

That is *jñāna*, the way of self-analysis through discrimination and dispassion, stripped to its barest essentials. All the rest of the Maharshi's message is an explanation, elaboration, elucidation, and what is most important, self-experimentation and actual realization of what has been said before.

Such is the principle, speaking very generally, on which the mysticism of the East operates. If one finds its practice too difficult, one can step down to a relatively less strenuous type of effort.

If the mystic would only cultivate the constant, deep contemplative, and repeated recollection (or remembrance) of the true nature of the *Self* until he has realized it, that alone would suffice. This method is called *abhyasa* and we also find it applied by Christian mystics for whom Christ represents the *Real Self*. For instance, we read in Brother Lawrence's *Practice of the Presence of God*: 'the least little remembrance will always be acceptable' (7th Letter). 'And being accustomed to think of Him often, you will find it easy to keep your mind calm' (8th Letter). 'We must often think of Him, and when we come to love Him, we shall then *also think of Him* often. . . .' (9th Letter). Even the *Gītā* says: 'Therefore at all times *remember* Me as the *Real Self*' (*tasmāt sarveṣu kāleṣu māmanusmara*).[1]

What the mystic must grasp is that this world or creation, being of the nature of phenomena, is, at least for the perceiver, nothing but a stream of thoughts. Thus the phenomenal world recedes from one's view as soon as one is free from thoughts. If at this stage consciousness has not also receded, then the mind is replaced by a fully awakened awareness of the *Self*, accompanied by a state which is only later describable as bliss. That is the Illumination of the mystics. It, therefore, stands to reason that every time one falls into or awakens from deep sleep, one experiences at the moment between these two states of consciousness, a fractional and fleeting replica of an Illumination. It is this partial and transient Illumination that gives to deep sleep the quality of rest, restoration, and peace which is only afterwards describable as a kind of bliss. A corollary of this is that a full

[1] *Gītā*, VIII, 7.

and permanent Illumination is an irreversible fact.[1] Thus for one who has experienced it, the state of wakefulness, sleep, *samādhi*, or physical death are as undifferentiated as the forward or backward movement of a train, its standing still at a station or being uncoupled from the engine, would be to a traveller fast asleep in it.[2]

It will be seen that though mysticism is predominantly a science, it is also an *art*. The art lies in being able to eliminate thoughts without losing wakeful consciousness. However difficult this may be in normal life, we learn from Tibetan manuscripts that in the moments immediately prior to physical death these technical difficulties are very considerably reduced. There is nothing supernatural about this. We have explained above that every time a change from one major kind of consciousness to another (such as from wakefulness to sleep) takes place, a partial and fleeting quasi-illumination bridges the transition. (Just as the driver of a car disconnects the engine through the clutch every time he changes gear.) Now death is an even more powerful change-over between states of consciousness, so that the intervening quasi-illumination is proportionately longer and less fleeting. Moreover, for physical and psychological reasons, the thoughts of a person about to die slowly still down. He has now only to do the other half and not let go of *waking* consciousness (i.e. not fall asleep or into a stupor) till the moment of physical death. Usually it is at this stage, when Enlightenment is a millionfold easier than otherwise, that the dying man is given a drug or injection to benumb his wakeful consciousness. This is a sad mistake for the opportunity that is lost is, from the mystic point of view, indeed golden. We read in Tibetan texts that just before death the patient should analyse his own mind. His thinking intellect, which is now devoid of particular thoughts, is not to be confused with the voidness of nothingness or with a blank. Indeed, the mystic consciousness in itself is about to dawn. It is a kind of *no-thing-ness* in which there is no thought yet without loss of waking consciousness. It is the intellect itself in its pristine thought-free state; unobstructed by thoughts or the ego, shining, thrilling and blissful. It is consciousness itself, *Turiya-turiyateeta* or the fourth state of consciousness resulting from a person being alive and awake yet without thoughts; the *All Good*, the *Self*. This realization is called the *dharma-kāya* state of perfect enlightenment. A person on the point of dying experiences this effortlessly as 'the Radiance of the Clear Light of Pure Reality'. All he has to do is to *recognize* it as the *Real Self* in a spontaneous, passive way without thinking about it.[3] As Brother Lawrence warns:

'. . . death follows us close, let us be well prepared for it, for we die but once, *and a miscarriage there is irretrievable.*' (4th Letter.)

[1] 'Just as a chicken cannot return into the egg-shell from which it has struggled out, so also one who has attained illumination does not fall back into the stage out of which he has evolved.' *Poems of the Tamil Mystics.*

[2] Cf. Ramana Maharshi's *Supplement* in Osborne's edition of the *Collected Works*, pp. 71–83.

[3] 'A holy inactivity': Brother Lawrence (2nd Letter).

Also the *Gītā*:

'And whoever, at the time of death, gives up his body and departs, think-ing of nothing except *Me* (the *Self*), he comes to My status of being (attains illumination), of that there is no doubt.' (VIII, 5.)

Memento mori! Ancient Indian and European philosophers certainly agreed on one point: philosophy, or love for wisdom, means reflecting on death.[1] Just as every process of dying is accompanied by a kind of replica-illumination so conversely, every process of Illumination is accompanied by a kind of replica-death.[2] That is the esoteric significance of the *purna-shava-āsana*, a kind of meditation on death. Its underlying purpose is to create a state resembling death as nearly as possible in order to bring about a similar state of the quasi-illumination which accompanies death. This is, however, dangerous because to attempt an artificially controlled psychosis can easily result in a real psychosis leading to incurable insanity. Even the safest form of mysticism is risky. In the process of eliminating particular thoughts as they arise, the hold on waking consciousness weakens and wakefulness itself may be eliminated. This results in an exceptionally deep sleep (*yoga-nidrā*) or a self-hypnotic state of lull (*mano-laya*) easily mistaken for genuine illumination. 'Many are called, but few are chosen.'

The mystic should never be misled into thinking that there are two selves in each person; one called the *Real Self*, and the other an ordinary self or the ego.

According to mysticism there is only one Self, and that is not the I but the Christ-consciousness in me (*Real Self*). The ego, being a zero when added to the one *Self* does not make two selves.[3] The difference between zero and one is greater than that between one and any other number because the former difference is not one of degree but of ontological essence. The one can become the many but never a zero, zero cannot add to the one.[4] For instance, we refer to sunlight and moonlight as if they were two but once moonlight has been traced to its source of origin we realize that there are not two self-luminous bodies, Sun and Moon, but only one, the Sun.[5] We understand then that they are not two lights but only one, the real one: sunlight. Yet in everyday life the apparent difference between the two is such that one is tempted to regard it as one of kind rather than of degree.

[1] 'No one really grows up, until he realizes he has to die': Richard Neuberger, U.S. Senator for Oregon.

[2] 'At the moment of death the soul experiences the same impressions as those who are initiated in the great Mysteries': Plutarch.

[3] 'The ego is only a reflection of the Self. If it completely vanishes, the Self remains over as the pure and perfect Reality.' Ramana Maharshi as quoted in *Kavyakantha Ganapati Muni*, VII, 5.

[4] See also *Gītā*, II, 16.

[5] 'The *Hridaya* (Real Self) is to the body as the Sun is to the Universe, the mind in the brain (meaning the thinking intellect or operations of thought) is as the Moon.' Ramana Maharshi as quoted in *Kavyakantha Ganapati Muni*, V, 13.

Again:

Supposing X, who is already married, marries two other women under the bogus names of Y and Z respectively. When this is found out there are not three imposters but one imposter (X) with two aliases. Punishment for bigamy will have to be undergone, not partly by a fictitious Y and partly by a fictitious Z, but only by X—who alone after all was the (relatively speaking) 'real' Y and Z.

Again:

Supposing by twilight I see something resembling a coiled up black cobra. I run away. I later recollect that I had seen there, earlier in the day, a disused bicycle tyre. I presume that the snake was near the tyre. Next morning in clear daylight, I see only the bicycle tyre, which had been left there and resembled a black snake. I am also told that as the place in question is in a cold district there are no snakes. Now, in actual fact, are there two separate independent things, a snake and a tyre, or only one—the tyre? My 'I' as a separate ego by itself is only a case of false identification like the snake that never was in the above example.

Thus to assert that there are two selves in every individual is like a man who believes he has two separate, independent faces every time he sees himself in a dream or in a mirror. In mysticism (rightly understood and correctly expounded as by Huxley and the Maharshi) an individual does not have even one self, let alone two. For the individual does not *have* a Self, he is!—and that *is* (for convenience's sake) is called the *Real Self*. The term is used only to dispel false notions of mistaken identity with other transitory or illusory self-hoods (such as 'my body is myself').

Correctly speaking, therefore, Mysticism does not imply searching for the *Self*, for as one *is* the *Self*, it cannot be something which gets lost or is found, but that one is searching for the *source* of the notion of Self-hood. Our own Self-hood, at all times and independent of everything else, is something uncontradictable and of spontaneous experience. Thus Being-in-itself is one and the same for all, directly experienceable (always in the present tense of the word) as our true-begotten state of origin. All other experiences are alien to our mystic Self-hood and merely grafted on our inborn primordial essence.

All mysticism, like the whole of Eastern wisdom, centres on the difference between the meaning of two words spelt almost alike. They are self (with a small 's') and Self (with a capital 'S'). Indeed the whole of Eastern wisdom is an attempt to explain the difference between these two words; between self and Self. Spell both with a small 's', or both with a capital 'S', and even the *Gītā* is reduced to chaos.[1]

Philosophy tries to understand the root idea by learning the meaning of

[1] Cf. 'The Self is the Lord of the self.' *Dhammapada*, v.160. 'The Self is the goal of the self.' *Ibid.*, v. 380. Also: 'For him who has conquered his self by the Self his Self is a friend but for him who has not possessed his Self, his very Self will act in enmity, like an enemy.' Radhakrishnan, *The Bhagavadgītā*, pp. 189–90.

the technical terms in and through which that root idea is, or has been expressed. This does not show much in the way of results. Mysticism has a far more efficient method. It takes uncritically the root idea for granted *for the time being*, and then describes it in technical terms taken from the personal theology of the mystic. The root idea, once known, no paradoxes remain; symbols become regular and mysticism plain. The root idea is: *the phenomenal world is an obstruction to Enlightenment*.

This root idea is subject to numerous qualifications and devotional terminology will reflect, by the terms used, the qualification to be emphasized. Thus this phenomenal world becomes *Mārā* the devil, the tempter, the Lucifer of Buddhist mysticism.[1] This same *devil* becomes the *Divine Mother* in Ramakrishna's mystic experiences. It also becomes in his parable the Mother who refused to give a penny (Enlightenment) to her child (*jīvā*) until it became unmanageably clamorous. This same devil turns into the wife of God in Ramakrishna's interpretation of the *Ramayana*: Lakman (*jīvā* or the individual) could not see *Rama* (Enlightenment), though the latter was only a few feet away from him, because *Sita* (the phenomenal world) was in the way. In Tantric esotericism this devil instead of being resisted, as in Buddhist mysticism, is thought of as the *feminine* aspect of the Creator,[2] i.e. as God's wife, mother, or sweetheart, and is reverently asked to stand aside (i.e. *requested* not to obstruct any more).[3] One will get lost in this maze and be unable to identify this devil dressed up as the divine wife if one has not fully grasped the root idea that the obstruction in every case is the presence of the phenomenal world. (The obstruction or obstructor need not *necessarily* be wicked.) This is just an illustration to show how the mastery of a single key idea reveals the inner significance of technical terms like *mārā*, *māyā*, *shakti* and a host of others. What is needed, therefore, is not a dictionary of terminology doctored to suit intellectuals but some acquaintance with root ideas—in other words one should also know the root of any frequently occurring theme or idea. Here philosophy and philology are intricately intertwined. Thus, when Pannini said: 'he who knows my Grammar knows God', it was not an empty boast but meant that the terminology of mysticism is philologically constructed of those spiritual and metaphysical ideas which lead to or aim at mystic union.

[1] Indicating that the qualification was putting stress on the obstruction aspect.

[2] The Creator is considered male, his creation female.

[3] This will also explain to the Western reader the meaning of what is meant by worshipping in the heroic aspect. At the lowest exoteric level it tries to sublimate sexual intercourse by assuming that the woman in the act is the feminine aspect (i.e. an obstacle on the way to Enlightenment). She is then requested to step aside and stop obstructing the Light (Enlightenment) in return for being propitiated. This quaint theory and practice can be understood only when one remembers that the phenomenal world is considered as the obstacle (to Enlightenment) on the one hand, whereas, on the other, the phenomenal world, being creation itself, is considered as a sort of coefficient of correlation to the Creator; is thought of as the Creator's feminine aspect. What is important to remember is that the real obstacle in every case is the phenomenal world no matter whether it is called the devil or the sweetheart of God.

The problem of terminology became more important as the belief grew that mysticism would be appreciated and accepted as soon as it was put on a scientific basis, and so in an academic garb! This problem of terminology gave rise to two further difficulties. The desire to present mysticism in a so-called scientific light led to emphasizing those aspects which were likely to win the acceptance of scientific opinion, and to suppressing or skipping over what was likely to become the target of sceptic satire. Thus even scholars tended to take refuge behind the respectability of epistemology, ontology and the like while topics like yoga, reincarnation and so on were relegated to writers of popular books. This led to two different levels of terminology: the strict, exact, academic one and the loose, ambiguous, popular one. But this was not the worst of it. What we wish to stress is that:

1. The *core* of mysticism is unchanging.
2. This core consists of a few major, indispensable root ideas.
3. This collection of root ideas is not a mere mixture; the ideas are intimately interconnected as elements in a chemical compound.
4. All ideas are not equally relevant to the study of mysticism but the absence of a single root idea would upset the balance at the centre, as these root ideas fit into each other like pieces of a jig-saw puzzle.
5. To put these root ideas into a fixed inelastic terminology of an academic-scientific type is a will-o'-the-wisp that has misled many. A less scientific method, and perhaps academically inexcusable, would be first to have a *prima facie* acquaintance with the root ideas. The terminology would then become a self-adjusting mechanism capable even of conducting a controversy over a root idea.

In our days when mysticism both in East and West is often used for worldly if not irreligious ends, the currency of mystic terms and ideas becomes seriously debased. 'Nay, fly to altars, there they'll talk you dead; For fools rush in where Angels fear to tread.'[1]

It is no longer possible to convey the holiness and sanctity inherent in mystic phraseology if it is constantly used for dogmatizing, proselytizing, and missionizing. T. S. Eliot referred to this terminological difficulty, while Heidegger used it as an excuse for refusing to write the third volume of his proposed trilogy. The translating of mystical terminology is not an exact but a very *exacting* science. On the face of it, the *Gītā* advises almost the very opposite of what conventionally ethical people would expect, when it counsels Arjuna to fight against his relatives, even killing them, if necessary.

The esoteric or mystic message of the *Gītā* is sheathed in a large number of carefully selected technical terms. For instance we find *nāsikāgram* mistakenly translated as the *tip* of the nose.[2] It means one end of the nose but everything has two ends, one of which being where it begins or originates. *Nāsikāgram* means the end of a person's nose as seen facing

[1] Pope.
[2] *Gītā*, VI, 13.

N

upwards: in other words the *root* of the nose—the space between the two eye-brows where the seat of the *Ājnā* lotus of *kundalini-yoga* is claimed to be. This interpretation is supported by another verse which mentions 'fixing the gaze between the eyebrows'.[1] To quote Richard Wilhelm's *The Secret of the Golden Flower:*

'When one fixes the thought on the midpoint between the two eyes, the Light streams in of its own accord.'

Then:

'But they [the Buddha and Lao-Tse] did not mean that one should fasten one's thoughts on the end of the nose.'

Again:

'It is only a matter of fixing one's thinking on the point which lies exactly between the two eyes. Then all is well.'[2]

Thus the end of the nose really means the *root* of the nose in the *Gītā* as well as in *The Secret of the Golden Flower*. And this is confirmed in the Bible, the source of all Christian mysticism.[3]

At first sight it seems that far too much importance is paid to which end of the nose is meant. But the answer lies in going back to root ideas. We have said before that in mysticism theory and practice are inseparably bound up. The root idea, therefore, is likely to have a theoretical and a practical counterpart. Philosophy needs to mention both parts. Thus:

Root idea:
(Theoretical counterpart):
Consciousness-in-itself (pure consciousness without thoughts) is the transcendental (ego-exterminated) state *turiyatita*, the fourth state of consciousness.

Root idea:
(Practical counterpart):
  (i) Concentration of thought (mentally) on and (physically) at a fixed point (*dharana*) leads to the desired thought-free state.
  (ii) Concentration *at* a fixed (physical) point enables mental concentration *on* a given point (in other words the mind is fixed unwaveringly on a single thought or idea).
  (iii) The ideal (physical) point to concentrate on is between the eyebrows (*Gītā*, V. 27).

[1] *Ibid.*, V, 27.
[2] Richard Wilhelm, *The Secret of the Golden Flower*, London, 1957, pp. 34–44.
[3] St Luke, xi, 34–5.

Therefore, if *nāsikāgram* means the end of the nose it refers to the root between the eyebrows and not to the tip. Concentration on the root end is supposed to prepare the individual psychophysically for the transcendental state; concentration on the tip would only make him squint.

A deep-seated misunderstanding of technical terms matures into a modern *prejudice* against mysticism and leads to an underestimation of the Christian contribution to spiritual insight. One does *not* have to accept root ideas unchallenged, but one should realize that they exist. After all a chemistry student must analyse many substances in order to advance in his studies. But how can he make a chemical analysis if he does not know the table of all the different elements along with their formulae? Undoubtedly he has to make many experiments and analyses in order to know more of his subject. But he cannot do this unless he knows certain things about his subject beforehand.

The second difficulty arises from technical terms sometimes appearing to mean almost the same thing. But vital consequences lie behind delicate distinctions. These similar but vitally different terms are used interchangeably even by responsible mystics. In a burst of enthusiasm love of God is often termed not *bhakti* or *bhava* but *prema* regardless of the finer shades of meaning that underly these worlds. Undoubtedly a swimming-pool and an ocean both contain water yet is there not a vast difference between them?

The present-day mystic who contributed most to clear up this mess, was Ramakrishna. He adopted the golden rule of starting with root ideas instead of sinking in the mire of terminology. His contribution is of special worth to Western scholars as he invariably defined not by words but by illustrations. Thus all possible errors of translation are reduced almost to zero. Then he gave every technical term its correct atomic weight in terms of philosophical understanding. He is the best antidote against the vagueness which arises by blurting the lines of distinction between two or more technical terms through indiscriminate use. Terminological misinterpretations make the West neglect its own mystic treasures. The Rev. Arthur Peacock says:

There is much evidence to suggest that in the last half-century the approach of Christians to non-Christian religions has undergone a radical change and that today within all folds of the Christian church there are men and women deeply concerned to gain an understanding of religions other than our own. . . . But while it can be shown that Christians have revealed a much more understanding approach to other religions there is less evidence to show that from other religions there comes equally a desire to gain a deeper appreciation of the Christian outlook.'[1]

Only a *mutually* understandable terminology of mysticism can open the eyes of the East to the West and, even more, of the West to the West. For example, thanks to Huxley, we are not only in a position to understand the

[1] *Forum*, September 1958, p. 35.

Gītā but also that Western masterpiece *The Cloud of Unknowing*. By stripping them of their theological technicalities we see that both recommend essentially the same ideas *and even the same practices*. It alway offers greater evidence of a given truth when two independent sources formulated at different times and in different *Weltanschauungen*, submit the same conclusions. This type of terminological rediscovery by the West of its own spiritual treatises will help it to get rid of its inferiority complex caused by the myth that the West is materialistic and the East mystical. By breaking down terminological barriers through penetrating analysis Huxley has helped to make interreligious friendship a practical possibility

Part IV

CONCLUSION

DEATH, IMMORTALITY, REBIRTH AND SALVATION IN THE
LIGHT OF A NEW EAST-WEST SYNTHESIS

CHAPTER 12

The New Synthesis

Using a cybernetic model of society, we might define progress as an increase in the capacity of a social system to receive and process information from within and without the system and to respond appropriately to it.[1]

If the difficulties of a comparative study of Eastern and Western philosophy are many and great, the need for such a cultural exchange today is even greater. This can best be judged by a statement made by the Advisory Committee of Unesco and called *The Guiding Principles of the Orient-Occident Major Project*. A close study of this report is an eye-opener.

The enormous importance given to the question of East-West synthesis by international organizations of a kind not likely to be much interested in philosophy, indicates that no pious wish for a sentimental exchange of cultural ideas is involved but that material interests, of a serious political value, are at stake.

All of a sudden the old delusion that philosophy belongs to an ivory tower, with which practical men of the world have nothing to do, seems to have been shattered. Comparative philosophy has become a subject of even political interest. An odd feature is that as soon as philosophy became comparative it achieved practical value. This admiration for its pseudo-practical values has found both a political and a cultural following. It is with the former aspect that the above Unesco statement deals. On the political side the realization came (exactly a century too late) that any war to master the world would have to be primarily one of ideologies. The best espionage would then be to find out the philosophy within the framework of which the ideologies of a people are susceptible. The value attached to this can be judged by what modern Governments spend on propaganda both inside and outside their country. Modern governments, therefore, have a vested interest in comparative philosophy. An example will make this clear. The Communist world would have a vested interest in a research in comparative philosophy, to show that Indian philosophy's emphasis on spiritual values is a myth and a sham leading to economic underdevelopment. Those who are opposed to Communism on religio-ideological grounds have an equally vested interest in proving that the spiritual message of Indian philosophy can be used to combat the atheistic arguments of Communism. This is only a rough general example and should not be overstressed. The war-makers of our times are not so much interested in acquiring territory as in possessing people's minds and controlling their way of thought. Now philosophy plays two distinct and

[1] Bellah, *Religion and Progress in Modern Asia*, New York, 1965, p. 170.

separate roles in this struggle for ideological empires. Its first role (and the one through which the study of comparative philosophy receives its present political importance) is that of a barometer to find out the philosophical weather in a given corner of the world. This gives the ideological world-conquerer an indication of how far it will accept his own ideology or resist that of his rivals. In this connection a knowledge of the philosophical vocabulary is a matter of some importance.[1] The terminology of the prevailing philosophy if borrowed by an ideological world power can be turned into a good instrument for infiltration.[2] The latter can then frame his ideology in such phrases as will present it in its most acceptable light to Eastern peoples. For example, instead of saying that an ideology will bring about 'the rule of the proletariat' in India, a better effect can be secured by rephrasing it: 'Will bring about *Ramraj*.'[3]

And so the advisory committee on the mutual appreciation of cultural values of the East and West held its second meeting in Paris. It devoted five sessions to a general discussion of two themes:

(a) The ideas that the Orient and Occident have formed of each other throughout history, how these ideas have been expressed, and their consequences for the development of mutual appreciation.

(b) How to formulate and encourage a *world viewpoint* based on the development of a mutual appreciation of cultural values.[4]

This discussion led to a *Joint Declaration* which the Committee adopted unanimously. It even recommended that the terms of this declaration should be the guiding principles of any action taken under the major project.[5]

From the discussion it emerged as a well-established fact that in certain countries, the co-existence of several cultures—both Western and Eastern —even if rooted in a recent period of foreign domination, has been achieved harmoniously; it has beneficial results and is completely accepted by the population as a factor of progress and enrichment, no matter how attached the people may be to the political independence they have regained.

An important point was that 'the contrast existing within each culture between its traditional values and modern living conditions is *greater* than the contrast between the cultures of East and West'. We all live under the increasing speed of *world evolution*.[6]

[1] The most important example in this respect is China. The Chinese language had no words equivalent to *democracy*, Collectivism, etc. The whole vocabulary of Communist jargon was built up by joining several words into one, according to their favourable or unfavourable *philosophical* and *not* philological basis.

[2] This is comparable to a more or less similar method used by the Gnostics to undermine the Church of Rome.

[3] The 'government' that would exist if the myth that the Golden Age of India will return, were to come true.

[4] What Radhakrishnan had been doing several decades before Unesco was formed.

[5] The East-West relationship.

[6] Compare this with Radhakrishnan and Huxley's ill concealed feeling of urgency and Sri Aurobindo's *Geometric Evolution*. It is interesting to note that delegates from utterly different countries at a semi-political international conference should voice

'This similarity between the situations and tasks with which the peoples of East and West are faced should help to constitute a solid foundation for their mutual understanding.'

As one member of the Committee said:

'We are all Eastern and Western, at one and the same time, both through our heritage and through the situation in which we find ourselves.'

Further: 'it is to the *masses* that this new state of mind has to be communicated'.

Again: 'The Unesco Major Project shall be the *Signal* for a new approach'.[1]

An extremely important paragraph in the Report revealed that:

'It is clear, however, that none of the complementary ideas of East and West, Europe and Asia, of Orient and Occident represent easily definable groups. Orient and Occident, especially, do not constitute entities in themselves and can be defined in relation to each other *only by means of the image that each forms of the other.*'[2]

Further: 'to speak of East and West *as if they were two entirely different worlds, separated by a clear boundary,* amounts to a certain human discrimination, or at least opens the door to the practice of such discrimination.'

The Report then draws attention to the danger of the subjective feeling of 'belonging more or less *exclusively* to one or the other of these two groups', and thereby 'conferring on the opposition of East and West a *reality which it does not possess'.*

The importance of the above can hardly be overestimated. It is a cause for great relief that the Committee took the view of Radhakrishnan, instead of the dangerous oversimplification of Professor F. S. C. Northrop. This Yale scholar and lover of the East has formulated both a theory and what he calls an *Algebra* of his own.[3] Following Einstein's lead in reducing

---

what Radhakrishnan and Aurobindo had long prophesied. An excellent illustration of Emerson's reinterpretation of Hegel's *Zeitgeist* as a cosmic will hinting at its future intentions through a subtle similarity in the conclusions of men, nations, events, and history.

[1] From the way the report re-echoes Radhakrishnan's words it seems the delegates came to the conference with a well versed, almost verbatim, if prefatory, command of his works ! ! !

[2] Italics mine.

[3] The Relation between Eastern and Western Philosophy in *Comparative Studies in Honour of Radhakrishnan's Sixtieth Birthday*, p. 363. See also Northrop's *The Meeting of East and West*, New York, 1946, and *The Logic of the Sciences and the Humanities*, Chapters XVI to XVIII, III to VI and XXIII to XXIV. For still more strenuous development of his argument see his chapter in *Philosophy: East and West*, edited by Charles A. Moore, Princetown University Press, 1940.

all physics to a single algebraic equation, Professor Northrop has tried to do the same with comparative philosophy and the result would look like a parody but for his obvious sincerity and good intentions. He reduces the entire issue to two algebraic oddities:

$$\text{Either 'W=E' or 'W+E'}$$

By 'W' he means Western philosophy. By 'E' he means Eastern wisdom.

He denounces the first, which he says is the standpoint of Radhakrishnan and Deussen.

He then champions the second of his algebraic equations (incomplete and unacceptable not only to philosophy but even to algebra) and dogmatically closes with:

'The whole truth is W+E, neither W=E nor is W merely instrumental to E.'

One who has lived in the East knows the dangers to which all such oversimplifications lead. That the Committee realize this is deeply satisfying. The Report says: 'To understand cultural values [philosophy is meant in this context] and appreciate them as matters of truth is to be aware of that which is universal in them . . . since cultural values abstracted from their universality quickly risk becoming a dead letter.' The Report stresses that Eastern cultures, just as those of the West, must be appreciated, not as peculiar curiosities but as expressions of human genius.

Further:

'The essential objective of Unesco's Major Project is represented by the still living traditions . . . these living and active traditions sometimes date from the most remote past, especially *as regards Asia*. [The Report warns that] No culture [Philosophy] should therefore be treated *simply* as a subject for study [and we are called upon] to play an active role in the common pooling of the *spiritual resources* of humanity.'

To encourage a more intensive study of comparative religion and philosophy, the advisory committee urgently appealed to everybody to 'respect the proper role of research workers' and even passed an express resolution to that effect. The conclusions of this international committee emphasize that researches in comparative religion and philosophy are a vital and world-wide need at present carrying practical, if not even political, consequences for the future.

The greatest difficulty in trying to make Eastern and Western philosophy understood by each other is that the very attitude which the latter praises as *scientific*, the former denounces as *useless argumentation*; the same attitude which the former praises as enlightening, the latter despises as *credulous*. The worst of it is that both sides use wrong arguments to support their case. The crux of this rather pseudo problem is that whereas the West prefers to know the method by which a given conclusion is arrived at, the East wants the answer *first* (which it checks in its own peculiar way) and is indifferent to method so long as the answers are right. This does not mean that it ignores method but, as the method may be more complicated to understand than its conclusion, leaves it to the specialist. This does not mean that Western philosophy is less valuable, but that since it has to reveal the method by which a given conclusion is arrived at, Western philosophy becomes complicated, too academic and, therefore, for the average reader, uninteresting—or as he puts it, too difficult.

Moreover, the average Westerner reads, as he proudly says, *critically*. This is not only right but an excellent attitude in which to read everything exoteric. But it leads to chaos when reading whatever is symbolically, or esoterically written. For instance, one cannot afford to read romantic poetry that way. Take Shelley's famous line:

> Like a poet *hidden* in the *light* of thought.

No average Western reader would complain that a thing cannot be hidden in light as the function of light is to reveal. Unfortunately, apart from the Bible and Romantic poetry, a Westerner seldom reads anything that is not exoteric. This also explains why the Bible is better understood and, therefore, more revered in the East.

If a thing is written esoterically, its meaning can only be understood by a reader who approaches it with the right attitude. Whatever that may be, the critical attitude is apparently not the right one. This does not mean that everything so written should be accepted as gospel truth, but that the reader *suspends* his inquiring faculty for the time being and so gives his subconscious mind a chance to vibrate in harmony with the subconscious mind of the writer when it was written. Then after a sufficient lapse of time, if the reader finds no intuitive response from his subconscious, it may be read critically. Criticism is not outlawed, it is only postponed. As the best part of Eastern wisdom is written esoterically its meaning can only be revealed if it is approached as if it were a friend instead of a book.[1]

Let us illustrate the different attitudes by an example: take a school text-book on mathematics. The correct answer to every problem is given at the end of the book so that the pupil can check his work. But the teacher will not be satisfied if the pupil gives the answers without showing how he worked them out. His attitude is comparable to that of Western philosophy.

Now if the last few pages of this text-book containing the answers are torn out and given to another pupil who has not seen the book before, he will be even more puzzled by this collection of answers than he would have been at the problems contained in the rest of the book. In the same way the Western reader of Eastern wisdom is perplexed by this collection of answers unaccompanied by the process through which they are reached.

Suppose during an examination in arithmetic the candidates want to check their answers. They ask each other in hurried whispers for the solution, hoping that the invigilator will not catch them. As the time is

---

[1] See the comments of C. G. Jung on the *I Ching* or *Book of Changes*.

short, and the position dangerous, what they want is a quick answer before the invigilator's attention is drawn. They would be dismayed if given a long explanation on how the answer should be reached. Such is the attitude of Eastern philosophy: method is *not* considered unimportant; it is so only because of the time available under the circumstances. The examination time is comparable to our own life-span, and the invigilator to death which may eliminate us from the examination at any moment. Therefore priority is given to answers and method is relegated to second place.

One result is that even the average individual in the East is able to take part in philosophical discussions. Conclusions being by nature concise are easier to understand and assimilate than method. For example, the conclusion of Einstein's *Theory of Relativity* is simple to understand and can be remembered by anybody who is prepared to take the method for granted.[1] But nobody except a mathematical genius can hope to follow the method by which Einstein came to this conclusion.

Another result is that by skipping the method the average person in the East is able to gather a far greater number of conclusions. Moreover, as conclusions are far more interesting to most people than metaphysical method, which requires long training and severe discipline, he does not find philosophy tedious as in the West, but as exciting as the average Western reader finds detective stories. This explains the paradox that although there is a very high percentage of illiteracy in Eastern countries, the average person there is well versed in many philosophical systems and enjoys discussing them. This ability and interest of the Eastern man in philosophy has been attributed by Western critics to a lack of vitamins, to poverty and a desire to escape from it, to frustration—in fact to everything except a genuine desire to know, or at least to think about, the unsolved problems of human existence which burn in his heart like a sacred flame. The Oriental is persecuted, to an extent which his Western critics can hardly imagine, by a craving to get at the root problems of the Why and Wherefore of his presence on this planet. He has, therefore, little patience for such inquiries of medieval scholastics as: 'how many angels can dance on the point of a needle?' or the modern: 'is a set of ordinary tea-sets an "extraordinary" set?'[2]

The second magnificent obsession in the East is the idea of the certain approach of death. Our time on earth being limited, and the number of things one can know being comparatively unlimited, the East prefers to concentrate on the relevant answers, provided they are correct or at least capable of being found correct by personal realization. *The important point of difference to note* is this:

In Western philosophy an idea is *not accepted* unless proved to be correct.

[1] $E = MC^2$. E = Energy; M = Matter; C = Speed of Light.

[2] 'In the Western World philosophers have too often confined their attention to debating whether or not there are such things as chairs or tables'. Tomlin, *The Great Philosophers of the Eastern World*, pp. 228–9.

In Eastern philosophy an idea is *not rejected* unless proved to be false. The burden of proving the negative is on the person denying.

The attitude of Western philosophy is:

No idea, statement, or theory can be accepted as true, or at all, unless conclusively proved to be so. What is *not proved* is to be treated as false.

The attitude of Eastern philosophy is:

An idea, statement, or theory which is not proved to be false may be accepted as true on a balance of probability. What is *not proved may* be accepted as true until proved to be false.[1]

Examples of two great not proved hypotheses are *karma*, the doctrine of automatic retribution, and *reincarnation*.

Both are mostly discredited in the West but widely accepted in the East. It makes a great difference which party you ask to prove the contrary but this does not necessarily make one superior to the other. As a rule, the burden of proof should be on the person denying the truth of a statement. Another thing to note is the measure of proof required. In *criminal* law it must be *conclusive* whereas in *civil* law a decision can be arrived at on a *balance of probabilities*.

Thus in Eastern philosophy the burden of proving the contrary is on the side which denies the truth of a given statement. The *measure* of proof required for its acceptance is a *balance of probability* in its favour.

That is also why the Buddha refused to answer when asked about the existence of God. He wanted to lay down a precedent, and a good one, which has become almost a tradition of Eastern wisdom. It can be reduced to the following rule:

As our life-span is limited, only those answers should be given or sought (first) which:

1. are either *immediately* applicable to or realizable by the individual; or
2. would automatically answer or give opportunity for answering other inquiries; or
3. would increase the probable life-span of the individual such as ethics and medicine; or
4. are not such answers as in order to be complete would require other questions to be asked.

In simpler words it means that questions should be answered in the order of their *urgency for that particular person*. For instance, supposing a man wants badly to go to London by a train leaving Glasgow at a fixed time. He has never been to London and if he misses this train he may never

[1] Philosophy, not science, is under consideration here.

again have an opportunity to go there. He reaches Glasgow station rather late and there is a very small chance of *just* catching the train if he hurries as much as possible. Now what is he likely to ask the railway-official when going past the controls? Would it not be:

'Which is the platform for the London train?' instead of questions like:
1. Is the Guildhall in London very big?
2. Will it take long to get there?
3. Is it a steam train or an electric one?
4. Will my fellow-passengers be friendly or talkative?
5. Will I like London?
6. How many times will the train stop?
7. Which is the longest street in London?
8. What is the price of fish there?

Now if he were to ask any of these eight questions instead of the previous one he would miss the train and lose all opportunity of getting to London. On the other hand the answers to the other eight questions could be obtained by catching the train. This is possible only if he gives top priority to the one question the answer to which can enable him to catch the train. It is not that the other questions should be ignored. They can and may be answered but only *after* he has caught the train.

In this example London represents the *goal* (of Eastern wisdom) to be reached in this life; to miss the train and so to lose all opportunity of getting to London is the symbol for death. Spiritual Enlightenment can be achieved only while we are alive; in order not to miss the train we should inquire only after the most indispensable answers (the knowledge of which would include the secret of immortality); if we get to London (know the full Truth), our other subsidiary questions will be answered, and in fact *can only* be answered by ourselves going to London.[1]

Another person (like the railway-official in our example) cannot answer all the questions even if he wants to (see questions 4 and 5 in our example).

I have given this analogy in great detail so that the Eastern man's craving for answers can be understood by his Western brother. It is not that the Eastern man ignores other questions but that he believes that by 'his own arrival at London' (by Self Realization which is also the final goal) the other problems will be either superfluous or solved.

In philosophy you cannot expect posterity to continue your researches

---

[1] 'The seeing of Reality, like a dream by one that's dumb, cannot be described *in language* to another'—Phadampa Sangay (English translation edited by Professor Evans-Wentz). This is exactly what Ludwig Wittgenstein tried to prove at the end of his *Tractus Logico-Philosophicus*. By a strange irony of fate his followers have twisted it to mean almost the very opposite of what he meant. What he meant was that the *Real* cannot be described in words. His followers perverted it to mean 'what cannot be described in words is not real' and formed a school of philosophy whose aim is to show that all that is known as philosophy is only an error of philology. See *Tractus Logico-Philosophicus*: 6· 51, 6· 52, 6· 521, 6· 522, 6· 5, 6· 432, 6· 4312, 6· 4311.

from where you left off in the same way as in science. This is because the products of science can be enjoyed or utilized without having to understand how they work. Results can be crystalized in an objective, concrete, physical form. For instance, if a scientist spends his whole life in trying to invent a motor, then after his death another scientist can continue from where he left off.[1] But in order to do that he must first understand and assimilate the work of the first scientist—and this is a time-consuming process which uses up part of a person's limited life-span. And so it may continue until after several generations the motor-car is a success. Thus perhaps the third generation from the first scientist will be able to use and enjoy the motor-car *without being under any compulsion to know how it came to be invented*. People can use the *results* of science even if they do not know how it works or how it is made. This is because these results, being objective and physical, can recapitulate in their objective existence (and often in their physical construction) the mental efforts of people now dead. But the products of philosophy being themselves mental, require mental effort (again a time consuming process) before even ready-made results can be assimilated. Philosophy, unlike scientific inventions, cannot be enjoyed at the expense of somebody else's mental effort. Perhaps that is why people have an aversion to it.

Moreover, philosophy and life are so intimately tied together that a person cannot pursue philosophic inquiry with the consolation that, even were he to die soon, a future generation might well solve the problem. The essence of philosophy for an individual includes of necessity the why and wherefore of his *own* existence. It will consciously or subconsciously form the basis on which he leads his life. It is his *Lebensanschauung* and is formulated and utilized in the very process of living. It is as intimately personal to him as his shadow. Even supposing that he can help posterity, posterity cannot help him. This has sometimes led to an unjust accusation against Eastern wisdom, that it is a study devoid of progress. The mistake here lies in thinking of progress as something outside oneself. Philosophy by its nature cannot produce this type of progress. In philosophy, as in religion, it is attained by each in himself and usually in terms of suffering.

Thus the attitude of Eastern wisdom is that only within the period of our *own* life-span is enlightenment possible and that our efforts, even if just

[1] So far, this can even be done in philosophy and so the distinction between what we try to show does not occur here but later on *after* the researches of science have taken a concrete (physical-objective) form: as in our example, the motor-car. It is not the continuation of inquiry but the use of its conclusions which is the point of departure. If a person were compelled to know and understand the mechanism and internal working of every invention and gadget before he was allowed to use it then the number of inventions he could possibly use in his (finite) lifetime would be considerably reduced. In that case would he not be impelled to select the most essential inventions? The conclusions of philosophy cannot be stored up in a physical form and left to be inherited by posterity. Posterity does not count here, nor is such a *divison of labour* possible as in science. Each individual must find what wisdom he can (and apply what he has found) before death overtakes him. Hence the feeling of extreme urgency.

'When half your Wisdom you must snatch, not take!'—Pope.

short of success, cannot be passed on to posterity. Posterity must begin where we began, at the beginning. This explains the feeling of urgency in Eastern wisdom which shows in its preference for answers, even when *not proved* as in *karma* and reincarnation. In the West, where philosophy and science are often intermixed, standards which are appropriate to the latter creep into the former where they are too rigid for growth. The Eastern viewpoint is well put in Milarepa's answer to Tsaphuwas: 'May thou, O learned one, trace out these things in standard books.'

This leads us to our next point of difference. Eastern wisdom is far more interested in the *noumenon*; whereas Western philosophy appears to be far more interested in the *phenomenon*. Theologically the Easterner believes that by being one with the Creator, Creation can be known and not vice versa as in Western philosophy and more particularly Western science. Let us look at it this way: a man wants to find out how much money the Shah of Persia has got—also how many palaces, secret apartments, diamonds, jewellery, etc., the latter has. But he must first try to become intimate with the Shah. Then the latter may disclose his possessions to him. But if, without ever having been introduced to the Shah, he tries to pry into his affairs he will not succeed and might get into trouble. In the same way Western science, *before* being acquainted with the divine, tries to analyse and inquire into the possessions of the divine—light, electricity, nuclear power, etc.—and from these fragmentary possessions expects to discover the essence of their Master (*noumenon*) who may be entirely different from his possessions (*phenomena*), just as the Shah of Persia as a human being is from his non-human possessions. I have given this analogy to explain why the orthodox East often despises modern knowledge and Western education as vain, dry, shallow, incomplete, even useless! The accusation is palpably unfair; why then is it made? Because from the Eastern standpoint all Western knowledge (including philosophy) appears analogous to finding out the essential nature of the Shah by a chemical analysis of his crown! This does not mean that a study of phenomena is by itself vain or useless. A whole world of difference depends on whether they are studied *before* or *after* being acquainted with the divine (knowledge of the noumenon). Apparently in the eyes of the East, the West does not seem to be acquainted with the divine.

At this stage the Western critic would retort that the divine is not capable of being *scientifically* known. At the most it can be taken on faith. Eastern wisdom answers as follows.

In order to know scientifically one must first make experiments. Even the most sceptical of scientists must have faith in some presupposed result otherwise he would not know with which experiment to begin. If Edison had not had faith in the possibility of an incandescent electric lamp, would he have had the energy or incentive to make the nine thousand and first experiment after nine thousand had failed? Moreover can a scientist even guess what *type* of experiment to conduct without faith in some hypothesis? Faith is, therefore, not incompatible with science but indispensable to it. Just as in order to study creation you have to make external (or laboratory) experiments, so in order to know the Creator you must make internal experiments (transcendental yoga; mysticism).

Western philosophy rightly insists on the discipline of logic. Eastern philosophy claims that logic is only one of several disciplines. Logic in itself prepares a person only for *intellectual* understanding. Total understanding (Self Realization) requires the rigours of other disciplines in addition to and not in substitution of logic. This aggregate of disciplines may roughly be called transcendental yoga, which should not be confused with what is *popularly* misnamed yoga.[1] Western philosophy never insists that its readers need anything besides intelligence in order to understand it, whereas Eastern wisdom refuses to reveal its secrets unless the student is willing to undergo such disciplines as ethical improvement, control over his appetites and emotions, and so on. It thinks it ridiculous to expect that supreme truths, the love and pursuit of which it calls wisdom, can be revealed to an ethically unripe person merely because he is clever at logic and epistemology! That at any rate is the Eastern viewpoint.[2]

It is, therefore, more convenient to divide Eastern wisdom into three broad divisions:

1. Ordinary exoteric philosophy, or philosophy as understood in the West, trying to understand the cosmos in the light of sense-acquired human knowledge.
2. Esoteric or yogic philosophy including philosophy accompanied by a specific system of introspective discipline which culminates in Enlightenment: trying to know the Creator.
3. *Post-Enlightenment* or *supra-yoga* philosophy: Creation and its *root* problems re-examined in the light of wisdom acquired from knowing the Creator. It consists mostly of the unpublished philosophy of Asia kept secret in closely guarded manuscripts or revealed in extremely esoteric books.[3]

[1] Yoga is a word which has lost all meaning because of indiscriminate use. By transcendental yoga we mean a systematized study (entirely disconnected with all supernatural or even supernormal phenomena) of the internal psychology of an individual's different levels of consciousness, made with the *exclusive* purpose of finding a method which will enable that individual to trace his identity to a particular stage of integral consciousness and thereby prepare him to *transcend* the limits of ordinary *sense-derived* knowledge.

[2] 'Philosophy carries us to the gates of the promised land, but cannot let us in; for that, insight or realization is needed'—*A Source Book in Indian Philosophy*, p. 355. (Radhakrishnan and Moore). This insight or realization is what transcendental yoga deals with.

[3] Whenever something worth while is found in Western philosophy, the custom is to broadcast it indiscriminately to all and sundry. In the East the tendency is to reveal exceptionally precious truths only to a selected few who are in some measure prepared to assimilate and appreciate them. Philosophy thereby retains its dignity as something worth striving for and does not degenerate (as in the West) into a subject to be passed at a university examination. As the East still prefers to keep fragments of its philosophy secret, a *complete* comparison of Eastern and Western philosophy is not yet possible.

As the last two categories are mostly missing in Western philosophy, a comparison with Eastern wisdom usually means a comparison of the *whole* of Western philosophy with only a *part* of Eastern philosophy. Eastern wisdom, like an iceberg, keeps the greater part of itself immersed and invisible.

What lies at the root of Eastern wisdom? What is the sum and substance of it all in one word? The answer is: *tattvajñāna*. This is three different words, each embodying one of the three *root* principles which together contain the innermost essence of Eastern wisdom. It can be analysed thus:

tat.   That element in man, and in other forms of creation originating in a birth, which is real, unchanging, permanent, eternal, essential, *sovereign*. It corresponds to the Soul or Holy Ghost of Christian Theology. It may, therefore, be considered as that which is divine in man by those who believe in the divine. Those who do not so believe should take it to mean whatever element in them, or in any other form of creation through birth, they consider to be most essential, longest lasting, or least subject to change. It is sometimes esoterically referred to as the Observer in *all Fields* (of observation); it is that element which is common to the essence of all birth-created forms.

tvam.   That with which a person identifies himself *when* he does not, has not, or is not '*identifying himself with tat*'. On the other hand the vast majority of us identify ourselves with the consciousness of existing as a separate person, with our own thoughts, moods, feelings, etc., which could not arise unless each of us took for granted the idea that I-exist. Hence for almost all of us, it is the ego-consciousness[1] which underlies all our thoughts that I exist. Thus instead of saying 'I think therefore I am' it would be more correct to say: 'I am: therefore all thoughts are conditional to this primal thought before even the idea of "I think" can arise.' When the axiomatic, and often subconscious, acceptance of the first combines with any thought whatsoever (including the thought 'I think') it gives rise to a phenomenon which makes one suppose that there is an 'I' who thinks. Or: 'I am!; therefore [it becomes possible that] I think.' In dreamless sleep one does not and cannot think yet the intuitive and axiomatic acceptance of the thought that 'I exist' continues.

Now if an individual has fallen into the habit of believing or thinking that his ego-consciousness is located in his body—or any particular physical part of it such as the heart or physical brain—then for him his *tvam* will be his physical body. Thus the *tvam* of each individual may differ depending on what he *habitually* identifies himself with. Thus it is the *Field-Observer* when the *tvam* of the individual is recognized as the ego-consciousness itself; merely the *Field* when located and habitually identified with something in particular such as, in almost all cases, the individual's physical body.

[1] The axiomatic acceptance of the intuition.

jñāna. Now it should be clear that if an individual were to identify himself with *tat* he would have no *tvam.* Therefore, to find one's *tat* is to lose one's *tvam*; to lose one's *tvam* is to find one's *tat.* For this purpose there are the different branches of *jñāna* or knowledge. For instance:

The problem of:	Gives rise to the study of:
What should one do or how should one behave before *tat* has been found?	*Nitishastra* (social ethics).
What is the relationship between *tvam* and *tat*?	Philosophy of the first type.[1]
How to lose one's *tvam*?	Philosophy of the second type.
How to find one's *tat*?	Philosophy of the second type, and/or religion as with the Christian saints.[2]
What after *tat* has been realized?	Philosophy of the third type.

The knowledge which *enables* one to realize the peculiar identity of *tvam* with *tat* is called *jñāna.* But the actual self-realized identification of the two is *vijñāna.* It is the fulfilment of *tattvajñana.* Merely to know that a cow is capable of giving milk is *jñāna*, but to milk her and nourish oneself on its vitamins that is *vijñāna.*

Thus the three words *tat, tvam, jñāna* have three other words corresponding to their fulfilment, namely:

1. *Samādhi.* Wherein the actual identification of *tvam* with *tat* takes place.
2. *Nityasuddhabodharupam.* Thought-free consciousness; experienced psychologically as a feeling of *timelessness* which remains during the temporary vacuum created during the above-mentioned *identification*— but before the resulting realization of it.
3. *Vijñāna.* The realization of identification *ex post facto.* That is to say, the *tvam's* realization of its identity with *tat ex post facto.*

This fulfilment of *tattvajñana* is the ideal which all Eastern wisdom considers to be the highest. (Whether it is called *vijñāna, tao, dharma-kāya* or *satori* is only a matter of terminology.) It is considered as the highest ideal and the sole purpose of existence in a human body. It is only because we each have the latent possibility to achieve *vijñāna* that life becomes a gift instead of a punishment. The various Eastern philosophies may differ in the names which they give to this goal and in their methods of attaining it;

---

[1] Please refer to our threefold classification of Eastern wisdom given above.

[2] The interested reader is advised to refer to St Ignatius Loyola's *Exercitia*, and *The Cloud of Unknowing.*

but they all agree that it is there, that it is reachable, that it *must* be reached; that *it* is the long sought for *Liberation*!

This gives to Eastern wisdom a unity and a purpose. However much one may disagree with it, it cannot be denied that it has a *precise* message to convey so that one may justly speak of a *spirit* of Eastern philosophy. As Charles A. Moore says: 'When one studies Oriental philosophy ... one is constantly reminded of a certain *spirit* pervading the whole, no matter how complex the content might appear.'[1] On the other hand there is no common, underlying element in Western philosophy to justify calling anything the *spirit* of Western philosophy.[2] This need not offend Western readers for it does not necessarily imply that their philosophy is inferior. The entire absence of any underlying characteristic which can be called the *spirit* of Western philosophy has been proved so conclusively by Professor Moore with so much evidence that I need not repeat it here.[3] I have already hinted what the *spirit* of Eastern philosophy is and how it can be compressed into that one word *tattvajñāna*. Now we are face to face with an important problem. We have shown that there is a central, fundamental idea common to all Eastern wisdom whereas this is not true of Western philosophy. Thus while Eastern wisdom, because of its unity of essence, is capable, when *taken as a whole*, of being compared and contrasted with some other major philosophy, the same cannot be done with Western philosophy *taken as a whole*. One can only take the different philosophies or systems contained in it one by one and then compare each with Eastern wisdom. This would avoid the enormous confusion to which the new-born science of comparative philosophy has given rise.

Contemporary Western thought begins with a reaction against the Hegelianism which pervaded the philosophical scene about fifty years ago. It was introduced into England and the English speaking world by Thomas Hill Green[4] (1836–82) who found in German idealism of Hegel's type a golden middle way between the two evils of naturalism and agnosticism. This kind of what is called 'Absolute Idealism', or 'Hegelianism modified by Anglo-Saxon caution'[5] was further developed by Francis Herbert Bradley (1864–1924) and fully expounded in his *Appearance and Reality*.

This book has been described as 'a spiritual tight-rope across a metaphysical abyss'. A more compromising attitude was taken by Bernard Bosanquet (1848–1923) who, however, inadvertently made concessions in-

---

[1] *Radhakrishnan: Comparative Studies in Philosophy Presented in Honour of his Sixtieth Birthday*, Chapter II.

[2] Except figuratively for convenience.

[3] *Ibid.*, pp. 43–86.

[4] 'It was with Green, and not before him, that German Idealism really began its mission on Anglo-Saxon soil. . . . He "opened the carefully guarded philosophical frontiers ... to the free entry of new ideas".' Rudolf Metz in *A Hundred Years of British Philosophy*, p. 268. An Italian observer, De Ruggiero, asserts, however, that the start came in 1874 by the publication of J. H. Stirling's *The Secret of Hegel*.

[5] Paton.

compatible with his own position.[1] The most noteworthy achievement of
J. M. E. McTaggart (1866–1925) was that he tried to make a synthesis
of German Hegelianism and its British modifications.[2]

Hegel's influence was even more profound in Italy where, as in the United
States, it was given a dynamic and voluntaristic bias as opposed to the
'block universe' conception of Bradley. It first entered the main stream of
Italian philosophy through men like Vico,[3] Spaventa, and Franceso de
Sanctis, and later found its way into the idealism of Benedetto Croce
(1866–1952).[4] The first book of his trilogy, *Filosofia dello Spirito* (Logic
as the Science of the Pure Concept), is both German and Hegelian in its
ideological emphasis.

Giovanni Gentile (1875–1944), a junior assistant of Croce and joint
editor with him of *La Critica*, carried this Hegelianistic neo-idealism to its
climax by indicating the unitary character of reality, thus paving the way
for his philosophy of self-consciousness. According to Gentile, 'the multi-
plicity is not indeed added to unity, it is absorbed in it. It is not $N+1$ but
$N=1$.'[5]

The Hegelian brand of idealism spread from England to the United
States where it started an intellectual renaissance causing revived and
intense interest in the works of Hegel, Kant and Fichte. The absolutism of
idealism was transformed by the American philosopher George Holmes
Howison (1834–1916) into what may be called a spiritual pluralism.
Howison's idealism is the result of Hegel's influence as modified by
Leibniz's theory of monads. Another important factor is his close friendship with the German philosopher Eucken, who also supported the theory of
personal idealism, or spiritual pluralism. Another famous American
philosopher to come under the influence of German idealism was Josiah
Royce (1855–1916). He had studied in Germany under Lotze, Wundt, and
Windelband. He transformed the Hegelian current into what he calls
'synthetic idealism' based upon a sympathetic criticism of realism,
mysticism and critical rationalism.

After the spread of Hegelian idealism came the reactions which it provoked. They mark the beginning of what is now called contemporary
Western philosophy. They led to pragmatism (as in America), realism (of
the G. E. Moore type), logical positivism, logical atomism, linguistic

---

[1] For a good exposition of Bosanquet's inconsistencies, see *Hegelian Cosmology*, by
Professor G. Watts Cunningham, p. 274.

[2] See his *A Commentary on Hegel's Logic*, p. 310.

[3] The famous novelist James Joyce claims Vico as one of his many influences.

[4] It is interesting to note that much of what Croce fancied to be his original discoveries had been anticipated by ancient Buddhist philosophy. There is an amusing
anecdote that when Croce, in one of his peevish moods, cancelled his engagement to
attend a forthcoming international philosophical congress, that outstanding genius of
Indian philosophy, Dasgupta, gave notice of his intention to challenge the originality
of Croce's ideas. This frightened Croce into attending the Congress, only to be defeated
in debate by Dasgupa.

[5] *The Theory of Mind as Pure Act*, Gentile, p. 32.

analysis and the like (as in England), existentialism (on the continent of Europe), and Marxism (later imported to serve as the State religion of Russia).

Pragmatism, as a philosophy, is as contemporary as only American civilization can be. It originated primarily as a polemic against the absolute idealism of the Hegelian school which had till then pervaded American thought. William James (1842–1910) was hostile to German metaphysics which he considered pedantic. He regretted the introduction of Hegelianism into America and sought to combat it. The seeds of combat had already been sown by Charles Sanders Peirce (1839–1914) who may be considered as the founder of pragmatism.

James took his lead from Peirce's essay 'How to Make Our Ideas Clear' published in the *Popular Science Monthly*.

In pragmatism we find that bitterly *anti-metaphysical* attitude which is now so characteristic of almost all contemporary Western philosophy. This pragmatism, in a somewhat altered form, became the 'instrumental-ism' of John Dewey (1859–1952). It also found its counterpart, in England, in the humanism of F. C. S. Schiller (1864–1937) which though patronizingly tolerant of Hegelian metaphysics, denies to all metaphysicians any claim to objective truth.

Logical positivism appears as a kind of by-product of the process of clearing up errors in the mathematics of the Hegelian period. The first blow was struck by Lobatchersky's non-Euclidean geometry, followed by Weierstrass's thesis on the differential and integral calculus. This was further reinforced by George Cantor's definition of continuity and by Frege's definition of cardinal numbers. The most decisive of all, however, was Frege's proof that arithmetic requires no concepts and no premises that are not to be found in deductive logic. Then this highly intricate branch of mathematics, under Carnap's influence, was used to fertilize logic, grammar and semantics. The result of this curious cross pollination became the philosophy, or sophistry, called logical positivism.

If all logical positivists had Russell's intellect, integrity, and reasonable-ness much could be said for it. Unfortunately that is not the case. For instance, Carnap goes to the extreme of claiming an error in syntax to be the *sole* cause of *all* philosophical problems. This quaint dogma was institutionalized into a kind of religion,[1] called *Der Wiener Kreis*, by such eminent men as Moritz Schlick, Otto Neurath, H. Feigl, K. Gödel, and P. Frank. We are told that logical positivism is more of a method than a result.

'A philosopher is a logical positivist if he holds that there is no special way of knowing that is peculiar to philosophy, but that questions of fact can only be decided by the empirical methods of science, while questions that can be decided without appeal to experience are either mathematical or

---

[1] It is exceedingly thought provoking to notice that both logical positivism and Marxism, though *prima facie* hostile to religion, themselves partake the nature of a religion.

linguistic. Many of them *would describe their position briefly as a determination to reject metaphysics.*[1]

As their doctrine is that all knowledge ultimately depends on sense-experience, a statement that cannot be verified by any sense-experience is neither true nor false but merely *nonsensical*. On the same grounds and arguing backwards they conclude that metaphysics is nonsensical. It will be noticed that they first give their own definition of both metaphysics and nonsensical—and then say that the one is the same as the other. Translated back into their own jargon this conclusion is a barefaced and pointless tautology:

Metaphysics	is	nonsensical
↓	↓	↓
That which is not verifiable by sense-experience	is	not capable of verification by sense-experience

It is curious that a school so antipathic to what it calls the pretentiousness of metaphysics should itself make use of such a high-flown and pretentious title as the International Encyclopedia of Unified Science.

Similarly while rejecting metaphysics it introduces a lot of other *metas*. Thus they say that philosophy as a branch of knowledge engaged in the formal analysis of science is a *meta*-science, propounding meta-theories in a meta-language. Philosophy as a meta-theory is then supposed to proceed in three directions: pragmatics, semantics, and logical syntax (*syntactics*), which are called collectively *semeotic*.[2]

While setting out to abolish all controversy in philosophy by turning it into an *exact* science (the Leibnizian 'Let us *calculate*'[3]), it is far from exact and seldom unanimous even among its closest followers. While they insist on abolishing such emotional or nonsensical concepts as *truth* (and the criterion of truth) they put redoubled emphasis on *verification*, which is only a Latin-derived word meaning the same thing! The most amusing part of it all, however, is that this so-called 'principle of verifiability' being itself neither a tautology nor an empirical fact, can only be, if not 'nonsense', a *metaphysical statement*. That logical positivism would turn out to be a myth and a sham was inherent in its own structure in spite of the sincerity, and possible good intentions, of its founders. As Christopher Candwell made clear in *Illusion and Reality*: 'Positivism is *always* dis-

---

[1] Russell in *Revue des Mathématiques*. (Italics mine.)

[2] C. W. Morris in *International Encyclopedia of Unified Science*, Vol. I, No. 2.

[3] It was Leibniz's contention that: 'If controversies were to arise, there would be no more need of disputation between two philosophers than between two accountants. For it would suffice to take their pencils in their hands, to sit down to their slates, and to say to each other . . .: *Let us calculate.*' *Leibnizens gesammelte Werke*, Vol. VII, p. 200.

honest, and from the start smuggles another reality (usually *the mind*) into the system of appearances in order to organize it and provide some standard of validity.'[1] The introduction of the word *mind* takes our attention back to Indo-Tibetan philosophy. Even assuming that the tenets of logical positivism are correct, there is no inevitable contradiction between it and Tibetan idealism. From the Indo-Tibetan point of view, logical positivism is only an infra-Bardo philosophy in so far as the latter confines itself to purely sense-derived empirical verifications. Nor can logical positivism (even supposing it were valid, which we have shown is not the case) attack the supra-Bardo philosophy of the East for much of it is empirically verifiable. Yoga, at its highest level, is not only a method; it is also an empirical verification. In fact, the too eager display of the latter has brought yoga into disrepute as a genuine method. Eastern wisdom stands or falls on the possibility and imperative need of *samādhi* or Enlightenment: that is to say consciousness in its pure state free of all thoughts whatsoever. At first sight one is tempted to argue that such a state is incapable of empirical verification. But the logical positivist fallacy is to consider only what can be proved as known. Now take the case of dreamless sleep, the existence of which no sane person will deny. Yet it is incapable of verification by pure sense-data. A person may see, hear, feel, taste and smell nothing and yet not be asleep. Conversely when a person is in dreamless sleep there is no means by which he can verify it. There is nothing by which he can demonstrate even to himself that he is in dreamless sleep. None of his five senses can tell him. And when he wakes up there is nothing by which he can prove that he was in that state, for it is equally possible that he has only forgotten that he had been dreaming. A dreamfree state of sleep cannot be proved empirically in the logical positivist way and yet who would be so ridiculous as to deny that such a state exists? In the same way *samādhi* or Enlightenment,[2] which resembles a thoughtfree state while fully awake, cannot be dismissed as nonsense just because it may not fulfil logical positivist idiosyncrasies. If the logical positivists mean that *samādhi* cannot be described in words, then they are right, but they have said nothing new. It was explained thousands of years ago in China that the *Tao* which can be *spoken* is not the *Tao*.

When the Buddha was approached with an offering of a golden flower by a student who asked to be taught the innermost core of his philosophy, he replied by holding up the flower and gazing at it in silence.[3] This

[1] Italics mine.

[2] Although the experience of *samādhi* cannot be described in words, words can be used to assert its existence as a fact.

[3] Jesus too replied to Pilate's question 'What is Truth?' by silence. This holy silence of Jesus is not to be confused with the ordinary silence of an adversary defeated in an argument and so with no reply. Here the silence *is* the reply. It means that words (or language) being an instrument subject to phenomena cannot convey the *Truth* which 'will make you free' from subjection to phenomena. That is what Wittgenstein probably meant when he said: 'There is indeed the inexpressible. This *shows* itself, it is the mystical.' The mystical reveals itself.

That is why the Truth of Christianity is also called the Revelation.

indicated that there are meanings in philosophy which cannot be conveyed through words. From this incident sprang and developed the philosophy of Zen which can beat logical positivism at its own game. What is best in logical positivism is only a new-fangled reformation of a very old metaphysics. The old metaphysical wine is in new mathematical bottles, the shape of which may *appear* anti-metaphysical but the contents are not. The positivist son does not recognize his metaphysical ancestor. As Radhakrishnan says: 'logical positivism is itself a kind of metaphysics, a sceptical metaphysics'.[1] But against this scepticism one can use the same retort as that of its venerable founder. When Bertrand Russell finds himself checkmated[2] by the logical monster of his own creation,[3] he replies: '. . . against the thorough-going[4] sceptic I can advance no argument except that I do not believe him to be sincere'. So we find ourselves back from knowledge to belief. This whole mathematical digression can only lead us from where we are, to where we are no better. What an irony of fate that what is called logical positivism should turn out to be so illogical and so irretrievably metaphysical. Indeed, such are the consequences (as Wittgenstein used to say) of 'being bewitched'.

Linguistic analysis is a sister branch of logical positivism and is called modern analytical philosophy or by some similar name. Its most able exponent, Ludwig Wittgenstein, was a person of transparent sincerity, a quality which has not been inherited by his followers. The start, however, was given by G. E. Moore who set out 'to refute idealism' and was refuted in turn by the unanalysable foundations of analysis. His thought is more ingenuous than ingenious. It is an inconclusive attempt to canonize 'common-sense' into a kind of realism based on two equally false assumptions: (1) the *reality* of relations and (2) that no relations are internal. This curious form of epistemological monism is a logical atomism based on mathematical logic. The principal characteristic of this school is the inordinate fuss they make about *language*. This 'Gospel according to Wittgenstein' is contained in a remarkable book, called *Tractus Logico-Philosophicus*, which should not be read either forwards or backwards (not that it would matter) but according to some occult decimal number attached to each paragraph. It is like one of those secret books on alchemy that may not be read by one who has not second sight, a sixth sense, or for that matter, a third eye! Even if one fails to be initiated by the *Tractus*, there is no harm

---

[1] *History of Philosophy Eastern and Western*, Vol. II, p. 442.

[2] '. . . uncompromising empiricism is untenable'—Russell in *Logic and Knowledge*, p. 381.

[3] '. . . no general proposition can be inferred to be *even probable* unless we postulate some *general* principle of inference which *cannot* be established empirically.' *Ibid.* (italics mine).

[4] This word *thorough-going* is rather telling. In practice it means that we should be unbendingly logical and sceptical, so long as the argument is in favour of the logical positivists, but should accept credulously what they say when any further logic or scepticism would upset their pet themes. In fairness, they did not invent this ingenious technique but only borrowed it (perhaps subconsciously) from the Marxist dictators.

in accepting the author's conclusion on faith. He himself confesses that his statements are nonsense. Or rather that all statements, since the world began, including his own, are nonsense because language, like some evil sorceress from the *Arabian Nights, bewitches* us all. But let us be fair and take Wittgenstein's own estimate of the achievements of this philosophy. He puts the question:

'What is your aim in philosophy?'

Answer:

'To show the fly the way out of the fly-bottle.'[1]

Question:

'What then, assuming this attempt, is a success?'

Answer:

'The fly must continue to remain in the same place and predicament *because* philosophy leaves everything as it is.'[2]

In spite of this kind of mumbo-jumbo Wittgenstein claims that: 'What *we* do is to bring words back from their metaphysical to their everyday usage.'[3] Now this is an obvious falsehood and can be proved to be so. For the linguistic philosophers when faced with common-sense statements pretend not to understand them unless put through some logical-mathematical ritual.[4] In fact the dangers of this linguistic solipsism are now clear even to its most partisan advocate, Bertrand Russell, who in this respect may be considered as Wittgenstein's philosophical godfather:

'This whole subject has become so technical, and so capable of quasi-mathematical definiteness, that it can hardly be regarded as belonging to philosophy . . . I think that on the same ground much of the recent work on logic, syntax, and semantics should be regarded as . . . not philosophical speculations.'[5]

Again:

'Absorption in language sometimes leads to a neglect of the connection of language with non-linguistic facts, although it is this connection which

---

[1] *Philosophical Investigations*, paragraph 309.
[2] *Ibid.*, paragraph 124.
[3] *Ibid.*, paragraph 116.
[4] See Tomlin's penetrating criticism of this pretention.
[5] Russell in *Logic and Knowledge*, 1950.

gives meaning to words and significance to sentences . . . [They] fight shy
of psychology and therefore have little to say about meaning or significance.
This makes them, in my opinion, somewhat narrow, and not capable of
producing an all round philosophy.'[1]

The fact, however, cannot be minimized that Wittgenstein was a great
philosopher. Not so much because of his *apparently* anti-mystical philosophy
but because he was himself a genuine mystic, as his life shows. He claimed
that we are bewitched, that 'a picture held us captive'.[2] Eastern wisdom
would agree with him; it calls this picture *māyā*, while Wittgenstein
called it language. But as long as we are bewitched we cannot know for
sure by what we are bewitched. All we can say is: 'let that which bewitches
be called X or Y or Z'. *Māyā* is only a name for this X. The practical
problem then is, how to pierce through and be free from this bewitchment
—that was Wittgenstein's goal. 'Philosophy is a battle against the bewitchment of our intelligence.'[3] This is also the goal of Eastern wisdom and
genuine yoga. The delusion is difficult to overcome because of *'the limits of
language'*.[4] That is why Eastern wisdom does not confine itself to verbal
theory but *insists* on practice and discipline (called yoga). Wittgenstein is
right, but in his own peculiarly muddled way which misleads his superficial followers. He is right when he says that: 'The sense of the world (of
phenomena) must lie outside the world (of phenomena, or bewitchment)'.[5]
That is to say in *samādhi*. Wittgenstein himself uses the telling word
illusion. To overcome this there is the yoga of knowing the Mind in its
nakedness; it is the clear seeing of Reality, it is that deliverance which the
Buddha declared as the goal of the *dharma*—it is that long sought for
Liberation.

Schopenhauer considered the need for metaphysics as that which
distinguishes man from the animal kingdom. When this natural hunger for
metaphysics is perverted or suppressed, it is a sign that evolution is
temporarily working in reverse. It, therefore, not only *heralds* the collapse
of civilization, as the famous philosopher R. G. Collingwood believed, but it
is also the very cause of such collapse. Metaphysics is to the soul what
physiology and hygiene are to the body. The present allergic attitude
towards metaphysics is, therefore, a symptom of spiritual amnesia. The
need for metaphysics, like that for sex, cannot be utterly uprooted, and if
repressed, crops up somewhere else, sooner or later, carrying retribution in
its wake. Philosophy and religion are legitimate channels for sublimating
the metaphysical urge. Contemporary philosophy, by denying it, has
brought about its own downfall. Man, anxious to know the meaning and
purpose of his existence, and having this aspiration frustrated by the
barrenness of legitimate philosophy, has turned more and more to its

---

[1] *Ibid.*

[2] *Philosophical Investigation*, paragraph 115.

[3] *Ibid.*, paragraph 109.

[4] *Ibid.*, paragraph 119.

[5] *Tractus Logico-Philosophicus*, 6. 41.

quacks.[1] Quack metaphysicians are doing a roaring trade at the very time when legitimate philosophy is dismissing metaphysics as superfluous. If this trend is continued, metaphysics will become the province and property of the quacks by right of prescription. Contemporary philosophy may flatter itself at having abolished metaphysics, but the very reverse may turn out to be the case. Metaphysics, when abolished officially, only goes underground and bides its time. The metaphysical revival, when it comes, as come it must, will send to obscurity many philosophers who today think they are writing for the future.

Our present philosophers lack that natural spontaneity which is the hallmark of first hand wisdom. They do not resemble venerable sages but extremely clever undergraduates. Can anyone say of a contemporary philosopher what Beethoven said of his music: 'He who understands my music will not be tormented by the everyday annoyances of human existence'? Our philosophers indulge in mental gymnastics which cannot be taken seriously outside a philosophical lecture-room or the quiet cloisters of Cambridge. No matter what they say, they make one feel that it is not something in which one can really believe. Consider Russell's *neutral monism*. It is sheer intellectual exercise for its own sake, but of anything even resembling philosophy, by any definition of that word, there is not even a trace. This kind of intellectual exhibitionism only indicates the spiritual immaturity of modern civilization, which delights in the immoderate use of that most powerful organ ever given to man, the thinking intellect. With the passing of time and the coming of maturity, a different ideal will take its place.

In addition to being vacillating, sceptical and incoherent, contemporary philosophy lacks that which alone can lend value to both life and philosophy.[2] This missing quality is: *aspiration*.

In the words of the Chorus Mysticus of Goethe's *Faust*, aspiration is an upward reach. Contemporary Western philosophy is itself rather Faustian.[3]

Now there is another school of thought which, though not directly in the mainstream of anti-Hegelian reaction, is an important branch of contemporary Western philosophy, *evolutionism*. Its founder, Herbert Spencer (1820–1903), wrote prior to the English reaction against positivism. In fact the latter affected his philosophical reputation. Now that positivism is back in England, ousting Hegelianism, Spencer may well become the idol of a second orgy of hero-worship. His contempt for metaphysics as a mirage is just what would delight the present linguistic positivists of England.[4]

[1] For a penetrating research on religious experiences, to show how deep seated the religious attitude is, see Rudolf Otto's *The Idea of the Holy*, which proves how very fundamental to our consciousness are awe and fascination for the numinous.

[2] Spengler prophesied that the final phase of Western civilization would be marked by utter scepticism.

[3] Spengler divided history into three periods of culture: *Apollonian, Magian* and *Faustian*. Our contemporary Western civilization is *Faustian*. Why? Because our present civilization is in the same condition as Faust was when Mephistopheles entered his study.

[4] F. C. S. Schiller, *Studies in Humanism*, pp. 17–19; see also pp. 182, 195, 211–2.

Before the tide turned, however, Spencer's positivist bases were attacked by Henri Bergson (1859–1941) in his *Creative Evolution*.

The Bergsonian revolution, headed by the concept of *élan vital* as the motive force of evolution, influenced another philosopher, C. Lloyd Morgan (1852–1936), in moulding his own theory of *emergent evolution*. But the boldest theory was put forward by Samuel Alexander (1859–1938), in his *Space, Time and Deity*, to the effect that *space-time*, which he considers to be the same as undifferentiated motion, is the very substance or thing out of which our world is made—the primeval matrix out of which the universe evolves. This is very similar to Hegel's idealism if the latter's Absolute is transferred to the bottom of the evolutionary ladder. No account of evolutionism is complete without mentioning the work of General Smuts. His *Holism and Evolution*, which appeared in 1926, discloses a serious misunderstanding of what the word *mind* is meant to signify. For instance, he says: 'Mind is not at the beginning, but at the end, but *Holism* is everywhere and all in all'.[1] The correct meaning of the word *mind* is vital to an understanding of the relationship between Eastern and Western philosophy. Here it is sufficient to quote Radhakrishnan:

'When the idealist affirms the primacy of mind, it is not the mind of this or that individual that is so posited, but the supreme mind (*Mind*).'[2]

From this idealistic, metaphysical, sort of evolutionism we now turn to that of Alfred North Whitehead (1861–1947), who is a central figure of the contemporary philosophical scene. He was Russell's teacher and co-author of the famous *Principia Mathematica*. He is a kind of two-way suspension-bridge—first from idealism-evolutionism to the iconoclastic zealots of ultra-modern philosophical analysis, and then from the mathematico-logical foxhole to a new, wide, all-embracing expanse of an almost Eastern metaphysics.

Just as Heidegger turns away from the professional philosophers and seeks his clue amongst the romantic poets, particularly Hölderlin,[3] so does Whitehead turn to poetry and Wordsworth. He says:

'It is important to ask what Wordsworth found in nature that failed to receive expression in science. . . . Is it not possible that the standardized concepts of science are only valid within narrow limitations, perhaps too narrow for science itself.'[4]

---

[1] *Holism and Evolution*, p. 335.

[2] *An Idealist View of Life*, p. 320.

[3] See Heidegger's *Hölderlin and the Essence of Poetry*.

[4] It is interesting to note that J. S. Mill, the famous philosopher of utilitarianism and logic, also found his consolation in the poetry of Wordsworth. Does it not show that logic, positivism, or a combination of them cannot satisfy the deepest needs of a human being? The abolition of metaphysics leaves a vacuum which nature abhors. Into this vacuum may rush in things more metaphysical than metaphysics itself. Take, for instance, the case of William James, the father of pragmatism, who found metaphysics too airy and then got entangled in spiritualism and the occult. Maugham

Whitehead began with a scientific materialism very similar to that of the Marxists, except that his conception of the world included fields of force and activity pervading all space. This idea of an infinite field of activity originated in physics through Fresnel's wave theory of light but did not become well-known till the formulation, by Maxwell, of electro-magnetic vector equations. However much Whitehead may deny Hegel, his philosophy of organism is a combination of Hegel's monism with the monadology of Leibniz, in the same way as it combines the Heraclitean inevitability of change with Plato's conception of the fundamental status of universals in reality.

Many of Whitehead's conclusions, perhaps quite unwittingly, confirm the findings of Eastern wisdom. This can best be explained by the theory that unknown even to himself he practised a form of yoga (the *dhyana* branch of *rāja yoga*). How so? It will be remembered that the golden secret of the psychological branches of yoga is the self-liberating power of the *concentrated* mind. Now it is more than probable that a thinker and mathematician of genius like Whitehead often had to concentrate exclusively on some particular point or problem. In this way he unknowingly submitted to the same kind of intellectual *tapasya* (rigorous discipline) as the yogi does intentionally. It may be that in one of his moods of extreme concentration (*pratyahara*), he reached the stage of *dharana*. For instance: 'My theme is the *energizing of a state of mind* in the modern world . . . and its impact upon other *spiritual* forces.'[1]

Wittgenstein is another example of one who probably practised a kind of yoga without realizing it. Observe both his and Whitehead's almost yogic conception of *solitariness:* '. . . the awful ultimate fact, which is the human being, consciously alone with itself, for its own sake. . . . Religion is what the individual does with his own solitariness. . . . Thus religion is solitariness, and if you are never solitary, you are never religious.[2]'

It may be noted that nowhere is the spiritual value of *solitariness* explained with greater care and detail than in Eastern wisdom.

Again, Whitehead says: 'Nature is . . . a totality including individual experiences, so that we must reject the distinction between nature as it really is and experiences of it which are purely psychological. Our experiences of the apparent world are nature itself.'[3] Yet all this has been anticipated by the *māyā* theory of Indian philosophy.[4] Whitehead lends Eastern wisdom additional authority by arriving independently at the same conclusions through modern science, mathematics and logic.

---

tells us of how he asked his brother (the famous novelist Henry James) to wait till six months after his death for (so unpragmatic a thing as) a message from the other world. Imagine this from one who found German idealism too much of a fairy-tale.

[1] *Science and the Modern World*, p. 4 (italics mine).

[2] *Alfred North Whitehead: An Anthology* (ed. Northrop and Gross), p. 472.

[3] *The Principle of Relativity*, p. 62 (italics mine).

[4] 'This world or *saṁsāra* is a process consisting of events, to use Whitehead's expressions.' Radhakrishnan, 'Fragments of a Confession', *Library of Living Philosophers*, Vol. 8, p. 27.

Whitehead's importance lies in that he is one of the very few contemporary Europeans who may be called a philosopher in the complete sense of the word. Like Plato, he takes into consideration all the different aspects. He himself described Western philosophy as foot-notes to Plato! Can it not be that *contemporary* Western philosophy is after all foot-notes to *Whitehead*?

Modern Europe may be said to begin at A.D. 1914. This is well brought out in a book called *The End of Laissez-faire* by that incomparable genius of economics, Lord Keynes. The end of *laissez-faire* is indeed the beginning of modern Europe as can be seen from the fact that what divides Europe today (along with the rest of the world) is essentially a difference of opinion on the virtues and extent of *laissez-faire*. 'Europe,' Metternich is supposed to have said, 'ends in the Reisenerstrasse!'—a street in Vienna where even today one can see the Russian church and the Russian embassy. At the Hungarian[1] frontier falls not an iron, but an ideological curtain which cuts off Europe from an ideological territory which rolls eastwards to the South China Sea. It can hardly be denied that the ideological difference between Western and Eastern Europe centres in its essence on a difference in *economic* theory and practice. All other differences can be traced to this origin: the relatively pro-*laissez-faire* West as compared to the relatively anti-*laissez-faire* Eastern Europe. This is the greatest event in the history of economic development since the Industrial Revolution. The significance of Lord Keynes's prophecy, however, was that he predicted the end of *laissez-faire* even in the West. The well known motto of economics today the world over is: 'Plan or no plan is no longer the question'. This has already led to the creation of welfare states in the West and communist Peoples' Republics in the East. In both, however, the State acquires exaggerated powers and the individual loses his identity in a sea of identities.[2] In this new religion of technocracy the individual's thought and life are put under continual psychological pressure. Man, made in the image of God, is supplanted by man made in the image of his passport or identity card, which latter the individual must always carry with him as if it were a holy document. The individual is *only* a citizen, and what is one amongst so many?

The result is that a new disease has become chronic in contemporary Europe: the nervous break-down, neurosis, or what may be better called quasi-insanity.

Now quasi-insanity is quite different from ordinary insanity total or partial. In it the individual is constantly subject to a mental strain which

[1] Hungarian is a non-European language. The Lithuanian language is entirely based on Sanskrit and so similar to it that Lithuanians can understand Sanskrit without previous study. The Lithuanian language being derived from Sanskrit enjoys the scientific exactness of the latter. Thus Kant, who was unaware of Sanskrit, said of the Lithuanian language that 'it possesses the key which will open all the enigmas, not only of philology, but also of history'.

[2] Observe that in contemporary European drama more than half the number of serious plays deal with the problem of identity.

makes him believe that he is, or is *about to go, insane*. It is insanity without the advantages of being insane. The individual's incapacity to believe in the benevolence and reality of anything divine in the cosmos leads to a failure of nerve, and the steady discontent which results can be kept at bay only by continuous extraversion.[1] Thus there is nothing which modern man avoids so carefully, and with so many subterfuges, as *introspection*. Given a choice between war and introspection, the average man would rather risk the horrors of war; but can he be blamed for that choice? The loss of personality, or personal identity (*psychosis*), is always more terrifying to the personality than the mere loss of his body through death. Not religion but *extraversion* is the opium of people today. Along with this is the need to focus attention on *youth*. For old age reminds the citizen of death, which again reminds him that the State, omnipotent as it is, has its membership restricted to those who are still alive. The citizen who has so long identified himself with the *Welfare* State fears nothing so much as the idea of being left out, of being *alone*. Modern man can face death, sometimes even heroically, but not *loneliness*. For that would make a mockery of all his past extraversion and disclose the scandal that the State, however 'welfare' it may be, is necessarily hostile to the individual's spiritual development. Were this known, the citizen would cry out like Cardinal Wolsey: 'Had I but serv'd my God [spiritual development] with half the zeal I serv'd my king [State], he would not . . . have left me naked. . . .' Not for nothing did Jesus say: 'Render unto Caesar the things that are Caesar's—give unto God, God's'. As soon as Europe became willing to barter the sayings of Jesus for those of writers of text-books on economics and sociology, its downfall was assured. Thus in 1917 the famous October Revolution took place, and in 1918 we find Spengler's *The Decline of the West*. Held captive by the need for extraversion and identity, Western civilization is today in the same position as Roman civilization at the time of St Augustine or Egyptian civilization at the time of Ipuwer.[2]

But what is most surprising is that the critics of Western civilization are unanimously pessimistic, forgetting that this very pessimism can bring about the collapse they fear. Nobody seems to realize that the picture of Western civilization today should give rise to unqualified optimism, for which there is much cause. Europeans themselves complain and lament that they are materialists, forgetting that a person who laments being a materialist has already ceased to be one. Moreover, the word materialist is very vague and can mean one or more of several propositions. A person does not cease to be a materialist by believing in God or Spirit—he must be able to realize that what he considers as non-God or non-spirit is only

[1] This extraversion has reached such limits in the U.S.A. that sociologists and literary critics bemoan that as the vast majority never read a book once they have left school, even literature may come to an end. Aldous Huxley therefore recommends the use of gramophone records (containing literature) instead of books.

[2] For an excellent revaluation of European civilization today, see Arnold Toynbee, *A Study of History*.

God or Spirit in disguise[1] (that is, disguised as matter). Thus the oft repeated accusation that Western civilization is materialistic is only a slogan devoid of metaphysical meaning. European civilization is as much or as little materialistic as any other. What the catchword probably means is that it is *materially* more advanced or prosperous. Now plenty and prosperity if wisely used lead to spiritual regeneration rather than to materialism. In the material prosperity of the West lies its greatest spiritual advantage. There are two reasons for this:

(i) Until primary wants are satisfied, the higher wants do not arise.[2] For example India today, faced by insurmountable economic difficulties, has to concentrate on producing the primary material requisites of well-being even at the cost of neglecting its spiritual heritage.[3] Only a society with a minimum of material prosperity can afford introspection. The West, because of this prosperity, has a golden opportunity of satisfying even its higher wants by the process of introspection. Critics may argue that even if the West has the opportunity for introspection it has not the inclination. But introspection is an *acquired* taste.

(ii) The West has had the opportunity to experience materialism to the full and has found it wanting. Through her material prosperity, she can discover that no amount of external plenty can satiate the gnawings of psychic poverty and discontent. Along with this material prosperity the West enjoys considerable freedom from sexual taboos and restraints. Thus it is in a better position to find out that with material plenty, as with sexual liberty, a time comes when the flesh can no longer allay the fever in

[1] This normally happens only through what the Bible calls the *beatific vision*. This *beatific vision* is, therefore, the goal of all human life. A civilization begins to decline when it neglects this goal or those who seek it. Thus if modern Europe had even one person like, say, St Thomas Aquinas, its civilization could be revivified. Thus the message of both Radhakrishnan and Huxley is that if we, or even a small minority of us, were to devote ourselves to the pursuit of this beatific vision, materialism would die a natural death and our civilization start progressing instead of declining.

[2] For example in the history of Greece we find that Sparta supplied the army and Athens the navy. When the need for war was over the Spartans returned to their land demobilized, poorer from the ravages of war and unstable employment. Athens, on the other hand, converted her navy into a mercantile fleet and prospered through international trade, thereby providing her people with the leisure and means for philosophical enquiry. Thus Socrates could reply to a Prince inviting him abroad: 'Meal, please your majesty, is a half penny a peck in Athens; and water I get for nothing'. It was in prosperous Athens, not in poor Sparta, that philosophy flourished. Material prosperity is the friend, not the foe, of spiritual regeneration.

[3] Another danger is that the pursuit of spiritual values in an environment of material poverty usually appears like sour grapes. It looks like making a virtue out of necessity: like pretending to a spiritual fortune in order to hide material poverty. (This makes even a genuine spiritual seeker uncertain in his subconscious mind). Marx could boldly call religion the opium of the masses *because the masses were poor*. Religion when practised by the rich can hardly be opium as Marx suggested.

P

the bone. The modern East has yet to make this discovery. It is tragic that just when the West is more or less abandoning materialism, having found it wanting, the modern East is drinking it to the dregs. The modern East can hardly be blamed for it. It is not possible to forgo the attractions of material security, comfort and luxury until one has enjoyed them to the full. In Jesus's parable of the prodigal son, we find that he only returns to his father after he has found harlots and husks equally wanting. Take, for example, a European country like Germany. Since 1914 it has experienced the First World War, the revolution, inflation, unemployment, the great depression, Nazism, the Second World War and its aftermath, the miraculous post-war prosperity. Opportunity enough, one would think, for finding out that 'husks and harlots' give no lasting satisfaction. The pleasures of materialism are attractive due to their novelty, and not because of their inherent quality. Modern Europe, therefore, offers ideal conditions for spiritual progress. If it does not take this opportunity it will have only itself to blame. It is a false conception that the European is by nature incapable of asceticism and renunciation so necessary on the spiritual path. During the last two wars many Europeans freely sacrificed possessions and human relationships to support an abstract idea. Critics may object that the West cannot cope with this problem if communist materialism overruns the whole world. But they underestimate the power of Eastern wisdom.[1] There is ample evidence to show that the average Russian hungers for mystic illumination. It is also known that he is, through Communism, extraordinarily well-disciplined. When Russian civilization meets Eastern wisdom (as in this small world it inevitably must), the disciplined Russian will find in yoga what he has been hungering for—and because of his previous training and discipline, he will be able successfully to put it into practice. The tide will then turn. It is not civilization, but materialism, that is on the decline. Both Communism and the West starve for something that will restore to them their lost reverence for wonder and ontological mystery. The modern West has the material requisites, Communism has the discipline, and the East its ancient wisdom in the training of mystic illumination. Thus it is not necessary to see doom in the future. A spiritual renaissance is the more probable alternative.[2] As Browning said: 'God's in his heaven, All's right with the world'.

The Marxist view is that a culture is only the superstructure of the material means of production. But the history of Indian culture proves that the preoccupation of the people has not been with the means of

[1] For instance, Aldous Huxley again and again cries out in alarm against mass-hypnosis and compelled indoctrination practised by modern states through psychological methods. His last book *Brave New World Revisited* is a plea for freedom from *brain-washing*. But yoga (i.e. *rāja yoga* or the yoga of psychological methods) discovered long ago methods whereby the individual can nullify such outside psychological compulsions. The famous English biologist, Sir Julian Huxley, recently advised scientists to make a more thoroughgoing research into Eastern yoga and mysticism.

[2] History shows that nothing brings a civilization so speedily to its ruin as lack of optimism for the future.

production so much as with the means of liberation from the world of phenomena (*moksha*). The East is saturated with a belief in the reality of the Unseen. A possible explanation could be that the early Aryans came to the Himalayas in the course of their migrations. It is a well-known fact that solitary mountain peaks invoke spiritually uplifting moods.[1] The ancient Indian civilization belongs to what Karl Jaspers calls the Axial period (800–200 B.C.). He says in *Von Ursprung und Ziel der Geschichte*:

'The India and China that we know were born from the Axial period, not primary but secondary, *spiritually* they penetrated the same depth as the West, which happened neither in Egypt nor Babylonia.'

The antiquity of India, which is as eerie and awe-inspiring as its esoteric philosophy, has been remarkably described by E. M. Forster in *A Passage to India*[2]:

'. . . the India we call immemorial came into being. But India is really far older. In the days of the prehistoric ocean the southern part of the peninsula already existed, and the high places of Dravidia have been land since land began, and have seen on the one side the sinking of a continent that joined them to Africa, and on the other the upheaval of the Himalayas from a sea. They are *older than anything in the world. . . . Yet even they are altering. . . .* Their main mass is untouched, but at the edge their outposts have been cut off. . . . *There is something unspeakable* in these outposts. They are like nothing else in the world, and a glimpse of them makes the breath catch. . . . they bear no relation to anything dreamt or seen . . . as if pilgrims, who generally seek the extraordinary, had here found too much of it. . . .

'It is as if the surrounding plain or the passing birds have taken upon themselves to exclaim *extraordinary*, and the word has taken root in the air, and been inhaled by mankind.'

The same may be said of Eastern wisdom, that it is extraordinary; there is something unspeakable in it; it is older than anything in the world; and yet it is altering.

A thorough study of ancient India would be of immense practical value to the India of today which needs something more than territorial unity to unite it. Territorial nationalism being short-lived cannot survive the shock of ideological nationalism—that is to say nationalism based on the infallibility of a common book such as Marx's *Das Kapital*. Now it is well-known that the present population of India (apart from Christians) consists of three major religious communities, Hindus, Moslems, and Parsees. Does ancient history show any signs that they had a common origin? If so it would be a great contribution to inter-religious friendship as every advance in the study of comparative religions leads to a corresponding

[1] Moses, Zoroaster, Christ, Mahommed: all had their moments of Enlightenment on some mountain peak or other.

[2] Part II, Chapter XII. (Italics mine.)

decline in religious fanaticism. Before examining the evidence we should point out that Radhakrishnan divides Indian philosophy into four periods:[1]

1. The Vedic Period (1500–600 B.C.)
2. The Epic Period (600 B.C.–A.D. 200)
3. The Sutra Period (from A.D. 200)
4. The Scholastic Period (from A.D. 200)

The history of Indian philosophy may be said to begin when the Aryans of Central Asia divided into two groups, the one spreading into Persia while the other came to India via Afghanistan. As Radhakrishnan says: 'It is now a commonplace of history that the Vedic Aryans and the Iranians descended from the same stock and exhibit great affinities and resemblance'.[2] Now the Vedas are popularly known to be *four* in number.[3] But as Radhakrishnan points out: 'The first three (*Rig, Yajur, Saman*) agree not only in their name, form and language, but in their contents also'.[4] We even notice that in spite of there being four Vedas, they are always referred to as the above mentioned three.[5]Thus the *Atharva* was probably not recognized as a Veda by itself until later. The very name *Atharva* being derived from 'to go' means that which comes after, that is to say, a *supplementary* Veda. Now the *Atharva* Veda is not a single book but consists of two different parts,[6] the *Bharagva* and the *Angirasa*. If these are counted as separate books there would be five Vedas. Evidence of this is found in the *Santi Parvan* (Chapter 335) where it is said:

'The four disciples of Vyasa, namely Sumantu, Vaisanspayana, Jaimini, and Paila, and the *fifth* one his son Suka, obtained a Veda each; and a sixth inheritance there was not to be had!'

As Bloomfield puts it:

'Occasionally, yet quite familiarly, the fourfold Veda is expanded into the

[1] *Indian Philosophy*, Volume I, p. 57.

[2] *Ibid.*, p. 74.

[3] *Ibid.*, p. 64.

[4] *Ibid.*

[5] *Shatapatha Brahmana* 4–6–7–1; also *Gītā*, IX: 17; IX: 20; IX: 21.

[6] Sayana in his Introduction to the Commentary on the *Atharva* Veda writes: 'Self-existent Brahma disciplined his energies for the purpose of creation. He perspired. The sweat divided into two streams. From one of them sprang up the great sage Bhrigu, and from the other Angirasa.' Now as the author of this Veda has a double name: Bhrigu-Angirasa—and as it is expressly stated that Bhrigu and Angirasa are two separate persons, it is evident that this Veda consisted of two distinct sections, *Bharagra* and *Angirasa* respectively. We find further evidence in the *Gopatha Brahmana* which relates that: 'On account of *tapas*, sweat is produced on Brahma's brow. More sweat breaks in streams. The waters are divided into the salty ocean and the sweet rivers. The sweet waters produced Bhrigu, and the salty waters Angirasa'— *Gopatha Brahmana*, 1–1–1, 15. See also Bloomfield, *Atharva Veda and Gopatha Brahmana*, pp. 106–8.

Atharvanic *Pentad* by dividing the *Atharva* Veda into two, the *Santa* (*Bharagva*) and the *Ghora* (*Angirasa*).'

Now the Persian philosopher Jilly says that 'the scripture of the Brahmins contains five parts. The *fifth* is forbidden to most Brahmins.'[1] And no wonder, because the *Bharagva* Veda represents the cult of *Asura* Worship (the Impersonal God). As this came in direct conflict with *Deva*-worshipping India, the *Bharagva* Veda fell into disrepute. But the only book in favour of *Asura* worship which could have existed at that time and which could have been accessible in India was the *Avesta* of Zarathustra. Therefore the *Avesta* must be the fifth Veda missing today. Then the grammarian Panini defined the *Avesta* as a collection of Mantras at a time when the word *Mantra* was synonymous with *Veda*. It is possible, therefore, that the *Bharagva* Veda was compiled by the sage Yamaswa round the nucleus of the *Gāthā* of Zarathustra.[2] Thus the Parsees and Hindus of today are the two sides of the same coin as far as the Vedas are concerned. This can be further corroborated if we accept the evidence of *Yasna* (48–10) where Zarathustra is called Ratus Naroish Nara, who was probably the Rishi Narayana in the *Māhābharata*. We have already explained that the *Gītā* is the substratum of Eastern wisdom. But it is mentioned again and again[3] that the philosophy of the *Gītā*:

1. had been previously taught by the sage Narayana[4] (Zarathustra?)
2. in the reign of King Vasu[5] (Vistaspa?)
3. in a country lying to the North-West of India[6] (Persia?)
4. where the people were very white in complexion[7] (pre-islamic Iranians?)
5. professed a culture based on self-expression[8] (*Asura*-type?)
6. and a religion that was essentially monotheistic[9] (Zarasthustrianism would be the only monotheistic religion that was in question.)

In this *Asura* versus *Deva* controversy, so deeply rooted in history, we find the seeds of a conflict which was not resolved until our own time. Religions have often been divided by some historians into two groups, Vedic Aryan and Semitic.

The latter includes Judaism, Christianity and Islam. But is Islam really Semitic? Historical evidence tends to show that it had more to do with Persia, which had an *Aryan*-Vedic culture, than with any other country. In fact, Allah declares in the Koran that the truest form of Islam will be found among the Persians, and not the Arabs.[10] Mohammed refers to the

---

[1] Nicholson, *Studies in Islamic Mysticism*, p. 133.

[2] See Jackson's *Zarathustra, the Prophet of Ancient Iran*, p. 117.

[3] *Santi Parvan*, 348–8; 348–53.

[4] *Ibid.*, 335–41; 336–3.

[5] *Ibid.*, 335–7.

[6] *Ibid.*, 335–10.

[7] *Ibid.*, 447–83.

[8] *Ibid.*, 448–1.

[9] See also Browne, *Literary History of Persia*, Vol. I, p. 203.

[10] *Koran*, Sura 47 verse 40.

Furkan (the scripture of *distinction* between righteousness and evil), as the original of the Koran.[1] But this is just what the *Gāthā* was then known as. To put the knowledge of the *Furkan* (*Gāthā?*) in the Arabic form, for the benefit of the Arabs who had not yet received any revelation, was what he conceived his function as a prophet to be.[2] It is also said that 'if knowledge were suspended from the ends of heaven, yet would the Persians achieve it'.[3] And that 'if *Faith* resided in the Pleiades, yet would the Persians reach it'.[4] And so Islam is not so much a Semitic as an Aryan religion of the *Asura* type. Thus the Hindus, Moslems, and Parsees of modern India have a common religious source in ancient Persia.

Is God with or without form? Personal or impersonal? Corporeal or incorporeal? Capable of finite representation or infinite? The supporters of the former point of view came to be known as Angirasas (derived from a word meaning fuel[5] or that which has been burnt), or image-worshippers; they represent the Deva cult with the first three Vedas as their Scripture.

The supporters of the latter points of view came to be known as *Bharagvas* (from *bhirgu*, to fry; the blaze of the flame).[6] They represent the Asura cult with the Avesta, or the *fifth* (*Atharva*) Veda, as their Scripture (*Furkan*).

The worshippers of the Deva cult had to suffer their idols being smashed by the foreign invaders of the Asura cult and from secession, within their own fold, by those who could not accept God as having form. The most famous of the latter group were Buddhists, and in contemporary India the two new sects, *Arya Samaj* and *Brahmo Samaj*.

Much bloodshed would have been saved if the iconomatic and iconoclastic worshippers of the same Supreme Being had had the benefit of Sri Ramakrishna's ingenious and illuminating explanation. Is the *Absolute* with form or formless? Both, says Ramakrishna. How can that be possible? Just as in an infinite formless ocean, an iceberg may be formed with a particular shape, but which, when melted, becomes once more identical with the infinite, formless ocean.

Thus in the religious history of India we find the iconomatic (Deva) school of thought steadily losing ground to the iconoclastic (Asura) type. Nowhere do we find an openly reverse process. Whenever the followers of

---

[1] Critics might object that the *Furkan* can just as well be the Christian Bible or the Jewish Tora. But the Koran expressly repudiates this in Chapter III verse 2 (*Imran*). Here is additional proof that the only other book historically possible would be the *Gāthā* which is, as we have shown, the elusive fifth Veda.

[2] *Koran*, Sura 12, verses 2–41: Sura 41, verses 42–6.

[3] Khuda Baksh: *Essays Indian and Islamic*. p. 63.

[4] Browne: *Literary History of Persia*, Volume 1, p. 264.

[5] Thus fuel being corporeal represents God with *form*. The blaze of the flame being incorporeal represents God as the formless Absolute. 'The sacrament of *upanayana* is of Indo-Iranian origin'—Radhakrishnan, *Religion and Society*, p. 135.

[6] 'In this *upanayana* ceremony the student (disciple) approached the teacher (Master) with fuel in his hands.' *Ibid.* Also: 'Fetch, dear boy, *fuel*, I shall initiate you.' *Chāndogya Upaniṣad*, IV. 4. 5.

the iconoclastic turn over to iconomatic it is only by means of some
religious subterfuge as in exoteric, ritualistic, Buddhism.

These two diverse trends meet in Sri Ramakrishna, the genius of modern
Indian philosophy. In his explanations we find the first logical argument in
favour of interreligious friendship as opposed to sentimental, humanitarian
arguments or those arising from inborn tolerance. With the advent of yoga,
the inconoclastic trend found its outlet in *jñāna* while the iconomatic trend
found refuge in *bhakti*. As Ramakrishna rightly points out, these two
different schools of yoga are not antagonistic; they differ only because they
are intended for two different types of individual. Although no serious
conflict should now take place, it is still quite natural for one who has been
brought up on *bhakti* yoga to retain an iconomatic preference (as is sometimes seen in Ramakrishna); and an iconoclastic preference in one who has
been inclined to *jñāna* yoga (as is sometimes displayed by Radhakrishnan).

Now in the last few decades something well-nigh impossible has occurred,
which can give Indian philosophy an almost empirically verifiable basis.
It had been said for a long time that success in *jñāna* includes *bhakti* as its
fruit and vice versa. But there was no outstanding figure for whom one
could claim success in either *bhakti* or *jñāna*, who could explain the inner
workings of both these systems. Then Sri Ramakrishna, the greatest
spiritual genius born in India since Gautama Buddha, mastered the
method of *bhakti* and at once succeeded with that of *jñāna*. Moreover he
was able to explain philosophically the inner workings of this oft-predicted,
but seldom observed, success. Very soon an equally noteworthy event took
place when Bhagavan Sri Ramana Maharshi mastered *jñāna* and was
immediately able to experience and explain the inner workings of *bhakti*.
This conclusively showed that the methods of *bhakti* and *jñāna* lead to the
same goal, and that on the successful completion of one the other is
mastered as well. This had been known before in a fumbling, theoretical
way; now the evidence was not only convincing—it had a personal radiance
of its own. To have two such spiritual giants as the Maharshi and Ramakrishna at almost the same time, and in the same country led to a serious
revival of interest in Vedānta in India and abroad. It was almost unbelievable that what had been taught in solitary forests by the sages of Vedic
India was realizable and attainable near the modern city of Calcutta! To
this twice blessed spiritual and philosophical renaissance, Radhakrishnan
adds a third name: Devandra(nath) Tagore, father of the Nobel Prize-
winning poet Rabindranath Tagore.[1] Devandranath's contribution was to
stress that *karma yoga* is intimately connected with *jñāna* and *bhakti*.
Moreover, considering the socio-economic condition of India, that method
or way is perhaps the most suitable of all the three. This was supported
strongly by Swami Vikekananda, the most influential philosopher of his
time. Radhakrishnan saw in it untold possibilities for the socio-economic
advancement of India, without losing in the process what he calls India's
spiritual heritage. In a commentary on a new translation of the *Gītā*
Radhakrishnan clarified the *karma* point of view with the same penetrating

[1] See also Zaehner, *Hinduism*, Oxford University Press, 1962.

exactness and acuteness with which Ramakrishna had explained the way
of *bhakti* and Sri Ramana Maharshi that of *jñāna*. Nor was that all. In the
process of showing that *karma-yoga* was on a par with *jñāna* and *bhakti*,
Radhakrishnan revealed another vital discovery that had been lying
latent: that *rāja-yoga* (contemplation) was equally on a par with *karma-
yoga* (action). Thus contemplation versus action is a constant theme in
Radhakrishnan's philosophy.[1] Things equal to the same thing are equal to
one another. In this case the end-product of the one is not only identical
with, but even includes, that of the other three. This conclusion, though
it sounds alarmingly simple, had far-reaching results. It freed the word
'yoga' from misunderstanding and disrepute. In popular conception,
particularly in the West, yoga meant usually *rāja-yoga* (the way of contemplation; inaction). That it could also mean *karma-yoga* (the way of
sublimating the ego through action) was not realized. This conflicted
sharply with the Indians of Radhakrishnan's generation who were burning
with zeal for social, political and economic reforms. They could not,
therefore, but disapprove of inaction whether contemplative or otherwise.[2] At the same time they were reluctant to part with anything that
could be described as belonging to the heritage of India. The problem was
how to combine spiritual enlightenment for the individual (hitherto expected mainly to come as the result of solitary contemplation) with such
social welfare for the masses as arose from industrialization and activity.
The way of *karma-yoga* (where action is not given up) appeared to be the
ideal solution and Radhakrishnan became its living prophet. As he often
emphasizes, *this is nothing new*. It is the central theme of the *Gītā* and the
story of king Janaka is an additional confirmation. Yet to the Western
world, which with the highly occidentalized East makes up practically the
whole world, it sounded as if it were something new;[3] strange, paradoxical, perhaps inconsistent but certainly enticing. Here for the first time
was a philosophy which hinted that, subject to a few technicalities,[4] it was
possible, indeed highly advisable, to eat your cake and have it. King
Janaka became the ideal to be followed.[5] Spiritual salvation in the process

[1] Radhakrishnan, *Religion and Society*, pp. 67–78.

[2] The action versus contemplation issue is also raised in the Bible in the story of
Martha and Mary. The anonymous author of *The Cloud of Unknowing* concludes
therefrom that contemplation is superior to action.

[3] It has always been mistakenly thought that a 'Yogi' is only a half-naked hermit
sitting on a solitary mountain peak in the Himalayas. That a Yogi (of the *karma-yoga*
type) can equally well be a business executive, the head of a state, or a field-marshal
(e.g. Arjuna) was never even considered.

[4] Which includes the giving up of all concern for the results of such action. As in
the vast majority of cases the fruit of action is itself the sole incentive for it, it is
obvious that this cannot be put into popular use. This aspect of the case has in no way
affected the optimism of its enthusiasts.

[5] It was (and still is) conveniently forgotten that King Janaka had to undergo
severe austerities and disciplinary training. The general of an army can perhaps be a
convinced follower of *karma-yoga*, as Arjuna was; but is it possible to imagine an army
of soldiers—all like Arjuna?

of social well-being! It was this current which produced Gandhiji, Tagore and Radhakrishnan. The same reasons which made it acceptable to the modernizing East made it attractive to the West—and thus the renaissance called Western Vedānta began. Yoga became respectable in the eyes of the extraverted West as soon as the reassurance was given that no *actual* parting from people and possessions was required. A mere inward renunciation was enough. The genuine student of yoga in India was also relieved of the common accusation from ill informed critics that he was seeking his personal salvation at the expense of neglecting the social good.[1] This exaggerated concern for 'the suffering masses of India—poor, starving and illiterate' came from all quarters,[2] Christian, secular and Communist. The Christian West was shocked by anyone who could think of meditation when there was so much of God's work to be done; the non-religious humanists insisted that contemplation, in search of what *they* thought inexistent, was a crime postponing, if not preventing, the instant realization of their welfare state Utopias. The Communists saw in contemplation an additional perverseness of the opium of the masses. Indeed, yoga and religion were in danger of being jettisoned altogether, had not Radhakrishnan and his like saved the situation by pointing out that *karma-yoga* was a solution as valid for society as for the individual.

Alas! man cannot serve two masters, God and Ego.[3] What was thrown out of the door as the individual's ego came back through the window disguised as society's ego. In the general confusion the Christ-aspect of *karma-yoga* was recrucified and the Barnabas (ego) set free again. The *karma-yoga* ideal is workable only if society consists largely of Arjunas, Janakas or Radhakrishnans.

Radhakrishnan describes the philosophical genius of India as arising from 'a desire to think, to dream and to meditate'. The philosopher is under a moral obligation to think, dream and meditate knowing full well that he will probably be ridiculed and derided for it unless he produces a sufficient number of pages full of erudite research. This obligation and the difficulties arising from it are magnified a thousand-fold in the present case because the essential message of both Radhakrishnan and Huxley—and the quintessence of all their philosophy—is that a person should put all activity aside and *first of all* acquire that inner experience which Radhakrishnan calls *realization of the supreme Self* (and which he maintains is the fundamental basis common to all religions). Huxley calls it *vertical self-transcendence* (which he maintains is the goal and essence of all philosophy). Now in Radhakrishnan's philosophy no one is qualified to talk or write about these things who has not himself had this inner experience.[4] Accord-

---

[1] Albert Schweitzer, Bertrand Russell, *et al.*

[2] The only outstanding exception was Aldous Huxley who as usual was not carried away by the sound and fury of social-welfare maniacs. See his *Time Must Have a Stop*, where such a maniac (Sebastian's father) comes to a sad end.

[3] That is the moral of Aldous Huxley's *The Grey Eminence*.

[4] In Indian philosophy anyone who reads or writes on *Religionsphilosophie* without having had this inner experience (comparable to the 'unless a man be born again' of

ing to Huxley, the writing of books is *horizontal self-transcendence* and only a step better than *downward self-transcendence* (the forgetting of one's ego in drink or sexual orgies). If it is too much to expect the author actually to have had this inner experience, he is at least expected to have given it his most sincere attention. This has nothing to do with the religious content of this or that particular Church. We are here concerned only with the practical possibilities for a contemplative life open to an average person living in a *western* city today. The proof of this is that almost all of Huxley's biographical and historical works deal with the life of Catholic saints while Radhakrishnan continually quotes Christian saints and mystics. Ideally the author should be a saint, but if he is not can he ever have this inner experience? He can in every case according to Huxley. Radhakrishnan, however, tends to follow the view of the *Kaṭha Upaniṣad*[1] that the Supreme Self reveals itself only to those whom it selects for the purpose, but the *possibility* of having this inner experience is the same for every individual.

The task of the sincere seeker who wants to write a book is to set out without further delay in quest for this inner experience: for that would conform with the philosophy of both these writers. If he will not or cannot do that, he should explore the whole subject at least *theoretically* and elucidate his findings. But he cannot hope for success if his *primary* goal is research and not the final experience.[2] He has to live in constant readiness for whatever degree of inner experience may be vouchsafed him. He has voluntarily to undergo a discipline that knows no indulgence. If (and it is a very big IF) one did have this inner experience, then according to Radhakrishnan one would write a much better book. But according to Huxley, the inner experience would be so deeply compelling and satisfying that one would be neither willing nor able to write. So the sincere author is on the horns of a very serious dilemma. If he does not obtain this inner experience, then he writes about what he neither knows nor understands. If he does obtain it then he knows and understands but is disinclined to write. 'How shall the absolute *Tao* be explained? He who speaks, knows not; he who knows, speaks not.' Huxley has dealt with this problem in his novel *Time Must Have a Stop* where Bruno explains the line of demarcation between a great artist and a saint. Huxley formulates his theory that all great artists have to keep a sharp look out in order to avoid becoming saints. According to him the birth of the saint (soul-consciousness) means the death of the artist (ego-manifestation).

The situation in which the research student finds himself would, therefore, be farcical, were the consequences not so grave. In fact, the bitter results of such a dilemma can only be appreciated by one who has lived in India

---

Christian theology) is compared to a merchant's camel which does not know the value of the treasure it carries on its back.

[1] *Kaṭha Upaniṣad*, I. 2. 23.

[2] 'The Self (Supreme Self, Soul, Christ-consciousness, Holy Ghost) reveals its true Character (only) to one that seeks it (the inner experience) *exclusively*.' (Italics mine)— Radhakrishnan, *The Principal Upaniṣads*, p. 620.

and seen the irony of spiritual giants on the one hand and mass illiteracy on the other. Radhakrishnan, however, anticipated this dilemma and found a way out. The solution according to Swami Vivekananda is 'to make the end also the means'.[1] Let us examine this sentence with some care as it affords, perhaps, the only way out of the dilemma, for it solves the average Westerner's most acute difficulty in accepting the life of the spirit. It also contains the essence of Radhakrishnan's message to the world. As it is a two-edged sword, one side of it applies to the West and the other to the *unwesternized* East. Let us reverse and re-examine this sentence: '*Make the means also the end*'. Here the word *end* refers to that inner experience which is considered to be the goal or purpose of existence in a human body. That this is so in all religions (Radhakrishnan's view) and also of all philosophy (Huxley's *philosophia perennis*) is not disputed by either of these two writers. In considering various methods of realizing or achieving this lofty and ultimate end, a very human error creeps in. It lies in thinking that human activity can be divided neatly into two separate water-tight compartments: one of activity directly motivated by this ultimate end, the other of activity motivated by the many different 'inferior' ends in view. Thus, for instance, in our example the author's efforts in his search for the inner experience would fall into the first compartment and his efforts at writing his book into the second. It is this hard and fast division of action which is the cause of our human enigmas. The most famous example of it in the West is Hamlet and in the East Arjuna; for both were princes and, therefore, men of action. The problem remains unsolved in Hamlet. The *Gītā* solves it not by destroying but by melting the division between the two compartments of action. It is as if a wall of ice between two containers of water were removed by heating the water in one of the compartments. By changing the motive with which actions in the second compartment are done the division between the two compartments disappears. Translated into practical terms it means that the author should seek to acquire that inner experience in, by, and through the writing of his book, thus 'making the end also the means'. The seeking of the inner experience and the writing of the book should no longer be considered as two separate kinds of activity. All action and all activity should lead to the realization of this inner experience. Thus without injustice to either side is solved the dilemma between God and mammon, between being a hermit in the Himalayas or a soldier on the battle-field, between activity in writing and serenity in contemplation. This is the only way to write about Eastern wisdom with a good conscience. To adopt any other method would be to act like the Arab who after shouting all day that a particular debtor was insolvent asked the latter to pay him a day's wages.[2] Thus the answer to the brutal *either/or* challenge of our times is: between two disadvantages choose neither, between two advantages, both.

Making the wisdom of the East intelligible to the West can be done by

[1] Or 'to make the means also the end'. So long as the two are made identical it matters not how the sentence is phrased.

[2] *Mystic Tales of the Arabs.*

drawing on the work of such writers as the West is acquainted with. If this wisdom is to receive a more sympathetic hearing (and that is the task to which both Radhakrishnan and Huxley have dedicated themselves) one must be able to place it within the framework of Christian theology and the experience of Christian saints and mystics. The fundamental difference between ancient and contemporary philosophy lies not in the content of metaphysical ideas but in the application of metaphysical wisdom to practical life. Radhakrishnan has spent all his energy in trying to convince the West, as well as the westernized East, that Indian philosophy, *amongst other things*, has at its disposal a *'practical'* remedy for the spiritual sickness arising from the West's short-sighted conception of utility. He traces the downfall of philosophy's reputation to the academic strait-jacket into which it has been put.[1] The inexorable law of nature is that what is totally superfluous shall be progressively exterminated. Radhakrishnan's idea is to save both philosophy and Western (meaning modern) civilization by making the *'practical'* advantages of the former apparent to the latter. That has always been the standpoint of Eastern wisdom through the ages. To divorce philosophy from life is to put both in danger. Like the bee, philosophy gives not only wax for light but also honey for nourishment. Two such philosophers as Radhakrishnan and Huxley have a joint message. Let us remember that their real motive for publishing their thoughts was not to contribute to learning but to help the rank and file of humanity. They both write under a feeling of urgency. Their books are filled with a sense of approaching crisis. Without putting it in words they imply unmistakably that we are living on the edge of a precipice at the foot of which is not death but *degradation*, of which death is only one among several forms. The real death is to miss that opportunity for Self Realization which life in a human body offers us all. We are living on the edge of a precipice in the sense that the *Zeitgeist*[2] has decided to make this task of Self Realization even more compelling.[3] As a result the consequences for man if he does not rise to the occasion will also be more drastic.[4] This, in

---

[1] The Society of Philosophical Inquiry which used to hold its meetings for over half a century in the U.S.A. had to close down in 1950 because of the *apathy* of the members toward philosophical thinking. It is also well-known that today in several institutions of learning the chair of philosophy is no longer filled.

[2] The issue of whether the *Zeitgeist* exists or not is neatly evaded by calling it the needs of the time or words to that effect. But Hegel's ghost is not an easy thing to exorcize.

[3] Very interesting to observe on this point is a remark made by Sri Aurobindo in his speech celebrating the first Independence Day of India. He showed how evolution does not proceed at an even arithmetical ratio but at a cumulative geometric one. Hegel's theory of the *Zeitgeist* appears to have found strong favour with both Aurobindo and Radhakrishnan and is noticeable when they discuss theories of evolution.

[4] This is also the idea which Bernard Shaw wanted to drive home. Bernard Shaw claimed *Back to Methuselah* as the only play which sincerely portrayed his 'philosophy'; the moral of this play is that the power which made man when the monkey did not come up to the mark, will make something more than man (the Superman?) if man does not come up to the mark.

turn, means that in the near future everything which is not directly concerned with man's reason for existence[1] will be exposed as self-defeating.
A ruthless nemesis is about to put every religion, philosophy, theory,
dogma, ideology etc. to the test. This is the challenge of our times and the
world has never faced a more serious one on such a scale. That is why both
these sages remind us in no uncertain terms of the Bible's words: 'Repent
and be saved': saved not from any physical terrors but from degradation
into any form of materialism, be it called pragmatism, communism,
utilitarianism or logical positivism, which would make us forget our
divine origin[2] and, therefore, our spiritual destiny which is to reclaim our
inherent if hidden divinity. Therefore our practical duty, particularly if
we are philosophers, is to put aside all intellectual gymnastics, and offer
something which the average man can grasp. The twentieth century is that
of the average man. The sense of urgency arises from the feeling that there
is no more time to waste. We can explain rationally why we are in this
precarious situation if we study the theory of the four *Yugas*, which is
translatable into terms of Western philosophy. It is only the *Zeitgeist*
divided into four stages with poetical descriptions ranging from gold to
iron. We are now in the *Kali Yuga* or Age of (spiritual) darkness.[3] Whether
we call it a *crisis* or *Kali Yuga*, no form of procrastination is permissible.

The reader should remember that as we are dealing here with such ulti-
mates as *God*, *Spirit*, *Soul* and *Life*, he cannot expect the same degree of
scientific accuracy as in a thesis on the effect of penicillin on rats, or on the
horse-power of a jet engine. Wisdom can stand the test of criticism, but not
the strain of scepticism. For in the realm of the spirit even a superstition,
in so far as it arises from faith (however misplaced it may be), is a force to
be reckoned with. We are dealing here with the imponderables of life,
which tend to be ignored precisely because they are imponderable. Is it not
like a man who dies by refusing to breathe for fear of inhaling germs?

We are not dealing with a philosophy meant for the quiet cloisters of
Cambridge or Heidelberg, but with a philosophy first given on the battle-
field of *Kurukaṣetra* by Krishna to Arjuna, while its latest version is
offered by Radhakrishnan and Huxley to a world which like Arjuna is
filled with despair at the approaching catastrophe. The battlefield looms
large in the background of their philosophy and its atmosphere is one of
constant emergency, alarm, and alert. To rephrase their message with
academic elegance in cool dispassionate tones would paint a false picture.

'To action alone hast thou a right and never at all to its fruits; let not the
fruits of action be thy motive; neither let there be in thee any attachment
to inaction.'[4]

[1] Self Realization or, theologically speaking, the fulfilment of God's purpose on
earth.

[2] Cf. 'God made man in his own image.'

[3] So spiritually bankrupt is this age in which we are living supposed to be, that by
Buddhist belief the Bodhisattvas expressly ask to be reborn at such a time so as to
help to dispel the materialistic darkness of such a period.

[4] *Gītā*, II, 47.

And again:

'One should not give up one's task though it may be defective, for all enterprises are clouded by defects as fire by smoke.'[1]

If, as Whitehead said, 'all Western philosophy is only foot-notes to Plato', the best of Eastern wisdom can only be a commentary on the *Gītā*. Arjuna is the symbol for those of us who feel lost and yet that they should not be lost, who cannot decide whether to fight or give way to despair. Action or inaction? To all these despondent Arjunas and hesitant Hamlets the *Gītā*, through Radhakrishnan, roars out anew its call to arms. We hear the cry. Can we resist the call? Did not Mohammed say: 'Paradise is under the shadow of swords'?

When people speak of a reconciliation between Eastern and Western philosophy, they usually mean a reconciliation between imaginary differences. Nothing so ruins the chances of a spontaneous and natural *rapprochement*, as the attitude that the two are different creatures to be brought under one yoke. Eastern and Western philosophy belong not only to the same genus but also to the same species. It is one creature not two. They are called by different names only in the sense that one state of an individual's mind can be called conscious, the other subconscious. A reconciliation here as elsewhere is a psychological rather than an historical event. But even considered historically such a *rapprochement* is not unique. Eastern and Western philosophy met when Cyrus conquered Ionia in 600 B.C.

'The Greek Philosophers, from the days of Thales, the head of the school of Miletus, came in contact with the Orient.'[2]

It is typical of the culture-nationalism of our times that even thought is chopped up and labelled American or British, Chinese or Indian philosophy and so on. In ancient times illumination from wherever it came, was called 'wisdom' and it remained at that. What makes the mingling of Eastern and Western philosophy appear so momentous is only the late-awakened, guilty conscience of the human race. A few decades ago, a colonial attitude was adopted towards everything which came from the East whether it was rice or cocoa, poetry or philosophy, the monsoon or the people. In the process the West, for the first time, gave a *new* religion to the East: the worship of the country whose passport one happens to carry.[3]

---

[1] *Ibid.*, XVIII, 48.

[2] *History of Philosophy Eastern and Western*, Vol. II, p. 12.

[3] This is not meant frivolously. The House of Lords, in the famous case of Lord Haw-Haw, ruled that a person owes allegiance to the country issuing a passport regardless of that person's origin or nationality. Failure to observe this resulted in a death sentence for Lord Haw-Haw. The passport is moreover a jealous god—it is a *sin* to love any country more than (or even as much as) the country issuing the passport.

This, like every other religion, found fertile soil in the East. Its fruit is the present day Afro-Asian monomania of patriotism and nationalism. This adolescent attitude still approaches comparative philosophy as if it were a kind of football-match between East and West. The danger point is reached when a philosophy is admired not because of its intrinsic worth but because it happens to be Indian, or condemned not because it is mediocre but because it is modern. The main point is that one should distinguish between a *rapprochement* deliberately contrived because of the increasing political importance of the Orient, and one that is the natural, inevitable process of conditions in the modern world. The *rapprochement*, or rather its beginning, is an accomplished fact and offers little room for controversy. The issue, however, is complicated by being confused with that of interreligious friendship. There are even observers to whom such a *rapprochement* is for some reason undesirable,[1] impractical[2] or dangerous.[3]

The most frequent argument advanced against a *rapprochement* by its critics can be reduced to this: a *rapprochement* is extremely undesirable if it is not a natural outcome. Such an outcome is not to be reckoned with because Western Christianity is something unique, completely different from the Eastern thought which preceded it.

Now there is no substance in the above argument. First of all Christianity, like all the great religions of the world, came from the East. In fact, Eastern wisdom prepared the ground for it. Nor is it, at its highest level, incompatible with Oriental thought. No less a sage than St Augustine wrote:

'That which is called the Christian Religion existed among the Ancients [the East], and never *did not exist, from the beginning of the human race* until Christ came in the flesh, at which time the true religion, *which already existed*, began to be called Christianity.'[4]

Another falsehood, or rather misunderstanding, which constantly creeps up clouding the *rapprochement* is that Eastern wisdom, being some kind of religion, competes with the exclusive claims of Christianity. For example, C. G. Jung says: 'You cannot be a good Christian, either in your faith or in your morality or in your intellectual make-up, and practise genuine yoga at the same time.'[5] Moreover if you happen to be a European, then for historical reasons ('which are written in your blood'[6]) your 'psychology' will be and remain 'thoroughly Christian'[7]—irrespective of your personal

---

[1] E. W. F. Tomlin, *The Great Philosophers of the Eastern World*, p. 283.

[2] Professor F. S. C. Northrop's essay on *The Relation between Eastern and Western Philosophy*.

[3] C. G. Jung's, 'Psychological Commentary' to *The Tibetan Book of the Great Liberation*, particularly pages xxxvi to xlix.

[4] St Augustine, *Epis. Retract.*, Book i.

[5] 'Psychological Commentary' to *The Tibetan Book of the Great Liberation*, p. lvi.

[6] *Ibid.*

[7] *Ibid.*, p. xxxvi.

wishes. All this arises from a total misunderstanding of what yoga is. It cannot be repeated too often that Eastern wisdom is *not* a religion. It can best be described as the *mechanism* or internal *machinery* of any and every religion. And even if a person does not believe in any religion or any God, it makes no difference to a wisdom which takes its stand on the fundamental and transcendental value of the ego-eliminated state. No matter how many different kinds of motorcar there may be, they all function because there is some connection between the engine and the wheels. It is the same with yoga. No matter what god, goal, or deity a religion posits, yoga is *only* concerned with showing an individual how to approach the god, goal, or deity which he happens to worship. As far as interreligious controversy is concerned, wisdom is as objective as pure mathematics. Moreover, Jung does not seem to realize that yoga can be one, or more, or all, of several yogas, including that of *bhakti*, of which he seems to be unaware. The Christian form of worship belongs to the sphere of *bhakti-yoga*. Jung's mistake is that he has narrowed the vast and varied field of Eastern wisdom to mean *only rāja-yoga*—the way of psychologically planned meditation. This becomes clear from his own description of what he thinks yoga to mean: 'If you can afford to seat yourself on a gazelle skin under a *Bo*-tree or in a cell . . .'[1] that is genuine yoga, but not if you live in 'Mayfair or Fifth Avenue, or in any other place which is on the telephone. . . .'[2] It is obvious that *karma-yoga* which can be practised all the better in 'Mayfair or Fifth Avenue' has also been left out.

A *rapprochement* is, then, inevitable in the sense that water, if *not obstructed*, will find its own level. As Radhakrishnan said, in his *Sir Edward Beatty Memorial Lectures*: 'When we take a long view of history we will find that there is not an Eastern view which is different from the Western view of life.' The greatest obstruction to a natural, smooth and self-adjusting *rapprochement* is the insistence that some such *rapprochement first* take place. All naïve attempts to impose a kind of international date-line on world-philosophy are bound to end in frustration; for wisdom is nothing if not universal in its scope and spirit. Eastern wisdom includes Western thought, and vice versa. Neither wisdom nor thought is capable of being brand-marked Eastern or Western. Why then do we do it? It is a temporary solution to bridge the gap until we are ripe for an integral worldview. Wisdom includes knowledge as well as a progressively increasing ability to know more. It is this ever-increasing capacity that facilitates deep rearrangements of inner structure and thus stimulates the growth of a radically new yet integral view of the world.

The Eastern sage finds deep consolation in philosophy because he takes it for granted that philosophy offers only what is unaged and unageing. Philosophy, if it is to be called wisdom, must first have conquered time. Its only excuse for existence is that it offers the essential as against the merely accidental, the eternal in place of the ephemeral, the transcendental instead of the transient. Eastern wisdom is not something in which theories,

[1] *Ibid.*, lvi.
[2] *Ibid.*

schools, and ideas can come and go out of fashion. Its cardinal problem is the *purpose of human life; the goal to be achieved by this opportunity of having been born in a human body*. It is not so much concerned with finding out what this purpose is, for it considers that as already found, as with *how to fulfil it*. The essence of Eastern wisdom is that each life has the same goal to strive for. In this respect we all have the same problem of how to achieve it. To pursue any other aim *at the expense of* this one is to risk frustration after frustration even unto death; or, in case of success, unending futility in the sense that boredom and discontent have not been banished once and for all.

Eastern wisdom argues: this goal, which every living being has to strive for, does not and cannot change with the passage of time. If philosophy merely means finding out *what* the purpose of human existence is, then, according to Eastern wisdom, this has already been discovered and there is nothing new left to contribute. Additional contributions to Eastern wisdom can, therefore, only deal with *how* to achieve this goal. If wisdom, whether in the East or elsewhere:

(i) denies that human life has a goal to strive for; or
(ii) denies that the above-mentioned is the goal of *all* human life for all time; or
(iii) gives priority to any other goal

then it cannot be said to be Eastern, in the innermost sense of that word, whatever other connection it may have with the East. If wisdom in any part of the world accepts this goal as the end-purpose of all human existence and deals with ways and means of realizing it, then it is part of the spiritual East. Eastern wisdom is not, therefore, monotonous or dogmatic. It deals with many problems and many aspects of a given problem. It is rich in interpretations and there is no topic under the sun with which it is not prepared to deal from a philosophical angle. But all this is subsidiary to its *central idea*. This has two different but related parts

(i) For what purpose, if any, is man (and creation) made?
(ii) How can man fulfil this purpose (thereby automatically deriving from life the utmost possible *satisfaction*, or 'the *Peace* that passeth understanding')?

The answer to the first question was found, and unanimously agreed upon, somewhere in the prehistoric past of Eastern wisdom. Philosophy in the East was no wild goose chase in pursuit of some hypothetical, controversial answer to the first question. It was the *answer* itself which formed the core, basis, and starting point of Eastern wisdom. Any further development was, and is of necessity, confined to the second question. Every age has its own peculiar difficulties and obstacles on the path leading to this goal, and the contemporary philosophy of every age concerned itself with the relative efficacy of different methods in overcoming obstacles on the way. But to

deny or replace this goal was, is, and will for ever remain entirely foreign
to the genius of Eastern wisdom. If a philosopher in the East were to hold
up any other ideal as the goal towards which all human life should aspire,
then it would cease to be Eastern wisdom and would become philosophy *in*
the East. However, the modern philosophy of the East, as represented by
Vedānta, boldly reaffirms this goal as the be-all and end-all of human life
on this planet. It is contemporary in method, presentation, interpretation,
and commentary but in substance and inner spirit it is lost in antiquity.
It is contemporary Indian philosophy's greatest contribution that it
reformulates a difficult to understand, prehistoric message in a way which
makes it understandable and acceptable to the present generation. Ignorance of the purpose of human life has never been treated as a valid excuse
for not having fulfilled it.

At first sight this may mislead one into believing that Eastern wisdom is
dogmatic and has nothing new to offer, being a monotonous repetition of
threadbare, dogmatic presuppositions. But in fact exactly the opposite is
true. One of the peculiarities of Eastern wisdom is that it sounds fresh in
spite of countless repetitions. It is capable of consoling doubtridden,
anxious men by diverting their attention from the uncertainties of change
to the certainty of the changeless. No reasonable person can expect much
consolation from a statement which is subject to alteration in the future.
If Eastern wisdom is to offer mankind a rock to lean upon, it must offer
what is not alterable with time. What is subject to time is subject to death.
The desire to triumph over death in some way or other was the origin of
Eastern wisdom. But to triumph over death one must triumph over time.
This led to the greatest of all discoveries in the ancient East—that man in
some curious way participates both in time and in the timeless. That aspect
of man which participates in time is called the *jīva*, that which stands outside of time is called the Ātman. Now a philosophy which sets out to show
how man can triumph over time cannot itself be subject to change.
According to Eastern wisdom only that which is changeless can be
essential, and therefore the real, and therefore the Truth. The acid test and
definition of Truth in this wisdom is: that which does not and cannot
possibly change. This does not mean that Eastern wisdom is superior or
everlasting as compared to Western philosophy. It is not a question of
being true to tradition that is at stake here. For Eastern wisdom stands
or falls on the validity of this single central concept that:

All human life has a goal to strive for compared to which all other human
goals are subordinate if not irrelevant.

If one denies that life has any goal, purpose, or meaning then neither life
nor philosophy, Eastern or otherwise, makes any sense. If the whole is
equal to zero, so is the part.

It can be argued that succeeding generations will differ as to what this
all-important goal is; that the goal to be striven for will differ according
to environment, race, temperament, time, etc. But the distinguishing

hallmark of Eastern wisdom is that there is no controversy whatsoever as to the goal. This strongly inclines one to believe that Eastern wisdom must be some fiercely dogmatic theology in disguise. But why should Eastern wisdom, which is usually so tolerant towards widely differing beliefs and allows a complete democracy of varying viewpoints, refuse to give any quarter here. The reason is that for it the individual is all important in his capacity as an individual. It is the goal for which everyone, *as an individual*, has to strive, for that is the main topic of Eastern wisdom and not the goal of any bundle of human beings such as society, nation, humanity, proletariat, species or the like. This means that when dealing with an individual as such, the fact of death has also got to be acknowledged. Any goal which refused to consider the *absolute certainty* that death comes to everybody everywhere, would be fraudulent. The goal of human life, therefore, whatever else it may include or omit, must provide some method or process for placing the individual beyond the reach of his more or less abrupt termination.[1] Physically and biologically this is neither possible nor desirable. The *only* solution is to trace a person's individuality to its roots. As death is so uncompromising and unbending, wisdom is compelled to be the same. As a result the individual, in every generation, is given something concrete to strive for. He is not left to think in despair that a philosopher in the future may evolve a system which will ridicule the goal on which he, at the moment, is asked to concentrate even at the cost of suffering and sacrifice. This removes wisdom from the status of a fashion parade at which contemporary theories and systems can be displayed. All wisdom is a race against death. While in the West the philosopher is more akin to the scientist, and philosophy more analogous to science, in the East he is closer to the mystic, and philosophy to enlightened mysticism. There is a very important difference between the mystic and the scientist which is comparable to that between the climate and the weather. For instance, many years ago scientists claimed that light consisted of particles, then they said it was made up of waves, now they say it is both. But the mystics of all generations are unanimous in their spiritual experience if not in their interpretations of it.[2] Those who want philosophy to be scientific forget that it would then be subject to the drawbacks of science. For the latter implies the *disinterested* pursuit of what is called truth for want of a better name. If disinterestedness is the test of scientific accuracy then Eastern wisdom is non-scientific, though not unscientific. Eastern wisdom is no disinterested pursuit of this, that or the other, It has a vested and exclusive interest, which is perhaps so selfish and ruthless as to be an obsession, in finding the *purpose*, followed by its *fulfilment*, of man's presence on this planet. Even were this goal not disputed, the critic would be justified in putting the following questions:

[1] No wonder that Jesus, who had to deal with the same problem of life everlasting and solved it successfully in his own way, said 'Heaven and Earth will pass away but my words will not pass away.' One can only defeat death by being even more inexorable than death itself!

[2] Cf. Joseph Politella, *Mysticism and Mystic Consciousness*, Kent State University Bulletin, Ohio, 1964 (Research Series 8).

(i) Why should the fulfilling of this goal be considered as the *only* purpose of life in a human body?

(ii) Why should it be regarded as the highest goal?

(iii) Why too, for *every* individual?

(iv) Why should this goal or purpose not change with the passing of time?

It is sufficient to point out that Eastern wisdom sees each individual as a kind of spiritual, psychological and chemical mixture of the *Self* and *not-self*. Life gives us the opportunity to extract and isolate the radium of the Self from the thousands of tons of dirt and mud which represent the not-self. Thus:

(i) It considers that to be the *only* purpose of human life because, from its point of view, once the process of Self Realization is complete, the answer becomes obvious in the process of realization itself. Any other goal can by definition lie only in the province of the not-self. Self and not-self must part either voluntarily, as in the realization of the *inner experience*, or, as for most of us, involuntarily in death. More important, if this were not the *only* goal then the individual would still remain *unsatisfied* after attaining it. If there was no one, single, exclusive goal in life, the individual would have to go through the endless torment of chasing one goal after another without obtaining any *lasting* satisfaction. If it were not the *only* goal, it would be no goal at all. For it means the attaining of something beyond which there is nothing further left to attain. An important corollary to this is that Self Realization does not lead to the boredom of having nothing to do, but to lasting satisfaction.[1] Otherwise we would be back in Schopenhauer's vicious circle of 'not to attain what we want leads to dissatisfaction; while satiety causes boredom'.[2] The *sole* purpose of human life is to attain that which brings unvarying satisfaction, regardless of whatever else may have been left undone; and its non-fulfilment invariably leads to discontent no matter what else may have been achieved.[3] This is why Eastern wisdom considers it to be the *highest* goal. Furthermore a study of Eastern wisdom, like learning how to drive a car, consists of *practice* as well as *theory*. Whoever pretends to understand Eastern wisdom by merely reading about it is like a person trying to learn swimming by taking a correspondence course. Innovations in wisdom are possible at the circumference but not at the centre. Those who accuse Eastern wisdom of being devoid of progress should bear in mind that progress beyond a peak may mean falling into a ravine. To go farther north than the North Pole would be to go South.

It is fatuous to pass off minor innovations as changes when the central current has not altered, and cannot possibly change without doing injustice to the subject. On the other hand one cannot deny that dynamic reinterpretations have taken place. It would be still greater folly to believe that Eastern wisdom is only a monotonous repetition of the old.

[1] 'He that drinketh of the water I give him will thirst no more.'
[2] See also Robert Louis Stevenson's Essay, *El Dorado*.
[3] *Gītā*, VI, 22.

It is *new* in the sense that every child that is born is new; it is *unvarying* in the sense that all children that are born are human beings with the characteristics common to human beings as such. This is indeed a great paradox of Indian philosophy: this old-newness or new-oldness. No Copernican Revolution, such as Kant claimed to have started, is here possible.

In every age, philosophers in the East have gone in search of new truths to discover. Their heroic attempts constitute the history of Eastern philosophy but not its conclusion. Its conclusion is that in the end they have all come back to the same key. Thus Radhakrishnan, in our own day, writes one more commentary on the *Gītā*; and Aldous Huxley calls it all Western Vedānta. Indeed it is in every way the *philosophia perennis*—this unchanging goal of wisdom in East and West. In wisdom, as in God, all is integrated.

CHAPTER 13

Behind the Veil of Magic

(Tibetan Mysticism and Modern Psychiatry: C. G. Jung and Evans-Wentz)

'Death?'—says one who has had this experience—'Die, I cannot anymore, for that belongs to my past like my youth and childhood.'[1]

People who quote Kipling's line 'East is East and West is West and never the twain shall meet' should consider the occasion when Professor Evans-Wentz from Oxford met Lama Kazi Dawa-Samdup of Tibet. The fruitful consequence of this East-West meeting were the four Tibetan Books published by the Oxford University Press:
1. *The Tibetan Book of the Dead.*
2. *The Tibetan Book of the Great Liberation.*
3. *Milarepa: Tibet's Great Yogi.*
4. *Tibetan Yoga and Secret Doctrines.*

No account of contemporary East-West philosophy would be complete without mentioning Evans-Wentz's lasting contribution, which has been appreciated by Western writers such as Carl G. Jung.[2] When it comes to esoteric philosophy, Evans-Wentz surpasses even Radhakrishnan in explaining the East in the light of the West. His most important contribution for our purposes, however, is his *Tibetan Book of the Dead* or more correctly the *Bardo Thödol*. It provoked much serious discussion in English-speaking countries in 1927, and Jung wrote of it:

'For years, ever since it was first published, the *Bardo Thödol* has been my constant companion, and to it I owe not only many stimulating ideas and discoveries, but also many fundamental insights.'[3]

From it Jung draws several vitally important conclusions which are indispensable for a proper understanding of the interrelationship between Eastern and Western philosophy, whether ancient or contemporary. But from our point of view it is especially valuable because it corroborates Radhakrishnan's philosophy of intuitional-absolute-idealism. This philosophy belongs to Berkeley's pattern as opposed to that of Locke and Hume. Bishop Berkeley founded a philosophical *Weltanschauung* which is almost

[1] Sri Ramana Maharshi.

[2] Aldous Huxley also appears to have been well acquainted with those books, especially with the *Bardo Thödol*. When he was at a critical stage during his mescalin experiment, his wife asked him questions precisely arising out of it. His *Time Must Have a Stop* was an attempt (rather immature) to portray Tibetan philosophy in the form of a novel.

[3] C. G. Jung, Foreword to *The Tibetan Book of the Dead*, London, 1957, p. xxxvi.

identical to that of the Indian Monists. Here we can observe a remarkable East-West correspondence. The Bishop arrives independently at the same conclusion as Vedānta. The most noteworthy Western philosopher in the Berkeley pattern was Fichte and it is interesting to note the almost exact resemblance of his philosophical *idea-ism*[1] to that of Milarepa. There is hardly any difference between the epistemology of Fichte and Milarepa,[2] although they had never heard of each other. It seems that Fichte's philosophy has not been properly understood and appreciated in the West. Perhaps future generations will find there a far more penetrating *Weltanschauung* than the West has yet produced. Berkeley, Fichte, Milarepa and Radhakrishnan form a kind of East-West chain in the history of philosophy, which for the want of a better name we call idea-ism. *The Tibetan Book of the Dead* is idea-ism's ingenious and most convincing defence. Only it does not claim to be such—like every oriental classic one has to read it between the lines. This remarkable book, while pretending to address a corpse on the nature of death, is really addressed to the living, and explains the value and purpose of life.[3] Assuming for a moment that idea-ism is true *then* by arguing backwards death would be exactly what the *Tibetan Book* describes it to be. Thus, if Radhakrishnan's readers have been convinced by what he says, they have only to read the *Tibetan Book* to find out what is waiting for them from the moment of death onwards. Radhakrishnan's philosophy and the Tibetan *Bardo Thödol* complete and complement each other like life and death. Radhakrishnan repeats again and again (to a *living* person, the reader) what the *purpose* of life is. The *Tibetan Book* repeats again and again (but pretending to address a dying person) what the *purpose* of life is. If he fails to achieve that purpose, the consequences attending his death have a common *idea-istic* metaphysical basis. That is to say, as life is *like* a dream, dream-like phenomena occurring after death cannot be intrinsically different from similar phenomena during life before death.

The Tibetan Book of the Dead provides the best testing ground for comparisons and contrasts between Eastern and Western philosophy. Moreover as Radhakrishnan does not hesitate to express his views about what death and the after-death state is like,[4] we have in the *Tibetan Book* our

---

[1] The word idea-ism or *Erscheinungslehre* is preferable to the word idealism which at least in English is seriously misleading.

[2] Here is an excellent opportunity for a student looking for a research subject in the history of philosophy. A comparison between Fichte and Milarepa is rich in untold possibilities.

[3] 'Under the guise of a science of death, the *Bardo Thödol* reveals the secret of life, and therein lies its spiritual value and its universal appeal.' Lama Anagarika Govinda, *The Tibetan Book of the Dead*, p. lxiii.

[4] In his book, *An Idealist View of Life*, Chapter VII, 'Human Personality and its Destiny', pp. 286–311, Radhakrishnan abandons his usual academic restraint and makes a series of bold statements relating to death, immortality, rebirth and the like. Some of these impetuous statements are amusingly unlike Radhakrishnan as when he is willing to accept love at first sight as evidence of rebirth (p. 289). This idea was the basis of Henry Rider Haggard's romances, *She* and *Ayesha*, or the *Return of She*.

best laboratory for testing theories about death and the hereafter.[1]

When people pretend to explain the after-death state it is usually from an occult, spiritualistic, supernatural or supernormal standpoint. *The Tibetan Book of the Dead* is the first record we have of a *purely philosophical* attempt at a coldly scientific, reasoned analysis of the after-death state uncontaminated by guesswork. It does not pretend to forecast what will happen after death, but, should anything happen, it explains what it *cannot* be otherwise than. For instance, no one can forecast *what* a person will dream tonight, but one can say that whatever he may dream it will consist of seeing, hearing, or feeling something and therefore will not be independent of imaginary sense impressions. In the same way one can without predicting the content of any particular dream, formulate a series of laws to which all dreams are subject. In much the same way the *Tibetan Book* avoids stating dogmatically what death is, but explains by a carefully worked process of *reductio ad absurdum* what death *cannot* be. For the first time the field of after-death possibilities is limited in range. Moreover this limitation of possibilities is reached without prejudice to the individual's religious views, cultural traditions, or eccentric superstitions.

Out of these four *Tibetan Books* two central facts emerge, which are in complete agreement with the ideas of both Radhakrishnan and Huxley:

1. The first all-important central idea is that every human life has a set purpose, which must be unconditionally fulfilled irrespective of whether the individual is aware of that purpose, or of the means of fulfilling it. No amount of useful or even benevolent activity can compensate for the failure to achieve that purpose. What is it? According to these four *Tibetan Books* it is to recognize 'the Clear Light of the Void'. What is this Clear Light of the Void? This brings us to the second point:

2. According to the *Bardo Thödol* any person (living or dead) can be either
   (1) experiencing (some thought, feeling, sensation etc.) while awake;
   (2) not experiencing anything while awake;
   (3) experiencing when not awake (in a dream);
   (4) neither experiencing nor awake (in dreamless sleep).

The (1) and the (3) together constitute what is called the *Bardo* which along with number (4) makes up the realm of *saṁsāra*. Opposed to this group of states of consciousness is (2) which constitutes *nirvāṇa*. Whereas all thoughts depend on a pre-existing consciousness, consciousness without thoughts—pure self-awareness—is not only possible but is the long-sought-for liberation itself. The *Tibetan Books*, like the Bible, claim that the Truth will make you free. The truth according to them is the *relative* reality of thoughts, and therefore all *Bardo-* phenomena, as compared to the *absolute* reality of 'consciousness-aware-of-nothing-but-itself'. Therefore in order to achieve this, a person must be: *alive*,[2] *awake*, fully conscious and yet at the same

---

[1] For it does not emphasize the contents of a stage of or belief in the hereafter, e.g. heaven, hell or purgatory, but the underlying structure itself.

[2] Thus the reading of the *Bardo Thödol* before a corpse is an excuse for driving home

time not thinking any thought whatsoever. This can be illustrated by an example. Imagine a film-projector for showing coloured slides, throwing pictures on a screen. If they follow one another quickly enough a scene is projected on the screen. If the slides are properly arranged in a set order, the scene will be more or less comprehensible.

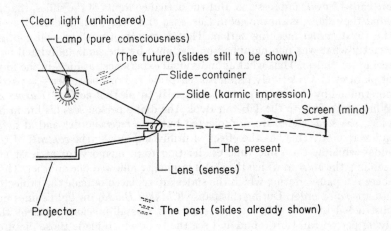

The light of the lamp before it meets the slide is comparable to the *clear light of the void*. This light is *pure consciousness* devoid of thoughts. It cannot be seen, and if seen would make no impression on the mind. It cannot be experienced *qua* experience. It is equivalent to pure Being. Being without any characteristics is equivalent to *no-thing*, but there is this difference—its presence is immediately indicated when it comes in contact with a coloured slide. The coloured slides are *karmic impressions* which magnified by the lens (senses) are projected on the screen (mind).

Now in our example there are two possibilities of 'recognizing' the light of the lamp in its original state.

1. Either make a pause during which no slide is put into the projector and recognize the light in the spotlessly reflected screen, or
2. Turn your head round and so to speak travel backwards with the light through the lens and then through the slide.

The first method is what the *Tibetan Book of the Great Liberation* explains as the 'seeing of reality' because the light is relatively real, while the pictures are relatively illusory.

The second method is what the *Tibetan Book of the Dead* suggests to the

---

the importance of being alive to those who are present and listening (e.g. mourners, relatives, etc.). That it cannot benefit a *dead* (as opposed to a dying) person should be clear for the common-sense reason, that the dead person is not likely to hear the book being read.

corpse, and illustrates what would happen were it possible. It is as difficult for the dead person to see through the *karmic* impression which is presented, as it is for a living person to accompany the projected light backwards into the lamp.

The order in which the slides have been arranged *before* projection is *karma*—here used in its popular but false meaning as destiny. Hence they are called *karmic* impressions. But the actual contents of the slides, that is, what they show, is *karmic not* in the sense of destiny, but as derived from the word *karma* meaning action. That is to say, the slides will contain exactly what was photographed on the film (by the same individual now seeing the slides). Thus what an individual experiences as life—in the form of pictures in a relatively regular order projected on the screen—is partly determined by destiny (*Karma* 1) and partly by his past actions (*Karma* 2). When, according to the Tibetan Book, the dying person sees his life in review, the *same* slides are re-projected but in a *reverse* order and at a far quicker speed. This has the effect of firmly impressing the *contents* of the slides while at the same time eradicating from memory, or at least enfeebling, the *order* in which the slides originally followed one another. Then there is a pause, during which the slides are replaced outside the projector in haphazard order. During this pause (*Chikhai Bardo*) the light shines unobstructed by any slide on the screen. At this all-precious moment the dying person can turn round and see the light which made those pictures possible. Thus even a very wicked person can win liberation because at this moment the slides—his *karma*—are not in operation. Once he realizes the light he also realizes that the pictures are not real happenings but projections.[1] Conversely, if he were to realize that the pictures are not real, but only projections, he could trace his way to the light. And that is exactly what the *Tibetan Book of the Dead* asks him to do now as the slides are reprojected in utterly haphazard order. But this is hardly possible now that the person is dead. This is the *Chönyid Bardo* not very different from haphazard projections during life as in dreams, psychoses, or insanity.[2]

An important philological truth which emerges from this philosophical presentation is that the word 'Self', or ego, is synonymous with the word 'life'. Thus the question 'What will happen to me after I die?' reveals its own answer.

As Radhakrishnan supports even the Rebirth (*Sidpa Bardo*) Theory;[3] his philosophy is in full agreement with these four *Tibetan Books*. This is because both he and they draw on a common source of wisdom, namely, the ancient esoteric philosophy of India which was later passed on to Tibet while it became obsolete in India because of foreign invasions. When the wave of ideological persecution swept over Tibet, the esoteric philosophy was literally buried underground to be rediscovered later on by *Tertons* or

---

[1] This is the truth that makes him free.

[2] See for instance H. G. Wells's *Christina Alberta's Father*, London, 1925.

[3] 'The self seeking for rebirth obtains embodiment in the frame offering the necessary conditions.' 'The Soul draws around it the forces necessary for its proper embodiment.' *An Idealist View of Life*, p. 296.

finders of buried treasure. Unfortunately in our own times another wave of persecution has swept across a large part of the globe including Tibet, and this time there is little chance of the esoteric philosophy being buried in safety for future generations. In this philosophy Materialism, whether it be Marxist Communism or Western Humanism, finds its deadliest foe. The *Tibetan Books*, therefore, symbolize a counter-challenge to all forms of materialism; and in changing the materialist's hard and indestructible matter into the fleeting state of the *Bardo*, it uses methods as scientific and accurate as the materialist's own mania for empirical truths can wish for.[1]

'A very justifiable fear of metaphysics', we are told, prevented Freud from reaching anything except an essentially negative valuation of the unconscious. As an introspective investigation into the nature of the sub-conscious mind plays a vital role in Eastern metaphysics, it is a Godsend to find a great psychologist who is also a philosopher well-versed in Eastern systems. Although Jung makes many mistakes, one definite fact emerges: that in the East as in modern Western existentialism, there is a very close interdependence between psychology and philosophy. In fact it is through psychological experiments and demonstrations that Eastern philosophy will one day attain the status of a universally accepted science in the modern world. Psychology, when equipped with the exactness and systematization of science, can be an indispensable aid in the proper understanding of Indo-Tibetan philosophy. Nor can it be otherwise when we realize that the two main considerations of Indo-Tibetan (hereafter referred to only as Eastern) philosophy are:

(i) our knowledge of the external world, especially when considered as nought but phenomena or *resembling* a prolonged dream-like state. It can hardly be denied that psychology is a great help in the study of any process of cognition, *a fortiori*, which is based on the *māyā*-philosophy of India.

(ii) The second principal theme is the winning of that Enlightenment which comes from realizing the *relative* unreality of *saṁsāric* existence because of its phenomena-based nature. This involves a study of the various states of consciousness which underlie and support the cognition of phenomena. And it is to psychology again that we must turn for a systematic study of the possibilities and nature of consciousness in its many aspects. A study of psychology enables us to understand how and in what way the various conclusions of Eastern philosophy were arrived at—and how, if at all, they can be checked and found correct, or contradictory. It can serve to check the vast balance-sheet of metaphysical conclusions. The modern psychologist should therefore not fear them like Freud, but face them like Jung. For our purposes

---

[1] For example the *Surangama Sutra* (the Essence of Mind) of the Buddha is a search for the correct difference of meaning between mind and *Mind* by a method as dialectical as any Marx ever used. It is, therefore, incorrect to believe that carefully reasoned analysis in a harsh dialectical way is a modern invention of Western philosophy. See also Charles Luk, *The Surangama Sutra*, London, 1965; and Eva Martin, *Reincarnation: the Ring of Return*, New York, 1965.

Jung's most important, and controversial, contributions are his commentaries on *The Tibetan Book of the Dead*, *The Tibetan Book of the Great Liberation* and *The Secret of the Golden Flower*. When we compare Chapter XIV of his *Seelenprobleme der Gegenwart*[1] with Part II, Chapter V of his *Aion*[2] we feel justified in having equated the Indian term Ātman (meaning *Real Self*) with Christ-consciousness. Here the word Christ means what St Paul described as the 'Christ in me', thus signifying the ego-free state of our innermost, and therefore essential or *real* being. And *Pure Being* is a fair equivalent for *Real Self*. Hence Christ-consciousness does not mean the consciousness of Christ but Christ *as* the very consciousness of *Pure Being*—man as he would be in the ego-eliminated state of Perfection. That is the state in which, according to St Thomas Aquinas,[3] man virtually, if not actually, surpasses even the angels.

It is indeed a pity that Jung's introduction to Zimmer's *Der Weg zum Selbst* is so disappointingly short, superficial, and insufficient. Let us, however, consider his 'Psychological Commentary' on the two *Tibetan Books* in some detail as it deserves repeated study.

Without Jung's enlightening commentary the *Bardo Thödol*, this very difficult book, would be still harder to understand. As for those who *pretend* to find it easy, one need only quote Jung: 'an idea that seems all too obvious to the enlightened European, because it reminds him of his own banal simplifications. But though the European can easily explain away these deities as projections, he would be quite incapable of positing them at the same time as real. The *Bardo Thödol* can do that, because in certain of its most essential metaphysical premises, it has the enlightened as well as the unenlightened European at a disadvantage.'[4]

Indeed the idea that something can be real and unreal at the same time is most allergic to the Western, 'either-or' type of thinking. As Professor Conger wrote: 'historically the West has been more concerned to introduce sharp distinctions . . . first, as to method, through the keen mind of Greece, with its distinctions of A and not-A. . . .'[5] But this superficial brilliance of the clear, but rather artificial, Athenian sun has to be paid for by a lack of subtlety; an inflexibility which hardens into an inability to understand the more profound and intuitional wisdom of religion and philosophy. This A versus not-A type of thinking develops quickly into the bigotry of 'all that is not-A is anti-A'. So that in our own day we hear such hysterical cries as 'whoever is not against communism is for it', or 'whoever is not baptized is an enemy of Christianity' and the like. This has gone to such extremes that Professor F. S. C. Northrop states that Eastern philosophy is mistaken because it refuses to be bigoted. He explains in

---

[1] *Psychologische Abhandlungen*, Vol. III.
[2] *Psychologische Abhandlungen*, Vol. VIII.
[3] *Summa Theologica*, i, q. 117, a.2, a d.3.
[4] 'Psychological Commentary', p. xxxvii.
[5] 'Radhakrishnan's World', *Library of Living Philosophers*, Volume 8, p. 111.

detail that *tolerance* need not necessarily be a virtue. In fact he claims that it is unsuitable to Western thinking and therefore hardly deserving to be classified as a virtue: '. . . to apply the doctrine of toleration . . . to Western beliefs and spiritual values . . . is to impose (an alien) theory of value where its application is inappropriate.'[1]

Jung's view is, however, more mature and so he is in a position to appreciate the 'magnificently affirmative both-and' of the *Tibetan Book*. He really expresses the heart of the matter when he says: 'Whenever the Westerner hears the word psychological, it always sounds to him like *only* psychological.'[2] And the same error crops up whenever such words as illusion, appearance, idea, *Erscheinung, māyā* or the like are used. It is this habit of putting on such inflexible mental strait-jackets that, more than anything else, prevents the West from getting an insight into the inner-most essence of Eastern philosophy. But as Jung says: 'Somehow we always have a wrong attitude to these things'.[3] But if we can put ourselves for a moment in the position of the dead man before whom the *Bardo Thödol* is being read, we may learn from its first paragraph that the *giver* of all *given* things (that is, given in the form of a series of tiny *karmic* impressions, magnified by the mind and *projected* by the senses) is within us as our Real Self. This, as Jung explains, 'is a truth which in the face of all evidence . . . is never known, although it is often so very necessary, indeed vital, for us to know it. . . . Perhaps it is not granted to many of us to see the world as something given. A great reversal of standpoint, calling for much sacrifice, is needed before we can see the world as given by the very nature of the soul.'[4] Here soul means ultimate Reality, hence Real Self.

To understand the purpose of human existence, or life, the dying person must realize that it is from this world of given things that liberation is sought. *The permanent Giver is sought; not his transitory 'gifts'.* The 'Giver' is consciousness; the 'gifts' are thoughts. The *Bardo Thödol* serves to recall this, at the crucial moment, to the dying person.

Although there may be a grain of truth in Jung's suggestion that we should read the *Bardo Thödol* backwards, we should not forget the purpose for which it is intended. It is a kind of last minute opportunity offered to one who has probably wasted many opportunities, not a textbook for an undergraduate in psychology. Moreover, according to the book itself, communication continues beyond physical death, even into the womb of the next physical rebirth! In the process, efforts are made to win the position most favourable to the spiritual evolution of the deceased, if full Enlighten-ment is not possible. It would not therefore help the dying man to hear it read backwards.[5] But there is no harm in a healthy living person reading it that way for psychological research. Jung has, however, done well in

---

[1] 'Eastern and Western Cultural Values', *Library of Living Philosophers*, Volume 8, p. 651.

[2] 'Psychological Commentary', p. xxxviii.

[3] *Ibid.*, p. xxxix.

[4] *Ibid.*, p. x.

[5] Jung himself admits this point on p. xlix.

interpreting *karma* in this context 'as *psychic heredity* in the very widest sense of the word'.[1]

Jung is right when he says that: 'fear of self-sacrifice lurks deep in every ego,'[2] and it is this which offers the most powerful resistance to any attempt at seeking Liberation. This also explains the statistical rarity of those who make a genuinely determined quest for Enlightenment even when they know the how and why of it. A willingness to die is required, and although there may be many who can part with their body with equanimity, it is much more difficult to die to one's ego: to part with one's likes and dislikes, caprices, idiosyncrasies and whims, and all that conflagration of a million and odd passionate trifles which taken together symbolize what is dearest to us.[3]

How natural and yet how ridiculous is this fear! Like a child unwilling to leave his broken toy with a shopkeeper who agrees to repair and improve it free of charge. Jung is however misleading when he contrasts this ego with the subconscious mind instead of with the Ātman, or, in this case, the Clear Light of the Void or pure consciousness. For this could mislead the reader into thinking that the Ātman is only his own subconscious mind. Clearly that is not what is meant. What Jung calls the *collective unconscious* is the *form-taking* attribute given out by the Universal Cosmic Mind during a period of active manifestation: it is a *māyā*-like instrument for expressing *māyā*. But the Ātman by definition transcends *māyā*; the Clear Light of the Void is beyond forms. Jung says 'that which is feared also belongs to the wholeness of the self'.[4] Yes, if it means the psychological self; but then not everyone will heed Jung's clear warning that:

'These things really are dangerous and ought not to be meddled with in our typically Western way. It is a meddling with fate which ... can let loose a flood of sufferings of which no *sane* person ever dreamed. These sufferings correspond to the *hellish* torments of the *Chönyid* state....'[5]

I have put the words 'sane' and 'hellish' in italics to give the shrewd reader a clue. Jung even goes so far as to explain *why* it is dangerous to play the fool with these high voltage, Tibetan yoga and Lamaist teachings:

'The deliberately induced psychotic state ... in certain unstable individuals might easily lead to a real psychosis ... the real nature of the danger: it is a

---

[1] *Ibid.*, p. xliii.

[2] *Ibid.*, p. xlvii.

[3] Isaac is the symbol for this in the biblical story of Abraham. Nothing was dearer to Abraham than Isaac and it was this that he was ordered to kill. As long as he was reluctant, he was compelled to kill—but as soon as he was prepared to forgo what was dearest to him, he was allowed to keep it. For it is not this or that which is dear to us but the ego which underlies all our likes and dislikes. It is this ego which has to be killed. Isaac is only a symbol for this ego (false self-hood or psychological personality; the *jiva* as contrasted with Ātman).

[4] *Ibid.*, p. xlvii.

[5] *Ibid.*, p. xlvi.

disintegration of the wholeness of the *Bardo* body. . . . The psychological equivalent of this dismemberment is psychic dissociation. . . . This . . . abolishes the normal checks imposed by the conscious mind and thus gives unlimited scope to the play of the unconscious dominants . . . (the stability of the ego is surrendered) to the extreme uncertainty of what must seem like a chaotic riot of phantasmal forms.'[1]

The author can vouch for the correctness of Jung's conclusions from his own first-hand experience when in India. He witnessed it happen to persons of whom he had intimate knowledge. He had no knowledge of Jung at that time, but independently came to the same conclusion.

To read the *Bardo Thödol* and its various commentaries makes one wonder whether death remains one of 'the Great Mysteries' after all. One is strongly inclined to agree with Jung that 'every serious minded reader must ask himself whether these wise old Lamas might not, after all, have caught a glimpse of the fourth dimension and twitched the veil from the greatest of Life's secrets'. Seeing the care and attention the Tibetans have devoted to solving this problem, the impartial and objective manner in which they have approached it, the subtleness of the method and the consistency of its conclusions, one can hardly deny the plausibility of success at the end. If to the West it appears fantastic that a problem like death can have any *scientifically acceptable* solution, we must not forget that the West has hardly taken an adult attitude towards the three great problems of Death, Evil, and Suffering. Even today an explanation of the last has not evolved beyond the *Book of Job*. One of the most respectable Sunday newspapers in London once decided to devote every week a *few lines* to an explanation of death. The first short article was contributed by Bertrand Russell, and though extremely mild, inoffensive, and unenlightening was worthy of respect. But it inadvertently upset the pet dogma of some church. Next week several pages were devoted to polemics against the famous philosopher. The problems of Death, Evil, and Suffering are not investigated properly in the West for fear of upsetting some long-held dogma, or else to avoid coming in conflict with a world-affirming optimism.[2] There is a reckless yes-saying to life in spite of all suffering—specially that of other people. Instead of a mere animalistic fondness for survival, the *Bardo Thödol* offers more profound reasons to explain our instinctive preference for what is called life. As Jung says:

'The supreme vision [the word vision should here be understood as "no visions", for this is the *Chikhai* state of the Clear Light. It is this utter lack of all visions that distinguishes it from other states. Thus this sentence should really begin: "The supreme *insight* . . ."] comes not at the end of the *Bardo*, but right at the beginning, in the moment of death [that is, before death—*during* life]. . . . The spiritual climax is reached at the moment

---

[1] *Ibid.*, p. xlvii.

[2] 'All animals, except Man, know that the purpose of life is to enjoy it.' Samuel Butler, *Hudibras*.

when life ends [i.e. is about to end]. . . . *Human life, therefore, is the vehicle of the highest perfection it is possible to attain.'*

Further:

'That is just what the dead [meaning not yet dead, but just about to die] man has to recognize, if it has not already become clear to him during life, that his own psychic self and the giver of all data [the Real Self] are one and the same.'[1]

In its latter capacity the former may use the *collective unconscious* as an organ, channel or instrument. In its essence it is, however, the pure (meaning thought-free) consciousness underlying both the conscious and the unconscious, or subconscious, mind of the individual.

In a preface addressed to the Eastern reader Jung describes his efforts as an attempt 'to build a bridge from the Shore of the Orient to the Shore of the Occident, and to tell of the various paths leading to the Great Liberation, the *Una Salus*'. Whether he succeeds or not, the attempt is praiseworthy and a sign of the cross-pollination which is steadily taking place.

Just as Evans-Wentz clarifies for the West the deep wisdom of Tibet, and Zimmer that of India, Richard Wilhelm elucidates the contribution of China. Not the political or geographical China but the real China which few know of, and Wilhelm was one of those few. The greatness of his achievement can hardly be assessed by one who has not travelled outside Europe.

Here again one must confess that it is well-nigh impossible to follow Wilhelm without Jung's commentaries. Much of the wisdom of China would stand in danger of being condemned as witchcraft or superstition if one did not take into consideration what Jung calls the *synchronistic* principle:

'Whatever is born or done this moment of time, has the qualities of this moment of time.'[2]

This after all is not so very different from Hegel's *Zeitgeist* and his philosophy of History. But Jung says that this type of thinking 'has been absent from the history of (Western) philosophy since the time of Heraclitus, and only reappears as a faint echo in Leibniz'.[3]

Wilhelm's *The Secret of the Golden Flower*[4] may be considered as the converse side of the *Bardo Thödol*, just as life is the converse, and not the reverse, of death. It should, therefore, be read together with the other

---

[1] 'Psychological Commentary', p. li.
[2] Memorial address delivered in Munich, May 10, 1930.
[3] *Ibid.*
[4] Known in Chinese as *T'ai I Chin Hua Tsung Chih*. The careful reader will find some remarkable facts by comparing the above with another but similar Chinese text called *Ch'eng Wei Shih Lun*.

Tibetan Book, on the 'Great Liberation', which, since it deals with Life, is a companion volume to the *Book of the Dead*. One is supposed to begin with the former and, if one fails, the latter is used at the crucial moment of death. The secret of the Golden Flower is the secret of the development of psychic forces latent in man. It is a kind of *rāja-yoga* in Chinese dress, draped with shrouds of mystery to avoid political interference. As Wilhelm explains, political and economic conditions in China led to the forming of 'a series of secret sects whose effort it was to achieve (by the practice of secret traditions from ancient times) a state of soul lifting them above all the misery of life'.[1] Although much of this was cant, humbug, and superstition, one should not leave out the small percentage devoted to *genuine* yoga consisting of psychologically planned meditations. It is not for nothing that Wilhelm comes to the same bold conclusion:

'East and West are no longer to remain apart.'[2]

Evans-Wentz's contribution was not confined to reconciling Eastern and Western philosophy, but reconciles the esoteric with the exoteric, the ancient with the modern, the scientific basis of religion with the religious aspirations of science. He has rescued what one may call the Wisdom of the East from sinking in the mire of exoteric interpretations.

We are amazed when we hear that in a poor country like Tibet such valuable natural resources as gold and oil remain unexploited. We now learn, thanks to Evans-Wentz, that there is something even more valuable which was till now literally buried in Tibet. This is the esoteric wisdom garnered by India through the ages and then slowly taken to Tibet by earnest and self-sacrificing scholars. Later it became disrupted in the land of its origin, for politico-historical reasons, but survived in Tibet when, for reasons of safety, it was literally buried underground. Even when it had been recovered, it was hardly to be expected, by Oriental standards, that it would be published for all and sundry. To the West it undoubtedly appears suspicious that anything which can add to the sum total of human knowledge should be kept secret. This is understandable since quacks often use mystification to boost the value of their wares, so that the very mention of the word *esoteric* brings disrepute in academic circles. But if we read Jung's commentaries on the *Tibetan Books* we see that there were very earnest and pressing reasons for keeping them more or less veiled from the general public. It is for the public's safety as such books really can be dangerous. Great wisdom is shown by the Catholic Church in putting on the Index all books that are *prima facie* dangerous or esoteric, but allowing them to be read against a permit issued to qualified persons. This is far more sensible than to let the public play havoc with things beyond its grasp. A certain amount of suffering, self-discipline or self-sacrifice should be made a condition prior to obtaining such books. The idea that any volume can be bought for money fosters the illusion that the

[1] *The Secret of the Golden Flower*, R. Wilhelm, London, 1957, p. 3.
[2] *Ibid.*, p. 11.

R

main thing is to acquire an important book which can then be read at leisure. The result is that more and more books are collected till their very quantity prevents their being read slowly and calmly, which alone would reveal the esoteric meaning hidden between the lines. However, in our modern civilization, what is one bad habit amongst so many! And indeed, it was because of the topsy-turvy nature of the modern world that Evans-Wentz was given permission by the Tibetan authorities to translate and publish the four books. This, considering Oriental standards, was an act of great self-sacrifice on the part of the Tibetan authorities—but one likely to go unappreciated where the publication of books, of whatever nature, is considered as a matter of course. Thus Evans-Wentz had a very delicate task before him, but the result of it has been an unqualified success.[1] As Aristotle said of his own works: 'They are published and not published.'

[1] Cp. 'Show us an arc of the curve, and a good mathematician will find out the whole figure. . . . Hence the perfect intelligence that subsists between wise men of remote ages. A man cannot bury his meanings so deep in his book, but time and like-minded men will find them.' Also: 'If a teacher has any opinion which he wishes to conceal, his pupils will become as fully indoctrinated into that as into any which he publishes.' Emerson's 'Essay on Spiritual Laws'.

CHAPTER 14

An Integral View of Life

(Apologia pro libro suo)

'To live alone one must be either a beast or a god—or one must be both; the latter is what we call a philosopher!'[1]

In one of Conan Doyle's short stories, Sherlock Holmes scoffs at the idea of vampires. There, at least, the infallible detective was wrong. There are such things as vampires. Why is it that nowadays we never see them; or, for that matter, ghosts, goblins, witches, fairies and the like? The supernatural with all its holy and unholy terrors has been exiled by the modern reader either to juvenile literature or to the publications of the Theosophical Society. The current Protestant theology in Germany is even pleading for the banishment of angels; and if you want to do the thing properly, get rid of God as well—say the Christian atheists.

A religion devoid of the supernatural element would find a large following today. If, however, the exiled 'supernatural' is reinstated in the disguise of a 'psychology of religion' (*Religionspsychologie*) then again one secures a large following. In other words, vampires are allowed to exist if they can be psychologically explained away.

The reason for this is that specialism (or treating a subject of study from one particular slant) has kidnapped philosophy and even raped it. Thus we have epistemology which only studies the process of cognition, linguistics which is obsessed only with an analysis of word structures and so on. The keynote everywhere is on analysis, and in order to analyse one must specialize. Yet it is the business of science not of philosophy to carry out analysis in the various specific fields of knowledge. The business of philosophy is synthesis not analysis; the *integral* interpretation of all experience not merely the analytic examination of the mode and process of experience or the study of any specific problem. Analysis belongs to logic and gives us (rational) thought; synthesis belongs to philosophy and gives us (integral) insight. Wisdom is the combination of rational thought with integral insight. Science is (as it should be) exact and precise; philosophy should be (but alas is not in our day) multifarious. Everybody wants to imitate the scientist because of the prestige supposedly attached to his status. Thus philosophers have been trying hard in our century to be mistaken for scientists. This has been successful as far as the lay public is concerned, for scientific pretensions pay off well. Even theology is belatedly entering the booming science-market.

Where pseudo-precision is so valued, the most deadly accusation is the

[1] Nietzsche.

charge of being many faceted or 'rambling'. Yet philosophy is supposed to be rambling; one ought to have the right to wander at will through the tidy rooms kept neat by that orderly charwoman called Science. How else are we to brain-storm our way to new ideas, into seeing new relationships between the various departments of knowledge? If philosophy is to deal with all aspects of life it should stop aping science; and an integral view of life is possible only where all aspects, rational and irrational, can be combined and compared with unfettered caprice. A fear of losing academic distinction frightens the professional philosopher; to this fear must be added an inferiority complex and a guilty conscience that he may not be doing anything useful. How else except by rambling does the professional philosopher expect to hit upon a lucky intuition that will reveal an aspect of totality till now overlooked? Leibniz coined the phrase *philosophia perennis*; the philosophy of the future must be a *philosophia totalis* or lose its vitality for ever. A discipline which is the result of mere repression, which renounces before the impact of total existence has been examined to the full, which is more afraid of the theoretical repercussion of vampires on its schematic thinking than of their existence, can no longer answer the riddles of life but is (as in German universities) an escape from the problems of daily living. What our philosophers sadly lack in East and West is spiritual virility. This virility can be had at a price, which is to give up this schoolmatronly craze for orderliness and have the courage to ramble; to give up system-building and get back to life in the raw. Is not life itself a rather rambling process? In a short time we will have electronic computers quite capable of solving the problems of epistemology, ontology and the like. What we need is a philosopher who cannot be replaced by a machine. With the invention of electronics, exactness and precision are out-of-date virtues. The world of tomorrow is wailing for its demon-lover with its atonal music, its aperspective paintings, its non-chronological (stream of consciousness) novels, its beat poetry, its psycho-cybernetic attitude to life. Shall we offer this world a philosophy fit only for the quiet cloisters of Cambridge? Is it any wonder that nobody is inclined to take philosophy seriously today? It is the one subject for which even the generous Ford Foundation will not give a grant. And yet the world is pining for a philosopher who will reveal to it the roots which struggle out of this stony rubbish.

In every age, it may be said, there is some type of philosophy which stands as representative and especially significant. Even philosophy has its heroes. In one age it will be the idealist, in another the pragmatist, in a third the positivist, in a fourth the scholar-saint, the materialist, and so on. What will be the significant characteristic of the philosophy of the age that is now coming to birth? The age which lies beyond Huxley and Jung, Marx and Einstein, depth psychology and interplanetary travel? This book has been my stuttering attempt to provide what may be the answer: the realization of an integral consciousness and its working out in all the manifold aspects of existence; a *philosophia totalis*; in form, an incoherent rambling—in content, the unity of many diverse currents reacting upon one another like a symphony with different movements. Although it may now be fashionable to discover new fads even in philosophy, one detects that they are not new but only attempts to revive dying ideologies. The really new philosopher must also play the prophet in an age too unsacrosanct for their coming. His task will be to restore the lost touch with cosmic evolution. Mankind is entering a new phase of evolution, a phase characterized by the birth pangs of a higher dimension of consciousness. The distinction between Eastern and Western, American and Chinese philosophy will very soon become a thing of the past. The philosophy of the future will be an integral one (regardless of the place where the body of the person setting forth his thoughts happened to be born). That we may enter the new era with confidence, we have examined at length modern philosophy in both East and West. In Part I we demonstrated the common substratum between East and West based on the spiritual experience of contact with the Higher Self present in each one of us. In the past, only sages, yogis, and mystics were the beneficiaries of the realized (integral) consciousness of this Higher Self. Now political democracy is being succeeded by a cosmic democracy; our century is that of the common man. The esoteric wisdom of the mystery temples, the rites of initiation and the rules of admittance are being replaced by the dynamics of a new era. The hero of our century, the common man, is now beginning (very slowly but still surely) to perceive the unstable foundations of human life and feels that anarchy and chaos lie deeper than the order he had been fooled into believing. The philosophical climate today has certain similarities with the period in which the Buddha lived and preached. At that time too, mankind was entering a new phase of cosmic evolution. But as those times were not of the common man, the integrated *nirvāṇa* consciousness remained the treasure of a deserving few. The Buddha revealed with penetrating exactness what our present day existentialist philosophers vaguely and morosely hint at. This was shown in Part II, Chapter 8 (b), above. Thus the integration of depth psychology and metaphysics can take place. This process and its philosophical framework was shown in Part III. The great mistake of philosophy has been to overlook and underestimate the volatile potentialities of the irrational. Man after all is not a rational animal. ('If passion never discomposed the mind . . .') He resembles a tiny craft of reason in a tossing and stormy sea of emotions and passion. Yet philosophy, till very recently, took little notice of man as he is in daily life, for it was too occupied with its model man and his place in the system of things. Before it could be shown that life cannot be press-ganged into a system it was necessary to exorcize Hegel's ghost out of European philosophy. How this was eventually brought about has been shown in Part IV, Chapter 12.

There have been men of integral vision in the past, but never until now could they be regarded as the true spokesmen of their age. In undertaking the immensely complex task of providing a thorough study of the integral consciousness in man, Radhakrishnan has written books of great importance to all who seek to understand and try to resolve the dilemmas of our time. That is why we have dealt with him so exhaustively throughout

Part II. Even Christian theology affirms the views he propounded [Part II, Chapters 8 (b) and 8 (c)]. This enables us to examine a problem which will be very much with us in the future, the possibility of tolerance (religious or otherwise) in a world torn by the struggle for men's minds [Part II, Chapter 7 (d)]. We examined the works of Aldous Huxley as a typical instance of the portrayal of integral consciousness in contemporary literature (Part III). The superman of Teilhard de Chardin and Aurobindo is, like the hero of Huxley's later novels, one who has attained this fourth dimension of consciousness. Christopher Isherwood (a milestone in English literature) gives us insight into such an awakening (Part III, Chapter 10). Here is a man who has been a saint in disguise for nearly the whole of his life, and suddenly he sees the chasm opening before him and cries that we have never been going anywhere. The integral consciousness is not a new or a fourth dimension of consciousness but the essential current underlying and supporting the other three states (waking, dream and deep sleep) of consciousness. That is integral consciousness seen from the subjective side as operating in an individual. This is nothing new. We have a clear exposition of it in the *Turiya* of the *Māṇḍūkya Upaniṣad* as early as 800 B.C. What is compellingly new in the present world situation is that man is being pressured by the forces of cosmic evolution into realizing this integration from the objective side. Rational thought (pragmatism, logical positivism, linguistic analysis *et. al.*) was the flowering of a form of consciousness that is now outdated. We need a breakthrough from this stick in the mud kind of philosophy. One cannot say that those foregone systems of thought were useless in themselves but only that they have outlived their utility because rational thought is no longer paramount. A psychic process on a cosmic scale is suddenly revealing (almost as if by the mutation of consciousness in the process of evolution) man's untold inner possibilities. *We have still to explore this Inner Space.* Man has been living on this planet for untold centuries with only a fragment of his full potentialities. When now and again an individual was able to exploit a little more than this fragment, he was hailed as a genius. Yet we are all geniuses in the chrysallis. No less an authority than Sir Julian Huxley speaks of *psychometabolism.*

'The other major tendency in biological evolution is the evolution of mind, a trend toward a higher degree of awareness. . . .
'Brains can be regarded as psychometabolic organs. . . . So brains, when highly developed, utilize the raw materials of simple experience and transform them into special systems of organized awareness. . . .
'The only primary reality we know is our subjective experience. . . . The only satisfactory approach to the problem is an evolutionary one. . . . We are simultaneously and indissolubly both matter and mind. . . . This provides a perfectly good analogy with the evolution of mind. . . . with the aid of its organ of awareness, it utilizes the raw material of its subjective experience and transforms it into characteristic patterns of awareness which then canalize and help to direct its behaviour. This I venture to call

psychometabolism. During the latter stages of evolution, an increasingly efficient type of psychometabolism is superimposed on and added to the universal physiological metabolism.'[1]

If what Huxley says here is scientifically accurate then one is justified in assuming that there is a plan behind the events which pattern life in the cosmos, and unless philosophy has learnt to discern this plan it cannot judge aright. The power behind evolution which guides the universe, dictates the form life may take on this planet, and watches over every embryo, will speak to the coming generation in more imperious tones and demonstrate its existence through events far more startling than a soft landing on the moon. Does this view of the future of mankind receive any corroboration from the professional historian? We get an inkling of this in Arnold Toynbee's doctrine of Challenge and Response followed up by his theory of creative minorities. The creative minority are the few individuals who have attained the integral consciousness before evolution has made it possible to all and sundry—as it shortly will. Such creative individuals have in the past been relatively rare (Zarathustra, Moses, Lao-Tse, the Buddha, Jesus, Mohammed and the like); they withdrew from society into solitude and there God or Grace, fasting or yoga, chance, or we know not what, gave them a certain additional insight, a new vitality (the more abundant life), a higher dimension of consciousness. This integral consciousness armed them with what Toynbee calls *mimesis* (a charismatic power to persuade) and they returned to society to stimulate their fellow men to rise to the occasion. ('Be ye therefore perfect. . . .') The aim of cosmic evolution is perfection, while frustrated achievement is tantamount to suffering. In the long run man cannot be content with anything short of perfection. (In Part II we explained *why* this is so; see the comparison between Radhakrishnan and Carlyle.) Only the angelic in him will be developed further as it ought to develop, only the bestial in him will perish as it ought to perish. This is the goal of cosmic evolution—and the only one that awaits us. Man's hopes are bent on perfection, and in his finest moments he has sought and worshipped a reality utterly perfect. This universal idea of infinite perfection arises *naturally* out of man's conative activity (be he saint or savage) and we surreptitiously recognize our own demand for it even while pretending to question its adequacy. The history of religions has seized upon this idea of perfection as the hallmark of saintliness and as the goal of life and of cosmic evolution. In the Chinese classics it is called *Li ki* (or complete); in the Buddhist canon it is called the Perfected One (*anuttara*, the beyondless) Aristotle speaks of *teleious* (that which has reached its goal, the complete, the perfect) as the lack-nothing; the Cathari and kindred sects called themselves *perfecti*. Man is now fed up with 'seeing as in a glass darkly' instead of face to face. If in religion we demand perfection, in philosophy we prize conclusiveness.

The more exalted the goal, the more despairing is our sense of ever

[1] Sir Julian Huxley, *Psychometabolism: Perspectives in Biology and Medicine*, London, 1964, pp. 399–432. See also my *Evolution und Gottesidee*, Ratingen, 1967.

attaining it. A lame, old man on the platform of a tube station may despair of ever reaching the street if he has never seen a moving staircase before. This has been mankind's lot till now. Only a few hardy and energetic souls climbed arduously to the surface and saw the sun in all its glory. Now very slowly and almost imperceptibly evolution has accelerated the stationary-seeming elevator belt on which mankind stands. Because we gaze around and see only chaos, the foolish idea that 'God is dead' arises. Because no hand stretches forth out of the Great Unknown to *pull* us up, we forget that we are, so to speak, being slowly *pushed* up from below.

Imagine a group of children imprisoned in a castle by the sea. There is a wall in the compound not too high for an average adult to look over but enough to prevent the children from seeing the sea.

As the children grow older and thereby taller, the greater are their chances of seeing the ocean; whoever succeeds even once is liberated from the castle almost immediately as if by magic. As the heads of the children approach the top of the wall their curiosity and longing grows all the more intense. Now many years ago there was a boy in the group who secretly kept a diary. One day he suddenly disappeared. Just before the others grew tall enough to see over the wall, they found this diary and read with astonishment a description of the sea. How could the writer have described several years ago what they are about to see? They read on and discover that the small boy who had seen the sea (and so been liberated) had been practising a strange method called leaping or high-jumping. Through a series of such leaps he had managed to gaze at the sea before his time and so had been able to describe what they themselves were soon to experience. He also gave in his diary not only a description of the sea but also a systematic method for learning how to jump high enough to look over the wall.

We ourselves resemble these children and evolution will soon make us tall enough to look over the wall—and what we shall see and experience will be the unbounded ocean (integral consciousness). How do we know? Because one of us (the philosopher of our age) has found a diary (a treasure trove of hidden wisdom) in which a description of what lies beyond the wall (beyond the pale of rational thought) has been left behind. Who wrote it? One who had seen (the sages and mystics of the past). How could he have seen what is hidden from us? Because he was more in earnest, he did something, he tried to jump harder whereas we confine our efforts to playing amusing games in the castle (worldly activities) or bashing each other over the head (war); specially if another's guess as to what may lie behind the wall happens to differ from our own. And the second half of the diary, explaining how one can learn to jump higher? That is mysticism and yoga. They show us how we can overcome the wall and gaze at the infinite (ocean) even before we have grown tall enough to glimpse this splendour. And having even once gazed at the infinite these enlightened sages and mystics were liberated from the dungeon for ever.

One would expect such a diary to be read with avid interest; that everyone will start learning how to jump higher. Alas, there are in our group ingenious people who suggest it is not necessary to see the ocean. Let us instead (they say) examine the diary's description of the sea for errors in syntax (linguistic analysis)!

> Of nought so certain as our reason still,
> Of nought so doubtful as of soul and will.

Then there are others who suggest that it would be the same thing if instead of gazing at the sea we were to look at a cup of salt water and multiply its extent in our imagination.

> Bounded by Nature, narrowed still by art,
> A trifling head and a contracted heart.

Yet the situation in which we are *now* placed is such that it matters little what we do or omit. As we grow taller inch by inch, as our heads begin to tower over the wall that we have grown by habit to love and revere, we will inevitably be confronted with the infinite. Some of the children in our group are already putting out their eyes for fear of growing taller.

> O would the sons of men once think their eyes
> And reason giv'n them but to study flies!
> See Nature in some partial narrow shape,
> And let the Author of the whole escape.

It is this 'not yet' of the highest spiritual experience that arouses our indignation or makes us give up the divine for lost. We overlook that this 'not yet' factor itself is by its own fiat a 'yet to be'. That explains why many an atheist secretly adores God in a different form—be it a picture by a master hand, a poem by Wordsworth, the piano playing of a genius, a walk through Richmond in spring, or even the façade of an old church. They call up feelings which everyday life does not as a rule evoke. There is a spiritual power in these moments so pregnant with integral consciousness, which can then reveal itself to the atheist as an ecstacy of beauty. For what after all is this God, seen after a close study of comparative religion, but the ideal of absolute perfection incorporated as an eternal reality? Even the so-called 'God denying' religions like Buddhism and Jainism ask us to strive for perfection, for *nirvāṇa*. Even Communism has its ideal of perfection (when, all conflicts being ended, the State automatically withers away) and, therefore, its God. Thus the ideal of perfection is the most convincing proof that we already own, though we do not possess, a consciousness that makes our mind refuse to be resigned to its own inconclusiveness. What the beat generation mistakenly but instinctively seeks in its excesses and use of psychedelic drugs is that same integral consciousness. We condemn their methods, yet their instinct is sure; they are more in touch with cosmic evolution. But because of a lack of discipline they ruin their chances. Nothing worth while ever came without self-control.

The scientific method is excellent but not exhaustive. Today it is being complemented, though not replaced, by other methods or even non-methods so that the overall world view is a more complete, integral one.

As soon as man began to rationalize, he discovered to his dismay that his reasoning faculty was severely limited and well-nigh useless in trying to arrive at the significance of our universe. Thus, in the West, man invoked the aid of imagination, intuition[1] and poetry just as in the East the aid of religion, mysticism, yoga and mythology were invoked. The alliance of reason with these other so-called primitive faculties gave rise to integral philosophy of the nature already described.

What is the value of integration in philosophy? What are the advantages of this type of thinking in the general scheme of life? It may be answered that poetry plays a very decided role as an interpreter between philosophy and wisdom. How close and vital is the connection between the two may be seen from the fact that Heidegger, the premier philosopher of our day, prefers to take his texts from romantic poets like Hölderlin rather than from the so-called rational philosophers.[2]

As Heidegger rightly says:

'the sensitive poet and the original thinker (philosopher) occupy neighbouring mountain peaks from which they can speak to one another across the space.'[3]

The modern contempt for the occult and the esoteric is due to their presenting to our proudly named Age of Science ideas which have only a vague indefinable existence, which are only suggestions, not even hypotheses.

There are ideas which admit of contradiction without being contradicted. When metaphysics tried to carry them from poetry and mythology into scientific realms, it was immediately snubbed—a blow from which it has not yet fully recovered. They found no place in science because they did not belong there. Yet they belong to another dimension of truth, poetic truth! These non-true (*not untrue*) ideas are the result of certain forces latent in the heart of man. They have always been treated with suspicion, and not without reason. For these ideas are not true in the sense that they can be so *proved* yet they are not un-true in the sense that they cannot be proved to be false. They are the unprovable non-truths of mythology which Plato described thus:

'Possibly, nay certainly, this is not true, but there is something more or less like it which is true.'

We must treat these ideas with suspicion and respect; somewhat as the West receives the envoys of the Kremlin.

[1] Its latest exponent was the great philosopher Bergson. Also see *From Intellect to Intuition* by Alice Bailey.

[2] 'Heidegger's Recall of Man to Being', Chapter V in *The Existentialists* by Professor James Collins, Henry Regnery and Co., Chicago, 1952.

[3] *Existence and Being* (translated into English by Scott, Hull and Crick), p. 391-2. The fact that this comparison appears in the postscript to *Was ist Metaphysik?* (5th ed. Frankfurt, 1949) rather than in the essays on Hölderlin indicates how close a bond exists between poetical and philosophical studies in Heidegger's opinion.

That is why the romantic poets had recourse to myth and symbols—because there is in man something which goes beyond exact science. As Renan wrote:

'Never has Man when in possession of a clear idea converted it into a myth.'

An integral philosophy reconciles the existence and development of myth, along with the quasi-philosophical truths contained in it, with the knowledge that it is only myth and not reality. In the realm of philosophy doubt need not have the sterilizing effect which it has in theology. The utility of an integral view requires that we hold two convictions:

(i) we must know that symbols are necessary; and
(ii) we must realize that they are only symbols.

Thus such a philosophy satisfies the fundamental intuitions of the human soul by, in Blake's words:

'displaying the Eternal Vision, the Divine similitude which if man ceases to behold he ceases to exist.'

Finally, it offers a criticism of life from the only point of view which, perhaps, is just, the intuitive one. The integral view passes judgement on philosophical, metaphysical, and religious ideas, accepting or rejecting them according to the richness of their content and their potentialities for beauty and harmony. We thus have a barometer for forecasting the coming philosophical weather of ideas. This an integral view can alone provide.

If the barrier of rational limitations can be broken only through intuition, then the latter is the bond between philosophy and the so-called primitive mind. For if intuition exists, it must have been strongest in the primitive period of humanity. As our knowledge of the primitive increases, we shall understand better the symbolism of philosophy. As our analysis of symbolism becomes more accurate, we shall understand more the profound meaning of primitive beliefs, the power of which made it possible for them to subsist in their crude forms in the midst of highly developed cultures and among gifted races, in ancient India and throughout the whole history of Africa.[1]

But even all this does not exhaust the manifold advantages. For there is still a whole range of facts as yet inaccessible to exact science, such as the subtler facts of abnormal psychology. Parapsychology is still in its infancy and so the portrayal of extremely subtle and powerful variations of human feeling and desire, which have such an important place in our life, is left to poetry, expressed through symbolism.

The philosopher observes and experiences long before the scientist, and his work, when it is integral, is based on experiment just as much as the

[1] D. Saurat, *Literature and Occult Tradition*, p. 161.

most exact sciences claim to be.[1] This type of integral observation is part of the indispensable patrimony of mankind, being the application of the ancient maxim 'know thyself'.

In our own times we are about to see a *volte face*. Metaphysics is supposed to be the tap root of philosophy's tree. But as Heidegger rightly asks, 'what about the soil?' Appeal is made to Descartes's famous comparison of philosophy to a great tree, the roots of which comprise metaphysics. Heidegger asks:

'What is the soil into which the roots of metaphysics are plunged? Unless this question is deliberately raised, philosophers will continue to regard the tree of philosophy as a self-sufficient organism instead of one that is nourished by a supporting earth and atmosphere.'[2]

What is this fertile soil of thought? Where is this wonder-working presupposition of metaphysics? Heidegger cannot find it in the writings of the rationalist philosophers. He has, therefore, to turn to Hölderlin and Romantic poetry for aid. This about-face from the rational to the romantic in our own day marks the triumph of *philosophia totalis* over the limitations of reason which hitherto have imprisoned the thinking intellect within the field of pure experience. Thus our search for first principles necessitates a progress from intellect to intuition; from philosophy to poetry, and most important of all from thinking to being. The Romantic poets, living at a time when Western philosophy had not yet advanced to the stage to which Heidegger has brought it, found in symbolism a language which could at once conceal and reveal.

Although at first sight it may appear far fetched and even unbelievable that there should be any bond of sympathy between the ideas of Eastern wisdom and those of European poetry, it becomes logical and indeed even inevitable when we examine the chain of causation, that mysterious factor in the history of ideas which links and unlinks all that is the most remote in time and place. The mistake lies in believing that an idea is geographical in place and conditional on time. An idea has its existence in one place only, the mind of man. The absurdity lies in branding ideas according to the place and time of the body of the thinker who had them. Thus an idea is branded as coming from the ancient East simply because the thinker to whom it occurred happened to live in the East at a particular time, now classified as ancient; similarly, the same idea when it occurs to, say, Shelley, is at once branded as English and Romantic just because Shelley happened to live during the Romantic Revival and was also English.

Once we accustom ourselves to think in terms of ideas, and not of the persons who had them, we realize at once that all ideas occur in the mind (not the brain), and we no longer restrict them according to geographical accidents and historical time-tables. Unfortunately we still refer to the ideas in relation to their thinkers instead of *in vacuo*.

[1] As the eminent scientist and botanist J. C. Bose once said: 'The Poet is intimate with truth, while the scientist approaches it awkwardly.'

[2] *Metaphysik*, p. 7.

Neoplatonism is the agency through which Eastern ideas penetrated into the Romantic Revival.

That Greek philosophy was influenced to a very great extent by Indian philosophy is now clearly established by Maulana Kalam Azad in the Preface to *History of Philosophy Eastern and Western*.[1] This very type of Greek philosophy pregnant with Eastern ideas and combined with Egyptian rites and mysticism found its outlet through Plotinus and was called Neoplatonism. Plotinus is, therefore, not only the father of European mysticism but also the indirect begetter of modern Romanticism. The main problems of soul, death and immortality, which were incorporated into Neoplatonism, were later re-exported farther west through the poetry of the Romantic Revival. Tied up with these problems of death and soul were those of evil and suffering which received special attention from Byron in *Cain* and *Manfred*, and from Shelley in *Prometheus Unbound*.

It must be mentioned to Schopenhauer's credit that he was the first person of note in Europe to grasp and appreciate these transoriental ideas without using the jargon of Neoplatonism or poetic-romantic symbolism. Fichte's system was even more drastically Eastern—one might almost say Tibetan. His philosophy if presented without his name and European setting is in essence indistinguishable from the esoteric system-philosophies of Tibet and the Far East.

However, the Romantic poets were poets and not philosophers, and so they used the vocabulary of myth and symbolism. Byron in *Cain* and *Manfred* exposed the weakness of Western philosophy on the problems of evil and suffering. The same *exposé* was repeated in a rational and philosophic setting by Jung in his *Answer to Job*. Jung stands in the same position to Shelley and Byron as Heidegger stands to Hölderlin. Both Jung and Heidegger express rationally what the poets before them had expressed intuitively. Western philosophy therefore always stood on one leg—that of optimism. The Romantic poets observed this lameness but were unable to provide another leg. It was only after Schopenhauer, *through his knowledge of Eastern philosophy*, that a note of pessimism entered Western philosophy. (And through it into Western literature as in the novels of Thomas Hardy which would have been improbable, if not impossible, prior to Schopenhauer's *Essays in Pessimism*.) This restored some balance to the optimistic disequilibrium. But it was at best a crutch and not another leg.

Neoplatonism, therefore, aroused the Eastern ideas that lay dormant in the minds of the Romantic poets; and once these were evoked the problem of suffering was bound to crop up, because it constitutes at least one-fourth of Eastern wisdom. The idea of the inevitability of suffering, when it is combined, as in Eastern wisdom, with a knowledge of or a belief in the *value* of suffering, leads to philosophical resignation. But the idea of the inevitability of suffering divorced from, or in ignorance of, the value of suffering leads not to resignation but to revolt. The Romantic poets were, therefore, open rebels. This spirit of revolt is symbolically expressed in

[1] Allen & Unwin, London, 1954.

Romantic poetry not in fragments but in all its awe-inspiring totality. Thus Cain and Manfred symbolize all mankind. They are symbols of man in revolt against the divine. In Shelley's *Prometheus Unbound* this idea of revolt is carried to its logical extreme; Prometheus forgives Jupiter or, symbolically speaking, Man forgives God for the suffering he causes in this world. The roles of conventional Christianity are reversed to such an extent that Nietzsche can cheerfully declare: 'God is dead'.

All this emotional storm was the result of having learnt the inevitability of suffering without having understood its value in the general scheme. This romantic revolt at the idea that anything so wonderful as man should be made to suffer reappears in a philosophical disguise in Jung's *Answer to Job*.

The origin of man, like that of the universe, is wrapped in impenetrable mystery. Yet we have reason to believe that in some remote past man was supremely happy and contented. Then for some unknown reason he forsook the happiness of pure Being which resulted in a great change for the worse. This is supported by the mythology of almost all countries especially India and the Orient. The goal before mankind now is to restore this former golden age which it has lost. That is the real unbinding (or liberation) of Prometheus (or the human race). His legend is universally acknowledged to be symbolic and only as such can it be satisfactorily explained.

Prometheus sometimes symbolizes the entire human race, or at least that portion of it which is anxious to break its fetters. The legend symbolizes the revolt against divine authority, *par excellence*. In the myth the poet finds an excellent outlet to vent his own feelings. There is something grand and awe-inspiring in defying authority, all the more so if it is the authority of the gods. Prometheus had defied them and, therefore, became the ideal romantic hero. The poets also wanted to defy the gods of their own time. What infuriates most philosophers is that although 'man is born free, he is everywhere in chains'. Man at his creation was endowed with the gift of perpetual happiness. He was not formed to be a sickly, suffering and above all, a mortal creature as we now see him to be. Thus the supereminence of man is like Lucifer's, one of pain.

To Shelley, man's highest duty was to refuse blind obedience irrespective of whether the authority was vested in wordly tyrants or in mythical gods. He considered religion, as it is practised, to be hostile and not friendly to the cultivation of those virtues which would bring about a world brotherhood through love. The most unique quality of his ideology is its *unworldliness* or rather otherworldliness. He saw in man a conflict between divine possibilities and animal limitations. He was not against the divine as such but only against that which would exploit the idea of the divine in order to support tyranny on earth.

In *Prometheus Unbound* Shelley combines the ideas of Aeschylus with the imagery of Sophocles, whereas the underlying philosophy is almost entirely Neoplatonic. Like Schopenhauer, he believed in the tremendous power of the human *will*. He believed that mankind had only *to will* that there should not be evil and automatically there would be none. He so believed in the perfectability of man that he was confident of the possibility of man eventually expelling evil from his own nature. The very foundation of Shelley's *Weltanschauung* is that it is possible to abolish evil from all creation and so restore mankind to the original golden age which is its birthright.

His favourite symbol was that of someone in constant warfare against the principle of evil. Laon, the enemy and victim of tyrants, is such a symbol. Saturn symbolizes the good, Jupiter the evil, usurping one, and Prometheus the redeemer of mankind who will lead it to a state beyond both good and evil. Both Blake and Shelley agree that man must be transported from the state where he is innocent through ignorance to where he is virtuous through wisdom. Prometheus typifies all humanity. Jupiter punishes him for his *Unbesonnenheit* by chaining him to a rock in the Indian Caucasus, where a vulture is expected to devour his ever renewed heart. However there is a rumour current in heaven prophesying the fall of Jove. Prometheus alone possesses the secret of averting that fall and obtains his freedom in exchange for it. But the most important point to note in Shelley is that Prometheus forgives Jupiter—and the very moment he does so, Jupiter is defeated. The tyrant is defeated through forgiveness. In other words it is the human which forgives the divine for all the tyranny the latter has practised upon it—and by forgiving the divine, excels it. This is the romantic *Weltanschauung* carried to its logical conclusion. The roles are reversed and the conventional criminal (a human sinner) not only becomes the judge, but even forgives the conventional judge (the divine) for having been so unmerciful in the past. The human pardon is the sentence of punishment imposed on the divine.

This ideology is neither new nor exceptional. And, if one accepts the premises from which the romantic poets begin their argument, it is even logically correct. Several hundred years before Shelley, Omar Khayyam wrote the following verse which Thomas Hardy, the last of the great romantics and the most pessimistic of all novelists, wanted to be read to him on his deathbed:

> O thou who man of baser earth did'st make
> And even with Paradise, devised the snake,
> For all the sins with which the face of man is blackened,
> Man's forgiveness give—and take![1]

In our own day Jung in his *Answer to Job* presented the same idea heavily dressed in psychological theories and Christian dogma. The sum and substance of it is that God, like any other patient in a psychiatrist's clinic, would be incomplete or not fully developed if he was only good and kind. Therefore, he must also have a cruel side which completely escaped the notice of Jesus Christ, who had not the good fortune to study psychology in Vienna! Man (as in Job) proves his superiority to God by forgiving Him. These are the kind of results we get from a philosophy which ignores an objective study of the problem of evil and suffering. How can a creation

[1] Fitzgerald's translation.

manifestly imperfect have a creator dogmatically omnipotent. Not finding an answer in conventional religion, the poets turned to romanticism. The symbolism of *Prometheus Unbound* is in the last analysis the calm and holy spirit of love, which in spite of all suffering keeps its faith in, and hopes for, the return of the golden age. When this prophecy is fulfilled, then love, unstained by any evil or pain, becomes the law of the universe.

My fruit is dreams, as theirs is bread[1]

Symbolically speaking, the intermediate supernatural powers which we find in Blake's poetry, and which are called the Eternals, represent the idea of the demiurge which often occurs both in Romantic poetry and in Eastern wisdom. This consists of a belief in an intermediate power between God as noumenon (inactive) and God as phenomena (active).[2] Pope tells us that the classical poets: 'Looked up from Nature to Nature's God'. But the romantic poets tend to interpose intermediary powers between God and *Natura naturans* (Nature as dynamic) or creation as a whole. This intermediary power or demiurge is thought of as a secondary (subordinate) creative and organizing aspect of God. This idea also occurs in Wagner's operas where demiurges called the *Norns* are empowered to do nothing except carry out decrees the causes of which are concealed in a higher source—the unfathomable.

The *Nornen* correspond to the Fates and the Furies of Greek mythology. These demiurgic powers can fulfil human requests. For example, they revive Helen for Faust and perform a similar feat in Byron's *Manfred*. The idea also occurs in Shelley's works where it is called Demogorgon, a secret and terrible power superior even to Jupiter, and capable of overthrowing him at the appointed hour. Whereas in Milton Demogorgon was only a dreaded name, he appears in Shelley as:

Ungazed upon and shapeless; neither limb,
Nor form, nor outline.[3]

He is the Prime Minister of the Absolute who proudly tells Jupiter that he is: 'Eternity, demand no direr name'.

In Blake, one of these intermediary powers falls and becomes the demiurge symbolized by Urizen (and alternatively by Albion).

This idea of the demiurge is well known in the pantheism of Western thought and is variously symbolized as:

the Norn	— Wagner
the Mothers	— Goethe
the Son	— Milton
the Soul of the World	— Shelley

[1] Francis Thompson

[2] In Chinese: the Tao-without-name and the Tao-with-name; Eckehart calls the former the Godhead and the latter God.

[3] *Prometheus Unbound*, ii. iv. 5.

Universal Man ⎫
Urizen   ⎬   — Blake
(Albion)   ⎭
Sapience   — Spenser
Natura naturans   — Whitman, Nietzsche, Hugo
the Fates and Furies — the ancient Greeks
Prajāpati   — ancient Indian philosophy
Matrona   — occult Jewish philosophy

The demiurge does not create the world but *becomes* it; by a cosmic manifestation God divides or rather projects himself into the Many. This, to
Blake, is the fall of the One into the Many, of unity into division, from
which all apparent evil seems to spring. The theme of the division of God,
followed by the reconstitution of God, is the central idea underlying all
Eastern wisdom.

In Blake the demiurges split themselves up 'in tears and cries' into male
and female.

> Eternity shuddered when they saw
> Man begetting his likeness
> on his own divided image.

Here man symbolizes the demiurge—just as in Goethe it is symbolized by
the Mothers who are those same primitive deities fecundated at the beginning
of the worlds by the demiurges, whose issue they are. This feminine aspect
also corresponds to Spenser's Sapience. The ideas of division and reproduc-
tion are closely allied to the incest theme which often occurs in Romantic
poetry, sometimes at the cosmic level and sometimes on the human plane.
There is an example of this in Wagner's *Walküre* where the two semi-divine
children of Wotan fecundate each other to reproduce Siegfried.

This aspect is in very close sympathy with a similar idea in Eastern
wisdom. We find in the *Satapatha* and *Aitareya Brahmanas* the story of
Prajāpati, the creator of the world, and Ushas, his daughter.

'Prajāpati conceived a passion for his own daughter. . . . May I pair with
her! Thus thinking he united with her.'[2]

This union results in the creation of all creatures, Ushas taking all the
female and Prajāpati the male forms.[3]

In Shelley the incest theme repeats itself on the purely human plane in
The Revolt of Islam. Laon and Cythna are also destined to regenerate the
world like Prajāpati and Ushas, and the parents of Siegfried.

What then is the symbolic meaning of the incest theme? The natural
consequence is, as in Neoplatonism, the theory of the reconstitution of the

[1] See Charles C. Osgood's *Studies in Philology* (University of North Carolina),
April, 1917, pp. 167–77.
[2] Max Müller's *Sacred Books of the East*, Vol. XII, pp. 208–9.
[3] *Attaveya Brahmano*, iii. 33.

S

Total God by the convergence of the separated atoms back to their source. According to the Romantic ideology, evil is the result of a universal struggle which will not cease till the male overtakes the female power and is harmoniously, once and for all, united to her; or, in Neoplatonic terminology, until the Many again becomes the One. This is the golden key with which we can unlock the symbolic hints of an integral consciousness in man.

'All Blake's writings are deeply mystical in thought and symbolic in expression, and this is true of the (apparently) simple little *Songs of Innocence*, no less than of the great, and partially intelligible prophetic books.'[1]

The *Songs of Innocence and Experience* are intended to show, as Blake himself said, 'two contrary states of the human soul'. The two Songs (or the series of songs) are therefore themselves symbols representing the possibilities for good and evil in human nature. By this symbolism Blake not only meant that the one cannot exist without the other but also that: 'without contraries [there] is no Progression'.[2] We are here reminded of Kant's analogy of the bird flying in thin air wrongly believing that it could fly even better in a vacuum and therefore hating the resistance of the atmosphere. For Blake the meaning of Christ's 'Love your enemy' seems to be 'convert resistance (the enemy) into power'. The human soul like Kant's bird can rise only when it meets with opposition which it turns into an uplifting force. The two Songs are, therefore, contrasted elements in a single pattern. By innocence Blake does not mean the innocence which comes through ignorance, but that which comes through wisdom. The human soul evolves from the innocence (born of ignorance) to the innocence (born of wisdom) via experience.

The human ego in its unevolved form searches for more and more experience for which it barters innocence. Life, therefore, challenges, exposes and destroys innocence. Burdened with sorrow the human ego oversatiated with experience longs for rest, for its original innocence. Thus childhood symbolizes that state of the human ego which may be found even in a mature person. Blake confirms the contention of Eastern wisdom that man has never really been separated from God.

In Eastern wisdom experience is a cruel necessity whereby man acquires insight. It is inevitably linked up with suffering as is wisdom with experience. Therefore the price of wisdom is suffering:

> What is the price of Experience?
> Do men buy it for a song
> Or wisdom for a dance in the street?
> Wisdom is sold in the desolate market where none come to buy
> And in the wither'd field where the farmer plows for bread in vain.[3]

[1] Spurgeon, *Mysticism and English Literature.*
[2] *The Marriage of Heaven and Hell.*
[3] *The Four Zoas.*

From the very moment of its birth a human creature is a prisoner in the field of pure experience. There is no alternative for him but to experience what he experiences. 'Therefore God becomes as we are, that we may be as he is.'[1]

It is difficult to understand Blake without understanding both mysticism and Fichte's philosophy. The ideas of Blake, Fichte and of Eastern thinkers form one school of philosophical thought which is diametrically opposite to what is known as materialism. They all centre around the ways in which man perceives the world. Just as Fichte's philosophy is the exact opposite of materialism, so Blake provides the exact contrast to its twin, positivism (the Comte-Spenserian conception of the world). It is important to bear in mind that these *a priori* assertions were for Blake not merely matters of belief, but of passionate knowledge. To him they were the very essence of existence.

The first of these fundamental beliefs is the unity of essence behind the diversity of forms. 'God is in the lowest effects as [in] the highest causes. He is become a worm that he may nourish the weak. . . . Everything on earth is the word of God and in its essence is God.'[2]

The second of these beliefs is the inherent divinity of man. This is most clearly brought out in *Everlasting Gospel* where God, speaking to Christ as the highest form of humanity, says:

> If thou humblest thyself, thou humblest me
> Thou also dwellest in Eternity.
> Thou art a man: God is no more:
> Thy own humanity learn to adore
> For that is my spirit of life.

This idea that every human soul is potentially divine has again a strong bond of sympathy with Eastern wisdom which has always rejected all belief in a vicarious salvation.

Symbolically interpreted Urisen is reason and Noah imagination. For Blake, imagination is the one sole reality because it releases man from his own self-made prison:

> I will go down to self-annihilation and eternal death
> Lest the last judgement come and find me unannihilate,
> And I be seiz'd and giv'n into the hands of my own selfhood.[3]

Because the language of imagination is art, it speaks through symbols, so that men imprisoned in their little selfhoods are reminded that Nature herself is a symbol. Thus things transient should remind us symbolically of things transcendental.

Once we get rid of the seemingly fixed reality of eternal things, which both Fichte and Eastern wisdom succeed in doing, they come to be considered

---

[1] Blake, *On Natural Religion.*
[2] *Notes on Lavater.*
[3] Blake, *Milton.*

only as symbols. Their essence of existence, and consequently their reality, is continually expanding:

> To open the eternal worlds, to open the immortal eyes
> of man inwards into the worlds of thought, into eternity,
> Ever expanding into the bosom of God, the human imagination.

Blake's symbolism can best be understood when taken in conjunction with his *Fourfold View of Nature*.

> Now I a fourfold vision see,
> And a fourfold vision is given to me.
> 'Tis fourfold in my supreme delight,
> And threefold in soft Beulah's night.
> And twofold always. May God us keep
> From single vision and Newton's sleep!

The single vision symbolizes that condition of mind which sees no farther than the concrete facts before it—in other words, the (Locke-Newtonian) mechanistic conception of the universe. The twofold vision is a *Weltanschauung* in which every external material thing is merely a symbol expressing a still greater essence behind it. Whereas in the fourfold view we have Father, Son, Holy Ghost and the Integral Consciousness through which the first three manifest themselves.

These four absolute principles reappear in a condensed and limited form in Blake's poetry as:

Reason	symbolized by	Urizen
Emotion	symbolized by	Lurah
Energy	symbolized by	Urthona
Sensation	symbolized by	Tharmas

These four principles are also found in the philosophy of the German mystic Jakob Boehme as contraction, expansion, rotation and integration.

Both Blake and Boehme have attacked the problem of good versus evil, and both have arrived at the same conclusion, so pithily described in the Upanishads as:

'If there is Evil, God is the author of it though untouched by it'

and again:

'Both gods and demons have one father.'

Evil must be embodied or experienced before it can be ejected. Thus Blake says:

'If the fool would persist in his folly he would become wise.'

According to Eastern wisdom everything has four dimensions, the fourth being Time. The past, present and future are not in watertight compartments but affect and influence one another, just as Virgil's heroes put those of Homer in the background and so give them a sense of the past. In fact this entire wisdom is a literary and philosophic projection of Einstein's *Theory of Relativity* into a sphere outside pure mathematics.

It must not be supposed that the study of Eastern wisdom will open a door through which the reader can leap out into the clear Athenian sun in which all the mystery of life and the cosmos will stand revealed in its sparkling clarity. Eastern wisdom is neither a magic charm nor a panacea. It is merely *one* amongst several ways of looking at life. It is a species of intuition and not a dogmatic rule; it is an apparatus of interpretation; a technique of practising religion in such a way as to establish a sort of telepathic communion with the innermost secret concealed in the cosmos.

To this we must add that the Eastern sages were all to a greater or lesser extent mystics. Now symbolism is of superlative importance in mysticism; indeed, symbolism and mythology are, as it were, the language of the mystic. This *necessity* for symbolism is an integral part of the belief in unity; for the essence of true symbolism rests on the belief that 'all things in Nature have something in common, something in which they are really alike'.[1] 'In order to be a true symbol, a thing must be partly the same as that which it symbolizes.'[2]

There is an excellent exposition of this aspect of symbolism in a paper by R. L. Nettleship.[3] He shows how every truth apprehended by finite intelligence *must* by its very nature only be the husk of a deeper truth, and *by the aid of symbolism* we are often enabled to catch the reflection of a truth which we are not capable of apprehending in any other way.

'As the essence of mysticism is to believe that everything we see and know is symbolic of something greater, mysticism is on one side the poetry of life.'[4]

The same holds good for philosophy which is in essence but the mysticism of nature (as with Schelling), ethics (Spinoza), or reason (Kant).

The philosopher approaches knowledge directly, the sage symbolically; but the oblique teaching of a sage impresses us more profoundly than the direct lesson of the philosopher, because the latter appeals principally to our reason (very limited as Kant has shown), whereas the sage touches our transcendental feeling. Thus in our own day we see a leading philosopher like Heidegger putting into a rational mould truths already expounded by the Romantic poet-sage, Hölderlin.

To the *scientist* the moon is a ball of matter following a fixed course of motion preordained by the laws inherent in its size, its gravity, and the

[1] *Mysticism in English Literature*, by C. F. E. Spurgeon, p. 9.
[2] *Ibid.*
[3] *Philosophical remains of R. L. Nettleship*, ed. A. C. Bradley, 1901, pp. 23–32.
[4] Spurgeon's *Mysticism in English Literature*, p. 12.

square-root of its distance from the sun, etc., etc. To the *poet* she is Cynthia[1] roaming in interstellar space, at her own caprice, in search of her beloved Endymion. The former is the result of observation and experiment; the latter is a pure flight of fancy—a Lamia!!!

This is what Keats had in mind when he wrote in *Lamia*

> . . . do not all charms fly
> At the mere touch of cold philosophy?

The word philosophy in this context should not be confused with philosophy as we understand it today. The old name for what we now call physics was natural philosophy. The neat and accurate division of sciences was still unknown, and what we now call chemistry, biology, botany, etc., was lumped together under the title natural philosophy or just philosophy for short.[2] What Keats here had in mind by philosophy was a picture of Newton and persons of his kind surrounded by bad smelling test tubes. As Forman quoted:

'He [Newton] has destroyed all the poetry of the rainbow by reducing it to prismatic colours.'

And again:

'The goblin is driven from the hearth and the rainbow is robbed of its mystery.'

Thus because of a semantic change in language it is necessary to interpret the word philosophy, as used in *Lamia*, not as we understand it today in the sense of the noble and disinterested pursuit of truth and wisdom, but as science, or more properly the scientific method. This last the Romantic poets conceived of as tinkering about with test-tubes, the needless building up of reservoirs of statistical material.

This is but one more aspect of the revolt against a mechanistic conception of the universe. Keats's remonstration against philosophy was directed solely against those abstract philosophers (who like Newton were really what we would call scientists) who held that because things do not cease to exist when we stop looking at them, therefore there must be some kind of *non-mental* reality behind our perception of them. Thus Locke, for instance, distinguishes the secondary qualities of perception from the primary qualities which he assigns to a substratum of substance. Locke's philosophy distinguishes sensation from reflection: the former is concerned with perception, the latter with the classification of sensations. Newton's corpus-

---

[1] Cp. 'Scientists should be trained to see the sun as a fact; artists to see it emotionally as beautiful.' N. Frye in *Fearful Symmetry*, p. 20.

[2] Here we are not referring so much to the times of Keats but to Burton's *Anatomy of Melancholy* from which this line has been derived by Keats (as is shown by Robert Gittings in his book on Keats *The Living Year*, Appendix 'A').

cular theory of light is derived from the same method of thought. It is, therefore, necessary to distinguish between *Truth* and mere *Fact*. If 'truth is beauty, and beauty truth', and if the rainbow is taken as an example of beauty, then on the same grounds but arguing backwards, it is the prismatic colours (being the Newtonian true composition of the rainbow) that should be beautiful—and the rainbow, though beautiful, is not true (as a rainbow) being merely a collection of prismatic colours.[1] The reason for this apparent incompability is that fact and truth are not necessarily the same. As Einstein has proved, truth is fact plus the individual perceiving it. In other words, 'the Observer enters into every Observation'.

Thus the *reality* of Lamia is as much in the eye of the beholder as her beauty is supposed to be. What appears as beauty to Lycius is a sham to Apollonius; what may appear as reality to a sage may be considered only as a mirage by the scientist. What the Romantic poets wanted to stress was that everything depended on the dimension of consciousness of the observer. In this they anticipated two centuries of science. They possessed the integral consciousness.

'Every eye sees differently. As the Eye such the object.'

> The Sun's Light when he unfolds it
> Depends on the Organ that beholds it.[2]

The rainbow is a kind of Lamia. A poet sees it as a thing of beauty and starts praising it.[3] The scientist (Apollonius) is infuriated because he knows it to be only an illusion of prismatic colours. He, therefore, concludes that the rainbow is not a fair lady, as the poet imagines her to be, but a serpent (a deceitful thing since a serpent is a symbol of guile and cunning). The scientist, therefore, rushes to enlighten him thinking it his sacred duty to save him. But such enlightenment is only disillusion to the poet, and in trying to save him he has merely hastened his end. For to the poet, imagination (Lamia) creates its own reality and, desire being a part of imagination, the world he desires is more real to him than the world we passively accept. Although the fact (the unreality of Lamia) is always the same, the poet's and the scientist's conceptions of truth are different—hence the tragedy. An Apollonius coming after Einstein should of course know that it is possible for a fact to be an illusion of prismatic colours at one level of sensory-impressions and yet a thing of beauty at another.

> *Gonzalo:* How lush and lusty the grass looks! How green!
> *Antonio:* The ground indeed is tawny.

[1] Cp. Blake's: 'Deduct from a rose its redness, from a lilly its whiteness, from a diamond its hardness, from a spunge its softness, from an oak its heighth, from a daisy its lowness, and rectify every thing in Nature as the Philosophers do, and then we shall return to chaos . . . O happy *Philosopher*.' Marg. to Lavater's *Aphorisms on Man* 532: Keynes's *The Complete Writings of William Blake*, p. 81.

[2] Blake's *Epigrams* as quoted by Frye in *Fearful Symmetry*, p. 19.

[3] My heart leaps up when I behold
A rainbow in the sky—Wordsworth

> *Sebastian:* With an eye of green in't.
> *Antonio:* He misses not much.
> *Sebastian:* No; he doth but mistake the truth totally.[1]

Again:

> Stop and consider! Life is but a day;
> A fragile dew-drop on its perilous way
> From a tree's summit; a poor Indian's sleep
> While his boat hastens to the monstrous steep
> Of Montmorenci.[2]

This transciency of human life, is a typically oriental thought found everywhere in Eastern writings from the *Rubaiyat* of Omar Khayyam to the *I Ching* in China. This was also a perpetual theme with the Romantic poets of the West and therefore indicates a strong bond of sympathy between the two. In our own day this theme is taken up by contemporary Western philosophers, for example Karl Jaspers's: '. . . *Nur ein Augenblick kann alles sein.*' (Only for a moment can existence be.) This 'fascination' for death is repeated in *The Fall of Hyperion*.

> . . . when suddenly a palsied chill
> Struck from the paved level up my limbs. . .
> I shriek'd, and the sharp anguish of my shriek
> Stung my own ears—I strove hard to escape
> . . . deadly was my pace . . .

Again:

> What am I that should so be saved from death,
> What am I that another death come not?

Notice that the question asked is not 'who am I?' but 'what am I?' indicating that the question is one relating to ultimate values. 'Who am I?' would imply an *a priori* acceptance that we are mortal human beings. 'What am I?' includes by implication a question as to the spiritual content of what constitutes a human being in the first place. We have already explained (in Part IV, Chapter 1) how very indispensable this question is for the practical realization of the integral consciousness inherent in man.

The answer of the goddess is indeed very illuminating:

> . . . Thou hast felt
> What 'tis to die and live again before
> Thy fated hour.

I venture to suggest that this is a reference to the Bird-Man ceremony of ancient Egypt, which commanded tremendous respect in the Greece of later times. The ceremony consisted in inducing a mysterious (yoga) trance, similar in all respects to actual death, whereby the soul was

---

[1] *The Tempest*, Act II, Scene I.
[2] Keats, *Sleep and Poetry*, Lines 85-90.

temporarily separated from the body and then restored to it again. The purpose was to instil in the mind of the initiate a fearlessness of death and the feeling of immortality.[1] We also know on good authority that it was customary for the the most outstanding Greek philosophers or mystics to visit Egypt on that account. In any case this ceremony is often mentioned in the Greek writings of those times.[2] It is another very interesting example of an ancient yogic idea finding its way into Western literature.

Another trait of Keats's symbolism is the idea of the fall of the gods which occurs notably in *Hyperion*. This idea is important as it recurs in modified forms in Shelley and Byron. Underlying it seems to be a belief that in the remote history of our unfortunate planet there was a time when all was well. It was the Golden Age of Saturn. The inevitable conclusion is that our own age is the very opposite of golden—there is a parallel idea in Indian philosophy and also in esoteric learning. According to this doctrine, our age, which we hail so proudly as one of reason, is called *Kali Yuga*, or the age of spiritual darkness. While with Keats there is this lament for a past golden age, in Shelley it takes a more active form, and the implied philosophy of *Prometheus Unbound* seems to be the restoration of this golden age on earth.

In Keats, the idea of the fall of the gods may also be ascribed to the fact that he unconsciously linked it up with the fall, or inversion in traditional values, which followed in the wake of the French Revolution. The idea of a past golden age can also be attributed to a too favourable reading of ancient Greek civilization—where all was golden in the clear Athenian sun. This cult of a past golden age, combined with a belief in its recurrence in the chequered history of mankind, had such a hold on poets that it should not be explained away too lightly, especially as it forms a powerful theme in the mythologies of almost all Eastern countries. Could it not be that the poets with their superior intuition were able to foresee something at which we with our rational apparatus can only guess?

Gilbert Murray attributed the fall of Greek civilization to 'a failure of nerve, an incapacity of the will to believe in the benevolence or reality of the gods'. T. S. Eliot says the same thing for Western civilization in *The Waste Land*:

> London bridge is falling down, falling down, falling down.

London bridge is a symbol for modern overmechanized civilization. The 'Waste Land' is London or for that matter any other huge impersonal city:

> Unreal city
> Jerusalem Athens Alexandria
> Vienna London
> Unreal.

[1] Egyptian paintings illustrating this Bird-Man ceremony are to be seen in the Mummy Room of the Eyptian section of the British Museum in London.

[2] 'At the moment of death the soul experiences the same impressions as those who are initiated into the great Mysteries.' Plutarch.

The influence of Eastern ideas in this poem is obvious, the *locus classicus* being the Da, Da, Da which occurs in Part V of the poem.

The triple Da, Da, Da, with its counterparts illustrates that every person's understanding of religious revelation is limited by the extent of his own (spiritual) evolution. The story in Indian philosophical-mythology[1] about this Da, Da, Da can be reinterpreted from Eliot's poem with slight alterations:

Thus, Prajāpati (Lord of all creatures) took gods, men, and demons (i.e. those desirous of self-improvement) as students of sacred knowledge. After some time they had to appear for an examination. The first to be examined were the gods. Prajāpati merely said 'Da!'[2]

'"Da" stands for *Datta*,' said the gods.[3] 'It means we should give' (that we should be generous; that we should answer prayers).

'Yes,' said Prajāpati, 'you have learnt well and have understood.'

Then came men (human beings). Prajāpati repeated: 'Da'.

'Da means *Dayadhvam*,' said the men.[4] 'It means we should be compassionate' (Christ's 'Love your enemy').

'Yes,' said Prajāpati, 'you too have understood.'

Then came the turn of the demons. Prajāpati repeated: 'Da'.

'Da stands for *Dāmyata*,' said the demons.[5] 'It means we should excercise self-control' (discipline our animal nature, evil lusts etc.).

'Yes,' said Prajāpati, 'you too have understood.'

Thus the single Da was interpreted in three different ways. Yet all three of them were considered to be valid, for their content was in proportion to the evolutionary needs of the three types of beings.

That is exactly what Eliot wants to say. It does not matter how we interpret religious experience. So long as our interpretation is in proportion to our experience, civilization can still be saved from the horrors of an agnostic Waste Land. The reason why the religions of the past did not succeed as they deserved was that they were too far ahead of evolution. Now evolution is catching up. Yet this kind of spiritual evolution is not feasible without bringing in the idea of reincarnation. Aurobindo thus succeeds where Teilhard de Chardin fails. Attaining the Superman with a higher dimension of consciousness can be a slow process spread over several lives.

T. S. Eliot opposed this notion that by some process either evolutionary or by trial and error (reincarnation), man one day will attain to a state of perfection. This he maintains is an illusion; according to the Christian doctrine and with particular reference to the Catholic Mass, Christ sacrificed his life in order that man may be redeemed.

[1] *Brihad-āranyaka Upaniṣad*, V., 2, I.

[2] From here on the order given is according to *The Waste Land* and not the Upanishads. According to the latter it is: (1) *Dāmyata* (2) *Datta* (3) *Dayadhvam*.

[3] In the Upanishads the gods explain 'Da' as *Dāmyata* or self-control.

[4] In the Upanishads the men explain 'Da' as *Datta* or Give.

[5] In the Upanishads the demons explain 'Da' as *Dayadhvam* or compassion.

And the entire drama of the Son of God's life is enacted where the wine symbolizes Christ's blood, and bread his body. During the ceremony the congregation partake of this wine and bread—the eternal reminder of the great sacrificer as a concession to human imperfectability. Eliot maintains that we are not sound, not 'substantial flesh and blood'!

> Our only health is the disease
> If we obey the dying nurse

The crux of the problem is to have the proper perspective, and the dying nurse is the one true Church which reminds the poet that death has been brought about by the disobedience of Adam to God; that is to say, of the human to the divine. Surprising as it may seem, this too is the central idea behind de Chardin's supposedly scientific thesis of the christification of matter. Even the idea of reincarnation was grasped by poets gifted with an integral consciousness. The two powerful themes in Shelley's *The Cloud* are death and change. Immortality lies in realizing that they are one and the same. This reminds us of reincarnation, of the impossibility of death in Nature. There is a very strong symbolical reference to reincarnation in the last two lines:

> Like a child from the *womb*, like a ghost from the *tomb*,
> I *arise* and *unbuild* it *again*.

Observe the italicized words: do they not conjure up a picture of rebirth? The indestructible essence takes on various shapes or forms from water to cloud; from womb to tomb, that is from birth to death. At death, the ghost or the essence arises to unbuild; to 'unbuild my own cenotaph' or come to life again; to repeat the process again.

The ghost or the essence or spirit of the previous embodiment or form now becomes the child from the womb (the same essence in its new embodiment or form). Observe, in particular, the use of the unique word unbuild, not destroy or demolish. To unbuild suggests a slow and *constructive* process. It is an attribute of life, not of death. Surely then to unbuild one's cenotaph would imply to live again.

The poem shows reincarnation at the physical level. It is a poetic formulation of that law of science developed by Newton and Einstein that: Matter can neither be created nor destroyed! Death is only a change of forms. What then is change? It is normally conceived in terms of a *thing* that changes, that is, in terms of something that persists through change so that we can say: 'this is the thing which yesterday was so-and-so and is today something else'.[1]

So does the sage in the midst of a constantly changing phenomenon, find something which retains its identity. This limitation inherent in the phenomenon of change itself is said to be found at the very fountainhead of philosophy.[2] In tracing Bergson's philosophy of change to the *Natur-*

---

[1] C. E. M. Joad's *Guide to Philosophy*, p. 170.
[2] F. W. Conner in *Cosmic Optimism*, p. 111.

philosophie of Schelling one should bear in mind that there are *two* elements: not only the 'eternal living deed', from which Bergsonism is supposed to be derived, but also 'the Eternal Changelessness of Neoplatonism or of the Vedānta'.[1]

Compare:

> Of the non-Existent there is no coming to be
> Of the existent there is no ceasing to be

And again:

Know thou, that by which all this is pervaded is indestructible. Of this immutable being, no one can bring about the destruction.[2]

This idea of an ultimate indestructible essence is often found in Shelley himself:

> The one remains, the many change and pass
> Heaven's light forever shines, earth's shadows fly . . .[3]

Compare Emerson's *Brahma*:

> If the red slayer think he slays
> Or if the slain think he is slain
> They know not well the subtle ways
> I keep and pass and turn again.

Thus when the physical texture of the cloud seemingly fades away, the vital essence of the cloud (what Shelley calls the 'I' in the poem) still survives and even laughs at its past form: 'I silently laugh at my own cenotaph'.

For: 'Rebirth is a law of nature. There is an objective connection between the various forms of life.'[4]

Thus the poet's love and fascination for Nature can partly be accounted for by the fact that it is in Nature that he first perceives the working of this principle of rebirth. 'Like corn a mortal ripens and like corn he is born again.'[5]

So in both Indian philosophy and Romantic poetry we find this shift in emphasis from a static to a dynamic conception of nature and the universe—from *natura naturata* to *natura naturans*. Creation is no longer a

---

[1] 'Bergson and Romantic Evolutionism', University of California *Chronicle*, XV (October 1913, p. 458). Neoplatonism is in fact the channel through which Indian ideas fertilize the *Philosophia Romantica*. As to the influence of Neoplatonism in Shelley, see *The Platonism of Shelley*, by Notopoulos.

[2] Radhakrishnan, *The Bhagavadgītā*, II, 16, 17.

[3] *Adonais*.

[4] Radhakrishnan, *The Bhagavadgītā*, p. 108.

[5] *Kaṭha Upaniṣad* I, 6.

given fact but a constantly recurring phenomenon.[1] This prepares us for an integral view of God and the world.

Why is it that the seed of the gall tree converts all the juices of the earth into bitterness, whereas the seed of the sugar cane converts them into sweetness? Is the reason to be found in the material elements of the seed or in the earth itself? Everyone feels that it would be madness to make such an assertion. What is the basis of the forces that are active in minerals? How can we account for the radical difference between the properties of chemical compounds and those of the combined materials? Why is it that fire flares when we strike a match? No chemist has yet discovered any fire in the match or on the rubbing surface, nor will he ever do so. What is the ultimate reason for the innumerable worlds which present themselves to us and which as fixed stars with their planets float at such distances from the earth, that a period of millions of years must be assumed as the time required by their light to reach us, although it travels at 186,000 miles a *second*? Indeed these stars are sometimes so remote that the rays of their light no longer reach our earth at all, either because they are moving away from us, or because their luminosity is no longer sufficient for such immense distances. What is the basis of the laws by which all those innumerable worlds rotate in space in perfect harmony so that none collides with the others? Certain orbits, as in the case of the planets of double stars and of many suns, are so complicated that, according to Littrow, mathematical analysis, in spite of its perfection, cannot determine these extremely complex movements. What is the origin of the laws that govern the universe? When the forms in which they manifest themselves perish, they disappear, but at once burst forth again when the conditions for them are laid down afresh, even though it be after billions of years. Thus they themselves are never destroyed, but simply become invisible.

Every thinking man has been most forcibly reminded of this total inadequacy of every knowable physical cause for its effect, and of the resultant necessity for postulating a hidden factor in world events, with the knowledge of which everything would be finally and completely clear, so that no more riddles and doubts would remain. *They* are the real and deepest reason for all belief in God, its unshakeable basis at all times. The concept of God in *this* sense is a necessary product of every well-regulated rational faculty. Indeed, to this extent one cannot speak merely of a *belief* in God, but even of an *implied knowledge* of Him. Therefore in this, and not in the necessity for a world-cause first in time, is to be found ultimately the fact that an awareness of God is ineradicably ingrained in man. That is why he cannot be permanently reconciled to any philosophical system which does not bring this awareness of God (integral consciousness) to maturity as its efflorescence.

[1] 'The Indian mind was all full of the idea of cyclic recurrence; everything was supposed to come round again. This is a very natural supposition for men to make.' H. G. Wells, *The Outline of History*, p. 397.

Index

GEORGE ALLEN & UNWIN LTD

Head Office
40 Museum Street, London, W.C.1
Telephone: 01-405 8577

Sales, Distribution and Accounts Departments
Park Lane, Hemel Hempstead, Herts.
Telephone: 0042 | 3244

Athens: 34 Panepistimiou Street
Auckland: P.O. Box 36013, Northcote Central N.4
Barbados: P.O. Box 222, Bridgetown
Bombay: 103/5 Fort Street, Bombay 1
Buenos Aires: Escritorio 454–459, Florida 165
Beirut: Deeb Building, Jeanne d'Arc Street
Calcutta: 285J Bepin Behari Ganguli Street, Calcutta 12
Cape Town: 68 Shortmarket Street
Hong Kong: 105 Wing On Mansion, 26 Hancow Road, Kowloon
Ibadan: P.O. Box 62
Karachi: Karachi Chambers, McLeod Road
Madras: 2/18 Mount Road, Madras
Mexico: Villalongin 32, Mexico 5, D.F.
Nairobi: P.O. Box 30583
New Delhi: 13–14 Asaf Ali Road, New Delhi 1
Philippines: P.O. Box 157, Quezon City D-502
Rio de Janeiro: Caixa Postal 2537-Zc-00
Singapore: 36c Prinsep Street, Singapore 7
Sydney N.S.W.: Bradbury House, 55 York Street
Tokyo: C.P.O. Box 1728, Tokyo 100-91
Toronto: 81 Curlew Drive, Don Mills

S. RADHAKRISHNAN

Religion in a Changing World

Throughout the world there is deep spiritual unrest and dissatisfaction with organized religions as they have come down to us. Those steeped in the spirit of science and modern thought are eagerly groping for a faith which will meet the demands of modern science and fulfil the hunger for the Unseen. Professor Radhakrishnan, who has devoted a lifetime to the study of the religious problems of the East and West, here sets forth his reflections on the religion of the future which will make for the development of a world community. The author evaluates the anti-metaphysical bias of our scientific age and interprets this outlook in positive rather than in negative terms, not as a loss of the sense of the spiritual but as a gain of the wholeness of experience. This book is written with deep religious feeling and will offer comfort to our bewildered generation, for it affirms the doubts and insecurities of modern man and points beyond them to the grounds for hope. It appreciates the intellectual difficulties of belief and gives the widest social content to religion.

'There is much that is inspiring and heartwarming in this little book.' *Expository Times*

'Here is an eloquent running commentary on the prospects for a spiritual interpretation of reality by a sensitive Hindu observer.' *Churchman*

East and West in Religion

'This is a great work, which will stand the test of time, and can be recommended to any seeker after truth.' *Everyman*

'Written with the author's usual distinction of style, and is only too short, not for his purpose, but for the reader's appetite.' *Guardian*

NINIAN SMART

The Yogi and the Devotee

This book, based on lectures given in Delhi, explores the relation between Christianity and Hinduism in a novel way. It does so by bringing to bear a general theory of the relation between religious experience and doctrines—a theory developed in the author's earlier book *Doctrine and Argument in Indian Philosophy*. It is argued that we need to present a new form of 'natural theology', which would indicate the relevance of religious experience and ritual to what is given in revelation. This may be the key to a new understanding between Christianity and Indian religions. The author also examines the lessons which Christians can learn from other faiths.

Ninian Smart, after learning Chinese in the army, served in Ceylon, and this first awakened his concern with understanding Eastern religions. In 1960 he was visiting lecturer at Banaras Hindu University. He has taught philosophy and history of religion at London, Birmingham and Wisconsin, and is now engaged in fashioning a Department of Religious Studies on somewhat revolutionary lines at the University of Lancaster.

Doctrine and Argument in Indian Philosophy

This book, addressed both to students of philosophy and to those interested in Indian religion and culture, has two unique features. The description of the various schools of Indian metaphysics, in the first part, includes an analysis of the religious factors which have determined their shape.

The second part describes arguments on particular topics, such as causation, epistemology and the existence of God. Readers can thus examine, independently of whether they agree with any of the traditional systems, the style and substance of Indian philosophical argumentation, and so may be stimulated to further explorations of a field which is duly neglected outside India.

SWAMI PRABHAVANANDA

Religion in Practice

Religion in Practice: a collection of twenty-five lectures delivered
to audiences in the United States over the past decade, is a manual
for spiritual living. Its author, Swami Prabhavananda, a senior monk
of the Ramakrishna Order of India, has lived and taught continuously
in the United States since 1923. He is today recognized as an outstanding scholar and translator (with Christopher Isherwood and
Frederick Manchester) of Hindu scriptures. During his years as a
teacher and spiritual adviser, he has consistently stressed the 'how'
of religion, avoiding for the most part complex theological questions
in preference to a direct and pragmatic approach to spiritual life.

This attitude is strongly evident in *Religion in Practice*, where
he insists again and again that in order for religion to be meaningful,
it must above all be practical. Abstruse and weighty philosophical
problems have no place in the Swami's view of man and God. His
main concern is the ways and means for man to realise God in this
very life. Men and women who feel drawn to a spiritual life, who
are prompted by a genuine urge to discover something higher in
themselves, will find rich meaning in Swami Prabhavananda's book.

The final portion of *Religion in Practice* contains a judicious
sampling of questions addressed to the Swami over the years, and
his answers to them. Most of the questions were asked by students
attending his evening study classes.

Christopher Isherwood, who has been both a disciple and literary
associate of Swami Prabhavananda for more than twenty years, has
contributed an interesting and instructive introduction.

'Each chapter contains solid food for thought; each casts fresh
light on the issues which are dealt with.'

The Inquirer

LONDON: GEORGE ALLEN & UNWIN LTD